THE BIOGRAPHICAL DICTIONARY OF SCIENTISTS

Physicists

THE BIOGRAPHICAL DICTIONARY OF SCIENTISTS

Physicists

General Editor
David Abbott PhD

BLOND EDUCATIONAL

First published in Great Britain in 1984 by
Frederick Muller Limited, 8 Alexandra Road,
Wimbledon, London SW19 7JZ.

Blond Educational is an imprint of Frederick
Muller Ltd

British Library Cataloguing in Publication Data

Biographical dictionary of scientists.
  1: Physicists
  1. Scientific—Biography
  I. Abbott, David
  509′.2′2   Q141

ISBN 0-584-70003-2

Made and printed in Great Britain by
Butler & Tanner Ltd, Frome and London

Contents

Acknowledgements

Many people are involved in the creation of a major new series of reference books. The general editor and the publishers are grateful to all of them and wish to thank particularly the contributing authors: Neil Ardley; Gareth Ashurst; Jim Bailey; Mary Basham; Alan Bishop; William Cooksey; David Cowey; Robert Matthews; Valerie Neal; Lucia Osborne; Helen Rapson; Mary Sanders; Robert Smith and David Ward. Our thanks are also due to Mick Saunders for his artwork and to Bull Publishing Consultants Ltd whose experience in the development of reference books has made a significant contribution to the series: John Clark; Kate Duffy; Nikki Okell; Hal Robinson and Sandy Shepherd.

Historical introduction

Physics is a branch of science in which the theoretical and the practical are firmly intertwined. It has been so since ancient times, as physicists have striven to interpret observation or experiment in order to arrive at the fundamental laws that govern the behaviour of the Universe. Physicists aim to explain the manifestations of matter and energy that characterize all things and processes, both living and inanimate, extending from the grandest of galaxies down to the most intimate recesses of the atom.

The history of physics has not been a straight and easy road to enlightenment. The exploration of new directions sometimes leads to dead ends. New ways of looking at things may result in the overthrow of a previously accepted system. Not Aristotle's system, nor Newton's, nor even Einstein's was "true"; rather statements, or "laws", in physics satisfy contemporary requirements or – in the existing state of knowledge – contemporary possibilities. The question that physicists ask is not so much "Is it true?" as "Does it work?"

Physics has many strands – such as mechanics, heat, light, sound, electricity and magnetism – and, although they are often pursued separately, they are also all ultimately interdependent. To pursue the history of physics, therefore, it is necessary to follow several separate chains of discovery and then to find the links between them. The story is of frustration and missed opportunities as well as of genius and perseverence. But however complex it may appear, all physicists seek or have sought to play a part in the evolution of an ultimate explanation of all the effects that occur throughout the Universe. That goal may be unattainable but the thrust towards it has kept physics as alive and vital today as it was when it originated in ancient times.

Force and motion

The development of an understanding of the nature of force and motion was a triumph for physics, one which marked the evolution of the scientific method. As in most other branches of physics, this development began in ancient Greece.

The earliest discovery in physics, apart from observations of effects like magnetism, was the relation between musical notes and the lengths of vibrating strings. Pythagoras (c.582–c.497 BC) found that harmonious sounds were given by strings whose lengths were in simple numerical ratios, such as 2:1, 3:2 and 4:3. From this discovery the belief grew that all explanations could be found in terms of numbers. This was developed by Plato (c.427–c.347 BC) into a conviction that the cause underlying any effect could be expressed in mathematical form. The motion of the heavenly bodies, Plato reasoned, must consist of circles, since these were the most perfect geometric forms.

Reason also led Democritus (c.470–c.380 BC) to propose that everything consisted of minute indivisible particles called atoms. The properties of matter depend on the characteristics of the atoms of which it is composed, and the atoms combine in ways that are determined by unchanging fundamental laws of nature.

A third view of the nature of matter was given by Aristotle (384–322 BC), who endeavoured to interpret the world as he observed it, without recourse to abstractions such as atoms and mathematics. Aristotle reasoned that matter consisted of four elements – earth, water, air and fire – with a fifth element, the ether, making up the heavens. Motion occurred when an object sought its rightful place in the order of elements, rocks falling through air and water to the earth, air rising through water as bubbles and fire through air as smoke.

There was value in all these approaches and physics has absorbed them all to some degree. Plato was essentially correct; only his geometry was wrong, the planets following elliptical, not circular, orbits. Atoms do exist as Democritus foretold and they do explain the properties of matter. Aristotle's emphasis on observation (though not his reasoning) was to be a feature of physics and many other sciences, notably biology, of which he may be considered the founder.

These ideas were, however, mainly deductions based solely on reason. Few of them were given the test of experiment to prove that they were right. Then came the achievements of Archimedes (c.287–212 BC), who discovered the law of the lever and the principle of flotation by measuring the effects that occur and deduced general laws from his results. He was then able to apply his laws, building pulley systems and testing the purity of the gold in King Hieron's crown by a method involving immersion.

Archimedes thus gave physics the scientific method. All subsequent principal advances made by physicists were to take the form of mathematical interpretations of observations and experiments. Archimedes developed the method in founding the science of statics - how forces interact to produce equilibrium. But an understanding of motion lay a long way off. In the centuries following the collapse of Greek civilization in around AD100, physics marked time. The Arabs kept the Greek achievements alive, but they made few advances in physics, while in Europe the scientific spirit was overshadowed by the "Dark Ages". Then in about 1200, the spirit of enquiry was rekindled in Europe by the import of Greek knowledge from the Arabs. Unfortunately, progress was hindered somewhat by the fact that Aristotle's ideas, particularly his views on motion, prevailed. Aristotle had assumed that a heavy object falls faster than a light object simply because it is heavier. He also argued that a stone continues to move when thrown because the air displaced by the stone closes behind it and pushes the stone. This explanation derived from Aristotle's conviction that nature abhors a vacuum (which is why he placed a fifth element in the heavens).

Aristotle's ideas on falling bodies were probably first disproved by Simon Stevinus (1548-1620), who is believed to have dropped unequal weights from a height and found that they reached the ground together. At about the same time Galileo (1564-1642) measured the speeds of "falling" bodies by rolling spheres down an inclined place and discovered the laws that govern the motion of bodies under gravity. This work was brought to a brilliant climax by Isaac Newton (1642-1727), who in his three laws of motion achieved an understanding of force and motion, relating them to mass and recognizing the existence of inertia and momentum. Newton thus explained why a stone continues to move when thrown; and he showed the law of falling bodies to be a special case of his more general laws. Newton went on to derive from existing knowledge of the motion and dimensions of the Earth-Moon system a universal law of gravitation, one which provided a mathematical statement for the laws of planetary motion discovered empirically by Johann Kepler (1571-1630).

Newton's laws of motion and gravitation, which were published in 1687, were fundamental laws which sought to explain all observed effects of force and motion. This triumph of the scientific method heralded the Age of Reason - not the Greek kind of reasoning, but a belief that all could be explained by the deduction of fundamental laws upheld by observation or experiment. It was to result in an explosion of scientific discovery in physics that has continued to this day. In the field of force and motion, important advances were made with the discovery of the law governing the pendulum and the principle of conservation of momentum by Christiaan Huygens (1629-1695) and the determination of the gravitational constant by Henry Cavendish (1731-1810).

The behaviour of matter

Physics is basically concerned with matter and energy, and investigation into the behaviour of matter also originated in ancient Greece with the work of Archimedes concerning flotation. As with force and motion, Simon Stevinus made the first post-Greek advance with the discovery that the pressure of a liquid depends on its depth and area. This achievement was developed by Blaise Pascal (1623-1662), who found that pressure is transmitted throughout a liquid in a closed vessel, acting perpendicularly to the surface at any point. Pascal's principle is the basis of hydraulics. Pascal also investigated the mercury barometer invented in 1643 by Evangelista Torricelli (1608-1647) and showed that air pressure supports the mercury column and that there is a vacuum above it, thus disproving Aristotle's contention that a vacuum cannot exist. The immense pressure that the atmosphere can exert was subsequently demonstrated in several sensational experiments by Otto von Guericke (1602-1686).

Solid materials were also investigated. The fundamental law of elasticity was discovered by Robert Hooke (1635-1703) in 1678 when he found that the stress (force) exerted is proportional to the strain (elongation) produced. Thomas Young (1773-1829) later showed that a given material has a constant, known as Young's modulus, that defines the strain produced by a particular stress.

The effects that occur with fluids (liquids or gases) in motion were then explored. Daniel Bernoulli (1700-1782) established hydrodynamics with his discovery that the pressure of a fluid depends on its velocity. Bernoulli's principle explains how lift occurs and led eventually to the invention of heavier-than-air flying machines. It also looked forward to ideas of the conservation of energy and the kinetic theory of gases. Other important advances in our understanding of fluid flow were later made by George Stokes (1819-1903), who discovered the law that relates motion to viscosity, and Ernst Mach (1838-1916) and Ludwig Prandtl (1875-1953), who investigated the flow of fluids over surfaces and made discoveries vital to aerodynamics.

The effects of light

The Greeks were aware that light rays travel in straight lines, but they believed that the rays originate in the eyes and travel to the object that is seen. Euclid (c.325–260 BC), Hero (fl. AD 60) and Ptolemy (fl. second century AD) were of this opinion although, recognizing that optics is essentially a matter of geometry, they discovered the law of reflection and investigated refraction.

Optics made an immense stride forward with the work of Alhazen (c. 965–1038), who was probably the greatest scientist of the Middle Ages. Alhazen recognized that light rays are emitted by a luminous source and are then reflected by objects into the eyes. He studied images formed by curved mirrors and lenses and formulated the geometrical optics involved. Alhazen's discoveries took centuries to filter into Europe, where they were not surpassed until the seventeenth century. The refracting telescope was then invented in Holland in 1608 and quickly improved by Galileo and Kepler, and in 1621 Willebrord Snell (1580–1626) discovered the laws that govern refraction.

The next major steps forward were taken by Newton, who not only invented the reflecting telescope in 1668, but a couple of years earlier found that white light is split into a spectrum of colours by a prism. Newton published his work in optics in 1704, provoking great controversy with his statement that light consists of a stream of particles. Huygens had put forward the view that light consists of a wave motion, an opinion reinforced by the discovery of diffraction by Francesco Grimaldi (1618–1663). Such was Newton's reputation, however, that the particulate theory held sway for the following century. In 1801 Young discovered the principle of interference, which could be explained only by assuming that light consisted of waves. This was confirmed in 1821, when Augustin Fresnel (1788–1827) showed from studies of polarized light, which had been discovered by Étienne Malus (1775–1812) in 1808, that light is made up of a transverse wave motion, not longitudinal as had previously been thought.

Newton's discovery of the spectrum remained little more than a curiosity until 1814, when Joseph von Fraunhofer (1787–1826) discovered that the Sun's spectrum is crossed by the dark lines now known as Fraunhofer lines. Fraunhofer was unable to explain the lines, but he did go on to invent the diffraction grating for the production of high-quality spectra and the spectroscope to study them. An explanation of the lines was provided by Gustav Kirchhoff (1824–1887), who in 1859 showed that they are caused by elements present in the Sun's atmosphere. With Robert Bunsen (1811–1899), Kirchhoff discovered that elements have unique spectra by which they can be identified, and several new elements were found in this way. In 1885, Johann Balmer (1825–1898) derived a mathematical relationship governing the frequencies of the lines in the spectrum of hydrogen. This later proved to be a crucial piece of evidence for revolutionary theories of the structure of the atom.

Meanwhile, several scientists investigated the phenomenon of colour, notably Young, Hermann von Helmholtz (1821–1894) and James Clerk Maxwell (1831–1879). Their research led to the establishment of the three-colour theory of light, which showed that the eye responds to varying amounts of red, green and blue in light and mixes mixing them to give particular colours. This led directly to colour photography and other methods of colour reproduction used today.

The velocity of light was first measured accurately in 1862 by Jean Foucault (1819–1868), who obtained a value within 1 per cent of the correct value. This led to a famous experiment performed by Albert Michelson (1852–1931) and Edward Morley (1838–1923) in which the velocity of light was measured in two directions at right angles. Their purpose was to test the theory that a medium called the ether existed to carry light waves. If it did exist, then the two values obtained would be different. The Michelson–Morley experiment, performed in 1881 and then again in 1887, yielded a negative result both times (and on every occasion since), thus proving that the ether does not exist.

More important, the Michelson–Morley experiment showed that the velocity of light is constant regardless of the motion of the observer. From this result, and from the postulate that all motion is relative, Albert Einstein (1879–1955) derived the special theory of relativity in 1905. The principal conclusion of special relativity is that in a system moving relative to the observer, length, mass and time vary with the velocity. The effects become noticeable only at velocities approaching light; at slower velocities, Newton's laws hold good. Special relativity was crucial to the formulation of new ideas of atomic structure and it also led to the idea that mass and energy are equivalent, an idea used later to explain the great power of nuclear reactions. In 1915 Einstein published his general theory of relativity, in which he showed that gravity distorts space. This explained an anomaly in the motion of Mercury, which does not quite obey Newton's laws, and it was dramatically confirmed in 1919 when a solar eclipse revealed that the Sun's gravity was bending light rays coming from stars.

Electricity and magnetism

The phenomena of electricity and magnetism are believed to have been first studied by the ancient Greek philosopher Thales (624–546 BC), who was considered by the Greeks to be the founder of their science. Thales found that a piece of amber picks up light objects when rubbed, the action of rubbing thus producing a charge of static electricity. The words "electron" and "electricity" came from this discovery, *elektron* being the Greek word for amber. Thales also studied the similar effect on each other of pieces of lodestone, a magnetic mineral found in the region of Magnesia. It is fitting that the study of electricity and magnetism originated together, for the later discovery that they are linked was one of the most important ever made in physics.

No further progress was made, however, for nearly 2,000 years. The strange behaviour of amber remained no more than a curiosity, though magnets were used to make compasses. From this, Petrus Peregrinus (*f.* 1200s) discovered the existence of north and south poles in magnets and realized that they attract or repel each other. William Gilbert (1544–1603) first explained the Earth's magnetism and also investigated electricity, finding other substances besides amber that produce attraction when rubbed.

Then Charles Du Fay (1698–1739) discovered that substances charged by rubbing may repel as well as attract in a similar way to magnetic poles and Benjamin Franklin (1706–1790) proposed that positive and negative charges are produced by the excess or deficiency of electricity. Charles Coulomb (1763–1806) measured the forces produced between magnetic poles and between electric charges and found that they both obey the same inverse square law.

A major step forward was taken in 1800, when Alessandro Volta (1745–1827) invented the battery. A source of current electricity was now available and in 1820 Hans Oersted (1777–1851) found that an electric current produces a magnetic field. This discovery of electromagnetism was immediately taken up by Michael Faraday (1791–1867), who realized that magnetic lines of force must surround a current. This concept led him to discover the principle of the electric motor in 1821 and electromagnetic induction in 1831, the phenomenon in which a changing magnetic field produces a current. This was independently discovered by Joseph Henry (1797–1878) at the same time.

Meanwhile, important theoretical developments were taking place in the study of electricity.

In 1827, André Ampère (1775–1836) discovered the laws relating magnetic force to electric current and also properly distinguished current from tension, or EMF. In the same year, Georg Ohm (1789–1854) published his famous law relating current, EMF and resistance. Kirchhoff later extended Ohm's law to networks, and he also unified static and current electricity by showing that electrostatic potential is identical to EMF.

In the 1830s, Carl Gauss (1777–1855) and Wilhelm Weber (1804–1891) defined a proper system of units for magnetism; later they did the same for electricity. In 1845 Faraday found that materials are paramagnetic or diamagnetic, and Lord Kelvin (1824–1907) developed Faraday's work into a full theory of magnetism. An explanation of the cause of magnetism was finally achieved in 1905 by Paul Langevin (1872–1946), who ascribed it to electron motion.

Electricity and magnetism were finally brought together in a brilliant theoretical synthesis by James Clerk Maxwell. From 1855 to 1873 Maxwell developed the theory of electromagnetism to show that electric and magnetic fields are propagated in a wave motion and that light consists of such an electromagnetic radiation. Maxwell predicted that other similar electromagnetic radiations must exist and, as a result, Heinrich Hertz (1857–1894) produced radio waves in 1888. X-rays and gamma rays were discovered by accident soon after.

The nature of heat and energy

The first step towards measurement – and therefore an understanding – of heat was taken by Galileo, who constructed the first crude thermometer in 1593. Gradually these instruments improved and in 1714 Daniel Fahrenheit (1686–1736) invented the mercury thermometer and devised the fahrenheit scale of temperature. This was replaced in physics by the celsius or centigrade scale proposed by Anders Celsius (1701–1744) in 1742.

At this time, heat was considered to be a fluid called caloric that flowed into or out of objects as they got hotter or colder, and even after 1798 when Count Rumford (1753–1814) showed the idea to be false by his observation of the boring of cannon, it persisted. Earlier Joseph Black (1728–1799) had correctly defined the quantity of heat in a body and the latent heat and specific heat of materials, and his values had been successfully applied to the improvement of steam engines. In 1824, Sadi Carnot (1796–1832), also a believer in the caloric theory, found that the amount of work that can be produced by an engine is related only to the temperature at which it operates.

Carnot's theorem, though not invalidated by the caloric theory, suggested that, since heat gives rise to work, it was likely that heat was a form of motion, not a fluid. The idea also grew that energy may be changed from one form to another (i.e. from heat to motion) without a change in the total amount of energy involved. The interconvertibility of energy and the principle of the conservation of energy were established in the 1840s by several physicists. Julius Mayer (1814–1878) first formulated the principle in general terms and obtained a theoretical value for the amount of work that may be obtained by the conversion of heat (the mechanical equivalent of heat). Helmholtz gave the principle a firmer scientific basis and James Joule (1818–1889) made an accurate experimental determination of the mechanical equivalent. Rudolf Clausius (1822–1888) and Kelvin developed the theory governing heat and work, thus founding the science of thermodynamics. This enabled Kelvin to propose the absolute scale of temperature that now bears his name.

The equivalence of heat and motion led to the kinetic theory of gases, which was developed by John Waterston (1811–1883), Clausius, Maxwell and Ludwig Boltzmann (1844–1906) between 1845 and 1868. It gave a theoretical description of all effects of heat in terms of the motion of molecules.

During the nineteenth century it also came to be understood that heat may be transmitted by a form of radiation. Pioneering theoretical work on how bodies exchange heat had been carried out by Pierre Prévost (1751–1839) in 1791, and the Sun's heat radiation had been discovered to consist of infrared rays by William Herschel (1738–1822) in 1800. In 1862 Kirchhoff derived the concept of the perfect black body - one that absorbs and emits radiation at all frequencies. In 1879 Josef Stefan (1835–1893) discovered the law relating the amount of energy radiated by a black body to its temperature, but physicists were unable to relate the frequency distribution of the radiation to the temperature. This increases as the temperature is raised, causing an object to glow red, yellow and then white as it gets hotter. Lord Rayleigh (1842–1919) and Wilhelm Wien (1864–1928) derived incomplete theories of this effect, and then in 1900 Max Planck (1858–1947) showed that it could be explained only if radiation consisted of individsible units, called quanta, whose energy was proportional to their frequency.

Planck's quantum theory revolutionized physics. It showed that heat radiation and other electromagnetic radiations including light must consist of indivisible particles of energy and not

of waves as had previously been thought. In 1905 Einstein found a ready explanation of the photoelectric effect using quantum theory, and the theory was experimentally confirmed by James Franck (1882–1964) in the early 1920s.

Another advance in the study of heat that took place in the same period was the production of low temperatures. In 1852 Joule and Kelvin found the effect named after them is used to produce refrigeration by adiabatic expansion of a gas, and James Dewar (1842–1923) developed this effect into a practical method of liquefying gases from 1877 onwards. Heike Kamerlingh-Onnes (1853–1926) first produced temperatures within a degree of absolute zero and in 1911 he discovered superconductivity.

Sound

Sound is the one branch of physics that was well established by the Greeks, especially by Pythagoras. They surmised, correctly, that sound does not travel through a vacuum, a contention proved experimentally by Guericke in 1650. Measurements of the velocity of sound in air were made by Pierre Gassendi (1592–1655) and in other materials by August Kundt (1839–1894). Ernst Chladni (1756–1827) studied how the vibration of surfaces produces sound waves, and in 1845 Christian Doppler (1803–1853) discovered the effect relating the frequency (pitch) of sound to the relative motion of the source and observer. The Doppler effect is also produced by light and other wave motions and has proved to be particularly valuable in astronomy.

The structure of the atom

The existence of atoms was proved theoretically by chemists during the nineteenth century, but the first experimental demonstration of their existence and the first estimate of their dimensions was made by Jean Perrin (1870–1942) in 1909.

The principal direction taken in physics in this century has been to determine the inner structure of the atom. It began with the discovery of the electron in 1897 by J. J. Thomson (1856–1940), who showed that cathode rays consist of streams of minute indivisible electric particles. The charge and mass of the electron were then found by John Townsend (1868–1937) and Robert Millikan (1868–1953).

Meanwhile, another important discovery had been made with the detection of radioactivity by Antoine Becquerel (1852–1908) in 1896. Three kinds of radioactivity were found; these were named alpha, beta and gamma by Ernest Rutherford (1871–1937). Becquerel recognized in 1900 that beta particles are electrons. In 1903 Rutherford explained that radioactivity is caused by the breakdown of atoms. In 1908 he identified alpha particles as helium nuclei, and in association with Hans Geiger (1882-1945) produced the nuclear model of the atom in 1911, proposing that it consists of electrons orbiting a nucleus. Then in 1914 Rutherford identified the proton and in 1919 he produced the first artificial atomic disintegration by bombarding nitrogen with alpha particles.

Rutherford's pioneering elucidation of the basic structure of the atom was aided by developments in the use of X-rays, which had been discovered in 1895 by Wilhelm Röntgen (1845-1923). In 1912 Max von Laue (1879-1960) produced diffraction in X-rays by passing them through crystals, showing X-rays to be electromagnetic waves, and Lawrence Bragg (1890-1971) developed this method to determine the arrangement of atoms in crystals. His work influenced Henry Moseley (1887-1915), who in 1914 found by studying X-ray spectra that each element has a particular atomic number, equal to the number of protons in the nucleus and to the number of electrons orbiting it.

In 1913, Niels Bohr (1885-1962) achieved a brilliant synthesis of Rutherford's nuclear model of the atom and Planck's quantum theory. He showed that the electrons must move in orbits at particular energy levels around the nucleus. As an atom emits or absorbs radiation, it moves from one orbit to another and produces or gains a certain number of quanta of energy. In so doing, the quanta give rise to particular frequencies of radiation, producing certain lines in the spectrum of the radiation. Bohr's theory was able to explain the spectral lines of hydrogen and their relationship, found earlier by Balmer.

These discoveries, made so quickly, seemed to achieve an astonishingly complete picture of the atom, but more was to come. In 1923, Louis De Broglie (1892-) found by combining the quantum theory with Einstein's mass-energy equation that electrons could behave as if they made up waves around the nucleus. This discovery was developed into a theoretical system of wave mechanics by Erwin Schrödinger (1887-1961) in 1926 and experimentally confirmed in the following year. It showed that electrons exist both as particles and waves. Furthermore it reconciled Planck's quantum theory with classical physics by indicating that electromagnetic quanta or photons, which were named and detected experimentally in X-rays by Arthur Compton (1892-1962) in 1923, could behave as waves as well as particles. A prominent figure in the study of atomic structure was Werner Heisenberg (1901-1976), who showed in 1927 that the position and momentum of the electron in the atom cannot be known precisely, but only found with a degree of probability or uncertainty. His uncertainty principle follows from wave-particle duality and it negates cause and effect, an uncomfortable idea in a science that strives to reach laws of universal application.

The next step was to investigate the nucleus. A series of discoveries of nuclear particles accompanying the proton were made, starting in 1932 with the discovery of the positron by Carl Andersson (1905-) and the neutron by James Chadwick (1891-1974).

This work was aided by the development of particle accelerators, beginning with the voltage multiplier built by John Cockcroft (1897-1967) and Ernest Walton (1903-), which achieved the first artifical nuclear transformation in 1932. It led to the discovery of nuclear fission by Otto Hahn (1879-1968) in 1939 and the production of nuclear power by Enrico Fermi (1901-1954) in 1942.

Modern physics

Physicists have advanced along several fronts in the second half of this century. A pioneering discovery of great consequence was made in 1948 with the invention of the transistor by John Bardeen (1908-), William Shockley (1910-) and Walter Brattain (1902-), and the subsequent development of microelectronic devices has been of immense importance. Superconductivity has been another field of activity, Bardeen and others achieving an explanation of this phenomenon in 1957. The tunnelling effect in superconductivity discovered by Brian Josephson (1940-) could lead the way to superfast computers. Another important practical development has been the invention of the laser by Theodore Maiman (1927-) in 1960 and the subsequent use of lasers in holography as predicted by Dennis Gabor (1900-1979) in 1947.

In theoretical physics, the main thrust forward continues to be in atomic structure. Physicists hope to be able to relate to each other the many different nuclear particles found in experiments involving high-energy accelerators. This may involve the assembly of all particles from hitherto undetected basic particles called quarks. It may also help to provide a unified view of the four basic forces, or interactions, in nature – gravity, electromagnetic interaction and the weak and strong nuclear forces. If so, a fundamental understanding of the nature of matter and energy may be in sight.

A

Abbe, Ernst (*1840-1905*), was a German physicist who, working with Carl Zeiss, greatly improved the design and quality of optical instruments, particularly the compound microscope. He indirectly had a great influence in various physical sciences, particularly in biology where the improved resolving power of his instruments permitted researchers to observe micro-organisms and internal cellular structures for the first time.

Abbe was born in Eisenach, Thuringia (now East Germany), on 23 January 1840, the son of a spinning-mill worker. On a scholarship provided by his father's employers he attended high school (graduating in 1857) and then went to study physics at the University of Jena. He gained his doctorate from Göttingen University in 1861 and three years later became a lecturer in mathematics, physics and astronomy at Jena, being appointed Professor in 1870. In 1866 he began his association with Carl Zeiss, an instrument manufacturer who supplied optical instruments to the university and repaired them. Abbe was appointed Director of the Astronomical and Meteorological Observatory at Jena in 1878. Two years earlier he had become a partner in Zeiss' firm, and in 1881 Abbe invited Otto Schott (1851-1935), who had studied the chemistry of glasses and manufactured them, to go to Jena, and the famous company of Schott and Sons was founded in 1884. On the death of Zeiss in 1888 Abbe became the sole owner of the Zeiss works. He established the Carl Zeiss Foundation in 1891, and in 1896 he formalized the association between the Zeiss works and Jena University by making the company a co-operative, with the profits shared between the workers and the university. He died in Jena on 14 January 1905.

The success of the Jena enterprise arose largely from the right combination of talents: Zeiss as the manufacturer; Abbe as the physicist/theoretician, who performed the mathematical calculations for designing new lenses; and Schott the chemist, who formulated and made the special glasses needed by Abbe's designs. Abbe worked out why, contrary to expectation, a microscope's definition decreases with a reduction in the aperture of the objective; he found that the loss in resolving power is a diffraction effect. He calculated how to overcome spherical aberration in lenses - by a combination of geometry and the correct types of glass. He also explained the phenomenon of coma (first recognized in 1830 by Joseph Jackson Lister (1786-1869), the father of the famous surgeon), in which even a corrected lens displays aberration when the object is slightly off the instrument's axis. It was overcome by applying Abbe's "sine condition", producing the so-called aplanatic lens. Finally Abbe calculated how to correct chromatic aberration, using Schott's special glasses and, later, fluorite to make microscope objective lenses, culminating in the apochromatic lens system of 1886.

In 1872 he developed the Abbe substage condenser for illuminating objects under high-power magnification. Among his other inventions were a crystal refractometer and, developed with Armand Fizeau, an optical dilatometer for measuring the thermal expansion of solids.

Alfvén, Hannes Olof Gösta (*1908-*), is a Swedish astrophysicist who has made fundamental contributions to plasma physics, particularly in the field of magnetohydrodynamics (MHD) - the study of plasmas in magnetic fields. For his pioneering work in this area he shared the 1970 Nobel Prize in Physics with the French physicist Louis Néel (1904-).

Alfvén was born in Norrköping, Sweden, on 30 May 1908 and was educated at the University of Uppsala, from which he gained his PhD in 1934. In 1940 he joined the Royal Institute of Technology, Stockholm, becoming Professor of Electronics in 1945 then Professor of Plasma Physics in 1963, this latter chair having been specially created for him. In 1967, however, after disagreements with the Swedish government, he obtained a professorship at the University of California, San Diego. Later he divided his time between the University of California and the Royal Institute.

Alfvén made his most important contributions in the late 1930s and early 1940s. Investigating the interactions of electrical and magnetic fields with plasmas (highly ionized gases containing both free positive ions and free electrons) in an attempt to explain sunspots, he formulated the frozen-in-flux theorem, according to which a plasma is - under certain conditions - bound to the magnetic lines of flux passing through it; later he used this theorem to explain the origin of cosmic rays. In 1939 he went on to propose a theory to explain aurorae and magnetic storms, a theory that greatly influenced later ideas about the Earth's magnetosphere. He also devised the guiding centre approximation, a widely used technique that enables the complex spiral movements of a charged particle in a magnetic field to be calculated relatively easily. Three years later, in 1942, he postulated that a form of electromagnetic wave would propagate through plasma; other scientists later observed this phenomenon in plasmas and in liquid metals. Also in 1942 Alfvén developed a theory of the origin of the planets in the solar system. In this theory (sometimes called the Alfvén theory) he hypothesized that planets were formed from the material captured by the sun from an interstellar cloud of gas and dust. As the atoms were drawn towards the Sun they became ionized and influenced by the Sun's magnetic field. The ions then condensed into small particles which, in turn, coalesced to form the planets, this process having occurred in the plane of the solar equator. This theory did not adequately explain the formation of the inner planets but it was important in suggesting the role of MHD in the genesis of the solar system.

Although Alfvén has studied MHD mainly in the context of astrophysics, his work has been fundamental to plasma physics and is applicable to the use of plasmas in experimental nuclear fusion reactors.

Alhazen (*c.965–1038*), was an Arabian scientist who made significant advances in the theory and practice of optics. He was probably the greatest scientist of the Middle Ages and his work remained unsurpassed for nearly 600 years until the time of Johann Kepler. His Arabic name was Abu ʼAlī al-Hassan ibn al-Haytham.

Alhazen was born in Basra (Al Basra, now in Iraq) in about 965. He made many contributions to optics, one of which was to contest the Greek view of Hero and Ptolemy (who flourished in the second century AD) that vision involves rays that emerge from the eye and are reflected by objects viewed. Alhazen postulated that light rays originate in a flame or in the Sun, strike objects, and are reflected by them into the eye. He studied lenses and mirrors, working out that the curvature of a lens accounts for its ability to focus light. He measured the refraction of light by lenses and its reflection by mirrors, and formulated the geometric optics of image formation by spherical and parabolic mirrors. He used a pin-hole as a "lens" to construct a primitive camera obscura. Alhazen also tried to account for the occurrence of rainbows, appreciating that they are formed in the atmosphere, which he estimated extended for about 15 km above the ground. He wrote many scientific works, the chief of them being *Opticae thesaurus* which was published in 1572 from a thirteenth-century Latin translation of his original Arabic version.

Alhazen spent part of his life in Egypt, where he fell foul of the tyrranical (and mad) Caliph al-Hakim. In a foolhardy attempt to impress the caliph, Alhazen claimed he could devise a method of controlling the flooding of the River Nile. To escape the inevitable wrath of the caliph for non-fulfilment of the promise, Alhazen pretended to be mad himself and had to maintain the charade for many years until 1021, when al-Hakim died. Alhazen died in Cairo in 1038.

Alter, David (*1807–1881*), was an American inventor and physicist whose most important contribution to science was in the field of spectroscopy.

Alter was born in Westmoreland County, Pennsylvania, on 3 December 1807. He had little early schooling but in 1828 he entered the Reformed Medical College, New York City, to study medicine, in which he graduated in 1831. Thereafter he spent the rest of his life experimenting and making inventions, working alone and using home-made apparatus. He died in Freeport, Pennsylvania, on 18 September 1881.

Alter made his most important contribution to physics in 1854, when he put forward the idea that each element has a characteristic spectrum, and that spectroscopic analysis of a substance can therefore be used to identify the elements present. He also investigated the Fraunhofer lines in the solar spectrum. Although the significance of this work was not recognized in the United States at that time, his idea was experimentally verified a few years later (about 1860) by Robert Bunsen (1811–1899) and Gustav Kirchhoff (1824–1887) and today spectroscopic analysis is extensively used in chemistry for identifying the component elements of substances and in astronomy for determining the compositions of stars.

Alter devoted most of his life, however, to making inventions, which included a successful electric clock, a model for an electric locomotive (which was not put into production), a new process for purifying bromine, an electric telegraph that spelled out words with a pointer, and a method of extracting oil from coal (which was not put into commercial practice because of the discovery of oil in Pennsylvania).

Ampère, André-Marie (*1775–1836*), was a French physicist, mathematician, chemist and philosopher who is famous for founding the science of electromagnetics (which he named electrodynamics) and who gave his name to the unit of electric current.

Ampère was born in Polémieux, near Lyons, on

22 January 1775. The son of a wealthy merchant, he was tutored privately and was, to a great extent, self-taught. His genius was evident from an early age, particularly in mathematics, which he taught himself and had mastered to an extremely high level by the age of about 12. The later part of his youth, however, was severely disrupted by the French Revolution. In 1793 Lyons was captured by the Republican army and his father – who was both wealthy and a city official – was guillotined. Ampère taught mathematics at a school in Lyons from 1796 to 1801, during which period he married (in 1799); in the following year his wife gave birth to a son, Jean-Jacques-Antoine, who later became an eminent historian and philologist. In 1802 Ampère was appointed Professor of Physics and Chemistry at the École Centrale in Bourg then, later in the same year, Professor of Mathematics at the Lycée in Lyons. Two years later his wife died, a blow from which Ampère never really recovered – indeed, the epitaph he chose for his gravestone was *Tandem felix* ("Happy at last"). In 1805 he was appointed an assistant lecturer in mathematical analysis at the École Polytechnique in Paris where, four years later, he was promoted to Professor of Mathematics. Meanwhile his talent had been recognized by Napoleon, who in 1808 appointed him Inspector-General of the newly formed university system, a post he retained until his death. In addition to his professorship and inspector-generalship, Ampère taught philosophy at the University of Paris in 1819, became Assistant Professor of Astronomy in 1820 and was appointed to the Chair in Experimental Physics at the Collège de France in 1824 – an indication of the breadth of his talents. He died of pneumonia on 10 June 1836 while on an inspection tour of Marseille.

Ampère's first publication was an early contribution to probability theory – *Considérations sur la théorie mathématique de jeu* (1802; *Considerations on the Mathematical Theory of Games*) in which he discussed the inevitability of a player losing a gambling game of chance against an opponent with vastly greater financial resources. It was on the strength of this paper that he was appointed to the professorship at Lyons and later to a post at the École Polytechnique in Paris.

In the period between his arrival in Paris in 1805 and his famous work on electromagnetism in the 1820s, Ampère studied a wide range of subjects, including psychology, philosophy, physics and, more important, chemistry. His work in chemistry was both original and topical but in almost every case public recognition went to another scientist; for example, his studies on the elemental nature of chlorine and iodine were cre-

dited to Humphry Davy (1778–1829). Ampère also suggested a method of classifying elements based on a comprehensive assessment of their chemical properties, anticipating to some extent the development of the Periodic Table later in that century. And in 1814 he independently arrived at what is now known as Avogadro's hypothesis of the molecular constitution of gases. He also analysed Boyle's law in terms of the isothermal volume and pressure of gases.

Despite these considerable and varied achievements, Ampère's fame today rests almost entirely on his even greater work on electromagnetism, a discipline that he, more than any other single scientist, was responsible for establishing. His work in this field was stimulated by the finding of the Danish physicist Hans Christian Oersted that an electric current can deflect a compass needle – i.e. that a wire carrying a current has a magnetic field associated with it. On 11 September 1820 Ampère witnessed a demonstration of this phenomenon given by Dominique Arago at the Academy of Sciences and, like many other scientists, was prompted to hectic activity. Within a week of the demonstration he had presented the first of a series of papers in which he expounded the theory and basic laws of electromagnetism (which he called electrodynamics to differentiate it from the study of stationary electric forces, which he called electrostatics). He showed that two parallel wires carrying current in the same direction attract each other, whereas when the currents are in opposite directions, mutual repulsion results. He also predicted and demonstrated that a helical "coil" of wire (which he called a solenoid) behaves like a bar magnet while it is carrying an electric current.

In addition, Ampère reasoned that the deflection of a compass needle caused by an electric current could be used to construct a device to measure the strength of the current, an idea that eventually led to the development of the galvanometer. He also realized the difference between the rate of passage of an electric current and the driving force behind it; this has been commemorated in naming the unit of electric current the ampere or amp (a usage introduced by Lord Kelvin in 1883). Furthermore, he tried to develop a theory to explain electromagnetism, proposing that magnetism is merely electricity in motion. Prompted by Augustus Fresnel (one of the originators of the wave theory of light), Ampère suggested that molecules are surrounded by a perpetual electric current – a concept that may be regarded as a precursor of the electron shell model.

The culmination of Ampère's studies came in 1827, when he published his famous *Mémoire sur la théorie mathématique des phénomènes électrodynamiques uniquement déduite de l'expérience* (*Notes on the Mathematical Theory of Electrodynamic Phenomena Deduced Solely from Experiment*), in which he enunciated precise mathematical formulations of electromagnetism, notably Ampère's Law – an equation that relates the magnetic force produced by two parallel current-carrying conductors to the product of their currents and the distance between the conductors. Today Ampère's law is usually stated in the form of calculus: the line integral of the magnetic field around an arbitrarily chosen path is proportional to the net electric current enclosed by the path.

Ampère produced little worthy of note after the publication of his *Mémoire* but his work had a great impact and stimulated much further research into electromagnetism.

Anderson, Carl David (*1905–*), is an American physicist who did pioneering work in particle physics, notably discovering the positron – the first antimatter particle to be found – and the muon (or mu-meson). He received many honours for his work, including the 1936 Nobel Prize in Physics, which he shared with Victor Hess.

Anderson was born in New York City on 3 September 1905, the son of Swedish immigrants. He was educated at the California Institute of Technology, from which he gained a BSc in physics and engineering in 1927 and a PhD in 1930. Thereafter he remained at the institute for the rest of his career, as a Research Fellow from 1930 to 1933, Assistant Professor of Physics from 1933 to 1939, and Professor of Physics from 1939 until his retirement in 1976. After retiring he was made an Emeritus Professor of the California Institute of Technology.

Anderson's first research – performed for his doctoral thesis – was a study of the distribution of photoelectrons emitted from various gases as a result of irradiation with X-rays. Then, as a member of Robert Millikan's research team, he began in 1930 to study gamma rays and cosmic rays, extending the work originally published by Skobelzyn, who had photographed tracks of cosmic rays made in a cloud chamber. Anderson devised a special type of cloud chamber that was divided by a lead plate in order to slow down the particles sufficiently for their paths to be accurately determined. Using this modified chamber he measured the energies of cosmic and gamma rays (by measuring the curvature of their paths) in strong magnetic fields (up to about 24,000 gauss, or 2.4 teslas). In 1932, in the course of this investigation, Anderson reported that he had found positively charged particles that occurred

as abundantly as did negatively charged particles, and that in many cases several negative and positive particles were simultaneously projected from the same centre. Anderson initially thought that the positive particle was a proton but, after determining that its mass was similar to that of an electron, concluded that it was a positive electron; he then suggested the name positron for this antimatter particle. Working with Neddermeyer, Anderson also showed that positrons can be produced by irradiation of various materials with gamma rays. In 1932 and 1933 other established scientists – notably Patrick Blackett, James Chadwick and the Joliot-Curies – independently confirmed the existence of the positron and, later, elucidated some of its properties.

In 1936 Anderson contributed to the discovery of another fundamental particle, the muon. While studying tracks in a cloud chamber, he noticed an unusual track that seemed to have been made by a particle intermediate in mass between an electron and a proton. Initially it was thought that this new particle was the one whose existence had previously been predicted by Hideki Yukawa (his hypothetical particle was postulated to hold the nucleus together and to carry the strong nuclear force). Anderson named the particle he had discovered the mesotron, which later became shortened to meson. Further studies of the meson, however, showed that it did not readily interact with the nucleus and therefore could not be the particle predicted by Yukawa. In 1947 Cecil Powell discovered another, more active type of meson that proved to be Yukawa's predicted particle. Anderson's particle – the role of which is still unclear – is now called the muon (or mu-meson) to distinguish it from Powell's particle, which is called the pion (or pi-meson).

Anderson, Philip Warren (*1923–*), is an American physicist who shared the 1977 Nobel Prize in Physics with Nevill Mott and John Van Vleck for his theoretical work on the behaviour of electrons in magnetic, non-crystalline solids.

Anderson was born in Indianapolis on 13 December 1923 and was educated at Harvard University, from which he gained his BS in 1943, MS in 1947 and PhD in 1949; he did his doctoral thesis under Van Vleck. Anderson's studies were interrupted by military service during part of World War II: from 1943 to 1945 he worked at the Harvard Naval Research Laboratories in Washington DC, becoming a Chief Petty Officer in the United States Navy. After obtaining his doctorate, in 1949, he joined the Bell Laboratories in New Jersey, becoming Consulting Director of Physics Research in 1976. In addition to this appointment he has been Joseph Henry Professor of Physics at Princeton University since 1975. Anderson has also visited several foreign universities: he was a Fulbright Lecturer at Tokyo University from 1952 to 1953; an Overseas Fellow at Churchill College, Cambridge, from 1961 to 1962; and Visiting Professor of Theoretical Physics at Cambridge from 1967 to 1975. He was a Fellow of Jesus College, Cambridge, from 1969 to 1975, and was made an Honorary Fellow in 1978.

Anderson has made many varied contributions, although most of his work has been in solid state physics. While studying under Van Vleck at Harvard, he investigated the pressure-broadening of spectral lines in spectroscopy and developed a method of deducing details of molecular interactions from the shapes of spectral peaks. In the late 1950s he devised a theory to explain superexchange – the coupling of the spins of two magnetic ions in an antiferromagnetic material through their interaction with a non-magnetic anion situated between them – and then went on to apply the Bardeen–Cooper–Schrieffer (BCS) theory to explain the effects of impurities on the properties of superconductors. In the early 1960s he investigated the interatomic effects that influence the magnetic properties of metals and alloys, devising a theoretical model (now called the Anderson model) to describe the effect of the presence of an impurity atom in a metal. He also developed a method of describing the movements of impurities within crystalline substances; this method is now known as Anderson localization.

In addition, Anderson has studied the relationship between superconductivity, superfluidity and laser action – all of which involve coherent waves of matter or energy – and predicted the existence of resistance in superconductors. Of more immediate widespread practical application, however, is his work on the semiconducting properties of inexpensive, disordered glassy solids; his studies of these materials indicate that they could be used instead of the expensive crystalline semiconductors now used in many electronic devices, such as computer memories, electronic switches and solar energy converters.

Ångström, Anders Jonas (*1814–1874*), was a Swedish physicist and astronomer, one of the early pioneers in the development of spectroscopy.

Ångström was born at Lögdö, Sweden, on 13 August 1814, the son of a chaplain. He was educated at the University of Uppsala, which awarded him his doctorate in physics in 1839; he began to lecture there in the same year. In 1843 he was appointed an observer at the Uppsala Observatory. In 1858 he was elected to the Chair

of Physics at the University, a post which he held until his death, at Uppsala, on 21 June 1874.

Ångström's first important work was an investigation into the conduction of heat and his first important result was to devise a method of measuring thermal conductivity, which demonstrated it to be proportional to electrical conductivity. Then, in 1853, he published his most substantial and influential work, *Optical Investigations*, which contains his principle of spectrum analysis. Ångström had studied electric arcs and discovered that they yield two spectra, one superimposed on the other. The first was emitted from the metal of the electrode itself, the second from the gas through which the spark passed. By applying Euler's theory of resonances Ångström was then able to demonstrate that a hot gas emits light at the same frequency as it absorbs it when it is cooled.

Ångström's early work provided the foundation for the spectrum analysis to which he devoted the rest of his career. He was chiefly interested in the Sun's spectrum, although in 1867 he investigated the spectrum of the Aurora Borealis, the first person to do so. In 1862 he announced his inference (in fact, it amounted to a discovery) that hydrogen was present in the Sun. In 1868 he published *Researches on the Solar System*, a famous work in which he presented measurements of the wavelengths of more than 100 Fraunhofer. The lines were measured to six significant figures in units of 10^{-8} cm. The unit of measure for wavelength of light, called the angstrom (Å, equal to 10^{-10} m), was officially adopted by 1907.

Another of Ångström's important contributions was his map of the normal solar spectrum, published in 1869, which remained a standard reference tool for 20 years.

Appleton, Edward Victor (*1892–1965*), was a British physicist famous for his discovery of the Appleton layer of the ionosphere which reflects radio waves and is therefore important in communications. He received many honours for his work, including a knighthood in 1941 and the Nobel Prize in Physics in 1947.

Appleton was born on 6 September 1892 in Bradford, Yorkshire. He attended Barkerend Elementary School from 1899 to 1903, then won a scholarship to Hanson Secondary School. A gifted student, he also won a scholarship to St John's College, Cambridge, in 1910 and graduated with first class honours in 1913. After a short period of postgraduate research with William Henry Bragg, Appleton became a signals officer in the Royal Engineers with the outbreak of World War I in 1914. This aroused his interest in radio and he began to investigate radio propagation when he returned to Cambridge after the war. In 1919 he was elected a Fellow of St John's College, and in the following year was appointed an Assistant Demonstrator at the Cavendish Laboratory. In 1924, when only 32 years old, he was appointed Wheatstone Professor of Physics at King's College, London, a post he held until 1936, when he was made Jacksonian Professor of Natural Philosophy at Cambridge. In 1939 he became Secretary of the Department of Scientific and Industrial Research, in which position he gained a reputation as an adviser on government scientific policy. During World War II, he was involved in the development of radar and of the atomic bomb. In 1949 he was made Principal and Vice-chancellor of Edinburgh University, a position he held until his death (in Edinburgh) on 21 April 1965. While at Edinburgh, he founded the *Journal of Atmospheric Research*, which became known as "Appleton's journal"; he remained its Editor-in-Chief for the rest of his life. Appleton began his research on radio when he returned to Cambridge after World War I. Initially he investigated (with Balthazar van der Pol Jr.) thermionic vacuum tubes – on which he wrote a monograph in 1932 – then in the early 1920s he turned his attention to studying the fading of radio signals, a phenomenon he had encountered while a signals officer during World War I.

The first transatlantic radio transmission had been made by Guglielmo Marconi in 1901, and to explain why this was possible (that is, why the radio waves "bent" around the Earth and did not merely go straight out into space) Oliver Heaviside and Arthur Kennelly postulated the existence of an atmospheric layer of charged particles (now called the Kennelly–Heaviside layer or E layer) that reflected the radio waves. Working with the New Zealand graduate student Miles Barnell – and using the recently set up BBC radio transmitters – Appleton proved the existence of the Kennelly–Heaviside layer. By periodically varying the frequency of the BBC transmitter at Bournemouth and measuring the intensity of the received transmission 100 km away, Appleton and Barnell found that there was a regular "fading in" and "fading out" of the signals at night but that this effect diminished considerably at dawn as the Kennelly–Heaviside layer broke up. They also noticed, however, that radio waves continued to be reflected by the atmosphere during the day but by a higher level ionized layer. By 1926 this layer, which Appleton measured at about 250 km above the Earth's surface (the first distance measurement made by means of radio), became generally known as the Appleton layer

(it is now also known as the F layer).

Appleton continued his studies of the ionosphere (as the charged layers of the atmosphere above the stratosphere are called), showing how they are affected by the position of the sun and by changes in the sunspot cycle. He also calculated their reflection coefficients, electron densities and their diurnal and seasonal variations. Further, he showed that the Appleton layer is strongly affected by the Earth's magnetic field and that although further above the Earth, it has a greater density and temperature than does the Kennelly–Heaviside layer.

Appleton's research into the atmosphere was of fundamental importance to the development of radio communications, and his experimental methods were later used by the British physicist Robert Watson-Watt – with whom Appleton had collaborated on several projects – in his development of radar.

Arago, (Dominique) François (*1786–1853*), was a French scientist who made contributions to the development of many areas of physics and astronomy, the breadth of his work compensating for the absence of a single product of truly outstanding quality. He was closely involved with André Ampère (1775–1836) in the development of electromagnetism and with Augustin Fresnel (1788–1827) in the establishment of the wave theory of light. Arago's political commitment demanded much time during his latter years, but he maintained a continuous flow of scientific investigations until almost the end of his life.

Arago was born in Estagel, France on 26 February 1786. He studied at the École Polytechnique in Paris and was then appointed to the Bureau of Longitudes. He travelled to the south of France and Spain with Jean Biot (1774–1862) in 1806, where they intended to measure an arc of the terrestrial meridian. Biot returned to France in 1807, but Arago continued his work amidst a deteriorating political situation. His return to France in 1809 was somewhat enlivened by a shipwreck and his subsequent near-escape from being sold into slavery in Algiers!

In the same year, Arago was elected to the membership of the French Academy of Sciences and became professor of analytical geometry at the École Polytechnique, a post he held until 1830. He became a fellow of the Royal Society of London in 1818, which awarded him the Copley medal in 1825 for his work on electromagnetism.

The year 1830 was one of several changes for Arago. He resigned his post at the École Polytechnique and succeeded Jean Fourier (1768–1830) as permanent secretary to the Academy of Sciences.

He also became director of the Paris Observatory and deputy for Pyrénées Orientales, a commitment he retained until 1852.

Arago's political affiliation was with the extreme left, and the political turbulence of 1848 saw him elected to a Ministerial position in the Provisional Government. It was under his administration that slavery was abolished in the French colonies. He resigned his post of astronomer in 1852 upon the coronation of Emperor Napoleon III, refusing to make an oath of allegiance to the Emperor. Arago's reputation protected him but he died soon afterwards in Paris on 2 October 1853.

Arago's one area of sustained scientific effort was the study of the nature of light. The controversy over the question of whether light behaves as a stream of particles or as a wave motion was one of the most hotly debated of the time. Arago initially sided with Biot in the particulate camp, but later took the other view with Baron Humboldt (1769–1859), Fresnel and others. In 1811, he invented the polariscope, with which he was able to measure the degree of polarization of light rays. From 1815, Arago worked with Fresnel on polarization and was able to elucidate the fundamental laws governing it. Fresnel's mathematical expertise complemented Arago's experimental ability in establishing the wave theory of light though, because of difficulties in explaining its transmission through the aether, Arago could not accept Fresnel's assertion that light moves in transverse waves.

In 1838, Arago published a method for determining the speed of light using a rotating mirror. He was interested to find out how the speed of light is affected by travelling through a medium such as water that is dense in comparison with air. The experiment was a crucial one in determining whether light is a wave motion or not, but sadly difficulties with his laboratory equipment, the 1848 Revolution and finally the loss of his eyesight in 1850 prevented Arago from completing the experiment. Leon Foucault (1819–1869) was able to do this for him, and he obtained results which confirmed the wave theory before Arago's death.

In 1820, Arago announced to the Academy of Sciences some observations on the effect of an electric current on a magnet which had been obtained by Hans Oersted (1777–1851). Arago himself turned to the study of electromagnetism, inspiring Ampère to do the same and producing many interesting results himself. Arago found in 1820 that an electric current produces temporary magnetization in iron, a discovery crucial to the later development of electromagnets and electric relays and loudspeakers. Then, in 1824, he discovered that a rotating non-magnetic metal disc, for example of copper, deflects a magnetic needle placed above it. This was a demonstration of electromagnetic induction, explained by Michael Faraday (1791–1867) in 1831.

Arago also investigated the compressibility, density, diffraction and dispersion of gases; the speed of sound, which he found to be 331.2 m/sec; lightning, of which he found four different types; and heat. His studies in astronomy included investigations of the solar corona and chromosphere, measurements of the diameters of the planets, and a theory that light interference is responsible for the "twinkling" of stars.

Arago's energy and enthusiasm, while directing him into a multiplicity of endeavours, acted as a catalyst in the achievement of several fundamental advances in the study of light and electromagnetism.

Archimedes (*c.287–212* BC), is generally considered to be the greatest mathematician and physicist of the ancient world. The details of his personal life, and many of the stories surrounding his achievements are of dubious authenticity. A biography of his life written by Heracleides (a friend of Archimedes) has been lost, so modern historians of science have to rely on the mathematical treatises that Archimedes is known to have published and on accounts of his life by Greeks who lived after his time. The reliability of at least parts of these accounts must be questioned, particularly those dealing with Archimedes' military exploits against the Romans during their siege of his home town Syracuse shortly before his death.

Archimedes is believed to have been born in 287 BC in Syracuse, Sicily, then a Greek colony. This date is based on the claim of a twelfth-century historian that Archimedes survived to the age of 75, for the date of his death in 212 BC is not questioned. His father was Phidias, an astronomer, and the family was a noble one possibly related to that of King Hieron II of Syracuse.

Alexandria was a great centre of learning for mathematicians, and Archimedes travelled there to study under Conon (*fl.c.*250 BC) and other mathematicians who had in turn studied under Euclid (*fl.c.*300 BC). Unlike most other disciples, Archimedes did not remain in Alexandria but returned to his home where he devoted the rest of his life to the serious study of mathematics and physics and, by way of recreation, to the design of a variety of mechanical devices which brought him great fame.

He chose only to publish the results of his scientific studies since only these, in his eyes, were worthy of serious consideration. His ability to invent and construct machinery was exploited during the Roman's siege of Syracuse from 215 to 212 BC. The siege is reported to have lasted such a long time because Archimedes was able to hold the Roman fleet at bay with a series of weapons which allegedly set fire to the ships or even caused them to capsize.

When the Roman sack of the city eventually came, Archimedes comported himself as the truly disinterested philosopher that he was. A Roman soldier came across him kneeling over a mathematical problem which he was examining, scratched out in the sand at the marketplace. Despite orders that Archimedes be taken alive and treated well, the impatient soldier – unable to remove him from his study – killed him on the spot.

Archimedes had decreed that his gravestone be inscribed with a cylinder enclosing a sphere together with the formula for the ratio of their volumes, this being the discovery that he regarded as his greatest achievement. His wish was evidently granted for Cicero found this gravestone in 75 BC, possibly confirming Plutarch's view that Archimedes himself thought highly only of his theoretical endeavours and disdained his practical inventions.

In physics, Archimedes is best known for his establishment of the sciences of statics and hydrostatics. In the field of statics, he is credited with working out the rigorous mathematical proofs behind the law of the lever. The lever had been used by other scientists, but it was Archimedes who demonstrated mathematically that the ratio of the effort applied to the load raised is equal to the inverse ratio of the distances of the effort and load from the pivot or fulcrum of the lever. Archimedes is credited with having claimed that if he had a sufficiently distant place to stand, he could use a lever to move the world.

This claim is said to have given rise to a challenge from King Hieron to Archimedes to show how he could move a truly heavy object with ease, even if he couldn't move the world. In answer to this, Archimedes developed a system of compound pulleys. According to Plutarch's Life of Marcellus (who sacked Syracuse), Archimedes used this to move with ease a ship which had been lifted with great effort by many men out of the harbour onto dry land. The ship was laden with passengers, crew and freight, but Archimedes – sitting at a distance from the ship – was reportedly able to pull it over the land as though it were gliding through water.

The best known result of Archimedes' work on hydrostatics is the so-called Archimedes Principle, which states that a body immersed in water

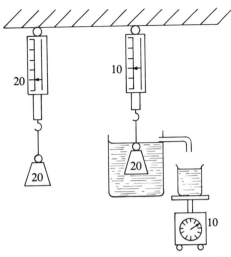

According to Archimedes' principle, the upthrust on an object immersed – or partly immersed – in a fluid is equal to the weight of the fluid displaced (and is independent of the weight of the object).

will displace a volume of fluid which weighs as much as the body would weigh in air. Archimedes is said to have discovered this famous principle when causing water to overflow from a bath. He was so overjoyed at the idea that he ran naked through the town crying "Eureka!" which, roughly translated, means "I've got it!". His interest in the problem is said to have been stimulated by the problem of determining whether King Hieron's new crown was pure gold or not. The king had ordered that this be checked without damaging the crown in any way. Archimedes realized that if the gold had been mixed with silver (which is less dense than gold), the crown would have a greater volume and therefore displace more water than an equal weight of pure gold. The story goes that the crown was in fact found to be impure, and that the unfortunate goldsmith was executed.

Among Archimedes' inventions was a design for a model planetarium able to show the movement of the Sun, Moon, planets and possibly constellations across the sky. According to Cicero, this was captured as booty by Marcellus after the sack of Syracuse. The Archimedes screw, which is an auger used to raise water for irrigation, is also credited to Archimedes, who is supposed to have invented it during his days in Egypt though he may simply have borrowed the idea from others in Egypt.

Archimedes wrote many mathematical treatises, some of which still exist in altered forms in Arabic. Among the areas he investigated were the value for π. Archimedes' approximation was more accurate than any previous estimate – he stated that the value for π lay between 223/71 and 220/70, the average of these two values being less than three parts in ten thousand different from the modern approximation for π. He also examined the expression of very large numbers, using a special notation to estimate the number of grains of sand in the Universe. The result – 10^{63} – may be far from accurate, but it showed that large numbers could be considered and handled effectively. Archimedes also evolved methods to solve cubic equations and to determine square roots by approximation, as well as formulas for the determination of the surface areas and volumes of curved surfaces and solids. In the latter area, Archimedes' work anticipated the development of integral calculus, which did not come for another 2,000 years. In his mathematical proofs Archimedes employed the methods of exhaustion and *reductio ad absurdum*, which were perhaps originally developed by Eudoxus and were also used by Euclid.

Surprisingly, in view of his reputation, Archimedes' work was not widely known in antiquity and little advance was made on it. It was preserved by Byzantium and Islam, from where it spread to Europe from the twelfth century onwards. Archimedes then had a profound effect on the history of science, for his method of finding mathematical proof to substantiate experiment and observation became the method of modern science introduced by Simon Stevinus, Johann Kepler, Galileo and Evangelista Torricelli among others in the late sixteenth and early seventeenth centuries.

Armstrong, Edwin Howard (*1890-1954*), was an American electronics engineer who worked almost exclusively in radio, developing the superheterodyne receiver and frequency modulation (FM) radio transmission.

Armstrong was born in New York City on 18 December 1890, the son of a publisher. As a child he had an intense interest in machines and mechanisms and by the age of 14, stimulated by reports of the work of Guglielmo Marconi (1874-1937), he was constructing wireless (radio) circuits for transmitters and receivers. After graduating from High School he attended the engineering department of Columbia University, New York, gaining a degree in electrical engineering in 1913. He became an instructor at Columbia, and during World War I he worked in the Laboratories of the US Signal Corps in Paris. In 1918, after the end of the war, he returned to Columbia University as an assistant to the physicist Michael Pupin (1858-1935), whom he eventually succeeded as Professor of Electrical Engineering in 1934.

During World War II he again carried out research for the military. His inventions earned him much money – he became a millionaire – but also involved him in expensive, protracted litigation and promotional costs. His health declined and he became depressed; at the end of January 1954 he committed suicide by jumping from the window of his New York apartment.

In 1912, while he was still a student at Columbia University, Armstrong designed and built a regenerative, or feed-back, radio receiving circuit that made use of the amplifying ability of the triode thermionic valve, called the Audion by its inventor Lee De Forest in 1906. The same circuit acted as an oscillator (transmitter) at high amplifications. He patented it, and for 14 years fought a series of legal battles about priority with De Forest. Armstrong finally lost the struggle in the Supreme Court, although the legal interpretation was not accepted by most of the scientists and engineers of the time who continued to uphold Armstrong's claim and awarded him the Franklin Medal for his invention.

The superheterodyne receiving circuit was developed by Armstrong during World War I in an attempt to make a receiver that could detect the presence of aircraft by means of the electromagnetic (radio) waves given off by the sparking of the ignition systems of their engines. Again he patented the idea, and sold patent rights and licences to major manufacturers, including RCA in the United States. During the 1920s, earnings from these sources made him a rich man.

At that time, radio broadcasting used amplitude modulation (AM), in which the audio signal varies the amplitude of a transmitted carrier wave. Electrical disturbances in the atmosphere caused by storms or electrical machinery also modulate the carrier wave, resulting in static interference at the receiver. In 1933 Armstrong, working with Pupin, developed and patented a method of radio broadcasting in which the transmitted signal is made to modulate the frequency of the carrier wave over a wide waveband. This method, called frequency modulation (FM), is unaffected by static and is capable of high-fidelity sound reproduction; it remains the basis of quality radio, television, microwave and satellite transmissions, although the high frequencies employed are generally limited to line-of-sight distances. FM broadcasting did not gain ground until after World War II, and then only after Armstrong had used much of his fortune in promoting it and in another round of legal actions about patent rights. Frustration and disenchantment with the attendant commercial, legal and financial problems probably led to his suicide.

B

Bacon, Roger (*c.1220–c.1292*), was an English philosopher and scientist who was among the first medieval scholars to realize and promote the value of experiment in reaching valid conclusions.

It is not certain when or where Bacon was born. One tradition says that he was born at Bisley in Gloucestershire, while another says he came from Ilchester in Somerset. His date of birth can only be guessed from his writing, in 1267, that he had learnt the alphabet forty years before. Bacon was educated in philosophy and mathematics at Oxford, and then lectured at the Faculty of Arts in Paris from about 1241. After about 1247, he returned to Oxford where he was inspired by the English scholar Robert Grosseteste (*c.*1168–1253) to cultivate the 'new' branches of learning – languages, mathematics, optics, alchemy and astronomy. In about 1257, he entered the Franciscan Order and, while a friar, appealed to Pope Clement IV to allow sciences a higher status in the curriculum of University studies. At the Pope's request, Bacon in 1266–67 wrote three volumes of an encyclopedia of all the known sciences: *Opus majus*, *Opus minus* and *Opus tertium*. In about 1268, he published fragments of another encyclopedia – *Communia naturalium* and *Communia mathematica*, and in 1272, *Compendium philosophiae*. Following the death of Pope Clement IV in 1268, Bacon lost papal protection and was imprisoned by the Franciscans at some time from 1277 to 1279, possibly for criticisms of the order's educational practices. Bacon languished in prison for as long as 15 years. His last work, on theology, was published in 1292. He is said to have died in the same year and was buried in the Franciscan church in Oxford.

Bacon in his writings states that he spent huge sums of money in acquiring "secret" books, in constructing instruments and tables, training assistants and in getting to know knowledgeable people. The experiments he performed and the knowledge he acquired earned him the title of *doctor mirabilis*. However little, if any, of his work was original. His main contribution was in optics, in which Robert Grosseteste acquainted Bacon with the work of Alhazen (*c.*965–1038). Bacon advocated the use of lenses as magnifying glasses to aid weak sight, and speculated that lenses might be used to make an instrument of great magnifying power – an indication of the telescope.

Bacon also described some of the properties of gunpowder in a volume written sometime before 1249, but there is no indication that he had any idea of its possible use as a propellant, only that it would explode and so could be used in warfare. He described early diving apparatus, in a passage where he referred to "instruments whereby men can walk on sea or river beds without danger to themselves" in 1240.

Bacon was an ardent supporter of calendar reform, suggesting the changes necessary to improve the calendar that were carried out by Pope Gregory XIII in 1582. He also promoted the use of latitude and longitude in map-making and, by estimating the distance of India from Spain, may have inspired Columbus' voyage to America, which was a search for a shorter westward route to India.

Bacon is sometimes referred to as one of the "forerunners" of science, but investigation does not show his scientific contribution to be very great. His importance in the history of science is due to his insistence on the use of experiment to prove an argument, a method that was not to flower until some three centuries later. Bacon also referred to the laws of reflection and refraction as being "natural laws" – that is, of universal application – a concept vital to the development of science.

Bainbridge, Kenneth Tompkins (*1904– *), is an American physicist best known for his work on the development of the mass spectrometer.

Bainbridge was born in Cooperstown, New York on 27 July 1904. He was educated at the Massachusetts Institute of Technology and at Princeton University, where he gained his MA in 1927 and a PhD in 1929. After working at the Bartol Research Foundation and at the Cavendish Laboratory in Cambridge, England, he became assistant professor of physics at Harvard University in 1934, associate professor in 1938 and professor from 1946 onwards. He has been professor emeritus since 1975. Bainbridge has held a number of important concurrent appointments. He worked in the radiation laboratory at MIT from 1940 to 1943 and then in the Los Alamos laboratory until 1945, when he directed the first atomic bomb test. He was awarded the Presidential Certificate of Merit for his work on radar in 1948.

The mass spectrometer or mass spectrograph was invented by Francis Aston (1877–1945) in 1919. In it, a beam of ions is deflected by electric and magnetic fields so that ions of the same mass are brought to a focus at the same point, enabling the masses of the ions in the beam to be determined. It proved the existence of isotopes. Aston's mass spectrometer was a velocity-focusing machine, meaning that it focused beams of

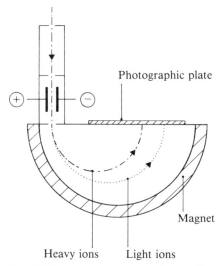

Photographic plate

Magnet

Heavy ions   Light ions

In Bainbridge's mass spectrograph, a collimated beam of positive ions of the same velocity is sorted into its component ions in a uniform magnetic field (at right-angles to the plane of the paper).

varying velocity but not varying direction. A direction-focusing machine, which focused beams of uniform velocity but varying direction, was developed by Arthur Dempster (1886–1950). Bainbridge's achievement in mass spectroscopy was to develop a double-focusing machine in 1936. It used successive electric and magnetic fields arranged in such a way that ion beams which are non-uniform in both direction and velocity can be brought to a focus. By the mid-1950s, instruments based on this principle were able to separate ions which differ in mass by only one part in 60,000.

Bainbridge is responsible for many of the innovations in the modern mass spectrometer, one of the most useful of analytical tools in physics, chemistry, geology, meteorology, biology and medicine.

Balmer, Johann Jakob (*1825–1898*), was a Swiss mathematics teacher who devised mathematical formulae that give the frequencies of atomic spectral lines.

Balmer was born in Lausen, near Basle, on 1 May 1825, the eldest son of a farmer who was also a member of the local administration of Basle. He went to school in Liestal, Basle, then in 1844 entered the Technische Hochschule in Karlsruhe, where he studied mathematics, geology and architecture. He subsequently spent a short time at the University of Berlin, then in 1846 returned to his old school in Basle to teach technical drawing while working towards his PhD, which he was awarded in 1849 by the Uni-

versity of Basle. In the following year he began teaching mathematics and Latin at a girls' school in Basle, a post he held for 40 years, until his retirement in 1890. From 1865 to 1890 he was also a part-time lecturer at Basle University, teaching projective geometry, which was the subject of a textbook he published in 1887. Balmer died in Basle on 12 March 1898.

Balmer was a mathematician by education and vocation and was not trained in physics. Nevertheless, he became interested in spectroscopy and – encouraged by J.E. Hagenbach-Bischoff, a professor at Basle University – began investigating the apparently random distribution of spectral lines. Spectroscopy was a relatively new discipline in the last quarter of the nineteenth century and, although it was known that excited molecules of a substance emit discrete, characteristic spectral lines, many scientists had failed to find a mathematical relationship between these lines. But in 1885 Balmer – then aged 60 – published an equation that described the four visible spectral lines of hydrogen (all that were then known) and also predicted the existence of a fifth line at the limit of the visible spectrum, which was soon detected and measured. He further predicted the existence of other hydrogen spectral lines beyond the visible spectrum. These lines were later found and named after their discoverers: the Lyman series (in the ultraviolet part of the spectrum), the Paschen series (in the infrared part of the spectrum), the Brackett series (infrared) and the Pfund series (infrared). The five lines in the visible part of the hydrogen spectrum are now known as the Balmer series, and are described by the formula:

$$v = R \left[\frac{1}{1^2} - \frac{1}{n^2} \right]$$

where v is the wave number, R is the Rydberg constant, and $n = 2, 3, 4 \ldots$

Balmer arrived at his formula (which has been modified only slightly in the light of later findings) solely from empirical evidence and offered no explanation as to why it gave the correct results. But it was later of crucial importance to Niels Bohr, who used it to support his model of atomic structure. Moreover, not until atomic theory had developed still further was a full explanation of Balmer's equation possible.

Balmer's last paper, which was published in 1897, contained equations to describe the spectral lines of helium and lithium.

Bardeen, John (*1908–   *), is an American physicist whose work on semiconductors, together with William Shockley (1910–   ) and Walter Brattain (1902–   ), led to the first transistor, an achievement for which all three men shared the 1956 Nobel Prize in Physics. Bardeen also gained a second Nobel Prize in Physics in 1972, which he then shared with John Robert Schrieffer (1931–   ) and Leon Cooper (1930–   ) for a complete theoretical explanation of superconductivity.

Bardeen, who is the only person thus far to be awarded two Nobel Prizes in Physics, was born in Madison, Wisconsin on 23 May 1908. He began his career with a BS in electrical engineering at the University of Wisconsin awarded in 1928. For the next two years, he was a graduate assistant working on mathematical problems of antennas and on applied geophysics, but it was at this stage that he first became acquainted with quantum mechanics. He moved to Gulf Research in Pittsburgh, where he worked on the mathematical modelling of magnetic and gravitational oil prospecting surveys, but the lure of pure scientific research became increasingly strong, and in 1933 he gave up his industrial career to enrol for graduate work with Eugene Wigner (1902–   ) at Princeton, where he was introduced to the fast developing field of solid state physics. His early studies of work functions, cohesive energy and electrical conductivity in metals were carried out at Princeton, Harvard and the University of Minnesota. From 1941 to 1945, he returned to applied physics at the Naval Ordnance Laboratory in Washington DC, where he studied ship demagnetization and magnetic detection of submarines.

In 1945 Bardeen joined the Bell Telephone Laboratory, and his work on semiconductors there led to the first transistor, an achievement rewarded with his first Nobel Prize in conjunction with Walter Brattain and William Shockley. He moved to the University of Illinois in 1951, where in 1957, along with Bob Schrieffer and Leon Cooper, he developed the microscopic theory of superconductivity (the BCS theory) that was to gain him a second Nobel Prize in 1972. Since 1975, he has been an emeritus professor at Illinois, and is now concentrating on theories for liquid helium-3 which have analogies with the BCS theory.

The electrical properties of semiconductors gradually became understood in the late 1930s with the realization of the role of low concentrations of impurities in controlling the number of mobile charge carriers. Current rectification at metal-semiconductor junctions had long been known, but the natural next step was to produce amplification analagous to that achieved in triode and pentode valves. A group led by William Shockley began a programme to control the number of charge carriers at semiconductor surfaces by varying the electric field. John Bardeen interpreted the rather small observed effects in terms of surface trapping of carriers, but he and Walter Brattain successfully demonstrated amplification by putting two metal contacts 0.05 mm apart on a germanium surface. Large variations of the power output through one contact were observed in response to tiny changes in the current through the other. This so-called point contact transistor was the forerunner of the many complex devices now available through silicon chip technology.

Ever since 1911, when Heike Kamerlingh-Onnes (1853–1926) first observed zero electrical resistance in some metals below a critical temperature, physicists sought a microscopic interpretation of this phenomenon of superconductivity. The methods that proved successful in explaining the electrical properties of normal metals were unable to predict the effect. At very low temperatures, metals were still expected to have a finite resistance due to scattering of mobile electrons by impurities. Bardeen, Cooper and Schrieffer overcame this problem by showing that electrons pair up through an *attractive* interaction, and that zero resistivity occurs when there is not enough thermal energy to break the pair apart.

Normally electrons repel one another through the Coulomb interaction, but a net attraction may be possible when the electrons are imbedded in a crystal. The ion cores in the lattice respond to the presence of a nearby electron, and the motion may result in another electron being attracted to the ion. The net effect is an attraction between two electrons through the response of the ions in the solid. The pairs condense out in a kind of phase transition below a temperature T_c (typically of the order of a few degrees K), and the involvement of the ions of the lattice in the interaction is confirmed by the dependence of T_c on the isotopic mass in the metal, i.e. T_c varies with variation of atomic vibration frequencies in the solid. The requirement of a finite energy to break up a so-called Cooper pair leads to a small energy gap below which excitations are not possible.

The BCS theory is amazingly complete, and explains all known properties associated with superconductivity. Although applications of superconductivity to magnets and motors were possible without the BCS theory, the theory is important for strategies to increase T_c as high as possible – if T_c could be raised above liquid nitrogen temperature, the economics of superconductivity would be transformed. In addition, the theory was an essential prerequisite for the prediction of Josephson tunnelling with its important applications in magnetometers, computers and determination of the fundamental constants of physics.

Both of Bardeen's achievements have important consequences in the field of computers. The invention of the transistor led directly to the development of the integrated circuit and then the microchip, which is making computers both more powerful and more practical. Superconductivity enables the basic arithmetic and logic operations of computers to be carried out at much greater speeds and may lead to the development of artificial intelligence.

Barkla, Charles Glover (*1877–1944*), was a British physicist who made important contributions to our knowledge of X-rays, particularly the phenomenon of X-ray scattering. He received many honours for his work on ionizing radiation, including the 1917 Nobel Prize in Physics.

Barkla was born on 7 June 1877 in Widnes, Lancashire. After studying at the Liverpool Institute, he went to University College, Liverpool, in 1895, where he studied under Oliver Lodge. He obtained his BSc in 1898 and his MSc in the following year. In the autumn of 1899 he went to Trinity College, Cambridge, where he researched under J. J. Thomson at the Cavendish Laboratory, but transferred to King's College, Cambridge in 1901 in order to sing in the choir. Nevertheless, he refused the offer of a choral scholarship, which would have enabled him to remain at Cambridge, and in 1902 returned to University College, Liverpool, as Oliver Lodge Fellow. In 1904 he was awarded a DSc and was regularly promoted, being appointed a Special Lecturer in 1907. He was made Professor of Physics at King's College, London, in 1909 and remained there until 1913, when he became Professor of Natural Philosophy at Edinburgh University, a position he held until his death on 23 October 1944.

Barkla's first major piece of research, which was carried out while he was a student at the Cavendish Laboratory, involved measuring the speed at which electromagnetic waves travel along wires of different thickness and composition. During his third year at Cambridge, he began investigating secondary radiation – the effect whereby a substance subjected to X-rays re-emits secondary X-radiation – a subject that he spent most of his subsequent career studying. He published his first paper on this phenomenon in 1903. In this paper he announced his finding that for gases of elements with a low atomic mass the secondary scattered radiation is of the same average wavelength as that of the primary X-ray beam to which the gas is subjected. He also found that the extent of such scattering is proportional to the atomic mass of the gas concerned. The more massive an atom, the more charged particles it contains and it is these charged particles that

are responsible for the X-ray scattering. Thus Barkla's work was one of the first indications of the importance of the amount of charge in an atom (rather than merely its atomic mass) in determining an element's position in the Periodic Table – a significant early step in the evolution of the concept of atomic number.

In 1904 Barkla found that, unlike the low atomic mass elements, the heavy elements produced secondary radiation of a longer wavelength than that of the primary X-ray beam. He also showed that X-rays can be partially polarized, thus proving that they are a form of transverse electromagnetic radiation, like visible light.

In 1907 Barkla began his most important research into X-rays, working at Liverpool with C. A. Sadler. They found that secondary radiation is homogeneous and that the radiation from the heavier elements is of two characteristic types. They also showed that these characteristics (that is, of a specific wavelength) radiations are emitted only after a heavy element is exposed to X-radiation "harder" (that is, of shorter wavelength, and therefore more penetrating) than its own characteristic emissions. This finding was the first indication that X-ray emissions are monochromatic.

Barkla named the two types of characteristic emissions the K-series (for the more penetrating emissions) and the L-series (for the less penetrating emissions). He later predicted that other series of emissions with different penetrances might exist, and an M-series – radiation with even lower penetrance than that of the K-series – was subsequently discovered. After about 1916, however, Barkla devoted his research to investigating a J-series of extremely penetrating radiations, the existence of which he had suggested. But the results of these studies could not be confirmed by other workers and the existence of the L-series was not and still is not, part of accepted theory. Nevertheless Barkla continued to adhere to his theory of the J-phenomenon, as a result of which he became increasingly isolated from the rest of the scientific community during his later years.

Becquerel, Antoine Henri (*1852–1908*), was a French physicist who discovered radioactivity in 1896, an achievement for which he shared the 1903 Nobel Prize in Physics with Pierre Curie (1859–1906) and Marie Curie (1867–1934). The Curies did not participate in Becquerel's discovery but investigated radioactivity and gave the phenomenon its name.

Becquerel was born in Paris on 15 December 1852 and educated at the École Polytechnique and École des Ponts et Chaussées, where he received a training in engineering. In 1875, he began private scientific research, investigating the behaviour of polarized light in magnetic fields and in crystals, linking the degree of rotation to refractive index. Both Becquerel's grandfather and father were respected physicists with positions at the Museum of Natural History and other institutions. On their deaths in 1878 and 1891 respectively, Becquerel succeeded to their posts. He became a member of the Academy of Sciences in 1889, a professor at the Museum in 1892 and at the École Polytechnique in 1895.

Becquerel then began the work for which he is remembered, not necessarily because of his position but because of the discovery of X-rays made by Wilhelm Röntgen (1845–1923) early in 1896. This prompted Becquerel to investigate fluorescent crystals for the emission of X-rays, and in so doing he accidentally discovered radioactivity in uranium salts in the same year. Pierre and Marie Curie then searched for other radioactive materials, which led them to the discovery of polonium and radium in 1898.

Becquerel subsequently investigated the radioactivity of radium, and showed in 1900 that it consists of a stream of electrons. In the same year, Becquerel also obtained evidence that radioactivity causes the transformation of one element into another. Following his award of the 1903 Nobel Prize in Physics jointly with the Curies, Becquerel became vice-president (1906) and president (1908) of the Academy of Sciences. He died soon after on 25 August 1908 in Brittany.

Becquerel's discovery of radioactivity was prompted by the mathematician Henri Poincaré (1854–1912), who told Becquerel that X-rays were emitted from a fluorescent spot on the glass cathode-ray tube used by Röntgen. This immediately suggested to Becquerel that X-rays might be produced naturally by fluorescent crystals, with which he was familiar through his father's interest in fluorescence. He therefore placed some crystals of potassium uranyl sulphate on a photographic plate wrapped in paper, and put it in sunlight to make the crystals fluoresce. When he developed the plate, Becquerel found it to be fogged, showing that a radiation resembling X-rays had penetrated the paper and exposed the plate. Becquerel then tried to repeat the experiment to make further investigations, but the weather was cloudy and the uranium crystals would not fluoresce as there was no sunlight. He put a wrapped plate and the crystals into a drawer and waited. The weather did not improve and Becquerel impatiently decided to develop the plate. To his astonishment, the plate had been strongly exposed to radiation. Clearly it was not connected with fluorescence, but was emitted naturally by the crystals all the time.

Becquerel studied the radiation and found that it behaved like X-rays in penetrating matter and ionizing air. He showed that it was due to the presence of uranium in the crystals, and subsequently found that a disk of pure uranium metal is highly radioactive. This led Pierre and Marie Curie to isolate polonium and radium, which is even more radioactive. Becquerel later subjected the radiation from radium to magnetic fields and was able to prove by the amount of deflection that it must consist of the electrons that had been discovered by J.J. Thomson (1856–1940) in 1897. Becquerel also discovered that radioactivity could be removed from a radioactive material by chemical action, but that the material subsequently regained its radioactivity.

Becquerel's discovery of radioactivity and its investigation by himself and the Curies caused a revolution in physics. It marked the beginning of nuclear physics by showing that atoms, and then nuclei within atoms, are made up of smaller particles. Furthermore, the spontaneous regeneration of radioactivity observed by Becquerel was evidence that one element can be transformed into another with the production of energy. A full explanation of radioactivity was achieved by Ernest Rutherford (1871–1937), leading eventually to nuclear fission and the production of nuclear energy.

Bernoulli, Daniel (*1700–1782*), was a Dutch physicist and mathematician who made important discoveries in hydrodynamics, anticipated the kinetic theory of gases, and investigated differential equations and probability theory.

Bernoulli was born in Groningen in Holland on 8 February 1700. He came from a famous family of mathematicians, his father being Johann (Jean) Bernoulli (1667–1748) and his uncle Jakob (Jacques) Bernoulli (1654–1705). Bernoulli's two brothers were also renowned mathematicians, as were two nephews and a cousin. However, Daniel Bernoulli was the only member of this gifted family to make a mark in physics.

He was educated at Basle, Switzerland, where in 1705 his father had assumed the professorship of mathematics that became vacant on the death of Daniel's uncle. Daniel was taught mathematics by his father and brother but studied medicine, obtaining his doctorate at Basle in 1721 with a thesis on respiration. In 1725, he won the first of a series of ten prizes awarded by the Paris Academy for papers on such diverse subjects as marine technology, navigation, oceanology, astronomy and medicine. In the same year, Bernoulli became professor of mathematics at St Petersburg in Russia and stayed there until 1733. This, his most creative period, saw the completion of his most famous work *Hydrodynamica*, published in 1738, and the production of fundamental work on oscillation and probability.

Bernoulli then returned to Basle to lecture in physiology and finally became professor of physics there in 1750. He remained at the university until 1776, giving lively lectures that apparently (for they have not survived) described many subsequent developments in physics that had not then been proved. He died on 17 March 1782 and is buried in Basle.

In physics, Bernoulli made an outstanding contribution in *Hydrodynamica*, which is both a theoretical and practical study of equilibrium, pressure and velocity in fluids. Bernoulli showed, in the principle given his name, that the pressure of a fluid depends on its velocity, the pressure decreasing as the velocity increases. This effect is a consequence of the conservation of energy and Bernoulli's principle is an early formulation of the idea of conservation of energy. *Hydrodynamica* also contains the first attempt at a thorough mathematical explanation of the behaviour of gases by assuming they are composed of tiny particles, producing an equation of state that enabled Bernoulli to relate atmospheric pressure to altitude, for example. This was the first step towards the kinetic theory of gases achieved a century later.

Daniel Bernoulli's main importance in the history of science is due to the exposition of the principle bearing his name, which governs fluid flow. It has many applications, not least in aerodynamics where it explains how a moving aerofoil experiences lift and produces flight.

Bethe, Hans Albrecht (*1906–*), is a German-born American physicist who is best known for his fundamental work on energy production in stars, for which, among many other honours, he received the 1967 Nobel Prize in Physics. He has also played an important role in trying to limit nuclear bomb testing and advising on nuclear disarmament.

Bethe was born on 2 July 1906 in Strasbourg (then in Germany, now in France), the son of a university professor. He was educated at the universities of Frankfurt and Munich, gaining his PhD from Munich (where he worked under Arnold Sommerfeld) in 1928. From 1928 to 1933 he lectured in physics at the universities of Frankfurt, Stuttgart, Munich and Tübingen then, with the coming to power of Adolf Hitler, moved to Britain, where he spent a year at Manchester University before moving to Bristol University in 1934. In the following year he emigrated to the United States (of which he later became a naturalized citizen) and joined the physics faculty of Cornell University, New York, where he was pro-

fessor of Physics from 1937 until his retirement in 1975. From 1943 to 1946 he was also Director of the Theoretical Physics Division of the Los Alamos Science Laboratory, working on the Manhattan Project to develop the atomic bomb, subsequently becoming a consultant to the Los Alamos Laboratory. He has also been a leader in emphasizing the social responsibilities of scientists: in 1958 he served as a delegate to the first International Test Ban Conference in Geneva and has since advised on nuclear disarmament.

Bethe made his most important contribution to science in 1938, when he worked out the details of the nuclear mechanisms involved in the production of stellar energy, a problem that had remained unsolved since Lord Kelvin and Hermann von Helmholtz had drawn attention to it some 75 years previously. Bethe's explanation, which is both precise and plausible, begins with the combining of a hydrogen nucleus (a proton) and a carbon-12 nucleus to form a nitrogen-13 nucleus. This initiates a series of reactions (in which three other protons are involved), the end result of which is the regeneration of carbon-12 and the conversion of the four protons to a helium nucleus (an alpha particle). Hydrogen is the fuel in this process, helium is the waste product and the carbon serves as the catalyst. He later proposed a second mechanism for stellar energy production involving the direct combination (in several stages) of hydrogen nuclei to form helium, a process that can occur at lower temperatures than those necessary for his first suggested mechanism.

Bethe has also studied electron densities in crystals, the order-disorder states in alloys, the operational conditions in nuclear reactors, the detection of underground explosions from seismographic records, and neutron stars (extremely dense stars in which the gravitational force is so strong that protons fuse with electrons to form neutrons).

Bhabha, Homi Jehangir (*1909–1966*), was an Indian theoretical physicist who made several important explanations of the behaviour of subatomic particles. He was also responsible for the development of research and teaching of advanced physics in India, and for the establishment and direction of the nuclear power program in India. He commanded wide respect in the international scientific community both for his contributions in the scientific sphere and also for his formidable skills as an administrator. He held many positions of responsibility at home and abroad, particularly in organizations concerned with the development of peaceful uses of atomic energy.

Bhabha was born in Bombay on 30 October

1909. He attended a number of schools in Bombay before entering Gonville and Caius College Cambridge in 1927 to study mechanical engineering. There his tutor in mathematics was Paul Dirac (1902–   ), who originated the relativistic electron theory that led to the prediction of antiparticles. Bhabha became fascinated by mathematics and theoretical physics and so, after earning his first class honours degree in 1930, he began to do research at the Cavendish Laboratories in Cambridge. He was also then able to tour Europe, meeting scientists of such importance as Wolfgang Pauli (1900–1958) and Enrico Fermi (1901–1954) and also visiting Niels Bohr's laboratory in Denmark. He was awarded his PhD in 1935, and remained at Cambridge until 1939 when he returned to India for a holiday.

He was still in India when World War II broke out. Unable to return to Cambridge, a readership at the Bangalore Institute of Science was created for him and he was put in charge of a department investigating cosmic rays. The renowned Indian physicist C.V. Raman (1888–1970) was the director of the Institute, and he had a profound influence on Bhabha. Bhabha determined to remain in India and advance the development of science and technology there.

In 1944 he proposed the establishment of a centre for the training of scientists in advanced physics and for the cultivation of research in that field as a stimulus for industrial development. The Tata Institute of Fundamental Research was established at Bombay in 1945 with Bhabha as director, a position he held until his death.

Bhabha later took on many responsibilities in the establishment of the Indian atomic energy programme and also became a figure of great importance in the international scientific community, serving as president of the United Nations Conference on the Peaceful Uses of Atomic Energy, first held in Geneva in 1955, and from 1960 to 1963 as president of the International Union of Pure and Applied Physics. He died tragically on 24 January 1966 in a plane crash on Mont Blanc.

Bhabha studied at the Cavendish Laboratories at a time of great advances in the understanding of the structure and properties of matter. He made major contributions to the early development of quantum electrodynamics, a part of high-energy physics. His first paper concerned the absorption of high-energy gamma rays in matter. A primary gamma ray dissipates its energy in the formation of electron showers. In 1935, Bhabha became the first person to determine the cross-section (and thus the probability) of electrons scattering positrons. This phenomenon is now known as Bhabha scattering.

Bhabha also studied cosmic rays and in 1937 suggested that the highly penetrating particles detected at and below ground level could not be electrons. In 1946, they were in fact found to be mu-mesons. Bhabha also put forward a theory proposing the existence of vector mesons, which were later identified in nuclear interactions. In 1938, he suggested a classic method of confirming the time dilation effect of the special theory of relativity by measuring the lifetimes of cosmic ray particles striking the atmosphere at very high speeds. Their lifetimes were found to be prolonged by exactly the amount predicted by relativity.

Bhabha was a skilled theoretician and a master administrator. His love for his native land stimulated him to the cultivation of educational and research facilities of the highest standard, and furthermore to the awakening of his government's awareness of the potential importance of atomic energy. He did everything in his power to ensure that India would become self-sufficient in all stages of the nuclear cycle so as not to be dependent on other nations. He spoke for all developing nations when he said in 1964 at the Third United Nations Conference on the Peaceful Uses of Atomic Energy that "no power is as expensive as no power".

Black, Joseph (*1728–1799*), was a Scottish physicist and chemist whose most important contribution to physics was his work on thermodynamics, notably on latent heats and specific heats.

Black was born in Bordeaux, France, on 16 April 1728. His father was from Belfast, but of Scottish descent, and was working in Bordeaux in the wine trade. Black went to Belfast to be educated, and then on to Glasgow University to study natural sciences and medicine. He moved to Edinburgh in 1751 to finish his studies, gaining his doctor's degree in 1754. Two years later he took over from William Cullen, his chemistry teacher at Glasgow, and was also offered the Chair in Anatomy. He soon changed this position for that of Professor of Medicine, and also practised as a physician. In 1766 he again followed Cullen as the Professor of Chemistry at Edinburgh University. Black died on 10 November 1799.

Until about 1760 Black devoted his research to chemistry but thereafter most of his work was in physics. He noticed that when ice melts it absorbs heat from its surroundings without itself undergoing a change in temperature, from which he argued that the heat must have combined with the ice particles and become latent. In 1761 he experimentally verified this hypothesis, thereby establishing the concept of latent heat (in the example of melting ice, the latent heat of fusion). In the following year he determined the latent heat of formation of steam (the latent heat of vaporization). Also in 1762 he described his work to a literary society in Glasgow, but did not publish his findings. In addition, he observed that equal masses of different substances require different quantities of heat to change their temperatures by the same amount, an observation that established the concept of specific heats (relative heat capacities).

Blackett, Lord Patrick Maynard Stuart (*1897–1974*), was a British physicist who made the first photograph of an atomic transmutation and developed the cloud chamber into a practical instrument for studying nuclear reactions. This achievement gained him the 1948 Nobel Prize in Physics. Blackett also discovered the phenomenon of pair production of positrons and electrons in cosmic rays.

Blackett was born in Croydon, Surrey on 18 November 1897. He did not initially go to university, but joined the Royal Navy in 1912 as a naval cadet. During World War I, he took part in the battles of the Falkland Islands and Jutland, and designed a revolutionary new gunsight. Attracted to science, Blackett resigned from the Navy after the war ended and embarked on a science course at Cambridge University, obtaining a BA degree in 1921. Continuing at the university, Blackett started research with cloud chambers under Ernest Rutherford (1871–1937) in the Cavendish Laboratory. In 1924, Blackett succeeded in obtaining the first photographs of an atomic transmutation, which was of nitrogen into an oxygen isotope. He continued to develop the cloud chamber and in 1932, with assistance from Guiseppe Occhialini, he designed a cloud chamber in which photographs of cosmic rays were taken automatically. Early in 1933, the device confirmed the existence of the positron (positive electron) proposed by Carl Anderson (1905–   ).

Blackett became professor of physics at Birkbeck College, London, in 1933 and continued his cosmic ray studies, demonstrating in 1935 the formation of showers of positive and negative electrons from gamma rays in approximately equal numbers. In 1937, he succeeded Lawrence Bragg (1890–1971) at the University of Manchester, continuing with his cosmic ray studies. During World War II, Blackett initiated the main principles of operational research, and afterwards returned to university life. At Manchester, his research team produced many important discoveries in studies involving cosmic radiation. Particles with a life span of 10^{-10} seconds were discovered. They became known as strange particles and included the negative cascade hyperon.

As a consequence of his research into cosmic rays, Blackett became interested in the history of the Earth's magnetic field and turned to the study of rock magnetism. He was appointed head of the physics department at Imperial College London, in 1953, where he built up a research team specializing in rock magnetism. On Blackett's advice, the government formed a Ministry of Technology in 1974, and he became president of the Royal Society in 1965 and a life peer in 1969. Blackett died on 13 July 1974.

In 1919, Rutherford explained the transmutation of elements from experiments in which he bombarded nitrogen with alpha particles. The oxygen atoms and protons produced were detected by scintillations in a screen of zinc sulphide. Blackett used a cloud chamber to photograph the tracks formed by these particles, taking more than 20,000 pictures and recording some 400,000 tracks. Of these, eight showed that a nuclear reaction had taken place, confirming Rutherford's explanation of transmutation. To reduce the huge number of observations, Blackett and Occhialini invented a cloud chamber that was automatically triggered by the arrival of a cosmic ray likely to cause a nuclear reaction in the chamber. Two geiger counters were attached to the chamber, the passage of the ray creating a current in the counters that operated the chamber. Pair production (the formation of showers of positrons and electrons from gamma rays), which Blackett discovered, was the first evidence that matter may be created from energy as Albert Einstein (1879–1955) had predicted in his special theory of relativity. The two particles subsequently rejoin and annihilate each other to form a gamma ray, thus converting mass back into energy.

Bohr, Aage Niels (*1922–   *); **Mottelson, Ben Roy** (*1926–   *); and **Rainwater, (Leo) James** (*1917–   *), are a group of Danish and American physicists who shared the 1975 Nobel Prize in Physics for their work on the structure of the atomic nucleus.

Aage Bohr is the son of Niels Bohr (1885–1962) and was born in Copenhagen on 19 June 1922 (the year that his father won the Nobel Prize in Physics). He was educated at the University of Copenhagen, and then worked for the Department of Science and Industrial Research in London from 1943 to 1945. From 1946 he worked at his father's Institute of Theoretical Physics in Copenhagen, and since 1956 he has been professor of physics at the University of Copenhagen. He was director of the Niels Bohr Institute (formerly the Institute of Theoretical Physics) from 1963 to

1970 and director of Nordita (Nordic Institute for Theoretical Atomic Physics) from 1975 to 1981. In addition to the Nobel Prize in Physics awarded in 1975, Bohr won the Atoms for Peace Award in 1969 and the Rutherford Medal in 1972. He has published *Rotational States of Atomic Nuclei* (1954) and *Nuclear Structure* Vol. I (1969) and Vol. II (1975) jointly with Ben Mottelson.

Ben Mottelson was born in Chicago, Illinois, on 9 July 1926. He was educated at Purdue University, where he gained a PhD in 1950. From 1950 to 1953, he was at the Institute of Theoretical Physics in Copenhagen, and he then held a position at CERN (European Centre for Nuclear Research) in a theoretical study group formed in Copenhagen. He has been professor at Nordita in Copenhagen since 1957. Mottelson became a Danish citizen in 1971, and has published several books and many scientific papers jointly with Bohr.

James Rainwater was born on 9 December 1917 in Council, Idaho. He gained a physics degree at the California Institute of Technology in 1939 and then read for his advanced degree at Columbia University. He remained there, rising to become Professor of Physics in 1952, a position he still holds. During the period 1942 to 1946, Rainwater worked for the Office of Scientific Research and Development (OSRD) and then the Manhattan Project, and he was director of the Nevis Cyclotron Laboratory from 1951 to 1953 and again from 1956 to 1961.

Aage Bohr, Ben Mottelson and James Rainwater shared the 1975 Nobel Prize in Physics for "the discovery of the connection between the collective motion and the particle motion in atomic nuclei and the development of the theory of the structure of the atomic nucleus, based on this connection". The three men had been working in loose collaboration for nearly 25 years. Niels Bohr had proposed that the particles in the nucleus of an atom are arranged like molecules in a drop of liquid. Exceptions to this rule were found and this led to the belief that the nuclear particles are arranged in concentric shells. Further studies showed that perhaps these shells were not spherically symmetrical. This suggestion was both unexpected and unattractive. In 1950, Rainwater wrote a paper in which he observed that most of the nuclear particles form an inner nucleus, while the other particles form an outer nucleus. Each set of particles is in constant motion at very high velocity and the shape of each set affects the other set. He postulated that if some of the outer particles moved in similar orbits, this would create unequal centrifugal forces of enormous power, which could be strong enough to permanently deform an ideally symmetrical nucleus. At that time, Aage Bohr was working with Rainwater as a visiting professor at the University of Columbia and was impressed by this theory. He began to work out a more detailed explanation of Rainwater's work after he returned to Denmark, and during the next three years he published results that he and his associate Ben Mottelson had obtained experimentally. These results proved the theoretical work.

The work of these three men achieved a deep understanding of the atomic nucleus and paved the way for nuclear fusion.

Bohr, Niels Henrik David (*1885–1962*), was a Danish physicist who established the structure of the atom. For this achievement he was awarded the 1922 Nobel Prize in Physics. Bohr made another very important contribution to atomic physics by explaining the process of nuclear fission.

Bohr was born in Copenhagen on 7 October 1885. His father, Christian Bohr, was professor of physiology at the University of Copenhagen and his younger brother Harald became an eminent mathematician. Niels Bohr was a less brilliant student than his brother but a careful and thorough investigator. His first research project, completed in 1906, resulted in a precise determination of the surface tension of water and gained him the gold medal of the Academy of Sciences. In 1911, he was awarded his doctorate for a theory accounting for the behaviour of electrons in metals.

In the same year, Bohr went to Cambridge, England, to study under J.J. Thomson (1856–1940), who showed little interest in Bohr's electron theory so, in 1912, Bohr moved to Manchester to work with Ernest Rutherford (1871–1937), who was making important investigations into the structure of the atom. Bohr developed models of the atom in which electrons are disposed in rings around the nucleus, a first step towards an explanation of atomic structure.

Bohr returned to Copenhagen as a lecturer at the University in 1912, and in 1913 developed his theory of atomic structure by applying the quantum theory to the observations of radiation emitted by atoms. He then went back to Manchester to take up a lectureship offered by Rutherford, enabling him to continue his investigations in ideal conditions. However, the authorities in Denmark enticed him back with a professorship and then built the Institute of Theoretical Physics in Copenhagen for Bohr. He became director of the Institute in 1920, holding this position until his death. The Institute rapidly became a centre for theoretical physicists from throughout the world, and such figures as Wolfgang Pauli (1900–1958) and Werner Heisenberg (1901–1976) developed Bohr's work there, resulting in the theories of quantum and wave mechanics that more fully explain the behaviour of electrons within atoms.

The year 1922 marked not only the award of the Nobel Prize for Physics but also a triumphant vindication of Bohr's atomic theory, which he used to predict the existence of a hitherto-unknown element. The element was discovered at the Institute and given the name hafnium.

In the 1930s, interest in physics turned towards nuclear reactions and in 1939 Bohr proposed his liquid-droplet model for the nucleus that was able to explain why a heavy nucleus could undergo fission following the capture of a neutron. Working from experimental results, Bohr was able to show that only the isotope uranium-235 would undergo fission with slow neutrons.

When Denmark was occupied by the Germans in 1940 early in World War II, Bohr took an active part in the resistance movement. In 1943, he escaped to Sweden with his family in a fishing boat – not without danger – and then went to England and on to the United States. He became involved in the development of the atomic bomb, helping to solve the physical problems involved, but later becoming a passionate advocate for the control of nuclear weapons. Among his efforts to persuade statesmen to adopt rational and peaceful solutions was a famous open letter addressed to the United Nations in 1950 pleading for an "open world" of free exchange of people and ideas.

In 1952 Bohr was instrumental in creating the European Centre for Nuclear Research (CERN), now at Geneva, Switzerland. He died in Copenhagen on 18 November 1962. In addition to his scientific papers, Bohr published three volumes of essays: *Atomic Theory and the Description of Nature* (1934), *Atomic Physics and Human Knowledge* (1958) and *Essays 1958–1962 on Atomic Physics and Human Knowledge* (1963).

Bohr's first great inspiration came from working with Rutherford, who had proposed a nuclear theory of atomic structure from his work on the scattering of alpha rays in 1911. It was not, however, understood how electrons could continually orbit the nucleus without radiating energy, as classical physics demanded. Ten years earlier Max Planck (1858–1947) had proposed that radiation is emitted or absorbed by atoms in discreet units or quanta of energy. Bohr applied this quantum theory to the nuclear atom to explain why elements emit radiation at precise frequencies that give set patterns of spectral lines. He postulated that an atom may exist in only a cer-

tain number of stable states, each with a certain amount of energy; the emission or absorption of energy may occur only with a transition from one stable state to another. Electrons normally orbit the nucleus without emitting or absorbing energy. When a transition occurs, an electron moves to a lower or higher orbit depending on whether it emits or absorbs energy. In so doing, a set number of quanta of energy are emitted or absorbed at a particular frequency. Bohr developed these ideas to show that the nuclei of atoms are surrounded by shells of electrons, each assigned particular sets of quantum numbers according to their orbits. Bohr's theory was used to determine the frequencies of spectral lines produced by elements and succeeded brilliantly. It also enabled him to explain the groups of the Periodic Table in terms of elements with similar electron structures, which led to the prediction and discovery of hafnium.

In developing a model for the nucleus, Bohr conceived of the nuclear particles being pulled together by short-range forces rather as the molecules in a drop of liquid are attracted to one another. The extra energy produced by the absorption of a neutron may cause the nuclear particles to separate into two groups of approximately the same size, thus breaking the nucleus into two smaller nuclei – as happens in nuclear fission. The model was vindicated when Bohr correctly predicted the differing behaviour of nuclei of uranium-235 and uranium-238 from the fact that the number of neutrons in each nucleus is odd and even respectively.

Niels Bohr gained not only a love of science from his father but also a philosophical insight into the nature of knowledge that enabled him to question accepted theories and seek new explanations. By reconciling Rutherford's nuclear model of the atom with Planck's quantum theory, he was able to produce a valid model for the atom completely at odds with classical physics. However, this did not prevent him from using a classical model to explain the structure and behaviour of the nucleus. Our present knowledge of the atom and the nucleus thus rests on the fundamental discoveries made by Bohr's restless and ingenious mind.

Boltzmann, Ludwig (*1844–1906*), was an Austrian theoretical physicist who contributed to the development of the kinetic theory of gases, electromagnetism and thermodynamics. His work in these fields led him to consider phenomena in terms of probability theory and atomic events, which led to the establishment of the branch of physics now known as statistical mechanics.

Boltzmann was born in Vienna on 20 February

1844 and educated at Linz and Vienna. He studied at the University of Vienna under Josef Stefan (1835-1893) and Josef Loschmidt (1821-1895), and received his PhD in 1866 from that institution. In 1867 Boltzmann became an assistant at the Physikalisches Institut in Vienna after which he held a series of professorial posts. He was professor of theoretical physics at the University of Graz from 1869 to 1873, of mathematics at the University of Vienna from 1873 to 1876, and of experimental physics at Graz from 1876 to 1879. He then became director of the Physikalisches Institut, moving in 1899 to Munich to become professor of theoretical physics at the University there. In 1894 went back to Vienna to succeed Stefan as professor of theoretical physics. During these years there was a heated and sometimes unpleasant scientific debate between the "atomists", championed by Boltzmann, and the "energeticists", one of whose spokesmen was Wilhelm Ostwald (1853-1932). Ernst Mach (1838-1916), one of the "energeticists", tried to reconcile the two schools of thought in an attempt to tone down the debate.

Boltzmann moved to the University of Leipzig in 1900, where he served as professor of theoretical physics. He suffered from depression and made an unsuccessful suicide attempt. He returned to his previous post at Vienna in 1902, with the added honour of the chair of natural philosophy from which Mach had just retired because of ill health. In 1904 Boltzmann travelled to the United States, lecturing at the World's Fair in St Louis and visiting Stanford and Berkeley, two prestigious campuses of the University of California. He still felt depressed at the hostility he sensed from some of his scientific colleagues, despite the fact that the revolutionary discoveries being made at the time about the structure of atoms and the properties of matter would ultimately support his theories. He committed suicide at Duino, near Trieste, on 5 September 1906, shortly before the discovery of Brownian motion, which led to a near universal acceptance of his kinetic and statistical theories.

Mechanics, dynamics and electromagnetism were all being developed when Boltzmann was a student. He made contributions to all of these areas during the course of his career. One of his most important sources of stimulation was the work of James Clerk Maxwell (1831-1879), whose investigations in the field of electromagnetism were not well known by European scientists. Boltzmann contributed greatly to the dissemination of Maxwell's work, particularly through a book on the subject published in 1891.

Boltzmann wrote his first paper on the kinetic theory of gases in 1859 while he was only a student. In 1868 he published a paper on thermal equilibrium in gases, citing and extending Maxwell's work on this subject. He was concerned with the distribution of energy among colliding gas molecules. He derived an exponential formula to describe the distribution of molecules which relates the mean total energy of a molecule to its temperature. It includes the constant k, now known as the Boltzmann constant, which is equal to $1.38 \times 10^{-23} \, \mathrm{JK}^{-1}$. This constant has become a fundamental part of virtually every mathematical formulation of a statistical nature in both classic and quantum physics.

Another important area of Boltzmann's investigation was thermodynamics. The second law of thermodynamics had been formulated in 1850 by Rudolph Clausius (1822-1888) and William Thomson (Lord Kelvin; 1824-1907). Boltzmann sought to find a mathematical description for the demonstration of the tendency of a gas to reach a state of equilibrium as the most probable state. In 1877 he published his famous equation, $S = k \log W$ (which was later engraved on his tombstone) describing the relation between entropy and probability.

Boltzmann also determined a theoretical derivation for Stefan's experimentally derived law of black body radiation. Stefan had shown that the energy radiated by a black body is proportional to the fourth power of its absolute temperature, and this is now often known as the Stefan–Boltzmann law. Boltzmann's investigation of the phenomenon was based on the second law of thermodynamics and Maxwell's electromagnetic theory.

Boltzmann's most enduring contribution arose from his pioneering work in the field of statistical mechanics. He had begun his study of the equipartition of energy, which resulted in the Maxwell-Boltzmann Distribution Law, early in his career. He demonstrated that the average amount of energy required for atomic motion in all directions is equal, and so formulated an equation for the distribution of atoms due to collision. This led to the foundation of statistical mechanics. This discipline holds that macroscopic properties of matter such as conductivity and viscosity can be understood, and are determined by, the cumulative properties of the constituent atoms. Boltzmann held that the second law of thermodynamics should be considered from this viewpoint. Boltzmann's work on the relationship between probability and entropy and on the inevitable and irreversible processes that must therefore occur, influenced Willard Gibbs (1839-1903), Max Planck (1858-1947) and others.

Boltzmann was a theoretician with great intuitive powers and vision. It is a tragedy that he did not live to see his work vindicated and the remarkable advances achieved by the "atomists" of the twentieth century.

Born, Max (*1882-1970*), was a German-born British physicist who pioneered quantum mechanics, the mathematical explanation of the behaviour of an electron in an atom. His version of quantum mechanics had a short reign as the most popular explanation and was soon displaced by the equivalent and more convenient wave mechanics of Erwin Schrödinger (1887-1961), which is in use today. The importance of Born's work was eventually recognized, however, with the award of the 1954 Nobel Prize in Physics, which he shared with Walther Bothe (1891-1957). (Bothe's share of the award was for his work on the detection of cosmic rays and was not connected with Born's achievements in quantum mechanics.) Born also made important advances in the understanding of the dynamics of crystal lattices.

Born was born in Breslau, Germany (now Wrocław, Poland) on 11 December 1882 into a wealthy Jewish family. His father was Professor of Anatomy at the University of Breslau, which Born later attended as well as the University of Göttingen, gaining his doctorate in physics and astronomy at Göttingen in 1907.

After periods of military service and various academic positions in Göttingen and Berlin, Born was appointed Professor of Physics at Frankfurt-am-Main in 1919. During this period, he became an expert on the physics of crystals. Following a meeting with Fritz Haber (1868-1934), who developed the Haber process for the synthesis of ammonia, Born became aware that little was known about the calculation of chemical energies. Haber encouraged Born to apply his work on the lattice energies of crystals (the energy given out when gaseous ions are brought together to form a solid crystal lattice) to the formation of alkali metal chlorides. Born was able to determine the energies involved in lattice formation, from which the properties of crystals may be derived, and thus laid one of the foundations of solid-state physics.

In 1921, Born moved from Frankfurt to the more prestigious university at Göttingen, again as professor. Most of his research was then concerned with quantum mechanics, in particular with the electronic structure of atoms. He made Göttingen a leading centre for theoretical physics and together with his students and collaborators - notably Werner Heisenberg (1901-1976) - he devised a system called matrix mechanics that accounted mathematically for the position of the electron in the atom. He also derived a technique, called the Born approximation method, for computing the behaviour of subatomic particles that is of great use in high-energy physics.

In 1933, with the rise to power of Adolf Hitler, Born left Germany for Cambridge, and in 1936 he became Professor of Natural Philosophy at Edinburgh University. He became a British citizen in 1939, and remained at Edinburgh until 1953, when he retired to Germany. The following year, Born received his Nobel award which, somewhat ironically, was for his discovery published in 1926 that the wave function of an electron is linked to the probability that the electron is to be found at any point. Born died at Göttingen on 5 January 1970.

Born was inspired by Niels Bohr (1885-1962) to seek a mathematical explanation for Bohr's discovery that the quantum theory applies to the behaviour of electrons in atoms. In 1924 Born coined the term "quantum mechanics" and the following year built on conceptual work by Werner Heisenberg to relate the position and momentum of the electron in a system called matrix mechanics. Wolfgang Pauli (1900-1958) immediately used the system to calculate the hydrogen spectrum and the results were correct. But about a year after this discovery, in 1926, Erwin Schrödinger expressed the same theory in terms of wave mechanics, which was not only more acceptable mathematically but enabled physicists to visualize the position of the electron as a wave motion around the nucleus, unlike Born's purely mathematical treatment. Born, however, was able to use wave mechanics to make a statistical interpretation of the quantum theory and expressed the probability that an electron will be found at a particular point as the square of the value of the amplitude of the wave at that point. This was the discovery for which he was belatedly awarded a Nobel Prize.

Bowden, Frank Philip (*1903-1968*), was an Australian physicist and chemist who worked mainly in Britain. He began his research career in electrochemistry, but early on became interested in surface studies and went on to make major contributions to the study of friction, lubricants and surface erosion as well as other related subjects.

Bowden was born in Hobart, Tasmania, on 2 May 1903. He received his BSc at the University of Tasmania in 1924. He continued his studies there and then in 1927 went to Cambridge University, where he began research in the department of colloid science. In 1935 Bowden became director of studies in natural sciences at Gonville and Caius College. He was then made a lecturer at Cambridge in 1937, a post he held until 1946.

In 1939 Bowden embarked on a lecture tour of the United States. He decided to return to Britain via Australia, and he was still there when World War II broke out in 1945. He was appointed head of the lubricants and bearings section for the Council for Scientific and Industrial Research at Melbourne University (which conducted research of great value to the war effort). When the war ended Bowden resigned his post in order to return to Cambridge to set up a similar research group there, and from 1946 to 1965 he was director of the laboratory for physics and chemistry of solids. A chair in surface physics was created for him in 1966. Bowden died in Cambridge on 3 September 1968.

Bowden's work in Tasmania and his early work at Cambridge was in the field of electrochemistry; specifically he was interested in the establishment of the hydrogen overpotential and in the effects of impurities on this process. He also worked on electrode kinetics. Although his electrochemical investigations continued until 1939, he began to publish papers on friction as early as 1931.

His early work in this topic demonstrated that the area of contact between two solid surfaces depends not only on details of their surface features but also on the magnitude of the load applied to them and on the hardness of the two surfaces. Since even a clean smooth metallic surface is irregular on an atomic scale, the area of contact where strong intermetallic forces might form is small. Therefore, sliding produces friction over only a small fraction of the total area of the surface, but can produce exceedingly high temperatures and even induce melting in hot spots. Another implication of this work was that a lubricant might be decomposed by heat at exactly the place where it is most needed.

Bowden's interest in skiing led him to realize that the thin layer of water between a ski or an ice-skate and the snow or ice is produced not by pressure due to the weight on them but to friction-induced heat caused by irregularities in the sliding surfaces. A variety of industries saw applications for Bowden's research in more serious areas, and his war research covered a broad range of areas of military significance. Machine and tool lubricants, flame-throwing fuels, the accurate measurement of shell velocities for gun calibration and the casting of aircraft bearings all came within their scope. Several ways of creating hot spots in a variety of materials were investigated, which had applications in the prevention of explosions due to frictional heating in munitions factories.

These research topics continued to be investigated by the research group which Bowden built up in Cambridge after the war. They took advantage of new techniques such as scanning electron microscopy, electron diffraction and high-speed photography in their investigations. The development of PTFE-coated metal appliances and devices was greatly accelerated by results obtained by Bowden and his team.

Boys, Charles Vernon (*1855–1944*), was a British inventor and physicist who is probably best known for designing a very sensitive apparatus (based on Henry Cavendish's earlier experiment) to determine Newton's gravitational constant and the mean density of the Earth. He received many honours for his work, including a knighthood in 1935.

Boys, the son of a clergyman, was born in Wing, Rutland, on 15 March 1855. He was educated at Marlborough College then in 1873 went to the Royal School of Mines, London, where he was taught physics by R. Guthrie (1833–1886) and chemistry by Edward Frankland (1825–1899). Although he received little formal instruction in mathematics, Boys taught himself calculus and designed an integrating machine that mechanically drew graphs of antiderivatives. He graduated in mining and metallurgy in 1876 and then, after a brief period working in a colliery, became an assistant to Guthrie, his former teacher, at the Royal College of Science in London. He was appointed Assistant Professor of Physics at the Royal College in 1889 but, opportunities for further promotion being rare, he resigned in 1897 to work for the Metropolitan Gas Board as a Referee. In 1920 he became one of the three Gas Referees that served all of Britain. He held this post until his formal retirement in 1939, although he continued to serve as an adviser to the Gas Board until 1943. In addition to his official appointments, from 1893 Boys pursued a lucrative business he had sufficient spare time to develop his scientific interests and to write several popular science books on subjects as diverse as soap bubbles, weeds and natural logarithms. He was also President of the Royal Society from 1916 to 1917. He died in Andover, Hampshire, on 30 March 1944.

Boys is known mainly as an inventor and designer of scientific instruments, in which area his most important contribution was probably his improved, extremely sensitive torsion balance, which he used to elaborate on Henry Cavendish's experiment to determine the gravitational constant and the mean density of the Earth. The novel feature of Boys' apparatus was his use of an extremely fine quartz fibre – ingeniously made by firing an arrow to the end of which was attached molten quartz – in the torsion balance. The properties of these fibres are such that Boys' balance was more sensitive, smaller and quicker to react than was Cavendish's original apparatus (which used copper wire). Testing his improved design in the basement of the Clarendon Laboratories in Oxford in 1895, Boys determined Newton's gravitational constant and calculated the mean density of the Earth as 5.527 times the density of water.

Boys' other work included the invention of a "radiomicrometer" (1890) to detect infrared radiation. This extremely sensitive instrument, consisting of a thermocouple and a galvanometer, was intended to measure the heat radiated by the planets in the Solar System. Using this device he calculated that Jupiter's surface temperature did not exceed 100°C; it is now thought to be below −130°C. He also developed a special camera to record fast-moving objects such as bullets and lightning flashes; designed a scientific toy using soap bubbles (called the Rainbow Cup, this device was later manufactured); and devised a calorimeter for determining the calorific value of coal gas (this subsequently became the standard instrument used to measure the calorific value of fuel gas in Britain). In addition, he performed a series of experiments on soap bubbles, which increased knowledge of surface tension and of the properties of thin films.

Bragg, William Henry (*1862-1942*), and **Bragg, (William) Lawrence** (*1890-1971*), father and son, were British physicists who pioneered and perfected the technique of X-ray diffraction in the study of the structure of crystals. For this work they were jointly awarded the 1915 Nobel Prize in Physics.

William Henry Bragg was born at Westward, Cumberland, on 2 July 1862. In 1881 he went to Cambridge University, obtaining a first-class degree in mathematics in 1885. He was immediately appointed Professor of Mathematics and Physics at the University of Adelaide, South Australia. It is said that he wondered why he was offered this appointment since he knew little physics, although he put this to right by reading important texts on the long sea journey to Australia. For many years William Henry Bragg did no research but concentrated on lecturing, although he did apprentice himself to a firm of instrument makers and subsequently made all the apparatus he required for practical laboratory teaching. Then in 1904 Bragg became president of the physics section of the Australian Association for the Advancement of Science and his opening address - on radioactivity - acted as the stimulus to begin original research. He found that radium produces alpha particles with a variety of energy ranges, confirming the theory of Ernest Rutherford (1871-1937) that the various disintegration products of the radioactive series should produce radioactivity of differing energy. Rutherford proposed Bragg for a fellowship of the Royal Society and in 1908 Bragg was appointed Professor of Physics at Leeds University, returning to Britain in 1909.

Bragg began to work on X-rays and, together with his son Lawrence, became convinced that X-rays behave as an electromagnetic wave motion. Using the skills at instrument making he had gained in Australia, Bragg constructed the first X-ray spectrometer in 1913. Both men used it to determine the structures of various crystals on the basis that X-rays passing through the crystals are diffracted by the regular array of atoms within the crystal.

During World War I, the Braggs' work on X-rays virtually ceased and William Henry Bragg devoted himself mainly to submarine detection. Both father and son were, however, awarded the 1915 Nobel Prize in Physics for their discovery, and in the same year William Henry Bragg became Professor of Physics at University College, London. After the war, he turned to the X-ray analysis of organic crystals. William Henry Bragg was knighted in 1920, and became Director of the Royal Institution in 1923 (instituting the famous series of Christmas lectures there) and then President of the Royal Society in 1935. He died in London on 10 March 1942.

William Lawrence Bragg was born at Adelaide on 31 March 1890. He studied mathematics at Adelaide University and continued in this subject at Trinity College, Cambridge. Then in 1910 he switched to physics at his father's suggestion, becoming interested in the X-ray work of Max von Laue (1879-1960), who claimed to have observed X-ray diffraction in crystals, and repeated many of von Laue's experiments. Lawrence Bragg was able to determine an equation now known as Bragg's Law that enabled both he and his father to deduce the structure of crystals such as diamond, using the X-ray spectrometer built by his father. In recognition of this achievement, Lawrence Bragg shared the 1915 Nobel Prize in Physics with his father, becoming the youngest person (at age 25) ever to receive the prize.

Lawrence Bragg then went on to determine the structures of such inorganic substances as silicates. In 1919, he became Professor of Physics at the University of Manchester and from 1938 to 1954 was Professor of Physics at Cambridge. He was knighted in 1941. Like his father before him, Bragg became Director of the Royal Institution in 1954 and he also devoted much energy to the popularization of science. Lawrence Bragg retired in 1966 and died in Ipswich on 1 July 1971.

Until the Braggs applied X-rays to the study of crystal structure, crystallography had not been concerned with the internal arrangement of atoms but only with the shape and number of crystal surfaces. The Braggs' work immediately gave a method of determining the positions of atoms in the lattices making up the crystals because they were able to relate the distance between the crystal planes or layers of atoms d to the angle of incidence of the X-rays θ and their wavelength λ, obtaining the simple equation $n\lambda = 2d\sin\theta$, where n is an integer. From the diffraction patterns obtained by passing X-rays through crystals, the Braggs were able to determine the dimensions of the crystal planes and thus the structure of a crystal. Furthermore, it gave a method for accurate determination of X-ray wavelengths.

The Braggs' pioneering discovery led to an understanding of the ways in which atoms combine with each other and also revolutionized mineralogy and later molecular biology, in which X-ray diffraction was crucial to the elucidation of the structure of DNA.

Branly, Edouard Eugène Désiré (*1844–1940*), was a French physicist and inventor who preceded Guglielmo Marconi in performing experiments resulting in the invention of wireless telegraphy and radio.

Branly was born in Amiens on 23 October 1844, the son of a teacher. He entered the École Normale Superieure in Paris in 1865, from which he gained his licence in physical and mathematical sciences in 1867 and his Aggregé in physics and natural science in 1868. He then joined the staff of the Lycée de Bourges but almost immediately afterwards returned to Paris to take charge of the physics laboratory at the Sorbonne, becoming its Adjunct Director in 1870. He then submitted his doctoral thesis to the Sorbonne, gaining his Docteur (medical) qualification in 1872 and his Docteur ès Sciences in 1873. In 1876 he was appointed Professor of Physics at the École Superieure de Sciences of the Catholic Institute in Paris through the influence of Abbot Hulst, who was then working at the Catholic Institute, and Henri-Étienne Sainte-Claire Deville, an eminent French chemist. From 1897 to 1916 Branly then worked as a medical professor of electrotherapy. It was not until 1898 that his work was recognized, with the award of the Houllevignes Prize by the French Academy of Sciences. Thereafter he received many other honours and, after his death in Paris on 24 March 1940, a national funeral was held for him in Nôtre Dame Cathedral.

Branly researched in various subjects, notably electricity, electrostatics (on which he wrote his doctoral thesis), magnetism and electrical dynam-

ics. His first task at the Catholic Institute, however, was to set up (with limited financial resources) a physics laboratory. (It was not until Frère Coty made a large donation in 1932 that the physics laboratory was adequately equipped, and all of Branly's work was carried out in very poor laboratory conditions.) His most important work – on wireless telegraphy – was performed in 1899, when he demonstrated the coherer, an invention of his that enabled radio waves from a distant transmitter to be detected. Once he had established the principle, however, he did not develop it further and the practical points were later taken up by Marconi, who was to share the 1909 Nobel Prize in Physics with Karl Braun for the invention of wireless telegraphy.

Braun, Karl Ferdinand (*1850–1918*), was a German physicist who is best known for his improvements to Guglielmo Marconi's system of wireless telegraphy, for which he shared (with Marconi) the 1909 Nobel Prize in Physics. He also made other important contributions to science, including the discovery of crystal rectifiers and the invention of the oscilloscope.

Braun was born in Fulda (now in West Germany) on 6 June 1850. He was educated at the universities of Marburg and Berlin, gaining his doctorate from the latter in 1872. His first job was assistant to Quinke at Würzburg University, after which he successively held positions at the universities of Leipzig, Marburg, Karlsruhe, Tübingen and Strasbourg; while at Strasbourg (from 1880 to 1883) he founded an Institute of Physics. In 1883 he was elected to the Chair in Physics at the Karlsruhe Technische Hochschule, a post he held until 1885, when he became Professor of Physics at Tübingen University. In 1895 he returned to Strasbourg University as Professor of Physics and Director of the Institute of Physics. In 1917 he went to the United States to testify in litigation about radio patents, but when the United States entered World War I he was detained as an alien in New York City and died there shortly afterwards, on 20 April 1918.

Braun began to study radio transmission in the late 1890s in an attempt to increase the transmitter range to more than 15 km (the maximum range then possible). He thought that the range could be increased by increasing the transmitter's power but, after working on Hertz oscillators, found that lengthening the spark gap to increase the power output was effective only up to a certain limit, beyond which power output actually decreased. He therefore devised a sparkless antenna (aerial) circuit in which the power from the transmitter was magnetically coupled (using electromagnetic induction) to the antenna circuit, instead of the antenna being connected directly in the power circuit. This invention, which Braun patented in 1899, greatly improved radio transmission, and the principle of magnetic coupling has since been applied to all similar transmission systems, including radar and television. Later Braun developed directional antennas.

Braun also discovered crystal rectifiers. In 1874 he published a paper describing his research on mineral metal sulphides, some of which, he found, conduct electricity in one direction only. His discovery did not find an immediate application, but crystal rectifiers ("cat's whisker") were used in the crystal radio receivers of the early 20th century – until they were superseded by more efficient valve circuits.

Braun's other principal contribution to science was his invention of the oscilloscope (1895), which he used to study high-frequency alternating currents. In his oscilloscope – which was basically an adaptation of the cathode-ray tube – Braun used an alternating voltage applied to deflection plates to deflect an electron beam within a cathode-ray tube. The Braun tube (as his invention was initially called) became a valuable laboratory instrument and was the forerunner of more sophisticated oscilloscopes and of the modern television and radar display tubes.

Brewster, David (*1781–1868*), was a British physicist who investigated the polarization of light, discovering the law named after him for which he was awarded the Rumford Medal by the Royal Society in 1819. He also helped to popularize science in his writings, and is perhaps best known as the inventor of the kaleidoscope.

Brewster was born in Jedburgh, Scotland, on 11 December 1781. His education was extended by reading his father's university notes on physics, his services as secretary to the local minister Thomas Somerville, and his friendship with James Veitch, an amateur astronomer. Brewster entered the University of Edinburgh in 1794 but never took his degree. He continued his studies, this time in divinity, and was awarded an honorary MA in 1800. He was later licensed to preach but was not ordained, and turned to publishing and teaching as the means of making a living.

One of Brewster's major concerns was increasing the public awareness of the importance of science. He edited a number of scientific periodicals and wrote many books and articles on science, including entries in the Encyclopaedia Britannica. He was also instrumental in the foundation of several academic organizations including the Edinburgh School of Arts in 1821, the Royal Scottish Society for Arts in 1821 and the

British Association for the Advancement of Science in 1831.

His achievements in optics were recognized by his election to many prestigious international scientific societies, including the Royal Society in 1815, and the French Institute. Brewster was knighted in 1832 and in 1859 made principal and later vice-chancellor of Edinburgh University. He died on 10 February 1868 in Allerby in Scotland.

With James Veitch, Brewster built many optical devices such as microscopes and sundials, developing an expertise that resulted in the invention of the kaleidoscope in 1816. In trying to improve lenses for telescopes, he became interested in optics and particularly in the polarization of reflected and refracted light. In 1813 he demonstrated, by studying the polarization of light passing through a succession of glass plates, that the index of refraction of a particular medium determines the tangent of the angle of polarization for light that transverses it. Brewster then sought an expression for the polarization of light by reflection and found, in 1815, that the polarization of a beam of reflected light is greatest when the reflected and refracted rays are at right angles to each other. This is known as Brewster's law, and it may be stated in the form that the tangent of the angle of polarization is numerically equal to the refractive index of the reflecting medium when polarization is maximum.

Brewster then worked on the polarization of light reflected by metals, and established the new field of optical mineralogy. By 1819 he had classified most crystals and minerals on the basis of their optical properties. During the 1820s he studied colour in the optical spectrum, finding that it could be divided into red, yellow and blue regions, and worked on absorption spectroscopy of natural substances, greatly extending the number of dark lines identified in spectra.

Brewster was an advocate of the particular theory of light on the basis of his experimental results. Although forced to admit that the wave theory did provide excellent explanations for certain observed phenomena, he clung to his views as he was philosophically unable to accept the wave theory because it assumed the existence of a hypothetical "ether".

Bridgman, Percy Williams (*1882–1961*), was an American physicist famous for his work on the behaviour of materials at high temperature and pressure, for which he won the 1946 Nobel Prize in Physics.

Bridgman was born on 21 April 1882 in Cambridge, Massachusetts. His father was a journalist and a social and political writer. He went to Harvard in 1900 and was awarded a PhD in 1908. He then began research work in the Jefferson Research Laboratory and spent his entire research life at Harvard University, starting as assistant professor in 1913. He became professor in 1919, Hollis Professor of Mathematics and Philosophy in 1927 and Higgins Professor in 1950. He retired to become Professor Emeritus in 1954. Suffering from an incurable disease, Bridgman killed himself at his home in Randolph, New Hampshire, on 20 August 1961.

At Harvard, it became clear that Bridgman was an excellent experimentalist and was skilled at handling machine tools and at manipulating glass. His experimental work on static high pressure began in 1908, and was at first limited to pressures of around 6,500 atmospheres. He gradually extended it to more than 100,000 atmospheres and eventually to about 400,000 atmospheres. Because this field of research had not been explored before, Bridgman had to invent much of his own equipment. His most important invention was a special type of seal in which the pressure in the gasket always exceeds that in the pressurized fluid. The result is that the closure is self-sealing – without this, his work at high pressure would not have been possible. He was later able to use the new steels and alloys of metals with heat-resistant compounds. His work involved measurement of the compressibilities of pressurized liquids and solids, and measurements of physical properties of solids such as electrical resistance. His discoveries included that of new high-pressure forms of ice. With the increase in range of possible pressures, new and unexpected phenomena appeared. He discovered that the electrons in caesium rearrange at a certain transition pressure. He pioneered the work to synthesize diamonds, which was eventually achieved in 1955. His technique was used to synthesize many more minerals and a new school of geology developed, based on experimental work at high pressure and temperature. Because the pressures and temperatures that Bridgman achieved simulated those deep below the ground, his discoveries gave an insight on the geophysical processes that take place within the Earth. His book *Physics of High Pressure* (1931) still remains a basic work.

Bridgman was an individualist. He published 260 papers, only two of which were with a co-author. He devoted himself to his scientific research, refusing to attend faculty meetings or to serve on committees. He disliked lecturing and did it badly. In 1914, however, during a course of lectures on advanced electrodynamics, Bridgman realized that many ambiguities and obscurities exist in the definition of scientific ideas and moved into the philosophy of science, publishing *The Logic of Modern Physics* in 1927.

Bullard, Edward Crisp (*1907-1980*), was a British geophysicist who, with the American Maurice Ewing, is generally considered to have founded the discipline of marine geophysics. He received many honours for his work, including a knighthood in 1953 and the Vetlesen Medal and Prize (the earth sciences equivalent of a Nobel Prize) in 1968.

Bullard was born in Norwich on 21 September 1907 into a family of brewers. He was educated at Repton School and Clare College, Cambridge, from which he graduated in physics in 1929. In 1931, after two years research at the Cavendish Laboratory, Cambridge, he became a demonstrator in Cambridge University's Department of Geodesy and Geophysics. During World War II he researched into methods of demagnetizing ships and of sweeping acoustic and magnetic mines. He then became the British Admiralty's Assistant Director of Naval Operational Research under P.M.S. Blackett, and later served on several committees concerned with combating German V-weapons. He continued to advise the Ministry of Defence for several years after the war. At the end of his wartime military service he returned to Cambridge as a Reader in Geophysics and soon became Head of Geophysics but, disillusioned by the university's tardiness in promoting growth in this subject area, went to Canada in 1948 to become Professor of Geophysics at the University of Toronto. He returned to England two years later, however, to take up the directorship of the National Physical Laboratory at Teddington. In 1957 he returned to Cambridge as Head of Geodesy and Geophysics, a position he held until his official retirement in 1974. On retiring he moved to La Jolla, California, where he continued to teach at the University of California (of which he had been a professor since 1963). He also advised the United States government on nuclear waste disposal. In addition to his academic and advisory posts, he played an active part in his family's brewing business and was a director of IBM (UK) for several years. Bullard died on 3 April 1980 in La Jolla.

Bullard's earliest work was to devise a technique (involving timing the swings of an invariant pendulum) to measure minute gravitational variations in the East African Rift Valley. Also before World War II he investigated the rate of efflux of the Earth's interior heat through the land surface and – influenced by the work of Ewing, a professor at Columbia University – he pioneered the application of the seismic method to study the sea floor. After the war, while at Toronto University, Bullard developed his "dynamo" theory of geomagnetism, according to which the Earth's magnetic field results from convective movements of molten material within the Earth's core. Also in this period - working at the Scripps Institute of Oceanography, California, in his summer vacations - he devised apparatus for measuring the flow of heat through the deep sea floor.

After returning to Cambridge he played a large part in developing the potassium-argon method of rock-dating. He also studied continental drift - before the theory became generally accepted. Using a computer to analyse the shapes of the continents, he found that they fitted together reasonably well, especially if other factors such as sedimentation and deformation were taken into account. Later, when independent evidence for these factors had been found, Bullard's findings lent considerable support to the continental drift theory.

C

Cailletet, Louis Paul (*1832-1913*), was a French physicist and inventor who is remembered chiefly for his work on the liquefaction of the "permanent" gases: he was the first to liquefy oxygen, hydrogen, nitrogen and air, for example.

Cailletet was born in Chatillon-sur-Seine on 21 September 1832, the son of an ironworks owner. He was educated at the college in Chatillon, the Lycée Henry IV in Paris and the École des Mines (also in Paris), after which he returned to Chatillon to manage his father's ironworks. Shortly afterwards he began his metallurgical studies, and later extended his research to the problems of liquefying gases. He died in Paris on 5 January 1913.

Investigating the causes of accidents that occurred during the tempering of incompletely forged iron, Cailletet found that many were due to the highly unstable state of the iron while it was hot and had gases dissolved in it. Also in the field of metallurgy he analysed the gases from blast furnaces. Other scientists had drawn off the gases under conditions that resulted in gradual cooling, which enabled the dissociated components in the gases to recombine. Cailletet, using a new technique by which the gases were cooled suddenly as soon as they had been collected, showed that the gases comprised of a large proportion of finely divided carbon particles, carbon monoxide, oxygen, hydrogen and a small proportion of carbon dioxide - a composition different from that obtained by the old sampling method. As a result of these and other metallurgical studies, Cailletet developed a unified concept of the role of heat in changes of state of metals,

and confirmed the views with which Antoine Lavoisier had introduced his *Traité élémentaire de chimie* in 1789. In 1883 Cailletet was awarded the Priz Lacaze of the French Academy of Sciences for his work in metallurgy.

Cailletet's best-known work, however, was on the liquefaction of gases. Until his studies (which were completed by 1878) several gases - including oxygen, hydrogen, nitrogen and air - were considered to be "permanent" because nobody had succeeded in liquefying them, despite numerous attempts involving the use of what were then considered to be extremely high pressures. Cailletet realized that the failure of these attempts was due to the fact that the gases had not been cooled below their critical temperatures (the concept of critical temperature - the temperature above which liquefaction of a gas is impossible - was put forward by the Irish chemist Thomas Andrews by 1869). In order to obtain the necessary amount of cooling, Cailletet employed the Joule-Thomson effect (the decrease in temperature that results when a gas expands freely), compressing a gas, cooling it, then allowing it to expand to cool it still further. Using this method he liquefied oxygen in 1877 and several other "permanent" gases in 1878, including hydrogen, nitrogen and air. (Raoul Pictet, working independently, also liquefied oxygen in 1877.)

Cailletet's other achievements included the installation of a 300 m-high manometer on the Eiffel Tower; an investigation of air resistance on falling bodies; a study of a liquid oxygen breathing apparatus for high altitude ascents; and the construction of numerous devices, including automatic cameras, an altimeter, and air sample collectors for sounding-balloon studies of the upper atmosphere. He was elected President of the Aero Club de France for these accomplishments.

Carnot, Nicolas Léonard Sadi (*1796-1832*), was a French physicist who founded the science of thermodynamics. He was the first to show the quantitative relationship between work and heat.

Sadi Carnot was born in Paris on 1 June 1796 into a distinguished family, his father Lazare Carnot and other relatives playing important roles in government. He was educated at the École Polytechnique in Paris from 1812 to 1814 and then at the École Genie in Metz until 1816. He became an army engineer, at first inspecting and reporting on fortifications and in 1819 transferring to the office of the general staff in Paris. Carnot had many interests, carrying out a wide range of study and research in industrial development, tax reform, mathematics and the fine arts. He was particularly interested in the problems of the steam engine and, in 1824, he published his classic work *Reflections on the Motive Power of Heat*, which was well received. He was then forced to return to active service in the army in 1827 but was able to resign a year later in order to concentrate on the problems of engine design and to study the nature of heat. In 1831, he began to study the physical properties of gases, in particular the relationship between temperature and pressure. Sadi Carnot died suddenly of cholera on 24 August 1832. In accordance with the custom of the time, his personal effects, including his notes, were burned. Only a single manuscript and a few notes survived, and Carnot's work was virtually forgotten. However it was rediscovered by Lord Kelvin (1824-1907), who confirmed Carnot's conclusions in his *Account of Carnot's Theorem* in 1849. He and Rudolph Clausius (1822-1888) then derived the second law of thermodynamics from Carnot's work.

In *Reflections*, Carnot reviewed the industrial, political and economic importance of the steam engine. The engine invented by James Watt (1736-1819), although the best available, had an efficiency of only 6 per cent, the remaining 94 per cent of the heat energy being wasted. Carnot set out to answer two questions:

1. Is there a definite limit to the work a steam engine can produce and hence a limit to the degree of improvement of the steam engine?
2. Is there something better than steam for producing the work?

Engineers had worked on problems like these before, but Carnot's approach was new for he sought a theory, based on known principles, that could be applied to all types of heat engines. Carnot's theorem showed that the maximum amount of work that an engine can produce depends only on the temperature difference that occurs in the engine. (In a steam engine, the hottest part is the steam and the coldest part the cooling water.) It is independent of whether the temperature drops rapidly or slowly or in a number of stages, and it is also independent of the nature of the gas used in the engine. The maximum possible fraction of the heat energy that is capable of being converted into work is represented by Carnot's equation $(T_1 - T_2)/T_2$, where T_1 is the absolute temperature of the hottest part and T_2 the temperature of the coldest part. Carnot's equation put the design of the steam engine on a scientific basis. Using experimental data and his own conclusions, he recommended that steam should be used over a large temperature interval and without losses due to conduction or friction.

In formulating his theorem, Carnot considered the case of an ideal heat engine following a reversible sequence known as the Carnot cycle. This cycle consists of the isothermal expansion and adiabatic expansion of a quantity of gas, producing work and consuming heat, followed by isothermal compression and adiabatic compression, consuming work and producing heat to restore the gas to its original state of pressure, volume and temperature. Carnot's law states that no engine is more efficient than a reversible engine working between the same temperatures. The Carnot cycle differs from that of any practical engine in that heat is consumed at a constant temperature and produced at another constant temperature, and that no work is done in overcoming friction at any stage and no heat is lost to the surroundings – so that the cycle is completely reversible.

At the time he wrote *Reflections*, Carnot was a believer in the caloric theory of heat, which held that heat is a form of fluid. But this misconception of the nature of heat does not invalidate his conclusions. Some notes which escaped destruction after Carnot's death indicate that he later arrived at the idea that heat is essentially work, or rather work which has changed its form. He had calculated a conversion constant for heat and work and showed he believed that the total quantity of work in the Universe is constant. It indicated that he had thought out the foundations of the first law of thermodynamics, which states that energy can never disappear but can only be altered into other forms of energy. Carnot's notes, however, remained undiscovered until 1878.

Carnot's work led Lord Kelvin, in 1850, to confirm and extend it. Rudolph Clausius made some modifications to it and Carnot's theorem became the basis of the second law of thermodynamics, which states that heat cannot flow of its own accord from a colder to a hotter substance.

The application of the science of thermodynamics founded by Sadi Carnot has been of great value to the production of power and also to industrial processes. To give one example, it has been useful in forecasting the conditions under which chemical reactions will or will not take place and the amount of heat absorbed or given out.

Cavendish, Henry (*1731-1810*), was a British physicist and chemist who made the first determination of the gravitational constant and thereby obtained the first-values for the mass and density of the Earth. He is also usually credited with the discovery of hydrogen. Cavendish was one of the few scientists to approach Newton's standard in both mathematical and experimental skills and

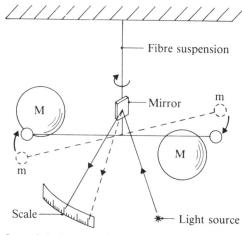

Cavendish determined the gravitational constant, G, using a torsion balance. He measured the deflection of the small masses m by the gravitational attraction of the large mass M. The method was later refined by Charles Boys.

was a major figure in eighteenth-century science. He devoted his entire life to the acquisition of knowledge, but published only those results that satisfied him completely. Most of his work, especially his experiments with electricity, were unknown for 100 years or more, so the immediate impact of his work was far less than it might have been.

Cavendish was born in Nice, France, on 10 October 1731. He was of aristocratic descent, his paternal grandfather being the Duke of Devonshire and his maternal grandfather the Duke of Kent. Cavendish attended Dr Newcome's Academy in Hackney, London, and then went on to Peterhouse College, Cambridge, in 1749. He left in 1753 without a degree, which was not an unusual practice at that time. He spent the rest of his life in London. His father encouraged his scientific interests and introduced him to the Royal Society, of which he became a member in 1760. Despite his active participation in the scientific community, Cavendish was a recluse and shunned most social contact, making no attempt to use a fortune of the order of a million pounds bequeathed to him.

Cavendish published his first paper, which demonstrated the existence of hydrogen as a substance, in 1776. He received the Copley Medal of the Royal Society for this achievement. His subsequent papers were few and far between, and included most notably a theoretical study of electricity in 1771, the synthesis of water in 1784 and the determination of the gravitational constant in 1798. He died alone in London on 24 February 1810.

It was only later that the enormous extent of Cavendish's researches became apparent in the manuscripts that he left behind. He had carried out experimental and mathematical investigations into all areas of science, but had neglected to publish most of his results. In the field of electricity in particular, he anticipated many discoveries made by others during and after his lifetime, but this was fully revealed only when James Clerk Maxwell (1831–1879) published Cavendish's electrical researches in 1879.

Cavendish's most important work in physics was on electricity and gravitation. His 1771 paper on the nature of electricity shows that he believed it to be an elastic fluid. He then worked on electricity for ten years, aiming to produce a sequel to Newton's *Principia* that would explain all electrical phenomena. But although this was his most concentrated research effort, Cavendish published nothing more about it. His fastidious attention to the details of his results and his thorough efforts to understand and unify all his observations frustrated this plan and he was not able to gain the overview that he sought. He tried unsuccessfully to uncover the relationship between force, velocity of current and resistance, although he found that electric fields obey the inverse square law and was able to produce some valuable work on conductivity. Much of the work done by Michael Faraday (1791–1867) and Charles Coulomb (1736–1806) and others during the next 50 years is foreseen in this early work by Cavendish, but none of his experiments were known until Maxwell edited and published them in 1879.

During the latter part of the 1780s, Cavendish worked on the production of heat and determined the freezing points for many materials, including mercury. He relied on some of the early work he had done on latent heats. One of the practical outcomes from these experiments was the explanation for some anomalous readings obtained when using mercury thermometers at low temperatures.

The five papers which Cavendish published during the last 25 years of his life all had an astronomical theme. By far the most important of these appeared in 1798, when he announced his determination of Newton's gravitational constant, thereby deriving the density and mass of the Earth. Newton's law of gravitation contained two unknowns: the gravitational constant and the mass of the Earth. Determining one would give the other. In what has become known as the Cavendish experiment, the gravitational constant was found.

Cavendish used an apparatus that had been devised by John Michell (1724–1793). It consisted of a delicate suspended rod with two small spheres made of lead attached to each end. Two large stationary spheres were placed in a line at an angle to the rod. The gravitational attraction of the large spheres caused the small spheres to twist the rod towards them. The period of oscillation set up in the rod enabled Cavendish to determine the force of attraction between the large and small spheres, which led him to determine the gravitational constant for Newton's equation, and thus the density of the Earth (about $5\frac{1}{2}$ times that of water) and its mass (6×10^{24} kg). The sensitivity of this apparatus was extraordinary, for the gravitational force involved was 500 million times less than the weight of the spheres, and Cavendish's results were not bettered for more than a century.

Cavendish was a great scientist and was honoured by the naming of the Cavendish Laboratories at the University of Cambridge in his memory. His contributions to science are notable for their quality and diversity. Had he permitted all his results to be published, the rate of advancement of physical science would undoubtedly have been greatly accelerated. He stands today as one of the giants of modern science.

Chadwick, James (*1891-1974*), was a British physicist who discovered the neutron in 1932. For this achievement he was awarded the 1935 Nobel Prize in Physics.

Chadwick was born at Bollington, Cheshire, on 20 October 1891. He began his scientific career at Manchester University, graduating in physics in 1911. Chadwick then continued at Manchester and, under Ernest Rutherford (1871-1937), investigated the emission of gamma-rays from radioactive materials. To gain further research experience, he went in 1913 to Berlin to work with Hans Geiger (1882-1945), the inventor of the geiger counter, where he discovered the continuous nature of the energy spectrum and investigated beta-particles emitted by radioactive substances. Chadwick was then interned as an enemy alien on the outbreak of World War I, living and working in a stable for the duration of the war. He still managed to do original research, however, and investigated the ionization present during the oxidation of phosphorus and the photochemical reaction between chlorine and carbon monoxide.

At the end of the war, Rutherford invited Chadwick to Cambridge. During this period, he determined the atomic numbers of certain elements by the way in which alpha-particles were scattered. He also established the equivalence of atomic number and atomic charge. With Rutherford, he produced artificial disintegration of

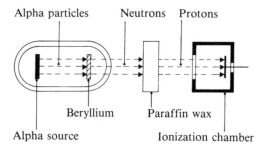

Chadwick discovered the proton by bombarding beryllium with alpha particles and allowing the neutrons produced to pass through a block of paraffin wax.

some of the lighter elements by alpha-particle bombardment.

His most famous achievement, the discovery of the neutron, came in 1932 after its existence had been suspected by Rutherford as early as 1920. In experiments in which beryllium was bombarded by alpha-particles, a usually energetic gamma-radiation appeared to be emitted. It was more penetrating than gamma-radiation from radioactive elements. Measurements of the energies involved and the conservation of energy and momentum suggested to Chadwick that a new kind of particle was being produced rather than radiation. The results pointed towards a neutral particle made up of a proton and an electron. Its mass should thus be slightly greater than that of the proton. Because the mass of the beryllium nucleus had not then been measured, Chadwick designed and carried out an experiment in which boron was bombarded with alpha-particles. This produced neutrons, and from the mass of the boron nucleus and other elements and the energies involved, Chadwick determined the mass of the neutron to be 1.0067 atomic mass units, slightly greater than that of the proton.

In the same year, Chadwick became professor of physics at the University of Liverpool. He ordered the building of a cyclotron and, from 1939 onwards, used it to investigate the nuclear disintegration of the light elements. During World War II, he was closely involved with the atomic bomb, and much of the research and calculation for the British contribution to the Manhattan Project was carried out at Liverpool under his direction. From 1943, he led the British team with the project in America.

In 1945 Chadwick was knighted, and in the same year he returned to Liverpool to continue his own research and to develop a research school in nuclear physics. He returned to Cambridge as Master of Gonville and Caius College in 1948, and stayed in this position until his retirement ten years later. He died on 24 July 1974.

The discovery of the neutron made by Chadwick led to a much deeper understanding of the nature of matter, explaining for example why isotopes of elements exist. It also inspired Enrico Fermi (1901–1954) and other physicists to investigate nuclear reactions produced by neutrons, leading to the discovery of nuclear fission.

Charles, Jacques Alexandre César (*1746–1823*), was a French physicist and mathematician who is remembered for his work on the expansion of gases and his pioneering contribution to early ballooning.

Charles was born in Beaugency, Loiret, on 12 November 1746. He became interested in science while working as a clerk in the Ministry of Finance in Paris. Stimulated by Benjamin Franklin's experiments with lightning and electricity, he constructed a range of apparatus which he demonstrated at popular public lectures. He also experimented with gases, and was elected to the French Academy of Sciences in 1795 and later became Professor of Physics at the Paris Conservatoire des Arts et Métier. He died in Paris on 7 April 1823.

The Montgolfier brothers made their first experiments with unmanned hot-air balloons at Viadalon-les-Annonay in June 1783. On hearing about them, Charles tried filling a balloon with hydrogen, and with the brothers Nicolas and Anne-Jean Robert made the first successful (unmanned) experiment in August 1783. In November of that year the Montgolfiers demonstrated their hot-air balloons in Paris, and on 1 December Charles and Nicolas Robert made the first manned ascent in a hydrogen balloon. In later flights Charles ascended to an altitude of 3,000 m. On a tide of public acclaim he was invited by King Louis XVI to move his laboratory to the Louvre - patronage that Charles was to regret ten years later during the French Revolution.

In about 1787 Charles experimented with hydrogen, oxygen and nitrogen and demonstrated the constant expansion of these gases, that is at constant pressure the volume of a gas is inversely proportional to its temperature. He found that a gas expands by 1/273 of its volume at 0°C for each Centigrade (Celsius) degree rise in temperature (implying that at −273°C, now known as absolute zero, a gas has no volume). He did not publish his results, but communicated them to the French physical chemist Joseph Gay-Lussac, who repeated the experiments and made more accurate measurements. Unknown to the two French scientists, John Dalton in England was also about to embark on similar research. Dalton deduced the same gas law in 1802, but the first to publish (six months later) was Gay-Lussac. For this reason, the law became known in France as Gay-Lussac's law but elsewhere it was, and still is, generally known as Charles' law. Incidentally, Gay-Lussac continued to emulate Charles by becoming a pioneer balloonist.

Charles devised or improved many scientific instruments. He invented a hydrometer and a reflecting goniometer, and improved the aerostat of Gabriel Fahrenheit (1686–1736) and the heliostat of W.J. vans' Gravesande (1688–1742).

Chladni, Ernst Florens Friedrich (*1756–1827*), was a German physicist who studied sound and invented musical instruments, helping to establish the science of acoustics.

Chladni was born in Wittenberg, Saxony (now in East Germany), on 30 November 1756. His father insisted that he study law at the University of Leipzig, from which he graduated in 1782. After his father's death in about 1785 Chladni changed to the study of science, concentrating on experiments in acoustics. He died in Brelau, Silesia (now Wrocław, Poland) on 3 April 1827.

Chladni's interest in sound stemmed from his love of music. In 1786 he began studying sound waves and worked out mathematical formulae that describe their transmission. His best-known experiment made use of thin metal or glass plates covered with fine sand. When a plate was made to vibrate and produce sound (for example by striking it or stroking the edge of the plate with a violin blow), the sand collected along the nodal lines of vibration, creating patterns called Chladni's figures. In 1809 he demonstrated the technique to a group of scientists in Paris.

He also measured the velocity of sound in various gases by measuring the change in pitch of an organ pipe filled with a gas other than air (the pitch, or sound frequency, varies depending on the molecular composition of the gas). He invented various musical instruments, including ones he called the clavicylinder and the euphonium. The latter consisted of rods of glass and metal that were made to vibrate by being rubbed with a moistened finger; he demonstrated it at lectures throughout Europe.

In 1794 Chladni published a book about meteorites (which he collected) and postulated that they come from beyond the Earth as debris of an exploded planet. Nobody accepted his theory until 1803, when the French physicist Jean Biot (1774–1862) confirmed that meteorites do, in fact, fall from the sky.

Clausius, Rudolf Julius Emmanuel (*1822–1888*), was a German theoretical physicist who is credited with being one of the founders of thermodynamics, and with originating its second law. His great skill lay not in experimental technique but in the interpretation and mathematical analysis of other scientists' results.

Clausius was born in Köslin in Pomerania, now Koszalin in Poland, on 2 January 1822. He obtained his schooling first at a small local school run by his father, and then at the Gymnasium in Stettin. He entered the University of Berlin in 1840, and obtained his PhD from the University of Halle in 1848. Clausius then taught at the Royal Artillery and Engineering School in Berlin, and in 1855 became Professor of Physics at the Zurich Polytechnic. He returned to Germany in 1867 to become Professor of Physics at the University of Würzburg, and then moved to Bonn in 1869 where he held the chair of physics until his death.

In 1870 the Franco-Prussian war stimulated Clausius to organize a volunteer ambulance service run by his students. He was wounded during the course of these activities, and the injury caused him perpetual pain. This, combined with the death of his wife in 1875, probably served to reduce his productivity during his later years. However, his scientific achievements were rewarded with many honours, including the award of the Royal Society's Copley Medal in 1879. Clausius died in Bonn on 24 August 1888.

Sadi Carnot (1796–1832), Benoit Clapeyron (1799–1864) and Lord Kelvin (1824–1907) had made contributions to the theory of heat and to changes of state. Clausius examined the caloric theory, eventually rejecting it in favour of the equivalence of heat and work. Drawing particularly on Carnot's and Kelvin's concept of the continuous degradation or dissipation of energy, Clausius formulated (in a paper published in 1850) the second law of thermodynamics and introduced the concept of entropy.

The word entropy derives from the Greek word for transformation, of which there are two types according to Clausius. These are the conversion of heat into work, and the transfer of heat from high to low temperature. Flow of heat from low to high temperature produces a negative transformation value, and is contrary to the normal behaviour of heat. Clausius deduced that transformation values can only be zero, which occurs only in a reversible process, or positive, which occurs in an irreversible process. Clausius therefore concluded that entropy must inevitably increase in the Universe, a formulation of the second law of thermodynamics. This law can also be expressed by the statement that heat can never pass of its own accord from a colder to a hotter body.

Entropy is considered to be a measure of disorder, and of the extent to which energy can be converted into work. The greater the entropy, the less energy is available for work. Clausius was opposed in his views by a number of scientists, but James Clerk Maxwell (1831–1879) gave Clausius considerable support in scientific argument on the subject.

Clausius did other work on thermodynamics, for example by improving the mathematical treatment of Helmholtz's law on the conservation of energy, which is the first law of thermodynamics; and by contributing to the formulation of the Clausius–Clapeyron equations which describe the relationship between pressure and temperature in working changes of state.

The second area to which Clausius made important contributions was the development of the kinetic theory of gases, which Maxwell and Ludwig Boltzmann (1844–1906) had done so much to establish. From 1857 onwards, Clausius examined the inner energy of a gas, determined the formula for the mean velocity and mean pathlength of a gas molecule, provided support for Avogardo's work on the number of molecules in a particular volume of gas, demonstrated the diatomic nature of oxygen, and ascribed rotational and vibrational motion (in addition to translational motion) to gas molecules. Clausius also studied the relationship between thermodynamics and kinetic theory.

Clausius' third major research topic was the theory of electrolysis. In 1857, he became the first to propose that an electric current could induce the dissociation of materials, a concept which was eventually established by Svante Arrhenius (1859–1927). Clausius also proposed that Ohm's law applies to electrolytes, describing the relationship between current density and the electric field.

Clausius was clearly a brilliant theoretician, but he showed a curious lack of interest in the developments which arose from his work. The results of Boltzmann, Maxwell, Willard Gibbs (1839–1903) and other scientists and the advancements in the field of thermodynamics, statistical mechanics and kinetic theory seem to have gone completely unnoticed by Clausius in his later years. One interesting consequence of the second law of thermodynamics is that as entropy increases in the Universe, less and less energy will be available to do work. Eventually a state of maximum entropy will prevail and no more work can be done: the universe will be in a static state of constant temperature. This idea is called 'the heat death of the universe' and although it seems to follow logically from the second law of thermodynamics, this view of the future is by no means accepted by cosmologists.

Cockcroft, John Douglas (*1897–1967*), was a British physicist who, with Ernest Walton (*1903–   *), built the first particle accelerator and achieved the first artificial nuclear transformation in 1932. For this achievement, Cockcroft and Walton shared the award of the 1951 Nobel Prize in Physics.

Cockcroft was born in Todmorden, Yorkshire, on 27 May 1897. He was admitted to Manchester University in 1914 to study mathematics but left a year later to volunteer for war service. He returned to Manchester in 1918 to attend the College of Technology and study electrical engineering, having gained an interest in this subject during his army service as a signaller. He obtained an MSc Tech in 1922 and then went to Cambridge University, taking a BA in mathematics in 1924. Cockcroft then remained at Cambridge, working at the Cavendish Laboratory under Ernest Rutherford (1871–1937). There he collaborated with Peter Kapitza (1894–   ) on the design of powerful electromagnets and then with Walton on the construction of a voltage multiplier to accelerate protons. With this instrument, the first artificial transformation – of lithium into helium – was achieved in 1932. Cockcroft and Walton then worked on the artificial disintegration of other elements such as boron.

During World War II, Cockcroft was closely involved with the development of radar and with the production of nuclear power, directing the construction of the first nuclear reactor in Canada. He returned to Britain in 1946 and was appointed first Director of the Atomic Energy Research Establishment at Harwell. Cockcroft was knighted in 1948, and in 1959 became Master of Churchill College, Cambridge. He received the Atoms for Peace Award in 1961 and was made President of the Pugwash Conference, an international gathering of eminent scientists concerned with nuclear developments, shortly before he died at Cambridge on 18 September 1967.

Cockcroft's background in electrical engineering was unusual for a nuclear physicist, but he was able to put it to good use when the need to increase the energy of particles used to bring about nuclear transformations became apparent in the late 1920s. Until then, only alpha particles emitted by radioactive substances were available. Cockcroft and Walton built a voltage multiplier to build up a charge of 710,000 volts and accelerate protons in a beam through a tube containing a high vacuum. They bombarded lithium in this way in 1932, and produced alpha particles (hel-

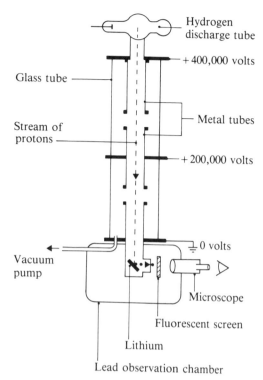

Cockroft and Walton's proton accelerator used a stream of protons (from a hydrogen discharge tube) which were accelerated to 8,000 km/sec by a high-voltage electric field. On striking a lithium plate, the protons split lithium atoms into two helium nuclei (alpha particles), detected by their scintillations on a fluorescent screen.

ium nuclei), thus artificially transforming lithium into helium. The production of the helium nuclei was confirmed by observing their tracks in a cloud chamber.

Cockcroft and Walton's voltage multiplier was the first of many particle accelerators. It was soon superseded by the cyclotron and led to accelerators of a wide range of energies. The development of the particle accelerator was essential to high-energy physics because it provided a means of studying subatomic particles that could not be produced in any other way, and it has also proved to be of great value in the production of radioactive isotopes.

Compton, Arthur Holly (*1892–1962*), was an American physicist who is remembered for discovering the Compton effect, a phenomenon in which electromagnetic waves such as X-rays undergo an increase in wavelength after having been scattered by electrons. For this achievement he shared the 1927 Nobel Prize in Physics with the British physicist C.T.R. Wilson. Compton was also a principal contributor to the development of the atomic bomb.

Compton was born at Wooster, Ohio, on 10 September 1892, the son of a philosophy professor at Wooster College who was also a Presbyterian minister. He was educated at his father's college, graduating in 1913 and going on to Princeton University, from which he gained his PhD three years later. He became a physics lecturer at the University of Minnesota, but left after a year to take up an appointment as an engineer in Pittsburgh for the Westinghouse Corporation. He travelled to Britain in 1919 and stayed for a year at Cambridge University, where he worked under Ernest Rutherford. In 1920 he returned to the United States and went to Washington University, St Louis, as Head of the Physics Department, moving to the University of Chicago in 1923 as Professor of Physics. Compton remained at Chicago for 22 years until, after the end of World War II in 1945, he returned to Washington University. He was Chancellor of the University from 1945 until 1953 and then became Professor of Natural Philosophy there, a position he held until 1961, when he became Professor at Large. He died in Berkeley, California, on 15 March 1962.

Compton began studying the scattering of X-rays by various elements in the early 1920s (using blocks of paraffin wax in which the carbon atoms' electrons deflected X-rays) and by 1922 he had noted the unexpected effects that the scattered X-rays show an increase in wavelength. He explained the Compton effect in 1923 by postulating that X-rays behave like particles and lose some of their energy in collisions with electrons, so increasing their wavelength and decreasing their frequency. He calculated that the change in wavelength, $\Delta\lambda$, is given by the equation

$$\Delta\lambda = (h/mc)(1 - \cos\theta)$$

where h is Planck's constant, m is the rest mass, c is the velocity of light and θ is the angle through which the incident radiation (e.g., X-rays) is scattered.

The chief significance of Compton's discovery is its confirmation of the dual wave/particle nature of radiation (later extended by Louis de Broglie in his hypothesis that matter can also have wave/particle duality). The behaviour of the X-ray, previously considered only as a wave, is explained best by considering that it acts as a corpuscle or particle - as a photon (Compton's term) of electromagnetic radiation. Quantum mechanics benefited greatly from this convincing interpretation. Further confirmation came from experiments using C.T.R. Wilson's cloud chamber in which collisions between X-rays and electrons were photographed and analysed. They could be interpreted as elastic collisions between two particles and measurements of the particle tracks in the cloud chamber proved the correctness of the mathematical formulation of the Compton effect.

In the early 1930s several scientists were debating the nature of cosmic rays. Robert Millikan had proposed that the rays are a form of electromagnetic radiation which, if this were true, would be unaffected by their passage from outer space through the Earth's magnetic field and should strike the Earth in undeflected straight lines. Other scientists, such as the German physicists Walther Bothe (1891–1957), postulated that the "rays" are made up of streams of charged particles which, therefore, should be deflected into curved paths as they traverse the Earth's magnetic field. Compton reasoned that the argument could be resolved by making cosmic-ray measurements at various latitudes, which he carried out during a long series of trips to various parts of the world to measure - or to organize dozens of other scientists to measure - comparative cosmic-ray intensities using ionization chambers. By 1938 he had collated the multitude of results and demonstrated a significant latitude effect by the Earth's field, proving that at least some component of cosmic rays consists of charged particles. He went on to confirm these findings by showing variations in cosmic-ray intensity with the rotation period of the Sun and with the time of day and time of year. One interpretation of these results suggests an extra-galactic source for cosmic rays.

During World War II Chicago University was the prime location of the Manhattan Project, the effort to produce the first atomic bomb, and in 1942 Compton became one of its leaders (as Director of the code-named Metallurgical Laboratory). He organized research into methods of isolating fissionable plutonium and worked with Enrico Fermi in producing a self-sustaining nuclear chain reaction, which led ultimately to the construction of the bombs that, used against Japan, effectively ended World War II. Compton's book *Atomic Quest* (1956) summarized this part of his career.

Coriolis, Gaspard Gustave de (*1792–1843*), was a French physicist who discovered the Coriolis force that governs the movements of winds in the atmosphere and currents in the ocean. Coriolis was also the first to derive formulae expressing kinetic energy and mechanical work.

Coriolis was born in Paris on 21 May 1792. From 1808, he studied there at the École Polytechnique and the École des Ponts et Chaussées, graduating in highway engineering. He returned to the École Polytechnique in 1816 as a tutor, and then became Assistant Professor of Analysis and Mechanics. In 1829 Coriolis accepted a Chair in Mechanics at the École Centrale des Arts et Manufactures and then, in 1836, he obtained the same position at the École des Ponts et Chaussées. In 1838 he became Director of Studies at the École Polytechnique. Often in poor health, he died in Paris on 19 September 1843.

From 1829, Coriolis was concerned that proper terms and definitions should be introduced into mechanics so that the principles governing the operation of machines could be clearly expressed and similar advances be made in technology as were being made in pure science. His teaching experience aided him greatly in this endeavour, and he succeeded in establishing the use of the word "work" as a technical term in mechanics, defining it in terms of the displacement of force through a certain distance. He proposed a unit of work called the dynamode, which was equal to 1,000 kg-m, but this unit did not enter general use.

Coriolis then proceeded to give the name kinetic energy to the quantity he defined as $\frac{1}{2}mv^2$, making the mathematical expression of dynamics much easier.

Coriolis went on to investigate the movements of moving parts in machines relative to the fixed parts and in 1835 made his most famous contribution to physics in a paper on the nature of relative motion in moving systems. Applying his ideas to the general case of rotating systems, Coriolis showed that an inertial force must be present to account for the relative motion of a body within a rotating frame of reference. This force is called the Coriolis force. It explains how the rotation of the Earth causes objects moving freely over the surface to follow a curved path relative to the surface, the Coriolis force turning them clockwise in the northern hemisphere and anticlockwise in the southern hemisphere. The Coriolis force therefore appears prominently in studies of the dynamics of the atmosphere and the oceans, and it is also an important factor in ballistics.

Coriolis was a scientist of acute perception who did much to clarify thought in the field of mechanics and dynamics. But for poor health, he might have realized his full potential and made an even greater contribution to science.

Coulomb, Charles (*1736–1806*), was a French physicist who established the laws governing electric charge and magnetism. The unit of electric charge is named the coulomb in his honour.

Coulomb was born in Angoulême on 14 June 1736 and educated at the École du Génie in Mézières, graduating in 1761 as a military engineer with the rank of First Lieutenant. After three years in France, he was posted to Martinique to undertake construction work and remained there from 1764 to 1772. Postings followed within France to Bouchain, Cherbourg, Rochefort and eventually to Paris in 1781.

In 1774, Coulomb had become a correspondent to the Paris Academy of Science. Three years later he shared the first prize in the Academy's competition with a paper on magnetic compasses and, in 1781, gained a double first prize with his classic work on friction. In the same year, he was elected to the Academy. During his years in Paris, his duties were those of an engineering consultant and he had time in hand for his physics research. The year 1789 marked the beginning of the French Revolution and Coulomb found it prudent to resign from the army in 1791. Between 1781 and 1806, he presented 25 papers (covering electricity and magnetism, torsion, and applications of the torsion balance) to the Academy, which became the Insitut de France after the Revolution. He was also a contributor to several hundred committee reports to the Academy on engineering and civil projects, machinery and instruments. In 1801 he became President of the Institut de France; he died in Paris on 23 August 1806.

Coulomb took full advantage of his various postings to pursue a variety of studies, including structural mechanics, friction in machinery and the elasticity of metal and silk fibres. In structural mechanics, he drew greatly on his experience as an engineer to investigate the strengths of materials and to determine the forces that affect materials in beams. In his study of friction, he extended knowledge of the effects of friction caused by factors such as lubrication and differences in materials and loads, producing a classic work that was not surpassed for 150 years. In both these fields, Coulomb greatly influenced and helped to develop engineering in the nineteenth century. He also carried out fundamental research in ergonomics, which led to an understanding not only of the ways in which people and animals can best do work but also, in influencing the subsequent research of Gaspard Coriolis (1792–1843), to a proper understanding of the fundamental nature of work.

Coulomb's major contribution to science, however, was in the field of electrostatics and magnetism, in which he made use of a torsion balance he invented and which is described in a paper of 1777. He was able to show that torsion suspension can be used to measure extremely small forces, demonstrating that the force of torsion is proportional to the angle of twist produced in a thin stiff fibre. This paper also contained a design for a compass using the principle of torsion suspension, which was later adopted by the Paris Observatory.

Coulomb was very interested in the work of Joseph Priestley (1733-1804) on electrical repulsion and in his paper of 1785 he discussed the adaptation of his torsion balance for electrical studies. He demonstrated that the force between two bodies of opposite charge is inversely proportional to the square of the distance between them. He also stated but did not demonstrate that the force of attraction or repulsion between two charged objects is proportional to the product of the charges on each. Coulomb's next paper, in 1787, produced proof of the inverse square law for both electricity and magnetism, and for both attractive and repulsive forces. A magnetic needle or charged pith ball was suspended from the torsion balance at a measured distance from a second similar needle or pith ball fixed independently, the torsion arm was deflected and the period of the resulting oscillations was timed. The experiment was repeated for varying distances between the fixed and oscillating bodies under test. Coulomb showed that if certain assumptions hold, the forces are proportional to the inverse square of the period and the period will vary directly as the distance between the bodies. The assumptions were (1) that the electrical or magnetic forces behave as if concentrated at a point, and (2) the dimensions of the bodies must be small compared with the distance between them. The results are embodied in Coulomb's law which states that the force between two electric charges is proportional to the product of the charges and inversely proportional to the square of the distance between them.

Coulomb went on to investigate the distribution of electric charge over a body and found that it is located only on the surface of a charged body and not in its interior.

Many of Coulomb's discoveries – including the torsion balance and the law that bears his name – had been made in essence by John Michell (1724-1793) and Henry Cavendish (1731-1810) in Britain. Michell died before completing his work and Cavendish neglected to publish his results, so Coulomb can truly be regarded as the principal scientist of his time. With his researches on electricity and magnetism, Coulomb brought this area of physics out of traditional natural philosophy and made it an exact science.

Cronin, James Watson (*1931–*). *See* Fitch, Val Lodgson.

Crookes, William (*1832-1919*), was a British physicist and chemist who, in a scientific career lasting more than 50 years, made many fundamental contributions to both sciences. He is best known in physics for his experiments with high-voltage discharge tubes and for inventing the Crookes radioscope or radiometer. Some of his experiments in physics might have resulted in major discoveries but these had to wait for later interpretation of the results by other scientists. Crookes never held a senior academic post, and carried out most of his researches in his own laboratory.

Crookes was born in London on 17 June 1832, the eldest of the 16 children of a tailor and businessman. Little is known of his early education but in 1848 he began a chemistry course at the new Royal College of Chemistry under August von Hofmann, who later made him a junior assistant, promoting him to Senior Assistant in 1851. Crookes' only academic posts were as Superintendent of the Meteorological Department at the Radcliffe Observatory, Oxford (1854-1855), and Lecturer in Chemistry at Chester Training College (1855-1856). He left Chester after only one year, dissatisfied at being unable to carry out original research and after having inherited enough money from his father to make him financially independent for life.

He returned to London and became secretary of the London Photographic Society and editor of its *Journal* in 1858. The following year he set up a chemical laboratory at his London home and founded as sole manager and editor the weekly *Chemical News*, which dealt with all aspects of theoretical and industrial chemistry and which he edited until 1906. Among his greatest achievements in chemistry was the discovery in 1861 of the element thallium using the newly developed spectroscope. He also applied this instrument to the study of physics. He was knighted in 1897 and made a Member of the Order of Merit in 1910. He died in London on 4 April 1919.

As part of his researches into the physical and chemical properties of thallium during the 1860s and 1870s, Crookes made an extremely accurate measurement of its atomic weight (relative atomic mass). This work involved weighing various samples of material in a vacuum, and he observed that when the delicate balance was counterpoised it occasionally made unexpected swings. He began to study the effects of light radiation on objects in a vacuum and in 1875 devised the radioscope (or radiometer). The instrument consists of a four-bladed paddle-wheel mounted horizontally on a pin-point bearing inside an evacuated glass globe. Each vane of the wheel is black on one side (making it a good absorber of heat) and silvered on the other side (making it a good reflector). When the radioscope is put in strong sunlight, the paddle-wheel spins round. Although little more than a scientific toy, it defied attempts to explain how it works until James Clerk Maxwell correctly showed that it is a demonstration of the kinetic theory of gases. The few air molecules in the imperfect vacuum in the radioscope bounce more strongly (with more momentum) off the heated, black sides of the vanes (than off the cooler, silvered sides), creating a greater reaction which "pushes" the paddle-wheel around. Crookes own observations were described in his paper "Attraction and Repulsion Resulting from Radiation" (1874).

During the 1870s Crookes' studies concerned the passage of an electric current through glass "vacuum" tubes containing rarified gases; such discharge tubes became known as Crookes tubes. The ionized gas in a Crookes tube gives out light – as in a neon sign – and Crookes observed near the cathode a light-free gap in the discharge, now called the Crookes dark space. He named the ion stream "molecular rays" and demonstrated how they are deflected in a magnetic field and how they can cast shadows, proving that they travel in straight lines. He made similar observations about cathode rays, but it was left to J.J. Thomson to understand the true significance of such experiments and to discover the electron (in cathode rays) in 1897. Crookes also noted that wrapped and unexposed photographic plates left near his discharge tubes became fogged, but he did not follow up the observation, which was later the basis of Wilhelm Röntgen's discovery of X-rays in 1895.

After 1900 Crookes turned his attention to uranium and radioactivity. As a result of this research, in 1903 he invented the spinthariscope, an alpha-ray detector. The instrument consists of a screen coated with zinc sulphide, which produces microscopic flashes of visible light when struck by alpha particles (helium nuclei) emitted by radioactive substances.

In the 1870s Crookes became extremely interested in spiritualism and published several papers that described experiments designed to investigate psychic phenomena. To many of his more conventional scientific colleagues this was akin to heresy!

D

Daniell, John Frederic (*1790–1845*), was a British meteorologist, inventor and chemist who is famous for devising the Daniell cell, a primary cell that was the first reliable source of direct current electricity. He received many honours for his work, including the Royal Society's Rumford and Copley medals, awarded in 1832 and 1837 respectively.

Daniell was born in London on 12 March 1790, the son of a lawyer. He received a private education, principally in the classics, after which he began working in a relative's sugar-refining factory. Early in his career he made the acquaintance of William Brande, Professor of Chemistry at the Royal Institution; the two men became lifelong friends, travelling together on several scientific expeditions and through their joint efforts reviving the journal of the Royal Institution. In 1831 Daniell was appointed the first Professor of Chemistry at the newly founded King's College, London, a post he held until his death (at a meeting of the Royal Society) on 13 March 1845.

Daniell made his best known contribution to science – the cell named after him – in 1836, only nine years before his death. The Italian physicist Alessandro Volta had invented (in 1797) a copper-zinc battery, which the English physicist William Sturgeon had improved by using zinc and mercury amalgam; but both these simple or voltaic cells suffered the severe disadvantage of producing a current that diminished rapidly. Daniell found that this effect (polarization) was

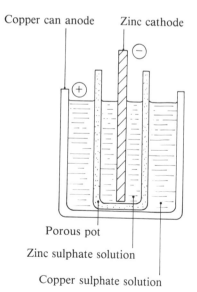

Copper can anode   Zinc cathode

Porous pot

Zinc sulphate solution

Copper sulphate solution

A Daniell cell has a zinc cathode immersed in zinc sulphate solution contained in a porous pot, surrounded by copper sulphate solution. The whole is contained in a copper can, which also forms the anode of the cell.

caused by hydrogen bubbles collecting on the copper electrode, thereby increasing the cell's internal resistance. In 1836 he proposed a new type of cell. The Daniell cell consists of a copper plate (anode) immersed in a saturated solution of copper sulphate and separated by a porous barrier (Daniell used a natural membrane), from a zinc rod (cathode) immersed in dilute sulphuric acid. The barrier prevents mechanical mixing of the solutions but allows the passage of charged ions. When the current flows zinc combines with the sulphuric acid freeing positively charged hydrogen ions which pass through the barrier to the copper plate. There they lose their charge and combine with copper sulphate, forming sulphuric acid and depositing copper on the plate. Negatively charged sulphate ions pass in the opposite direction and react with the zinc to form zinc sulphate, therefore no gases are evolved at the electrodes and a constant current is produced. Daniell's cell stimulated research into electricity – including his own investigations into electrolysis – and was later commercially used in electroplating and glyphography (a process giving a raised relief copy of an engraved plate for use in letterpress printing)

Daniell's other work included the development of improved processes for sugar manufacturing; investigations into gas generation by the distillation of resin dissolved in turpentine; and inventing a new type of dew-point hygrometer for measuring humidity (1820) and a pyrometer for measuring the temperatures of furnaces (1830). He also studied the behaviour of the Earth's atmosphere; gave an explanation of trade winds; researched into the meteorological effects of solar radiation and of the cooling of the Earth; suggested improvements for several meteorological instruments; and pointed out the importance of humidity in the management of greenhouses.

Davisson, Clinton Joseph (*1881-1958*), was an American physicist who made the first experimental observation of the wave nature of electrons. For this achievement, he was awarded the 1937 Nobel Prize in Physics with George Thomson, who made the same discovery independently of Davisson.

Davisson was born in Bloomington, Illinois, on 22 October 1881. He attended local schools before gaining a scholarship for his proficiency in mathematics and physics in 1902 to the University of Chicago, where he studied under Robert Millikan (1868–1953). In 1905 Davisson was appointed part-time instructor in physics at Princeton University while continuing his studies at Chicago, gaining a BS degree from Chicago in 1908, followed by a PhD in 1911 for a thesis on

"The Thermal Emission of Positive Ions from Alkaline Earth Salts". Davisson then spent six years as an instructor in the Department of Physics at the Carnegie Institute of Technology in Pittsburgh. He was able to spend the summer of 1913 in the Cavendish Laboratories at Cambridge working under J.J. Thomson (1856–1940). Refused enlistment in the army in 1917, he accepted wartime employment in the engineering department of the Western Electric Company (later Bell Telephone) in New York. At the end of the war, although offered an assistant professorship at the Carnegie Institute, Davisson remained at Bell Telephone where he was able to work on research full-time. He stayed there until his retirement in 1946, when he became a Visiting Professor of Physics at the University of Virginia, Charlottesville. He retired from this position in 1949 and died on 1 February 1958.

Davisson's work at Western Electric was concerned with the reflection of electrons from metal surfaces under electron bombardment. In April 1925, an accidental explosion caused a nickel target under investigation to become heavily oxidized. Davisson removed the coating of oxide by heating the nickel and resumed his work. He now found that the angle of reflection of electrons from the nickel surface had changed. Davisson and his assistant Lester Germer (1896–1971) suspected that the change was due to recrystallization of the nickel, the heating having converted many small crystals in the target surface into several large crystals.

A year later, Davisson attended a meeting of the British Association for the Advancement of Science where he received details of the theory proposed by Louis De Broglie (1892–   ) that electrons may behave as a wave motion. Davisson immediately believed that the effects he had observed were caused by the diffraction of electron waves in the planes of atoms in the nickel crystals, just as X-ray diffraction had earlier been observed in crystals by Max Von Laue (1897–1960) and William Henry Bragg (1862–1942) and William Lawrence Bragg (1890–1971).

To resolve this question, Davisson and Germer used a single nickel crystal in their experiments. The atoms were in a cubic lattice with atoms at the apex of cubes, and the electrons were directed at the plane of atoms at 45° to the regular end plane. Electrons of a known velocity were directed at this plane and those emitted were detected by a Faraday chamber. In January 1927, results showed that at a certain velocity of incident electrons, diffraction occurred, producing outgoing beams that could be related to the interplanar distance. The wavelength of the beams was determined, and this was then used with the known velocity of the electrons to verify De Broglie's hypothesis. The first work gave results with an error of 1–2 per cent but later systematic work produced results in complete agreement. Similar experiments at higher voltages using metal foil were carried out later the same year at Aberdeen University, Scotland, by George Thomson (1892–1975, the son of J.J. Thomson). The particle-wave duality of subatomic particles was established beyond doubt, and both men were awarded the 1937 Nobel Prize in Physics.

Davisson's experimental findings that electrons have a wave nature confirmed and established theoretical explanations of the structure of the atom in terms of electron waves. This understanding proved vital to investigations into the nature of chemical bonds, and to the production of high magnifications in the electron microscope.

De Broglie, Louis (*1892–*   ), is a French physicist who first developed the principle that an electron or any other particle can be considered to behave as a wave as well as a particle. This wave–particle duality is a fundamental principle governing the structure of the atom, and for its discovery, De Broglie was awarded the 1929 Nobel Prize in Physics.

De Broglie was born in Dieppe, France, on 15 August 1892, the second son of a noble French family and as such expected to have a distinguished military or diplomatic career. It was perhaps fortunate that his elder brother Maurice, who pioneered the study of X-ray spectra, had pursued his scientific interests to considerable success against the wishes of his family, his only compromise being a relatively short naval career. Nevertheless, in 1909 Louis entered the Sorbonne in Paris to read history. A year later when he was eighteen he began to study physics. It had been his intention to enter the diplomatic service but he became so interested in scientific subjects, partly through the influence of Maurice whom he helped in his extensive private laboratory at the family home, that he took a physics topic for his doctoral dissertation rather than that on French history which the Sorbonne first offered. This dissertation was submitted in 1924, but before that De Broglie began exploring the ideas of wave–particle duality. Following the award of his doctorate, De Broglie stayed on at the Sorbonne until 1928. He moved to the Henri Poincaré Institute in 1932 as Professor of Theoretical Physics, retaining this position until 1962. Since 1946, he has been a senior adviser on the development of atomic energy in France.

In 1922, De Broglie was able to derive Planck's formula $E = hv$, where E = energy, h = Planck's constant and v is the frequency of the radiation, using the particle theory of light. This probably suggested the idea of wave–particle duality to him because it prompted the question of how a particle could have a frequency. Using this idea and Einstein's mass–energy equation $E = mc^2$, he derived $E = mc^2 = hv$. Now, mc is the momentum of the particle and C/v is the wavelength of the associated wave, λ. Hence the momentum $= h/\lambda$. This relation between the momentum of the particle and the wavelength of the associated wave is fundamental to De Broglie's theory.

The extension of this idea from light particles (photons) to electrons and other particles was the next step. Niels Bohr (1885–1962) in his model of the atom found that the angular momentum of an electron in an atom must be $nh/2\pi$, where n is a whole number. De Broglie showed that this expression for the angular momentum of the electron could be derived from his momentum–wavelength equation if an electron wave exactly makes up the circular orbit of the electron with a whole number of wavelengths and produces a standing wave, i.e. $n\lambda = 2\pi r$ where r is the radius of the orbit. Otherwise interference would take place and no standing wave would form. De Broglie's idea gave a further explanation of Bohr's model of the atom. Much of this work was described in his doctoral dissertation, although some of it was published in 1923.

If particles could be described as waves then they must satisfy a partial differential equation known as a wave equation. De Broglie developed such an equation in 1926, but found it in a form which did not offer useful information when it was solved. A more useful wave equation was developed by Erwin Schrödinger (1887–1961) later in 1926.

The experimental evidence for De Broglie's theory was obtained by Clinton Davisson (1881–1958) and George Thomson (1892–1975) in 1927. These two men independently produced electron diffraction patterns, showing that particles can produce an effect which had until then been exclusive to electromagnetic waves such as light and X-rays. Such waves are known as matter waves.

De Broglie's discovery of wave–particle duality enabled physicists to view Einstein's conviction that matter and energy are interconvertible as being fundamental to the structure of matter. The study of matter waves led not only to a much deeper understanding of the nature of the atom but also to explanations of chemical bonds and the practical application of electron waves in electron microscopes.

Throughout his life, De Broglie has been concerned with the philosophical issues of physics and he is the author of a number of books on this subject. He pondered whether the statistical results of physics are all that there is to be known or whether there is a completely determined reality which our experimental techniques are as yet inadequate to discern. During many of his years as a professional scientist, he inclined to the former view but his later writing suggests his belief in the latter.

Democritus (*c.460-370* BC), was a Greek philosopher who is best known for formulating an atomic theory of matter and applying it to cosmology.

Little is known of Democritus' life. He was probably born in Abdera, Thrace, in about 460 BC. He became a rich man, and travelled far from his native Greece, particularly to Egypt and the East. In his long lifetime, Democritus is reputed to have written more than 70 works, although only fragments of them have survived. He died, aged 70, in about 370 BC.

Democritus believed that all matter – throughout the Universe, solid or liquid, living or non-living – consists of an infinite number of tiny indivisible particles which he called atoms. According to the theory, atoms cannot be destroyed (an idea similar to the modern theory of the conservation of matter) and exist in a vacuum or "void", which corresponds to the space between atoms. Atoms of a liquid, such as water, are smooth and round and so they easily "roll" past each other and the liquid is formless and flows. A solid, on the other hand, has angular, jagged atoms that catch onto each other and hold them together as a solid of definite form. Atoms differ only in shape, position and arrangement. Thus the differences in the physical properties of atoms account for the properties of various material substances. When atoms separate and rejoin, the properties of matter change, dissolving and crystallizing, dying and being reborn. Even new worlds can be created by the coming together in space of a sufficient number of similar atoms.

It is tempting, with the benefit of modern scientific knowledge, to overemphasize the apparent foresight of Democritus' theories. Remarkable although they undoubtedly were, they were a product of his mind and had no basis in experiment or scientific observation. Eventually they were superseded by other philosophies, and atomism was discarded as a theory until revived 800 years after Democritus by such scientists as Galileo Galilei.

Désormes, Charles Bernard (*1777-1862*), was a French physicist and chemist whose principal contribution was to determine the ratio of the specific heats of gases. He did this and almost all of his scientific work in collaboration with his son-in-law Nicolas Clément (1779-1841).

Désormes was born in Dijon, Côte d'Or, on 3 June 1777. He was a student at the École Polytechnique in Paris from 1794, when it opened, and subsequently worked there as a demonstrator. Désormes met Clément at the École Polytechnique, beginning a scientific collaboration that lasted until 1824. He left the École in 1804 to establish an alum refinery at Berberie, Oise, with Clément and Joseph Montgolfier (1740-1810), who had earlier pioneered balloon flight.

Clément and Désormes published their most famous work on specific heat in 1819. This memoir led to the election of Désormes (but not of Clément) to the Academy of Sciences in Paris. Désormes' scientific productivity subsequently declined and in 1830 he turned his efforts entirely to politics. He was elected counsellor for Oise in 1830 and, after three consecutive attempts to enter Parliament in 1834, 1837 and 1842, finally was elected to the Constituent Assembly in 1848, in which he sat with the Republicans. He died in Verberie on 30 August 1862.

The period of Désormes' life in which he was actively involved in scientific study was comparatively short. It began in 1801, when he commenced his joint work with Clément. In this and the following year, they correctly determined the composition of carbon disulphide (CS_2) and carbon monoxide (CO). There was a certain amount of acrimonious debate with Claude Berthollet (1748-1822) over the work on carbon disulphide, as he contended that it was in fact identical to hydrogen sulphide (H_2S). In 1806, Clément and Désormes made an important contribution in the field of industrial chemistry by the elucidation of all the chemical reactions that take place during the production of sulphuric acid by the lead chamber method, in particular clarifying the catalytic role of nitric oxide in the process. This improved the production of sulphuric acid, which was of great benefit to the chemical industry. In 1813 they made a study of iodine and its compounds.

From 1812 onwards, Clément and Désormes worked together on heat. Their first achievement in this field was to make an accurate estimate of the value for absolute zero. They also studied steam engines, showing that an engine would develop more power if the steam could undergo maximum expansion.

In 1819 Désormes and Clément published a classic paper describing the first determination of γ, the ratio of the specific heat capacity of a gas at constant pressure (C_p) to its specific heat capacity at constant volume (C_v). They did this by allowing a quantity of gas to expand adiabatically, thus lowering its temperature and pressure, and then to heat up to the original temperature without expanding, thus increasing its pressure. The ratio is found by a simple calculation involving the pressures that are produced. This method was not significantly improved until 1929.

Sadi Carnot (1796–1832), who attended Clément's lectures, was probably inspired by the work of Clément and Désormes to develop his fundamental theorem on the motive power of heat.

Dewar, James (*1842–1923*), was a British physicist and chemist with great experimental skills that enabled him to carry out pioneering work on cryogenics, the properties of matter at extreme low temperatures. Dewar is also remembered for his invention of the Dewar vacuum flask, which has been adapted for everyday use as the thermos flask.

Dewar was born at Kincardine-on-Forth, Scotland, on 20 September 1842. He went to local schools until he contracted rheumatic fever in 1852, which required a long convalescence at home. He was nevertheless able to enter the University of Edinburgh in 1859, where he studied physical science and later worked as a demonstrator. In 1867, Dewar presented models of various chemical structures at an exhibition of the Edinburgh Royal Society. This work interested Friedrich Kekulé (1829–1896), who invited Dewar to Ghent in Belgium for the summer. Dewar then returned to Edinburgh, and continued as an assistant until 1873, holding a concurrent post as a lecturer at the Royal Veterinary College from 1869. The Jacksonian Professorship of Natural Experimental Philosophy and Chemistry at the University of Cambridge was offered to Dewar in 1875, followed two years later by the Fullerian Professorship of Chemistry at the Royal Institute in London. Dewar occupied both these chairs until his death. In 1877, he was also elected a Fellow of the Royal Society, which later awarded him the Rumford Medal for his research on the cryogenic properties of matter. Dewar was appointed to a government committee on explosives from 1888 to 1891, and in 1889 invented the important explosive cordite in collaboration with Frederick Abel (1827–1902). Dewar was knighted in 1904 and died in London on 27 March 1923.

Dewar's early work in Edinburgh concerned several branches of physics and chemistry. In 1867, he worked on the structures of various organic compounds and during his visit to Ghent may have suggested the structural formula for benzene that is credited to Kekulé. He also proposed formulas for pyridine and quinoline. In 1872, Dewar invented the vacuum flask as an

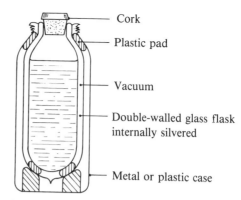

Cork
Plastic pad
Vacuum
Double-walled glass flask internally silvered
Metal or plastic case

A Dewar, or vacuum, flask has double walls silvered on the inside and containing a vacuum. The silvering reduces heat transfer by radiation, and the vacuum prevents conduction or convection.

insulating container in the course of an investigation of hydrogen-absorbed palladium. In collaboration with Peter Tait (1831–1901), he found that charcoal could be used as an absorbent to improve the strength of the vacuum. The vacuum prevented heat conduction or convection, so heat loss could occur only by radiation. The reflective silver layer on the walls of a vacuum flask are designed to minimize this.

When Dewar went to Cambridge in 1875, he began a long-term collaborative project on spectroscopy with George Liveing (1827–1924). They examined the correlation between spectral lines and bands and molecular states, and were particularly concerned with the absorption spectra of metals.

Dewar's move to the laboratories of the Royal Institution in London in 1877 marks the beginning of his main work on the liquefaction of gases and an examination of cryogenic properties. In that year, Louis Cailletet (1832–1913) and Raoul Pictet (1846–1929) in France had succeeded in liquefying oxygen and nitrogen, two gases that had resisted Faraday's attempts at liquefaction. Dewar first turned to the production of large quantities of liquid oxygen, examining its properties. He found in 1891 that both liquid oxygen and ozone are magnetic. His vacuum flasks were invaluable in this work because they enabled him to preserve the very cold liquids for longer than would otherwise have been possible.

Dewar developed the cooling technique used in liquefaction by applying the Joule-Thomson effect, whereby expansion of a compressed gas results in a lowering of temperature due to the energy used in overcoming attractive forces between the gas molecules. By subjecting an already chilled gas to this process, he became the first to produce liquid hydrogen in 1895, though only in small quantities; then by using bigger apparatus he made larger amounts in 1898. He proceeded to examine the refractive index of liquid hydrogen, and a year later succeeded in solidifying hydrogen at a temperature of $-259°C$.

Every gas had now been liquefied and solidified except one - helium. Dewar tried to liquefy helium, but was unsuccessful because his sample was contaminated with neon which froze at the low temperature and blocked the apparatus. Heike Kamerlingh Onnes (1853-1926) managed to liquefy helium using Dewar's techniques in 1908, and Dewar was then able to achieve temperatures within a degree of absolute zero ($-273°C$) by boiling helium at low pressure.

Dewar investigated properties such as chemical reactivity, strength and phosphorescence at low temperature. Substances such as feathers, for example, were found to be phosphorescent at these temperatures. From 1892 to 1895, he studied with John Fleming (1849-1945; the inventor of the thermionic valve) the electric and magnetic properties of metals at low temperatures. They predicted that electrical resistance becomes negligible at extremely low temperatures, this phenomenon of superconductivity subsequently being detected by Onnes in 1911.

During the World War I cryogenic research, being very expensive, had to be suspended. Dewar turned to the study of thin films, and later to the measurement of infra-red radiation. He was a scientist with tremendous experimental flair and patient application.

Dirac, Paul Adrien Maurice (*1902-   *), is a British theoretical physicist of great international standing. He has played a pivotal role in the development of quantum electrodynamics, being responsible for the introduction of concepts such as electron spin and the magnetic monopole. Dirac's most important achievement has been to predict the existence of antiparticles. For his contributions to theoretical physics, he shared the 1933 Nobel Prize in Physics with Erwin Schrödinger (1887-1961).

Dirac was born in Bristol on 8 August 1902. He attended Bristol University from 1918 to 1921, taking a degree in engineering but also attending lectures on philosophy. He then spent two further years at Bristol studying mathematics, and in 1923 transferred to the University of Cambridge, where he was introduced to the work of Niels Bohr (1885-1962) and Ernest Rutherford (1871-1937) on the structure of the atom. Dirac continued to study projective geometry, however, a tool he found most useful in his later research.

Dirac completed his PhD thesis in 1926. He then began to travel, visiting major centres for theoretical physics including the Institute of Theoretical Physics at Copenhagen and the University of Göttingen. There Dirac met and worked with the leading figures in the developing field of quantum mechanics, such as Niels Bohr, Wolfgang Pauli (1900-1958), Max Born (1882-1970) and Werner Heisenberg (1901-1976), with whom Dirac had already built up a lengthy correspondence.

St John's College at Cambridge University elected Dirac a Fellow in 1927, and in 1928 he formulated the relativistic theory of the electron from which he predicted the existence of the positron. The impact of the theory was profound and brought Dirac wide recognition. In 1932 he became Lucasian Professor of Mathematics at Cambridge, a post he held until 1969. In 1933 the positron was discovered and Dirac won the Nobel Prize in Physics. He was awarded the Royal Society's Royal Medal in 1939 and the Copley Medal in 1946. In 1969 he was made the first recipient of the Oppenheimer Prize. Since 1971, Dirac has been Professor of Physics at Florida State University.

During the late 1920s, there was an intense burst of activity in the field of theoretical physics. In 1923 Louis De Broglie (1892-   ) proposed a model of the electron which ascribed to it wave-like properties. This was a major break from the Bohr model of the atom. Schrödinger extended De Broglie's work by considering the movement of a particle in an electromagnetic field, thereby establishing the subject now known as of wave mechanics. Heisenberg also worked on this subject and developed a non-relativistic model of the electron.

Dirac was perturbed by a number of features of Heisenberg's theory. He was dissatisfied with its non-relativistic form and wished to integrate it with special relativity. Consideration of these problems enabled Direct in 1928 to formulate the relativistic theory of the electron. Apart from its mathematical elegance, an attribute Dirac constantly strove for in his work, the theory was also astonishingly fertile. The model was able to describe many quantitative aspects of the electron, including properties that were entirely new. These included the half-quantum spin and magnetic moment of the electron. Dirac's model was also able to account perfectly for certain anomalies in the hydrogen spectrum. Perhaps the most significant prediction to arise from Dirac's relativistic wave equation of the electron was the proposal of the positive electron, the positron.

Dirac found that the matrices describing the electron contained twice as many states as were expected. He proposed that positive energy states in the matrices described the electron, and that the negative energy states described a particle with a mass equal to that of an electron but with an opposite (positive) charge of equal strength, i.e. an antiparticle of the electron. He predicted that an electron and its antiparticle, later called the positron, could be produced from a photon. This was soon confirmed by both Carl Anderson (1905–) and Patrick Blackett (1897–1974), who independently discovered the positron in 1932 and 1933. This led to the prediction of the existence of other antiparticles, such as the antiproton. This was discovered by Emilio Segrè (1905–) and co-workers in 1955. Dirac's relativistic wave equation was also able to give a quantitative explanation for the Compton effect, and furthermore enabled Dirac to predict the existence of the magnetic monopole. This has proved to be more elusive than the positron and has not been irrefutably detected even to this day.

Dirac was eager to learn new mathematical methods, and he studied the mathematics of eigenvalues and eigenvectors which Schrödinger had found so useful. In examining the uses of these, he noticed that those particles with half-integral spins (e.g. the electron) which obeyed Pauli's exclusion principle also obeyed statistical rules different from the other particles. The latter class of particles obeyed statistical rules developed by Satyendranath Bose (1894–1974) and Albert Einstein (1879–1955). Dirac worked out the statistics for the other particles, only to discover that Enrico Fermi (1901–1954) had done very similar work already. Since the two scientists developed the theory independently, it is usually called Fermi-Dirac statistics to honour both. Fermi-Dirac statistics are of great value in nuclear and solid-state physics and are used, for example, to determine the distribution of electrons at different energy levels.

During recent years Dirac's work has returned principally to the field of mathematics. He has been working on the large number hypothesis. This hypothesis deals with pure, dimensionless numbers such as the ratio of the electrical and gravitational forces between an electron and a proton, which is 10^{39}. This ratio, perhaps coincidentally or perhaps not, also happens to be the age of the Universe when it is expressed in terms of atomic units.

If there is some meaningful connection between these two values, there must be a connection between the age of the Universe and either the electric force or the gravitational force. It is possible, therefore, that the gravitational force is not constant but is decreasing at a rate proportional to the rate of ageing of the Universe.

Another interesting fact is that the number of particles in the Universe (10^{78}) is equal to the square of the age of the Universe. This implies that matter may be being continuously created. This idea was earlier proposed in the steady state hypothesis of Thomas Gold (1920–), although it assumed that the gravitational force remains constant with time.

Dirac was responsible for the formulation of equations that were essential to the development of quantum theory, and for the reconciliation of relativity with quantum theory resulting in the formulation of the relativistic wave theory for the electron. He is one of the giants of twentieth-century physics.

Doppler, (Johann) Christian (*1803–1853*), was an Austrian physicist who discovered the Doppler effect, which relates the observed frequency of a wave to the relative motion of the source and the observer. The Doppler effect is readily observed in moving sound sources, producing a fall in pitch as the source passes the observer, but it is of most use in astronomy where it is used to estimate the velocities and distances of distant bodies.

Doppler was born in Salzburg, Austria, on 29 November 1803, the son of a stonemason. He showed early promise in mathematics, and attended the Polytechnic Institute in Vienna from 1822 to 1825. He then returned to Salzburg and continued his studies privately while tutoring in physics and mathematics. From 1829 to 1833, Doppler went back to Vienna to work as a mathematical assistant and produced his first papers on mathematics and electricity. Despairing of ever obtaining an academic post, he decided in 1835 to emigrate to the United States. Then, on the point of departure, he was offered a professorship of mathematics at the State Secondary School in Prague and changed his mind. He subsequently obtained professorships in mathematics at the State Technical Academy in Prague in 1841, and at the Mining Academy in Schemnitz in 1847. Doppler returned to Vienna the following year and, in 1850, became Director of the new Physical Institute and Professor of Experimental Physics at the Royal Imperial University of Vienna. He died from a lung disease in Venice on 17 March 1853.

Doppler explained the effect that bears his name by pointing out that sound waves from a source moving towards an observer will reach the observer at a greater frequency than if the source is stationary, thus increasing the observed frequency and raising the pitch of the sound. Similarly, sound waves from a source moving away from the observer reach the observer more slowly, resulting in a decreased frequency and a lowering of pitch. In 1842, Doppler put forward this explanation and derived the observed frequency mathematically in Doppler's principle.

The first experimental test of Doppler's principle was made in 1845 at Utrecht in Holland. A locomotive was used to carry a group of trumpeters in an open carriage to and fro past some musicians able to sense the pitch of the notes being played. The variation of pitch produced by the motion of the trumpeters verified Doppler's equations.

Doppler correctly suggested that his principle would apply to any wave motion and cited light as an example as well as sound. He believed that all stars emit white light and that differences in colour are observed on Earth because the motion of stars affects the observed frequency of the light and hence its colour. This idea was not universally true as stars vary in their basic colour. However Armand Fizeau (1819–1896) pointed out in 1848 that shifts in the spectral lines of stars could be observed and ascribed to the Doppler effect and hence enable their motion to be determined. This idea was first applied in 1868 by William Huggins (1824–1910), who found that Sirius is moving away from the solar system by detecting a small red shift in its spectrum. With the linking of the velocity of a galaxy to its distance by Edwin Hubble (1889–1953) in 1929, it became possible to use the red shift to determine the distances of galaxies. Thus the principle that Doppler discovered to explain an everyday and inconsequential effect in sound turned out to be of truly cosmological importance.

Einstein, Albert (*1879–1955*), was a German-born American theoretical physicist who revolutionized our understanding of matter, space and time with his two theories of relativity. Einstein also established that light may have a particle nature and deduced the photoelectric law that governs the production of electricity from light-sensitive metals. For this achievement, he was awarded the 1921 Nobel Prize in Physics. Einstein also investigated Brownian motion and was able to explain it so that it not only confirmed the existence of atoms but could be used to determine their dimensions. He also proposed the equivalence of mass and energy, which enabled physicists to deepen their understanding of the nature of the atom and explained radioactivity and other nuclear processes. Einstein, with his extraordinary insight into the workings of nature, may be

compared with Isaac Newton (whose achievements he extended greatly) as one of the greatest scientists to have lived.

Einstein was born in Ulm, Germany, on 14 March 1879. His father's business enterprises were not successful in that town and soon the family moved to Munich, where Einstein attended school. He was not regarded as a genius by his teachers; indeed there was some delay because of his poor mathematics before he could enter the Eidgenössosche Technische Hochschule in Zurich, Switzerland, when he was 17. As a student he was not outstanding and Hermann Minkowski (1864–1909), who was one of his mathematics professors, found it difficult in later years to believe that the famous scientist was the same person he had taught as a student.

Einstein graduated in 1900 and after spending some time as a teacher, he was appointed a year later to a technical post in the Swiss Patent Office in Berne. Also in 1901 he became a Swiss citizen and then in 1903 he married his first wife, Mileva Marić. This marriage ended in divorce in 1919. During his years with the Patent Office, Einstein worked on theoretical physics in his spare time and evolved the ideas that were to revolutionize physics. In 1905 he published three classic papers on Brownian motion, the photoelectric effect and special relativity.

Einstein did not, however, find immediate recognition. When he applied to the University of Berne for an academic position, his work was returned with a rude remark. But by 1909 his discoveries were known and understood by a few people, and he was offered a junior professorship at the University of Zurich. As his reputation spread, Einstein became full Professor or Ordinariat, first in Prague in 1911 and then in Zurich in 1912, and he was then appointed Director of the Institute of Physics at the Kaiser Wilhelm Institute in Berlin in 1914, where he was free from teaching duties.

The year 1915 saw the publication of Einstein's general theory of relativity, as a result of which Einstein predicted that light rays are bent by gravity. Confirmation of this prediction by the solar eclipse of 1919 made Einstein world famous. In the same year he married his second wife, his cousin Elsa, and then travelled widely to lecture on his discoveries. One of his many trips was to the California Institute of Technology during the winter of 1932. In 1933 Adolf Hitler came to power and Einstein, who was a Jew, did not return to Germany but accepted a position at the Princeton Institute for Advanced Study, where he spent the rest of his life. During these later years, he attempted to explain gravitational, electromagnetic and nuclear forces by one unified field theory. Although he expended much time and effort in this pursuit, success was to elude him.

In 1939, Einstein used his reputation to draw the attention of the President of the United States to the possibility that Germany might be developing the atomic bomb. This prompted American efforts to produce the bomb, though Einstein did not take part in them. In 1940 Einstein became a citizen of the United States. In 1952, the state of Israel paid him the highest honour it could by offering him the presidency, which he did not accept because he felt that he did not have the personality for such an office. Einstein was a devoted scientist who disliked publicity and preferred to live quietly, but after World War II he was actively involved in the movement to abolish nuclear weapons. He died at Princeton on 18 April 1955.

Einstein's first major achievement concerned Brownian motion, the random movement of fine particles which can be seen through a microscope and was first observed in 1827 by Robert Brown (1773–1858) when studying a suspension of pollen grains in water. The motion of the particles increases when the temperature increases but decreases if larger particles are used. Einstein explained this phenomenon as being the effect of large numbers of molecules bombarding the particles. He was able to make predictions of the movement and size of the particles, which were later verified experimentally by the French physicist Jean Perrin (1870–1942). Experiments based on this work was used to obtain an accurate value of the Avogadro number, which is the number of atoms in one mole of a substance, and the first accurate values of atomic size. Einstein's explanation of Brownian motion and its subsequent experimental confirmation was one of the most important pieces of evidence for the hypothesis that matter is composed of atoms.

Einstein's work on photoelectricity began with an explanation of the radiation law proposed in 1901 by Max Planck (1858–1947). This is $E = hv$, where E is the energy, h is a number known as Planck's constant and v is the frequency of radiation. Planck had confined himself to black-body radiation, and Einstein suggested that packets of light energy are capable of behaving as particles called "light quanta" (later called photons). Einstein used this hypothesis to explain the photoelectric effect, proposing that light particles striking the surface of certain metals cause electrons to be emitted. It had been found experimentally that electrons are not emitted by light of less than a certain frequency v^0; that when electrons are emitted, their energy increases with an increase in the frequency of the light; and that an increase in light intensity produces more electrons but does not increase their energy. Einstein suggested that the kinetic energy of each electron, $\frac{1}{2}mv^2$, is equal to the difference in the incident light energy hv and the light energy needed to overcome the threshold of emission hv^0. This can be written mathematically as $\frac{1}{2}mv^2 = hv - hv^0$ and this equation has become known as Einstein's photoelectric law. Its discovery earned Einstein the 1921 Nobel Prize in Physics.

Einstein's most revolutionary paper of 1905 contained the idea which was to make him famous, relativity. Up to this time, there had been a steady accumulation of knowledge which suggested that light and other electromagnetic radiation does not behave as predicted by classical physics. For example, no method had been found to determine the velocity of light in a single direction. All the known methods involved a reflection of light rays back along their original path. It had also proved impossible to measure the expected changes in the speed of light relative to the motion of the Earth. The Michelson-Morley experiment had demonstrated conclusively in 1881 and again in 1887 that the velocity of light is constant and does not vary with the motion of either the source or the observer. To account for this, Hendrik Lorentz (1853–1928) and George Fitzgerald (1851–1901) independently suggested that all lengths contract in the direction of motion by a factor of $(1 - v^2/c^2)^{\frac{1}{2}}$, where v is the velocity of the moving body and c is the speed of light.

The results of the Michelson-Morley experiment confirmed that no "ether" can exist in the Universe as a medium to carry light waves, as was required by classical physics. This did not worry Einstein, who viewed light as behaving like particles, and it enabled him to suggest that the lack of an ether removes any frame of reference against which absolute motion can be measured. All motion can only be measured as motion relative to the observer. This idea of relative motion is central to relativity, and is one of the two postulates of the special theory, which considers uniform relative motion. The other is that the velocity of light is constant and does not depend on the motion of the observer. From these two notions and little more than school algebra, Einstein derived that in a system in motion relative to an observer, length would be observed to decrease by the amount postulated by Lorentz and Fitzgerald. Furthermore, he found that time would slow by this amount and that mass would increase. The magnitude of these effects is negligible at ordinary velocities and Newton's laws still held good. But at velocities approaching that of light, they become substantial. If a system were to move at the velocity of light, to an observer its length would be zero, time would be at a stop and its mass would be infinite. Einstein therefore concluded that no system can move at a velocity equal to or greater than the velocity of light.

Einstein's conclusions regarding time dilation and mass increase were later verified with observations of fast-moving subatomic particles and cosmic rays. Length contraction follows from these observations, and no velocity greater than light has ever been detected. Einstein went on to show in 1907 that mass is related to energy by the famous equation $E = mc^2$. This indicates the enormous amount of energy that is stored as mass, some of which is released in radioactivity and nuclear reactions, for example in the Sun. One of its many implications concerns the atomic masses of the elements, which are not quite what would be expected by the proportions of their isotopes. These are slightly decreased by the mass equivalent of the binding energy that holds their molecules together. This decrease can be explained by, and calculated from, the famous Einstein formula.

Minkowski, Einstein's former teacher, saw that relativity totally revised accepted ideas of space and time and expressed Einstein's conclusions in a geometric form in 1908. He considered that everything exists in a four-dimensional space-time continuum made up of three dimensions of space and one of time. This interpretation of relativity expressed its conclusions very clearly and helped to make relativity acceptable to most physicists.

Einstein now sought to make the theory of relativity generally applicable by considering systems that are not in uniform motion but under acceleration. He introduced the notion that it is not possible to distinguish being in a uniform gravitational field from moving under constant acceleration without gravitation. Therefore, in a general view of relativity, gravitation must be taken into account. To extend the special theory, he investigated the effect of gravitation on light and in 1911 concluded that light rays would be bent in a gravitational field. He developed these ideas into his general theory of relativity, which was published in 1915. According to this theory, masses distort the structure of space-time.

Einstein was able to show that Newton's theory of gravitation is a close approximation of his more exact general theory of relativity. He was immediately successful in using the general theory to account for an anomaly in the orbit of the planet Mercury that could not be explained by Newtonian mechanics. Furthermore, the general theory made two predictions concerning light and gravitation. The first was that a red shift is produced if light passes through an intense gravitational field, and this was subsequently detected in astronomical observations in 1925. The second was a prediction that the apparent positions of stars would shift when they are seen near the Sun because the Sun's intense gravity would bend the light rays from the stars as they pass the Sun. Einstein was triumphantly vindicated when observations of a solar eclipse in 1919 showed apparent shifts of exactly the amount he had predicted.

Einstein later returned to the quantum theory. In 1909, he had expressed the need for a theory to reconcile both the particle and wave nature of light. In 1923, Louis De Broglie (1892-   ) used Einstein's mass-energy equation and Planck's quantum theory to achieve an expression describing the wave nature of a particle. Einstein's support for De Broglie inspired Erwin Schrödinger to establish wave mechanics. The development of this system into one involving indeterminacy did not meet with Einstein's approval, however, because it was expressed in terms of probabilities and not definite values. Einstein could not accept that the fundamental structure of matter could rest on chance events, making the famous remark "God does not play dice". Nevertheless, the theory remains valid.

Albert Einstein towers above all other scientists of the twentieth century. In changing our view of the nature of the Universe, he has extended existing laws and discovered new ones, all of which have stood up to the test of experimental verification with ever-increasing precision. The development of science in the future is likely to continue to produce discoveries that accord with Einstein's ideas. In particular, it is possible that relativity will enable us to make fundamental advances in our understanding of the origin, structure and future of the Universe.

Fabry, Charles (*1867–1945*), was a French physicist who specialized in optics. He is best remembered for his part in the invention and then in the investigations of the applications of the Fabry-Pérot interferometer and etalon.

Fabry was born in Marseilles on 11 June 1867. He and his two brothers all became prominent mathematicians or physicists. Fabry attended the École Polytechnique in Paris from 1885 to 1889, and despite becoming interested in astronomy along with his brothers, his studies under Macé de Lépinay took him into the field of optics. After completing his degree at the École Polytechnique,

Fabry went on to take a doctorate in physics at the University of Paris in 1892. He then did some teaching at lycées in Pau, Bordeaux, Marseilles, Nevers and Paris, before joining the Faculty of Science at the University of Marseilles in 1894.

The next 25 years saw Fabry concentrating on research and teaching in Marseilles, where he was elected to the Chair of Industrial Physics in 1904. The Ministry of Inventions recalled him to Paris in 1914 in order to investigate interference phenomena in light and sound waves, and in 1921 Fabry returned to Paris on a more permanent basis as Professor of Physics at the Sorbonne. He was later also made Professor of Physics at the École Polytechnique, and the first Director of the Institute of Optics. In 1935 Fabry became a member of the International Committee on Weights and Measures at the Bureau de Longitudes, but he retired in 1937 and died in Paris on 11 December 1945.

Fabry's research was dedicated to devising methods for the accurate measurement of interference effects, and to the application of this technique to a broad range of scientific subjects. His interest in interference was apparent very early in his career, his doctoral thesis having been concerned with various theoretical aspects of interference fringes.

Alfred Pérot (1863–1925) and Fabry invented the interferometer which was named after them in 1896. It is based on multiple beam interference and consists of two flat and perfectly parallel plates of half-silvered glass or quartz. A light source produces rays which undergo a different number of reflections before being focused. When the rays are reunited on the focal plane of the instrument, they either interfere or cohere, producing dark and light bands respectively. When the light source is monochromatic, as for example with a laser or a mercury vapour lamp, the Fabry-Pérot interference fringes appear as sharp concentric rings. A non-monochromatic source produces a more complex pattern of concentric rings. If the two reflecting plates are fixed in position relative to one another, the device is called a Fabry-Pérot etalon. If the distance between the plates can be varied, the apparatus is a Fabry-Pérot interferometer.

These devices can be used to distinguish different wavelengths of light from a single source, and are accurate to a resolving power of one million. The Fabry-Pérot interferometer has a resolving power 10 to 100 times greater than a prism or a small diffraction grating spectroscope, and is more accurate that the device used by Michelson and Morley in their classic experiment intended to detect the motion of the Earth through the hypothetical ether.

Fabry and Pérot worked together for a decade on the design and uses of their invention. One of their achievements was the setting of a series of standard wavelengths. Then in 1906 Fabry began to collaborate with Henri Buisson. By 1912 study of the spectra of neon, krypton and helium enabled them to confirm a broadening of lines predicted by the kinetic theory of gases. In 1914, they used the interferometer to confirm the Doppler effect for light, not with stellar sources as had until then been necessary but in the laboratory.

Applications to astronomy were also explored, including the measurement of solar and stellar spectra, and photometry. An issue of practical importance in biology, medicine, astronomy and of course physics was the identification of the material responsible for the filtering out of ultraviolet radiation from the sun. In 1913 Fabry was able to demonstrate that ozone is plentiful in the upper atmosphere and is responsible for this.

Fahrenheit, Daniel Gabriel (*1686–1736*), was a Polish-born Dutch physicist who invented the first accurate thermometers and devised the Fahrenheit scale of temperature.

Fahrenheit was born at Danzig (now Gdansk), Poland, on 14 May 1686. He settled in Amsterdam in 1701 in order to learn a business, and became interested in the manufacture of scientific instruments. From about 1707 he spent his time wandering about Europe, meeting scientists and other instrument makers and gaining knowledge of his trade. In 1717 he set himself up as an instrument maker in Amsterdam, and remained in Holland for the rest of his life. Fahrenheit published his methods of making thermometers in the *Philosophical Transactions* in 1742 and was admitted to the Royal Society in the same year. He died at The Hague on 16 September 1736.

The first thermometers were constructed by Galileo Galilei (1564–1642) at the end of the sixteenth century, but no standard of thermometry had been decided upon even a century later. Galileo's was a gas thermometer, in which the expansion and contraction of a bulb of air raised or lowered a column of water. Because it took no account of the effect of atmospheric pressure on the water level, it was very inaccurate. Guillaume Amontons (1663–1705) improved the gas thermometer in 1695 by using mercury instead of water and having the mercury rise and fall in a closed column, thus avoiding effects due to atmospheric pressure.

Fahrenheit's first thermometers contained a column of alcohol which expanded and contracted directly in the same way as modern thermometers. Fahrenheit came across this instrument in 1708 when he visited Claus Roemer (1644–1710), who had devised the thermometer in 1701. Roemer had developed a scale of temperature in which the upper fixed point, the boiling point of water, was 60° and the lower, the temperature of an ice-salt mixture, was 0°. Body temperature on this scale was $22\frac{1}{2}°$ and the freezing point of water came to $7\frac{1}{2}°$.

Fahrenheit took up Roemer's ideas and combined them with those of Amontons in 1714, when he substituted mercury for alcohol and constructed the first mercury-in-glass thermometers. Fahrenheit found that mercury was more accurate because its rate of expansion, although less than that of alcohol, is more constant. Furthermore mercury could be used over a much wider temperature range than alcohol. In order to reflect the greater sensitivity of his thermometer, Fahrenheit expanded Roemer's scale so that blood heat was 90° and the ice-salt mixture 0°; on this scale freezing point was 30°. Fahrenheit later adjusted the scale to ignore body temperature as a fixed point so that the boiling point of water came to 212° and freezing point was 32°. This is the Fahrenheit scale that is still in use today.

Using his thermometer, Fahrenheit was able to determine the boiling points of liquids and found that they vary with atmospheric pressure. In producing a standard scale for the measurement of temperature as well as an accurate measuring instrument, Fahrenheit made a very substantial contribution to the advance of science.

Faraday, Michael (*1791–1867*), was a British physicist and chemist who is often regarded as the greatest experimental scientist of the 1800s. He made pioneering contributions to electricity, inventing the electric motor, electric generator and the transformer and discovering electromagnetic induction and the laws of electrolysis. He also discovered benzene and was the first to observe that the plane of polarization of light is rotated in a magnetic field.

Faraday was born in Newington, Surrey, on 22 September 1791. His father was a poor blacksmith, who went to London to seek work in the year that Faraday was born. Faraday received only a rudimentary education as a child and although he was literate, he gained little knowledge of mathematics. At the age of 14, he became an apprentice to a bookbinder in London and began to read voraciously. The article on electricity in the *Encyclopedia Britannica* fascinated him in particular, for it presented the view that electricity is a kind of vibration, an idea that was to remain with Faraday. He also read the works of Lavoisier and became interested in chemistry, and carried out what scientific experiments he could put together with his limited resources. He was aided by a manual dexterity gained from his trade, which also stood him in great stead in his later experimental work.

In 1810 Faraday was introduced to the City Philosophical Society and there received a basic grounding in science, attending lectures on most aspects of physics and chemistry and carrying out some experimental work. He also attended the Royal Institution, where he was enthralled by the lectures and demonstrations given by Humphry Davy (1778–1829). He made notes eagerly, assembling them at work into finely bound books. In 1812 Faraday came to the end of his apprenticeship and prepared to devote himself to his trade, not expecting to make a career in science. Almost immediately, however, there came an extraordinary stroke of luck. Davy was temporarily blinded by an explosion in a chemistry experiment and asked Faraday to help him until he regained his sight. When he recovered, Faraday sent Davy the bound notes of his lectures. Impressed by the young man, Davy marked him out as his next permanent assistant at the Royal Institution and Faraday took up this post in 1813.

This was remarkably good fortune for Faraday, because Davy was a man of wide-ranging interests and great scientific insight as well as a brilliant exponent of ideas. Furthermore, Davy undertook a tour of France and Italy from 1813 to 1815 to visit the leading scientists of the day, including the pioneer of current electricity Alessandro Volta (1745–1827). Faraday accompanied Davy, gaining an immense amount of knowledge, and on his return to London threw himself whole-heartedly into scientific research.

Faraday remained at the Royal Institution and made most of his pioneering discoveries in chemistry and electricity there over the next 20 years. He became a great popularizer of science with his lectures at the Royal Instituion, which he began in 1825 and continued until 1862. His fame grew rapidly, soon eclipsing even that of Davy, who became embittered as a result. But the strain of his restless pursuit of knowledge told and in 1839 Faraday suffered a breakdown. He never totally recovered but at the instigation of Lord Kelvin (1824–1907), returned to research in 1845 and made his important discoveries of the effect of magnetism on light and developed his field theory. In the 1850s, Faraday's mind began to lose its sharp grip, possibly as a result of low-grade poisoning caused by his chemical researches, and he abandoned research and then finally lecturing. He resigned from the Royal Institution in 1862 and retired to an apartment provided for him at Hampton Court, Middlesex, by Queen Victoria. He died there on 25 August 1867.

Faraday was mainly interested in chemistry during his early years at the Royal Institution. He investigated the effects of including precious metals in steel in 1818, producing high-quality alloys that later stimulated the production of special high-grade steels. Faraday then investigated chlorine, which Davy had shown to be an element, producing the first compounds of chlorine and carbon in 1820. He also carried out research into gases and oils used for heating and lighting, which led to the discovery of benzene in 1825. Faraday also investigated the effects of low temperature and pressure on gases, first liquefying several gases (including chlorine) in 1823, and he prepared the first heavy lead glass in 1824, which led to improvements in optical instruments.

But Faraday's interest in science had been initiated by a fascination for electricity and he eventually combined the knowledge that he gained of this subject with chemistry to produce the basic laws of electrolysis in 1834. But his first major electrical discovery was made much earlier, in 1821, only a year after Hans Oersted (1777–1851) had discovered with a compass needle that a current of electricity flowing through a wire produces a magnetic field. Faraday was asked to investigate the phenomenon of electromagnetism by the editor of the *Philosophical Magazine*, who hoped that Faraday would elucidate the facts of the situation following the wild theories and opinions that Oersted's sensational discovery had aroused. Faraday conceived that circular lines of magnetic force are produced around the wire to explain the orientation of Oersted's compass needle, and therefore set about devising an apparatus that would demonstrate this by causing a magnet to revolve around an electric current. He succeeded in October 1821 with an elaborate devise consisting of two vessels of mercury connected to a battery. Above the vessels and connected to each other were suspended a magnet and a wire; these were free to move and dipped just below the surface of the mercury. In the mercury were fixed a wire and a magnet respectively. When the current was switched on, it flowed through both the fixed and free wires, generating a magnetic field in them. This caused the free magnet to revolve around the fixed wire, and the free wire to revolve around the fixed magnet.

This was a brilliant demonstration of the conversion of electrical energy into motive force, for it showed that either the conductor or the magnet could be made to move. In this experiment, Faraday demonstrated the basic principles governing the electric motor and although practical motors subsequently developed had a very different form

to Faraday's apparatus, he is nevertheless usually credited with the invention of the electric motor.

Faraday's conviction that an electric current gave rise to lines of magnetic force arose from his idea that electricity was a form of vibration and not a moving fluid. He believed that electricity was a state of varying strain in the molecules of the conductor, and this gave rise to a similar strain in the medium surrounding the conductor. It was reasonable to consider therefore that the transmitted strain might set up a similar strain in the molecules of another nearby conductor – that a magnetic field might bring about an electric current in the reverse of the electromagnetic effect discovered by Oersted.

Faraday hunted for this effect from 1824 onwards, expecting to find that a magnetic field would induce a steady electric current in a conductor. In 1824, François Arago (1786–1853) found that a rotating non-magnetic disc, specifically of copper, caused the deflection of a magnetic needle placed above it. This was in fact a demonstration of electromagnetic induction, but nobody at that time could explain Arago's wheel (as it was called). Faraday eventually succeeded in producing induction in 1831. In August of that year, he wound two coils around an iron bar and connected one to a battery and the other to a galvanometer. Nothing happened when the current flowed through the first coil, but Faraday noticed that the galvanometer gave a kick whenever the current was switched on or off. Faraday found an immediate explanation with his lines of force. If the lines of force were cut – that is, if the magnetic field changed – then an electric current would be induced in a conductor placed within the magnetic field. The iron core in fact helped to concentrate the magnetic field, as Faraday later came to understand, and a current was induced in the second coil by the magnetic field momentarily set up as current entered or left the first coil. With this device, Faraday had discovered the transformer, a modern transformer being no different in essence even though the alternating current required had not then been discovered.

Faraday thus is also credited with the simultaneous discovery of electromagnetic induction, though the same discovery had been made in the same way by Joseph Henry (1797–1878) in 1830. However, busy teaching, Henry had not been able to publish his findings before Faraday did so, although both men are now credited with the independent discovery of induction.

Faraday's insight enabled him to make another great discovery soon afterwards. He realized that the motion of the copper wheel relative to the magnet in Arago's experiment caused an electric current to flow in the disc, which in turn set up a magnetic field and deflected the magnet. He set about constructing a similar device in which the current produced could be led off, and in October 1831 built the first electric generator. This consisted of a copper disc that was rotated between the poles of a magnet; Faraday touched wires to the edge and centre of the disc and connected them to a galvanometer, which registered a steady current. This was the first electric generator, and generators employing coils and magnets in the same way as modern generators were developed by others over the next two years.

Faraday's next discoveries in electricity, apart from his major contribution to electrochemistry, were to show in 1832 that an electrostatic charge gives rise to the same effects as current electricity, thus proving that there is no basic difference between them. Then in 1837 he investigated electrostatic force and demonstrated that it consists of a field of curved lines of force, and that different substances take up different amounts of electric charge when subjected to an electric field. This led Faraday to conceive of specific inductive capacity. In 1838, he proposed a theory of electricity based on his discoveries that elaborated his idea of varying strain in molecules. In a good conductor, a rapid build-up and breakdown of strain took place, transferring energy quickly from one molecule to the next. This also accounted for the decomposition of compounds in electrolysis. At the same time, Faraday rejected the notion that electricity involved the movement of any kind of electrical fluid. In this, he was wrong (because the motion of electrons is involved) but in that this motion causes a rapid transfer of electrical energy through a conductor, Faraday's ideas were valid.

Faraday's theory was not taken seriously by many scientists, but his concept of the line of force was developed mathematically by Kelvin. In 1845, he suggested that Faraday investigate the action of electricity on polarized light. Faraday had in fact already carried out such experiments with no success, but this could have been because electrical forces were not strong. Faraday now used an electromagnet to give a strong magnetic field instead and found that it causes the plane of polarization to rotate, the angle of rotation being proportional to the strength of the magnetic field.

Several further discoveries resulted from this experiment. Faraday realized that the glass block used to transmit the beam of light must also transmit the magnetic field, and he noticed that the glass tended to set itself at right-angles to the poles of the magnet rather than lining up with it as an iron bar would. Faraday showed that the differing responses of substances to a magnetic field depended on the distribution of the lines of force through them, and not on the induction of different poles. He called materials that are attracted to a magnetic field paramagnetic, and those that are repulsed diamagnetic. Faraday then went on to point out that the energy of a magnet is in the field around it and not in the magnet itself, and he extended this basic conception of field theory to electrical and gravitational systems.

Finally Faraday considered the nature of light and in 1846 arrived at a form of the electromagnetic theory of light that was later developed by James Clerk Maxwell (1831–1879). In a brilliant demonstration of both his intuition and foresight, Faraday said "The view which I am so bold to put forth considers radiation as a high species of vibration in the lines of force which are known to connect particles, and also masses of matter, together. It endeavours to dismiss the ether but not the vibrations." It was a bold view, for no scientist until Albert Einstein (1879–1955) was to take such a daring step.

Michael Faraday was a scientific genius of a most extraordinary kind. Without any mathematical ability at all, he succeeded in making the basic discoveries on which virtually all our uses of electricity depend and also in conceiving the fundamental nature of magnetism and, to a degree, of electricity and light. He owed this extraordinary degree of insight to an amazing talen for producing valid pictorial interpretations of the workings of nature. Faraday himself was a modest man, content to serve science as best he could without undue reward, and he declined both a knighthood and the Presidency of the Royal Society. Characteristically, he also refused to take part in the preparation of poison gas for use in the Crimean War. His many achievements are honoured in the use of his name in science, the farad being the SI unit of capacitance and the Faraday constant being the quantity of electricity required to liberate a standard amount of substance in electrolysis.

Fermi, Enrico (*1901–1954*), was an Italian-born American physicist best known for bringing about the first controlled chain reaction (in a nuclear reactor) and for his part in the development of the atomic bomb. He also carried out early research using slow neutrons to produce new radioactive elements, for which work he was awarded the 1938 Nobel Prize in Physics.

Fermi was born in Rome on 19 September 1901, the son of a government official. He was educated at the select Reale Scuola Normale Superior in Pisa (which he attended from 1918) and went on to the University of Pisa, receiving his

PhD in 1929 for a thesis on X-rays. He then travelled to Göttingen University, where he worked under Max Born, and to Leiden University, where he studied with P. Ehrenfest. He became a mathematics lecturer at the University of Florence in 1924, and two years later he was appointed Professor of Theoretical Physics at Rome University. Fermi married a Jew (in 1928) and during the 1930s became alarmed by increasing antisemitism in Fascist Italy under Benito Mussolini. After the Nobel Prize ceremony in Stockholm in 1938 Fermi did not return to Italy but went with his wife and two children to the United States, where he took up an appointment in New York at Columbia University. In 1941 he and his team moved to Chicago University where he began building a nuclear reactor, which first went "critical" at the end of 1942. He became involved in the Manhattan Project to construct an atomic bomb, working mainly at Los Alamos, New Mexico. At the end of World War II in 1945 Fermi became an American citizen and returned to Chicago to continue his researches as Professor of Physics. He died there, of cancer, on 28 November 1954.

Fermi first gained fame soon after his Rome appointment with his publication *Introduzione alla Fisica Atomics* (1928), the first textbook on modern physics to be published in Italy. His experimental work on beta-decay in radioactive materials provided further evidence for the existence of the neutrino (as predicted by Wolfgang Pauli) and earned him an international reputation. The decay, which takes place in the unstable nuclei of radioactive elements, results from the conversion of a neutron into a proton, an electron (beta particle) and an antineutrino.

Following the work of the Joliot-Curies, who discovered artificial radioactivity in 1934 using alpha-particle bombardment, Fermi began producing new radioactive isotopes by neutron bombardment. He found that a block of paraffin wax or a jacket of water round the neutron source produced slow, or "thermal", neutrons which are more effective at producing such elements. This was the work that earned him the Nobel Prize. He did, however, misinterpret the results of experiments involving neutron bombardment of uranium, and it was left to Lise Meitner and Otto Frisch to explain nuclear fission in 1938.

In the United States Fermi continued the work on the fission of uranium (initiated by neutrons) by building the first nuclear reactor, then called an atomic pile because it had a moderator consisting of a pile of purified graphite blocks (to slow the neutrons) with holes drilled in them to take rods of enriched uranium. Other neutron-absorbing rods of cadmium, called control rods,

could be lowered into or withdrawn from the pile to limit the number of slow neutrons available to initiate the fission of uranium. The reactor was built on the squash court of Chicago University, and on the afternoon of 2 December 1942 the control rods were withdrawn for the first time and the reactor began to work, using a self-sustaining nuclear chain reaction. Two years later the Americans, through a team led by Arthur Compton and Fermi, had constructed an atomic bomb, which used the same reaction but without control, resulting in a nuclear explosion.

Element number 100, discovered in 1955 a year after Fermi died, was named fermium, and his name is also honoured in the fermi, a unit of length equal to 10^{-15} m.

Fitch, Val Lodgson (*1923–*), and **Cronin, James Watson** (*1931–*), are American physicists who shared the 1980 Nobel Prize in Physics for their work in particle physics.

Fitch was born in Merriman, Nebraska, on 10 March 1923. He was educated at McGill University, where he obtained his BEng in 1948. He gained a PhD from Columbia University in physics in 1954. From 1954 to 1960 Fitch rose from Instructor to Professor of Physics at Princeton University, and since 1976 he has been Cyrus Fogg Bracket Professor of Physics at Princeton. He was a member of the President's Scientific Advisory Committee from 1970 to 1973.

Cronin was born in Chicago, Illinois, on 29 September 1931. He was educated at the Southern Methodist University, obtaining a BS in 1951. He then gained an MS from the University of Chicago in 1953 and a PhD in physics in 1955. From 1955 to 1958, he was an assistant physicist at the Brookhaven National Laboratory. Cronin then went to Princeton University, becoming Professor of Physics in 1965. Since 1971, he has been Professor of Physics at the University of Chicago.

The discovery for which Fitch and Cronin received the 1980 Nobel Prize in Physics was first published in 1964, and at that time was regarded as a bombshell in the field of particle physics. It is surprising that their work was not rewarded earlier.

Until 1964, it was not possible to distinguish unambiguously between matter and antimatter outside of our own galaxy and a few nearby galaxies. In 1964, Cronin, Fitch and their colleagues had set up an experiment with the proton accelerator at the Brookhaven Laboratory in New York to study the properties of K° mesons. These are neutral, unstable particles with a mass equal to approximately half that of the proton, and had been discovered earlier in the interactions of particles from outer space with the Earth's atmosphere. $K°$ is a mixture of two "basic states" which have a long and a short lifetime and are therefore called $K°_L$ and $K°_S$ respectively. These two basic states can also mix together to form not $K°$ but an anti-matter particle (anti-$K°$), and $K°$ can oscillate from particle to anti-particle through either of its basic states. This is a unique phenomenon in the world of particle physics.

A rule called CP-conservation states how $K°_L$ and $K°_S$ should decay (C stands for conjugation and P for parity). Charge conjugation changes all particles to antiparticles. Parity concerns handedness and is like a mirror reflection – all positive points in a three-dimensional co-ordinate system (x, y, z) are changed to $(-x, -y, -z)$ by a parity operation. The conservation rule means that these two operations when applied together do not alter an interaction, such as the decay of an unstable particle. What Cronin and Fitch found to their surprise was that a $K°_L$ meson can decay in such a way as to violate CP-conservation about 0.2 per cent of the time. Their results were verified at other accelerators and many strange explanations were provided. The conclusion that had to be drawn was that decays of $K°_L$ mesons do violate CP-conservation and so are different from all other known particle interactions.

While it was relatively simple to confirm these results, it has proved much more difficult to explain them. The latest theories seem to view particles as being built up from six basic different entities called quarks. Earlier theories based on four quarks did not explain CP-violation satisfactorily. There is firm evidence for the existence of five kinds of quark, but the search for the sixth has so far been unsuccessful – and there may be more. CP-violation could explain why we exist at all. Scientists are puzzled why matter seems to dominate over antimatter, when all the theories suggest that matter and antimatter should have been formed in equal amounts. CP-violation could help to solve this problem, since if antiparticles decay faster than particles, they would totally disappear.

The work of Cronin and Fitch is recorded as a classic piece of research and their findings have had impact on an outstanding controversy about the symmetry of nature. They have shown for the first time that left-right assymmetry is not always preserved when some particles are changed in state from matter to antimatter.

FitzGerald, George Francis (*1851-1901*), was an Irish theoretical physicist who worked on the electromagnetic theory of light and radio waves. He is best known, however, for the theoretical phenomenon called the Lorentz-FitzGerald con-

traction which he and, independently, Hendrik Lorentz proposed to account for the negative result of the famous Michelson-Morley experiment on the velocity of light.

FitzGerald was born in Dublin on 3 August 1851. He was a nephew of the physicist George Stoney, and received his initial education at home, tutored by the sister of the mathematician George Boole. He entered Trinity College, Dublin, in 1867 (at the age of only 16) and graduated four years later. FitzGerald went on to study mathematical physics, and in 1877 received a Fellowship of Trinity College. He became Erasmus Smith Professor of Natural and Experimental Philosophy there in 1881, an appointment he retained until he died, in Dublin, on 22 February 1901.

FitzGerald predicted that a rapidly oscillating (i.e., alternating) electric current should result in the radiation of electromagnetic waves – a prediction proved correct in the late 1880s by Heinrich Hertz's early experiments with radio, which Fitz-Gerald brought to the attention of the scientific community in Britain.

At that time, one school of thought among physicists postulated that electromagnetic radiation – such as light – had to have a medium in which to travel. This hypothetical medium, termed the "ether", was supposed to permeate all space and in 1887 the American physicists Albert Michelson and Edward Morley conducted an experiment intended to detect the motion of the Earth through the ether. They measured the velocity of light simultaneously in two directions at right-angles to each other, but found no difference in the values – the velocity was unaffected by the Earth's motion through the ether. FitzGerald proposed in 1892 that the Michelson-Morley result – or lack of result – could be accounted for by assuming that a fast-moving object diminishes in length, and that light emitted by it does indeed have a different velocity but travels over a shorter path, and so seems to have a constant velocity no matter what the direction of motion. (Only an observer outside the moving system would be aware of the reduction in light velocity; within the system the contraction would also affect the measuring instruments and result in no change in the perceived velocity.) He worked out a simple mathematical relationship to show how velocity affects physical dimensions. The idea was independently arrived at and developed by the Dutch physicist Hendrik Lorentz in 1895, and it became known as the Lorentz-FitzGerald contraction. In 1905, four years after FitzGerald's death, the contraction hypothesis was incorporated and given a different interpretation in Albert Einstein's general theory of relativity.

Fizeau, Armand Hippolyte Louis (*1819-1896*), was a French physicist who was the first to measure the speed of light on the Earth's surface. He also found that light travels faster in air than in water, which confirmed the wave theory of light, and that the motion of a star affects the position of the lines in its spectrum.

Fizeau was born in Paris on 23 September 1819 into a wealthy family. He began to study medicine, his father being Professor of Pathology at the Paris Faculty of Medicine, but was forced to abandon his medical ambitions through ill health. Fizeau then turned to physics, studying optics at the Collège de France and taking a course with François Arago (1786-1853) at the Paris Observatory.

Fizeau's principal contributions to physics and astronomy cover a fairly short period of time and include the first detailed photographs of the Sun in 1845, the proposal that a moving light source such as a star undergoes a change in observed frequency that can be detected by a shift in its spectral lines in 1848, the first reasonably accurate determination of the speed of light in 1849, and the discovery that the velocity of light is greater in air than in water in 1850. Many of his discoveries were made in collaboration with Léon Foucault (1819-1868).

In recognition of his work, Fizeau gained the first Triennial Prize of the Institut de France in 1856. He became a member of the Academy of Sciences in 1860, rising to become its president in 1878, and he was awarded the Rumford Medal of the Royal Society in 1866. Fizeau died at Venteuil on 18 September 1896.

Inspired by Arago, Fizeau began to research into the new science of photography in 1839, improving the daguerrotype process. The fruitful collaboration with Foucault commenced at this time, leading them to develop photography for astronomical observations by taking the first detailed pictures of the Sun's surface in 1845. The two men went on to study the interference of light rays and showed how it is related to the wavelength of the light. They also found, in 1847, that heat rays from the Sun undergo interference and that radiant heat therefore behaves as a wave motion.

These latter results greatly strengthened the view that light is a wave motion, an issue that was being hotly debated at the time following the experiments of Thomas Young (1773-1829) and Augustin Fresnel (1788-1827) that had established the wave theory earlier in the century. In 1838, Arago had proposed an experiment to settle the question by measuring the velocity of light in air and in water. The wave theory demanded that light travels faster in air and the particle theory required it to travel faster in water. Arago's proposal was to reflect light from a rotating mirror, the amount of deflection produced being related to the velocity of light.

In 1847, Fizeau and Foucault split up their partnership. Foucault persevered with Arago's suggestion but Fizeau decided to try a simpler method. In 1849, he sent a beam of light through the gaps in the teeth of a rapidly rotating cog wheel to a mirror 8 km away. On returning, the beam was brought to the edge of the wheel, the speed being adjusted so that the light was obscured. This meant that light rays which had passed through the gaps were being blocked on their return by the adjacent teeth as they moved into the position of the gaps. The time taken for the teeth to move this distance was equal to the time taken for light travel 16 km to the mirror and back. Fizeau's wheel had 720 teeth and rotated at a rate of 12.6 revolutions per second. By a simple calculation, he obtained the value of 315,000 km a second for the speed of light. Although five per cent too high, this was the first reasonably accurate estimate, previous values having been obtained by inaccurate astronomical methods.

In collaboration with Louis Bréguet (1804-1883), Fizeau now applied himself to Arago's proposal and set about measuring the speed of light in air and water. Using a rotating-mirror apparatus and dividing the light beam so that half passed through air and half through a tube of water, Fizeau showed in 1850 that light travels faster in air. Foucault reached the same conclusion in the same way at the same time, and the wave theory of light was finally confirmed.

Another important experiment conducted by Fizeau in 1851 was one in which he determined the amount of drift of light waves in a transparent medium which is in motion. According to a theory given by Fresnel, the velocity of drift of waves in a medium moving with velocity u is $(1-1/\eta^2)u$, where η is the refractive index of the medium. Fizeau arranged two tubes side by side and water was forced at a considerable speed (as much as 7 m per second) along one tube and back by the other, while a beam of light was split into two parts which were sent through the tubes, one with the stream and the other against it. They were then brought together again and tested for interference produced by any difference in time traversed arising from the motion of the water. The result gave exactly the formula quoted above.

Earlier, in 1848, Fizeau made a fundamental contribution to astrophysics by suggesting that the Doppler effect would apply to the light received from Stars, motion away from the Earth

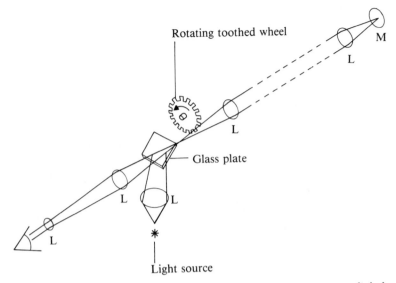

Rotating toothed wheel

M

L

L

Glass plate

L L

L

✳

Light source

Fizeau's method of measuring the velocity of light used a system of lenses (L) to transmit a light beam nearly 9 km, where a mirror (M) reflected it back along the same path to the eyepiece of a telescope. The speed of the rotating toothed wheel was adjusted until a tooth blocked the returning beam, so that the out-and-back time could be calculated for the beam along a total path of more than 17 km.

causing a red shift in the spectral lines and motion towards the Earth producing a blue shift. Fizeau may have been unaware of Doppler's discovery of the effect in sound in 1842 and of his erroneous theory relating the colour of stars to their motion. Fizeau's discovery is now the basis of the principal method of determining the distances of galaxies and other distant bodies.

Fizeau was able to finance his experiments from his personal wealth, and this enabled him to develop experimental methods that were later refined by others, particularly Foucault and Albert Michelson (1852-1931), leading to accurate values for the velocity of light and the consequent development of relativity.

Fortin, Jean Nicholas (*1750-1831*), was a French instrument maker who made precision equipment for many of the most eminent French scientists of his time, although he is remembered today for the portable mercury barometer, which is named after him.

Little is known of Fortin's life. He was born in Mouchy-la-Ville, Île de France, on 8 August 1750. He worked in Paris as a member of the Bureau de Longitudes, having been helped in his early career by Antoine Lavoisier, for whom he made several scientific instruments. During his later years Fortin worked for the Paris Observatory, constructing instruments for astronomical studies and surveying. His only known publication is an

abridgment of John Flamsteed's *Atlas Celeste*, which was published in 1776. Fortin died in Paris in 1831.

One of Fortin's major early achievements was his construction of a precision balance for Lavoisier; it consisted of a metre-long beam mounted on steel knife-edges and was able to measure weights as little as 70 mg. He made the first version of this balance in 1778, and another in 1799 for the Convention Committee on Weights and Measures; this latter version incorporated a comparator for standardizing weights. In the same year he adjusted the weight standard, the platinum kilogram, which was stored in the French National Archives.

Fortin is best known, however, for his barometers, although he did not make many of them. In 1800 he designed a portable mercury barometer that incorporated a mercury-filled leather bag, a glass cylinder in the cistern, and an ivory pointer for marking the mercury level. The mercury level could also be adjusted to the zero mark, and any barometer that possesses this feature is now known as a Fortin barometer. Fortin did not inevent these features but he was the first to use them together in a sensitive portable barometer.

Fortin also made apparatus used by Joseph Gay-Lussac in experiments on gas expansion; for Pierre Dulong and François Arago's investigation of the validity of the Boyle-Mariotte law; for Jean Biot and Arago's expedition to Spain in 1806 to measure the arc of the terrestrial meridian; and numerous other instruments, including various clocks.

Foucault, Jean Bernard Léon (*1819–1868*), was a French physicist who invented the gyroscope, demonstrated the rotation of the Earth, and obtained the first accurate value for the velocity of light.

Foucault was born in Paris on 19 September 1819. He was educated at home because his health was poor and went on to study medicine, hoping that the manual skills he developed in his youth would stand him in good stead as a surgeon. But Foucault soon abandoned medicine for science and supported himself from 1844 onwards at first by writing scientific textbooks and then popular articles on science for a newspaper. He carried out research into physics at his home until 1855, when he became a physicist at the Paris Observatory. He received the Copley Medal of the Royal Society in the same year, and was made a member of the Bureau des Longitudes in 1862 and the Académie des Sciences in 1865. He died of a brain disease in Paris on 11 February 1868.

Foucault's first scientific work was carried out in collaboration with Armand Fizeau (1819–1896). Inspired by François Arago (1786–1853), Foucault and Fizeau researched into the scientific uses of photography, taking the first detailed pictures of the Sun's surface in 1845. In 1847, they found that the radiant heat from the Sun undergoes interference and that it therefore behaves as a wave motion. Foucault parted from Fizeau in 1847, and his early work then propelled him in two directions.

Making the long exposures required in those early days of photography necessitated a clockwork device to turn the camera slowly so that it would follow the Sun. Foucault noticed that the pendulum in the mechanism behaved rather oddly and realized that it was attempting to maintain the same plane of vibration when rotated. Foucault developed this observation into a convincing demonstration of the Earth's rotation by showing that a pendulum maintains the same movement relative to the Earth's axis and the plane of vibration appears to rotate slowly as the Earth turns beneath it. Foucault first carried out this experiment at home in 1851, and then made a spectacular demonstration by suspending a pendulum from the dome of the Panthéon in Paris. From this, Foucault realized that a rotating body would behave in the same way as a pendulum and in 1852, he invented the gyroscope. Demonstrations of the motion of both the pendulum and gyroscope proved important to an understanding

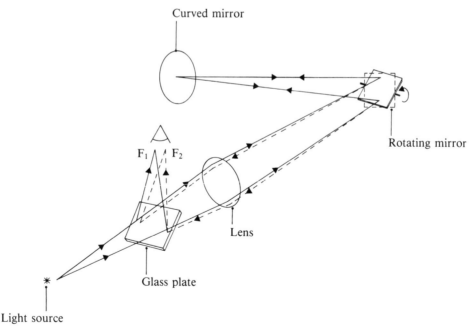

Foucault measured the velocity of light by directing a converging beam of light at a rotating plane mirror, situated at the radius of curvature of a spherical mirror which reflected the light back along the same path. The change in angle of the rotating mirror displaced the focus of the returning beam from F_1 to F_2, and from this displacement and the mirror's rotational speed the velocity of light was calculated.

of the action of forces, particularly those involved in motion over the Earth's surface.

Foucault's other main research effort was to investigate the velocity of light. Both he and Fizeau took up Arago's suggestion that the comparative velocity of light in air and water should be found. If it travelled faster in water, then the particulate theory of light would be vindicated; if the velocity were greater in air, then the wave theory would be shown to be true. Arago had suggested a rotating mirror method first developed by Charles Wheatstone (1802-1875) for measuring the speed of electricity. It involved reflecting a beam of light from a rotating mirror to a stationary mirror and back again to the rotating mirror, the time taken by the light to travel this path causing a deflection of the image. The deflection would be greater if the light travelled through a medium that slowed its velocity. Fizeau abandoned this method after parting from Foucault and developed a similar method involving a rotating toothed wheel. With this, he first obtained in 1849 a fairly accurate numerical value for the speed of light.

Foucault persevered with the rotating mirror method and in 1850 succeeded in showing that light travels faster in air than in water, just beating Fizeau to the same conclusion. He then refined the method and in 1862 used it to make the first accurate determination of the velocity of light. His value of 298,000 km per second was within one percent of the correct value, Fizeau's previous estimate having been about 5 per cent too high.

Foucault also interested himself in astronomy when he went to work at the Paris Observatory. He made several important contributions to practical astronomy, developing methods for silvering glass to improve telescope mirrors in 1857 and for accurate testing of mirrors and lenses in 1858. In 1860, he invented high-quality regulators for driving machinery at a constant speed and these were used in telescope motors and also in factory engines.

Foucault's outstanding ability as an experimental physicist brought great benefits to practial astronomy and also, in the invention of the gyroscope, led to an invaluable method of navigation. It is ironic that he missed the significance of an unusual observation of great importance. In 1848, Foucault noticed that a carbon arc absorbed light from sunlight, intensifying dark lines in the solar spectrum. This observation, repeated by Gustav Kirchhoff (1824-1887) in 1859, led immediately to the development of spectroscopy.

Franck, James (*1882-1964*), was a German-born American physicist who provided the experimental evidence for the quantum theory of Max Planck (1858-1947) and the quantum model of the atom developed by Niels Bohr (1885-1962). For this achievement, Franck and his co-worker Gustav Hertz (1887-1975) were awarded the 1925 Nobel Prize in Physics.

Franck was born in Hamburg on 26 August 1882. On leaving school, his father (a prosperous banker) sent him to Heidelberg University in 1901 to read law and economics as a preparation for his entry into the family firm, considering the status of scientists to be very lowly indeed. Fortunately, at Heidelberg Franck met Max Born (1882-1970) and a lifelong friendship was begun. Born, also from a wealthy Jewish family, had full parental approval for his career and this eventually convinced Franck's father to allow his son to follow a scientific career. At first it was to be geology, but this quickly turned to chemistry and then to physics when he went to Berlin University in 1902. It was there that Franck obtained his doctorate in 1906 for research into ionic mobility in gases.

Franck was awarded the Iron Cross during World War I, and from 1916 he worked at the Kaiser Wilhelm Institute of Physical Chemistry under Fritz Haber (1868-1934) on the study of gases, becoming head of the physics division there in 1918. Two years later, Franck became Professor of Experimental Physics at the University of Göttingen, where Born had just taken the chair of theoretical physics. At Göttingen, Franck and Hertz undertook the work on the quantum theory that gained them the 1925 Nobel Prize in Physics. Franck remained there until 1933, when Adolf Hitler came to power. Although allowed to retain his position because of his distinguished war record, Franck was told to dismiss other Jewish members of his Institute in the University. Franck refused to do this and left Germany, going at first to Copenhagen and then to the United States, where he became Professor of Physics at Johns Hopkins University in Baltimore in 1935. This was followed by a move to Chicago in 1938, where Franck was appointed Professor of Physical Chemistry.

During World War II, Franck became an American citizen and carried out metallurgical work related to the production of the atomic bomb. He became aware of the devastating power of this weapon and, in a document that became known as the Franck Report, he and other scientists suggested that it should first be demonstrated to the Japanese on unpopulated territory. Franck retired from the University of Chicago in 1949. Numerous honours were accorded him in these late years by academics and universities in both the United States and Europe. The city of

Göttingen, as part of its thousandth anniversary in 1953, made Franck and Born honorary citizens and Franck died there on 21 May 1964 while visiting friends.

In his major contribution to physics, Franck investigated the collisions of electrons with noble gas atoms and found that they are almost completely elastic and that no kinetic energy is lost. With Hertz, he extended this work to other atoms. This led to the discovery that there are inelastic collisions in which energy is transferred in definite amounts. For the mercury atom, electrons accept energy only in quanta of 4.9 electron volts. For such collisions to be inelastic, the electrons need kinetic energy in excess of this figure. As the energy is accepted by the mercury atoms, they emit light at a spectral line of Å 2537. This was the first experimental proof of Planck's quantum hypothesis that $E = hv$ where E is the change in energy, h is Planck's constant and v the frequency of light emitted. These experiments also tended to confirm the existence of the energy levels postulated by Bohr in his model of the atom. For this work, Franck and Hertz shared the 1925 Nobel Prize in Physics.

Franck also studied the formation, dissociation, vibration and rotation of molecules. With Born he developed the potential energy diagrams that are now common in textbooks of physical chemistry. From the extrapolation of data regarding the vibration of molecules obtained from spectra, he was able to calculate the dissociation energies of molecules. Edward Condon (1902-1974) interpreted this method in terms of wave mechanics, and it has become known as the Franck-Condon principle.

During his later years at Göttingen and at Baltimore, Franck carried out experiments on the photodissociation of diatomic molecules in liquids and solids and this led to an interest in photosynthesis. Research in this field was dominated by organic chemists and biochemists and Franck found himself involved in much controversy. His research led him to believe in a two-stage mechanism within the same molecule for the photosynthetic process, when the established view was that two different molecules are involved.

Franklin, Benjamin (*1706-1790*), was the first great American scientist. He made an important contribution to physics by arriving at an understanding of the nature of electric charge as a presence or absence of electricity, introducing the terms "positive" and "negative" to describe charges. He also proved in a classic experiment that lightning is electrical in nature, and went on to invent the lightning conductor. Franklin also

mapped the Gulf Stream, and made several useful inventions, including bifocal spectacles. In addition to being a scientist and inventor, Franklin is widely remembered as a statesman. He played a leading role in the drafting of the Declaration of Independence and the Constitution of the United States.

Franklin was born in Boston, Massachusetts, of British settlers on 17 January 1706. He started life with little formal instruction and by the age of ten he was helping his father in the tallow and soap business. Soon, apprenticed to his brother, a printer, he was launched into that trade, leaving home shortly afterwards to try for himself in Philadelphia. There he set himself up as a printer and in 1724 was sent to London to prospect for presses and types. However, this turned out to be a ruse of the city governors to get rid of him – why, is obscure. Nevertheless, Franklin, without funds or introductions, soon found himself work and put the next two years to good use in becoming a skilled printer.

Back in Philadelphia, Franklin's fortunes progressed. His own business prospered and he was soon active in journalism and publishing. He started the *Pennsylvania Gazette*, but is better remembered for *Poor Richard's Almanack*, a great collection of articles and advice on a huge range of topics, "conveying instruction among the common people". Published in 1732, it was a great success and brought Franklin a considerable income. Public affairs also proved to be his metier and gradually Franklin became enmeshed in all sorts of progressive undertakings. He was Clerk of the Pennsylvania Assembly as well as Postmaster of Philadelphia, and founded the American Philosophical Society in 1743 and in 1749 a college that later became the University of Pennsylvania. He was elected to the Pennsylvania Assembly in 1751 and as a politician became concerned with the government of the colony from Britain. These activities by no means affected his scientific investigations, however, and his major work on electricity was done in this period.

In 1757, Franklin travelled again to Britain, this time with proper credentials as the Agent of the Pennsylvania Assembly, and stayed on and off until 1775, attending meetings of the Royal Society as well as campaigning for the independence of the American colonies as their leading spokesman in Britain. He was awarded the Copley Medal of the Royal Society in 1753 and elected to the Society in 1756, the subscription of 25 guineas being waived in honour of his achievements.

Back in America, Franklin helped to draft the Declaration of Independence in 1776 and was one of its signatories. He then travelled to France to enlist help for the American cause in the Revolutionary War that followed, successfully organizing nearly all outside aid. He played a central part in the negotiation of the peace with Britain, signing a treaty that guaranteed independence in 1783. Franklin, though now well over 70, continued to play an active part in the affairs of the new nation. He became president of Pennsylvania, worked hard to abolish slavery, and in 1787 guided the Constitutional Convention to formulate and ratify the Constitution. He died soon after in Philadelphia on 17 April 1790.

In 1746, his business booming, Franklin turned his thoughts to electricity and spent the next seven years in the execution of a remarkable series of experiments. Although he had little formal education, his voracious reading habits gave him the necessary background and his practical skills, together with an analytical yet intuitive approach, enabled Franklin to put the whole topic on a very sound basis. It was said that he found electricity a curiosity and left it a science.

By the time of Franklin's entry to the field, the notions of charged bodies, insulators and conductors were established, though what was being "charged" or "conducted" was a matter of speculation. One of Franklin's earliest observations was of the ability of a pointed metal object to discharge an electrified conductor. A bodkin was used to discharge metal shot on a dry glass base. An earthed bodkin discharged the shot either touching it or as much as 8 inches (20 cm) distant, but an insulated bodkin had no effect. A man on an insulated base could electrify a glass tube by rubbing, and "communicate" the charge to another man similarly insulated. These experiments led Franklin to the fundamental conclusion that electricity is a single fluid that flows into or out of objects to produce electric charges. This naturally led to the introduction of the terms positive and negative, a positive charge being an excess of electricity and a negative charge a corresponding deficiency of electricity. But Franklin had no way of knowing in which direction the electric fluid moved, and he made an arbitrary choice of which bodies became positive and which negative. In fact, electric charge moves to his negatively charged bodies, which is why the electron is given a negative charge. However, Franklin made a fundamental discovery when he realized that the gain and loss of electricity must be balanced - the concept of conservation of charge. And his notion that the so-called electrical fire is fundamental to all matter, his "one-fluid" theory, brings us right up to the twentieth century.

The Leyden jar, which was invented in 1745, was an ideal proving ground for the clarification of these ideas. Franklin was able to show that the two coatings were oppositely charged, and that one had to be earthed while the other was being electrified. And finally he showed that the "power is in the glass" - an appreciation of the importance of the dielectric later to be fully discussed by Michael Faraday (1791-1867). This work led to the first plate condenser or capacitor, which contained glass sheets between lead plates - the Franklin panes. This device simplified electrical experiments by allowing the glass and lead components to be separated and increased in number, and gave rise to a "battery" of condensers.

These fundamental ideas led to Franklin's most famous work of all - that on lightning - and his invention of the lightning conductor. Although not the first to wonder about thunder and lightning in connection with electricity, Franklin showed that the thunderclouds are indeed seats of electric charge whose behaviour is like charged bodies and that pointed conductors can dissipate the charge or carry it to earth safely.

The sentry-box or Philadelphia experiment, which was devised by Franklin but first performed in France in 1752, caused a sensation. A man on an insulating base stood inside a sentry-box, which had a pointed rod some 10 m long fixed to its roof and insulated from it. The box itself was sited on a high building. Franklin suggested that a man could draw charge from a thundercloud by presenting an earthed wire to the rod, the man being protected by a wax handle. Sparks a few centimetres long were obtained. A later worker who did not fully observe the safety precautions laid down by Franklin was electrocuted. Later that year (1752), Franklin himself carried out his famous experiments with kites. By flying a kite in a thunderstorm, he was able to charge up a Leyden jar and produce sparks from the end of the wet string, which he held with a piece of insulating silk. The lightning conductor used everywhere today owes its origin to these experiments so long ago. Furthermore, some of Franklin's last work in this area demonstrated that while most thunderclouds have negative charges, a few are positive - something confirmed in modern times.

Of the rest of Franklin's work, staggering in its diversity, interest and humanity, we can give only a summary here. His interest in atmospheric electricity led him to recognize the aurora borealis as an electrical phenomenon, postulating good conditions in the rarefied upper atmosphere for electrical discharges, and speculating on the existence of what we now call the ionosphere. An interest in meteorology followed naturally from this. Franklin explained whirlwinds and water-spouts as being due to very rapid air circulation leading to low pressure in axial regions. He also pondered (long before the eruption of Krakatoa) on the effect of volcanic activity on weather.

Franklin's interest in heat and insulation led him to study clothing, air circulation and the cooling effect of perspiration. He was very enthusiastic about health-improving activities, especially swimming, wrote on lead poisoning, gout, sleep, and was a late convert to inoculation. There was a fashion to apply electric-shock treatment in cases of paralysis but Franklin remained a sceptic and Mesmer and his followers were discredited. In a very modern comment, Franklin wondered about the possible psychological value of such treatment.

The Pennsylvanian fireplace – a stove with underfloor draught – was a great success in 1742. Franklin refused a patent and showed his magnanimity of nature when a London manufacturer made a lot of money out of a "very similar" model. "Not the first instance . . ." he said quietly in his autobiography. It was recognition enough to be imitated.

Franklin was also influential in areas of physics other than electricity. Unfashionably for the time, he rejected the particle theory of light, being unable to account for the vast momentum that the particles should possess if they existed. This view inspired Thomas Young (1773–1829) to his fundamental work on the wave theory early in the following century, and the concept of light particles having momentum was used by Louis De Broglie (1892–) to establish the wave nature of the electron more than a century later still. But in considering heat, Franklin's views were less helpful to the course of science. Franklin suggested a famous experiment to demonstrate conductivity in which rods of different metals are heated at one end and wax rings placed at the same distance along the rods fall off at different times as heat spreads through the rods at different rates. This led Franklin to speculate that heat is a fluid like electricity, and aided development of the erroneous caloric theory of heat.

Always interested in the sea, Franklin produced the first chart of the Gulf Stream following observations made in 1770 that merchantmen crossed the Atlantic Ocean from east to west in two weeks less than the mail ships – the former keeping to the side of the current, not fighting it. In 1775 he used a thermometer to aid navigation in the warm waters of the Gulf Stream and, as late as 1785, was devising ways of measuring the temperature at a depth of 30 m. Finally Franklin also busied himself with such diverse topics as the first public library, bifocal lenses, population control, the rocking chair and daylight-saving time.

Benjamin Franklin is arguably the most attractive and interesting figure in the history of science, and not only because of his extraordinary range of interests, his central role in the establishment of the most powerful nation on Earth, and his amazing willingness to risk his life to perform a crucial experiment – a unique achievement in science. By conceiving of the fundamental nature of electricity, he began the process by which a most detailed understanding of the structure of matter has been achieved.

Fraunhofer, Joseph von (*1787–1826*), was a German physicist and optician who was the first person to investigate the dark lines in the spectra of the Sun and stars, which are named Fraunhofer lines in his honour. In so doing he developed the spectroscope, and he later became the first to use a diffraction grating to produce a spectrum from white light. These achievements were made and used by Fraunhofer mainly to improve his optical instruments, and his work laid the basis for subsequent German supremacy in the making of high grade scientific and optical instruments.

Fraunhofer was born in Straubing on 6 March 1787. His education was limited and he started work in his father's glazing workshop at the age of 10. After his father's death in 1798, he was apprenticed to a Munich mirror-maker and glass-cutter, and in 1806, he entered the optical shop of the Munich Philosophical Instrument Company, which produced scientific instruments. There Fraunhofer developed an expertise in both the practice and theory of optics. Under Pierre Guinand, a master glass-maker, Fraunhofer acquired practical knowledge of glass-making and combined this with his grasp of optical science to improve the fortunes of the company. This success brought him promotion within the firm and, by 1811, he had become a director.

Still highly active in business, Fraunhofer made his discovery of the dark lines in the Sun's spectrum in 1814, and invented the diffraction grating in 1821. In 1823, Fraunhofer accepted the post of Director of the Physics Museum of the Bavarian Academy of Sciences in Munich. But he contracted tuberculosis two years later and died in Munich on 7 June 1826, at the early age of 39.

Although he had had little formal education, Fraunhofer sought to understand optical theory and apply it to the practical work of constructing lens combinations of minimum aberration. At that time, there was little high-quality crown and flint glass and methods of determining the optical constants of glass were crude, limiting the size and quality of lenses that could be produced and also confining instrument makers to trial-and-error methods of construction. Fraunhofer approached lens-making according to optical theory and set out to determine the dispersion powers and refractive indices of different kinds of optical glass with greater accuracy. In collaboration with Guinand, he also sought to improve the quality of the glass used to make lenses.

In 1814, Fraunhofer began to use two bright yellow lines in flame spectra as a source of monochromatic light to obtain more accurate optical values. Comparing the effect of the light from the flame with the light from the Sun, he found that the solar spectrum is crossed with many fine, dark lines. A few of these had been seen by William Woolaston (1766–1828) in 1802, but Fraunhofer observed 574 lines between the red and violet ends of the spectrum.

In this way, Fraunhofer was able to make very accurate measurements of the dispersion and refractive properties of various kinds of glass, and in so doing he developed the spectroscope into an instrument for the scientific study of spectra.

In 1821, Fraunhofer examined the patterns that result from light diffracted through a single slit, and related the width of the slit to the angles of dispersion of the light. Extending from a large number of slits, he constructed a grating of 260 parallel wires and made the first study of spectra produced by diffraction gratings. The presence of the solar dark lines enabled him to note that the dispersion of the spectra is greater with a diffraction grating than with a prism. Fraunhofer examined the relationship between the dispersion and the separation of the wires in the grating, and concluded that the dispersion is inversely related to the distance between successive slits in the grating. By measuring the dispersion, he was able to determine the wavelengths of light of specific colours and the dark lines.

Fraunhofer also constructed reflection gratings, enabling him to extend his studies to the effect of diffraction on oblique rays. By using the wave theory of light, he was able to derive a general form of the grating equation that is still in use today.

Fraunhofer never published his researches into glassmaking nor the methods that he developed for calculating and testing lenses, viewing them as trade secrets. This work enabled him to develop telescopes of unsurpassed quality, leading to important discoveries in astronomy. But Fraunhofer did publish his work on diffraction gratings, which was important in the development of spectroscopy, a vital tool in the elucidation of atomic structure much later. He also published his observations of the dark lines in the spectrum, although he could not provide an explanation of them. This was achieved by Gustav Kirchhoff (1824–1887) in 1859.

The dark lines crossing the Sun's spectrum indicate the presence in the Sun's atmosphere of certain elements in the vapour state. The vapours in the chromosphere are cooler than the lower photosphere of the Sun and they absorb their own characteristic wavelengths from the Sun's continuous spectrum according to Kirchhoff's law – a substance which emits light of a certain wavelength at a given temperature will also absorb light of the same wavelength at that temperature. Some of the wavelengths emitted are absorbed by the vapours in the chromosphere as the Sun's light passes through them, producing the dark lines. It therefore became possible to identify the elements in the Sun's atmosphere from a study of the Fraunhofer lines, and hydrogen and helium were both shown to be present – in fact, this was how helium was first discovered. The same method is also applied to other stars.

Fraunhofer's insistence on high-quality craftmanship thus led to discoveries and developments in science on both a cosmological as well as an atomic scale.

Fresnel, Augustin Jean (*1788–1827*), was a French physicist who established the transverse-wave theory of light in 1821.

Fresnel was born on 10 May 1788 in Broglie, Normandy. His parents provided his early education themselves and, at the age of 12, he entered the École Centrale in Caen where he was introduced to science. In 1804 Fresnel entered the École Polytechnique in Paris intending to become an engineer. Two years later he went to the École des Ponts et Chaussées for a three-year technical course which included experience in practical engineering. Completing the course successfully, he became a civil engineer for the government.

Fresnel then worked on road projects in various parts of France, but became interested in optics. When Napoleon returned to France from Elba in 1815, Fresnel deserted his government post in protest. He was arrested and confined to his home in Normandy, taking advantage of this enforced leisure to develop his ideas on the wave nature of light into a comprehensive mathematical theory.

Napoleon's return proved to be short-lived and Fresnel was soon reinstated into government service. His scientific investigations were curtailed from then on and all his work was done in his spare time. But his achievements were great, rewarding Fresnel with unanimous election to the Academie des Sciences in 1823 and, just before he died, the Rumford Medal of the Royal Society. Fresnel had been continually plagued with ill-health, tuberculosis eventually causing his death at Ville D'Avray, near Paris, on 14 July 1827 at the early age of 39.

Fresnel began his investigations into the nature

of light convinced that the wave theory was correct because of its essential simplicity. He was not aware of earlier work by Christiaan Huygens (1629–1695) and Thomas Young (1707–1783) advocating a wave nature for light, and sought to establish his own ideas in a study of diffraction. Fresnel was soon able to demonstrate mathematically that the dimensions of light and dark bands produced by diffraction could be related to the wavelength of the light producing them if light were to consist of waves.

Huygens had believed that light consists of longitudinal waves like sound waves, and Fresnel endeavoured to refine his mathematical explanation on this basis. He ran into formidable difficulties but then became aware of new discoveries indicating that light may be polarized by reflection. Fresnel plunged into a mathematical explanation for this phenomenon and concluded in 1821 that polarization could occur only if light consists of transverse waves. Few agreed with him because of difficulties in conceiving of the nature of a medium to carry transverse waves. Fresnel was able to show, however, that his theory convincingly explained the phenomenon of double refraction and it rapidly gained acceptance.

Neither the particle theory nor the longitudinal wave theory could explain double refraction. Fresnel showed that light could be refracted through two different angles because one ray would consist of waves oscillating in one plane while the other ray consisted of waves oscillating in a plane perpendicular to the first one. The understanding of polarized light came to have important applications in organic chemistry (in optical isomerism) and was later carried beyond the visible spectrum to lay the groundwork for the theoretical uncovering of a wide range of radiation by James Clerk Maxwell (1831–1879).

Fresnel is also remembered for the application of his new ideas on light to lenses for lighthouses. He produced a revolutionary design consisting of concentric rings of triangular cross-section, varying the overall curvature to produce lenses that required no reflectors to produce a bright parallel beam.

Frisch, Otto Robert (*1904–1979*), was an Austrian-born British physicist who first described the fission of uranium nuclei under neutron bombardment, coining the term "fission" to describe the splitting of a nucleus.

Frisch was born in Vienna on 1 October 1904. He displayed surprising skills in mathematics at a very early age, but when he entered the University of Vienna in 1922 he studied physics, being awarded his PhD in 1926. The next year he began

work in the optics division of the Physikalische Technische Reichsanstalt in Berlin on a new light standard to replace the candle power.

In 1930 Frisch moved to Hamburg to become an assistant to Otto Stern (1888–1969), where they did research into molecular beams. Then in 1933 Frisch, being Jewish, was fired because of the racial laws the Nazis introduced following Adolf Hitler's rise to power. He moved to the department of physics at Birkbeck College, London, and a year later went to the Institute of Theoretical Physics in Copenhagen.

The German occupation of Denmark at the beginning of World War II forced Frisch to move once again and he was offered posts in Britain, first at Birmingham University and then in 1940 at Liverpool, where facilities such as a cyclotron were available for nuclear research. In 1943 he became a British citizen, which enabled him to become part of the delegation of British scientists sent to the Los Alamos nuclear research base in the United States. There he supervised the Dragon experiment, which led to the first atomic bomb. At the end of World War II, Frisch returned to Britain to become Deputy Chief Scientific Officer at the newly established Atomic Energy Research Establishment at Harwell, near Oxford. He remained there until 1947 when he became Jacksonian Professor of Natural Philosophy at Cambridge University. He retired in 1971 and died after an accident in Cambridge on 22 September 1979.

In 1938 Frisch was spending a holiday in Sweden with Lise Meitner (1878–1968), his aunt and herself a well-known physicist. She received a letter from two of her colleagues, Otto Hahn (1879–1968) and Fritz Strassmann (1902–   ), which stated that the bombardment of uranium nuclei with neutrons had resulted in the production of three isotopes of barium, a much lighter element. Frisch and Meitner realized that this meant that the uranium nucleus had been cleaved. They calculated that the collision of a neutron with a uranium nucleus might cause it to vibrate so violently that it became elongated. If the nucleus stretched too much, the mutual repulsion of the positive charges would overcome the surface tension of the nucleus and it would then break into two smaller pieces, liberating 200 MeV of energy and secondary neutrons. Frisch coined the term of nuclear fission for this process, after the use of that term to describe cell division in biology.

During his wartime researches in Britain, Frisch worked on methods of separating the rare uranium-235 isotope that Niels Bohr (1885–1962) had calculated would undergo fission. He also calculated details such as the critical mass needed to produce a chain reaction and make an atomic bomb, and was instrumental in alerting the British government to the need to undertake nuclear research. Then at Los Alamos, Frisch designed the Dragon experiment, which involved the dropping of a slug of fissile material through a hole in a near-critical mass of uranium. This allowed the scientists to study many details of a near-critical mass which they would not otherwise have been able to investigate. At the first test explosion on 16 July 1945, Frisch conducted experiments from a distance of 40 km.

When Frisch moved to Harwell after the war, he did some mathematical work on chain reactions and supervised the building of the laboratories. At Cambridge he was mainly concerned with teaching and the development of automatic devices to evaluate information produced in bubble chambers, which are used to study particle collisions.

Frisch was a talented experimental physicist, who partly by virtue of his fortunate position – both geographical and temporal – was able to contribute to and observe some of the most dramatic developments in the history of science.

G

Gabor, Dennis (*1900–1979*), was a Hungarian-born British physicist who invented holography, a method of producing three-dimensional images using laser light. For this achievement, he was awarded the 1971 Nobel Prize in Physics. He conceived the idea of holography in 1947, many years before the invention of the laser on which it depends.

Gabor was born in Budapest on 5 January 1900. He was educated at the Technical University in Budapest and then at the Technische Hochschule of Berlin in Charlottenberg, from which he received a diploma in electrical engineering in 1924. He took his doctorate in 1927, developing a highspeed oscillograph to monitor high-voltage transmission lines, and then worked as a research engineer in Berlin. In 1933 he fled from Nazi Germany and went to Britain, where he remained for the rest of his life, becoming a British subject. He first worked in private industry as a research engineer, and in 1949 joined Imperial College of Science and Technology as a Reader in Electronics. In 1958 he became Professor of Applied Electron Physics at Imperial College and then on retirement in 1967 a Senior Research Fellow. From 1976 until his death, Gabor was Professor Emeritus of Applied Electron Physics at the University of London. He died in London on 8 February 1979.

In 1947 Gabor realized that a beam of coherent light reflected from an object contains information on the shape of the object. In coherent light all the waves are exactly in phase with each other. A coherent beam reflected from an object travels a varying number of wavelengths to an observer, depending on the distances to the surfaces of the object. In holography, this beam exposes a photographic plate or film. To make it produce information on the shape of the object, the plate is also illuminated by a beam of coherent light coming directly from the light source. This interferes with the reflected beam, producing an interference pattern that is recorded in the photographic plate. No lenses are required. The interference pattern produced depends on the amplitude of the light waves in the reflected beam at the surface of the plate, which in turn depends on the distance of each part of the plate from each part of the object. It therefore contains information on the shape of the object.

The pattern is called a hologram, and appears as an apparently meaningless pattern of whirls when the plate is developed. But when it is placed in a beam of coherent light and the viewer looks through the hologram, a three-dimensional image of the object is seen. If the viewer moves, a different perspective of the object is obtained. The reason for this is that the eyes look through different parts of the hologram and view separate interference patterns made by light rays reflected from the object at different angles. The light source reconstitutes two images, one for each eye, and a three-dimensional image is seen exactly as if the real object were before the viewer.

Gabor invented this method before coherent light sources became available, calling it holography from the Greek word *holos*, meaning whole. He conceived it as a method of improving the resolving power of the electron microscope, which uses electron beams and not light rays. Gabor managed to develop the basic technique of holography using conventional light sources, which produce incoherent light, the waves being out of phase with one another. He filtered the light to produce some degree of coherence, but the results were very crude. But with the invention of the laser in 1960, a source of high intensity coherent light became available and holography became feasible. Many applications have subsequently been found for holography, including information storage and component testing, and it may well prove possible to use it to develop a system of three-dimensional television or motion pictures.

Galileo (*1564-1643*), was an Italian physicist and astronomer whose work founded the modern scientific method of deducing laws to explain the results of observation and experiment. In physics, Galileo discovered the properties of the pendulum, invented the thermometer, and formulated the laws that govern the motion of falling bodies. In astronomy, Galileo was the first to use the telescope to make observations of the Moon, Sun, planets and stars.

Galileo was born in Pisa on 15 February 1564. His full name was Galileo Galilei, his father being Vincenzio Galilei (*c*.1520-1591), a musician and mathematician. Galileo received his early education from a private tutor at Pisa until 1575, when his family moved to Florence. He then studied at a monastery until 1581, when he returned to Pisa to study medicine at the university. Galileo was attracted to mathematics rather than medicine, however, and also began to take an interest in physics. In about 1583 he discovered that a pendulum always swings to and fro in the same period of time regardless of the amplitude (length) of the swing. He is said to have made this discovery by using his pulse to time the swing of a lamp in Pisa Cathedral.

Galileo remained at Pisa until 1585, when he left without taking a degree and returned home to Florence. There he studied the works of Euclid (*fl.*300s BC) and Archimedes (287-212 BC), and in 1586 extended Archimedes' work in hydrostatics by inventing an improved version of the hydrostatic balance for measuring specific gravity. At this time, Galileo's father was investigating the ratios of the tensions and lengths of vibrating strings that produce consonant intervals in music, and this work may well have demonstrated to Galileo that the validity of a mathematical formula could be tested by practical experiment.

In 1589 Galileo became Professor of Mathematics at the University of Pisa. He attacked the theories of Aristotle (384-322 BC) that then prevailed in physics, allegedly demonstrating that unequal weights fall at the same speed by dropping two cannon balls of different weights from the Leaning Tower of Pisa to show that they hit the ground together. Galileo also published his first ideas on motion in *De Motu* (*On Motion*) in 1590.

Galileo remained at Pisa until 1592, when he became Professor of Mathematics at Padua. He flourished at Padua, and refined his ideas on motion over the next 17 years. He deduced the law of falling bodies in 1604 and came to an understanding of the nature of acceleration. In 1609 he was diverted from his work in physics by reports of the telescope, which had been invented in Holland the year before. Galileo immediately constructed his own telescopes and set about observing the heavens, publishing his findings in *Sidereus nuncius* (*The Starry Messenger*) in 1610. The book was a sensation throughout Europe and brought Galileo immediate fame. It resulted in a lifetime appointment to the University of Padua, but Galileo rejected the post and later in 1610 became mathematician and philosopher to the Grand Duke of Tuscany, under whose patronage he continued his scientific work at Florence.

In 1612 Galileo returned to hydrostatics and published a study of the behaviour of bodies in water in which he championed Archimedes against Aristotle. In the following year, he performed the same service for Nicolaus Copernicus (1473-1543), publicly espousing the heliocentric system. This viewpoint aroused the opposition of the Church, which declared it to be heretical and in 1616 Galileo was instructed to abandon the Copernican theory. Galileo continued his studies in astronomy and mechanics without publicly supporting Copernicus although he was personally convinced. In 1624 Urban VIII became pope and Galileo obtained permission to present the arguments for the rival heliocentric and geocentric systems in an impartial way. The result, *Dialogue Concerning The Two Chief World Systems*, was published in 1632, but it was scarcely impartial. Galileo used the evidence of his telescope observations and experiments on motion to favour Copernicus, and immediately fell foul of the Church again. The book was banned and Galileo was taken to Rome to face trial on a charge of heresy in April 1633. Forced to abjure his belief that the Earth moves around the Sun, Galileo is reputed to have muttered "*Eppur si muove*" (*Yet it does move*).

Galileo was sentenced to life imprisonment, but the sentence was commuted to house arrest and he was confined to his villa at Arcetri near Florence for the rest of his life. He continued to work on physics, and summed up his life's work in *Discourses And Mathematical Discoveries Concerning Two New Sciences*. The manuscript of this book was smuggled out of Italy and published in Holland in 1638. By this time, Galileo was blind but he still continued his scientific studies. In these last years, he designed a pendulum clock. Galileo died at Arcetri on 8 January 1642.

Galileo made several fundamental contributions to mechanics. He rejected the impetus theory that a force or push is required to sustain motion, and identified motion in a horizontal plane and rotation as being "neutral" motions that are neither natural nor forced. Galileo realized that gravity not only causes a body to fall, but that it also determines the motion of rising bodies and furthermore that gravity extends to the centre of the Earth. He found that the distance travelled by a falling body is proportional to the square of the time of descent. Galileo then showed that the motion of a projectile is made up of two components: one component consists of uniform motion in a horizontal direction and the other component is vertical motion under acceleration or deceleration due to gravity. This explanation was used by Galileo to refute objections to Copernicus based on the argument that birds and clouds would not be carried along with a turning or moving Earth. He explained that a horizontal component of motion provided by the Earth always exists to keep such objects in position even though they are not attached to the ground.

Galileo came to an understanding of uniform velocity and uniform acceleration by measuring the time it takes for bodies to move various distances. In an era without clocks, it was difficult to measure time accurately and Galileo may have used his pulse or a water clock – but not ironically, the pendulum – to do so. He had the brilliant idea of slowing vertical motion by measuring the movement of balls rolling down inclined planes, realizing that the vertical component of this motion is a uniform acceleration due to gravity while the horizontal component is a uniform velocity. Even so, this work was arduous and it took Galileo many years to arrive at the correct expression of the law of falling bodies. This was presented in the *Two New Sciences*, together with his derivation that the square of the period of a pendulum varies with its length (and is independent of the mass of the pendulum bob). Galileo also deduced by combining horizontal and vertical motion that the trajectory of a projectile is a parabola. He furthermore realized that the law of falling bodies is perfectly obeyed only in a vacuum, and that air resistance always causes a uniform terminal velocity to be reached.

The other new science of Galileo's masterwork was engineering, particularly the science of structures. His main contribution was to point out that the dimensions of a structure are important to its stability: a small structure will stand whereas a larger structure of the same relative dimensions may collapse. Using the laws of levers, Galileo went on to examine the strengths of the materials necessary to support structures.

Galileo's other achievements include the invention of the thermometer in 1593. This device consisted of a bulb of air that expanded or contracted as the temperature changed, causing the level of a column of water to rise or fall. Galileo's thermometer was very inaccurate because it neglected the effect of atmospheric pressure, but it is histor-

ically important as one of the first measuring instruments in science.

In astronomy, Galileo's achievements were to discover mountains on the Moon, sunspots, the phases of Venus and the four largest (Galilean) satellites of Jupiter. Galileo also saw Saturn to be oval in shape, an observation that Christiaan Huygens (1629-1695) later showed to be caused by its rings, and found that the Milky Way is composed of stars. These discoveries were made in 1609 and 1610.

Galileo was a pugnacious and sarcastic man, especially when confronted with those who could not or would not admit the validity of his observations and arguments. This characteristic symbolizes his position in the history of science, for with Galileo the idea that experiment and observation can be used to prove the validity of a proposed mathematical description of a phenomenon really became a working method in science. Although he built on the views and work of Archimedes and Copernicus, in his achievements Galileo can be considered to have founded not only classical mechanics and observational astronomy, but the method of modern science overall. In mechanics Isaac Newton (1642-1727) developed Galileo's work into a full understanding of inertia, which Galileo had not quite grasped, and arrived at the basic laws of motion underlying Galileo's discoveries.

Galvani, Luigi (*1737-1798*), was an Italian anatomist who, accidentally and without realizing it, discovered current electricity. The galvanometer, which detects electric current, is named after him.

Galvani was born in Bologna on 9 September 1737. He took a degree in medicine at the University of Bologna in 1759 and became a lecturer in anatomy there in 1762, following publication of a paper on human bone. In 1767 he produced an important treatise on the anatomy of birds and then in the 1770s turned to a study of the action of nerves and muscles. In 1775 Galvani was appointed Professor of Anatomy at Bologna and in 1782 became Professor of Obstetric Arts at the Institute of Science in Bologna. His work on electricity dates from the 1780s and was published in 1791. Disagreements on the interpretation of his findings and the loss of his academic position clouded his later years, and Galvani died in poverty and disappointment on 4 December 1798.

In the course of experiments on dead frogs, Galvani found that an electric charge produced by a static electricity machine caused the muscles in the frogs to twitch. He reasoned that lightning, which Benjamin Franklin (1706-1790) had shown to be electrical in nature in 1752, would produce electric charges in the air and that the frogs could be used as a detector of electricity to confirm this. Galvani therefore hung up some frogs by brass hooks on some iron railings outside his home during a thunderstorm, and noticed that the muscles contracted as he anticipated. He then observed that the muscles of the frogs continued to twitch when the storm ceased. He repeated the experiment indoors and found that contractions occurred when a metal plate or rod was touched to a frog and to a hook of another metal inserted into the frog. The effect did not occur with non-conductors.

Being an anatomist rather than a physicist, Galvani was convinced that the phenomenon he had discovered was due to animal electricity. He reasoned that the muscles of the frog contained a reservoir of electric fluid of animal origin, and that touching the metals to the frog enabled the electricity to flow in a similar way to the discharge of a Leyden jar, causing the muscles to contract.

This idea was contested by Alessandro Volta (1745-1827) in 1793, who was able to show that a flow of electricity occurs when two metals are brought in contact with moisture and he later constructed the first electric battery.

Galvani had in fact become the first person to generate an electric current, which was produced by the brass-iron junction in the moist tissue of the frog, and he is now credited with the discovery of current electricity. He himself always resisted this view, preferring to regard his observations as being due to animal electricity. Galvani later found that electric fishes produce electricity in their muscles, and regarded this as proof of his interpretation. Although Volta's explanation of current electricity was correct, Galvani's work on animal electricity did prove to be of great value in zoology.

Gamow, George (*1904-1968*), was a Russian-born American physicist who provided the first evidence for the big-bang theory of the origin of the Universe. He predicted that it would have produced a background microwave radiation, which was later found to exist. Gamow was also closely involved with the early theoretical development of nuclear physics, and he made an important contribution to the understanding of protein synthesis.

Gamow was born in Odessa on 4 March 1904. He attended local schools and first became interested in astronomy when he received a telescope from his father as a gift for his thirteenth birthday. In 1922 he entered Novorossysky University, but he soon transferred to the University of Leningrad where he studied optics and later cosmology, gaining his PhD in 1928. Gamow then went

to the University of Göttingen, where his career as a nuclear physicist really began. His work impressed Niels Bohr (1885-1962) who invited Gamow to the Institute of Theoretical Physics in Copenhagen. There he continued his work on nuclear physics and he also studied nuclear reactions in stars. In 1929 Gamow worked with Ernest Rutherford (1871-1937) at the Cavendish Laboratory, Cambridge. His work there laid the theoretical foundations for the artificial transmutation of elements, which was achieved in 1932.

Gamow returned to Copenhagen in 1930. From 1931 to 1933 he served as Master of Research at the Academy of Science in Leningrad and then, after being denied permission by the Soviet government to attend a conference on nuclear physics in Rome in 1931, he used the Solvay Conference held in Brussels in 1933 as an opportunity to defect. He settled in the United States where he held the chair of Physics at George Washington University in Washington from 1934 until 1956. He then held the post of Professor of Physics at the University of Colorado until his death. In 1948 Gamow was given top security clearance and worked on the hydrogen bomb project at Los Alamos, New Mexico. Later in life, he gained considerable fame as an author of popular scientific books, being particularly well-known for the "Mr Tompkins" series. He was awarded the Kalinga Prize by UNESCO in 1956 in recognition of the value of his popular scientific texts. Gamow died in Boulder, Colorado, on the 20 August 1968.

Gamow's work can be broadly divided into two main areas: his theoretical contributions to nuclear physics, and astronomy. Some of his studies fell outside both of these disciplines.

His first major scientific work was his theory of alpha-decay, which he produced in 1928 while at the University of Göttingen. He was able to explain why it was that uranium nuclei could not be penetrated by alpha particles that have as much as double the energy of the alpha particles emitted by the nuclei. This, he proposed, was due to a "potential barrier" which arose due to repulsive Coulomb and other forces. The model represented the first application of quantum mechanics to the study of nuclear structure, and was simultaneously and independently developed by Edward Condon (1902-1974) at Princeton University.

During his visits to Copenhagen in 1928 and 1930, Gamow continued his work on nuclear physics and in particular on the liquid drop model of nuclear structure. This theory held that the nucleus could be regarded as a collection of alpha particles which interacted via strong nuclear and

Coulomb forces. His work under Rutherford in 1929 was concerned with the calculation of the energy which would be required to split a nucleus using artificially accelerated protons. This work led directly to the construction of a linear accelerator in 1932 by John Cockcroft (1897–1967) and Ernest Watson (1903–   ), in which protons were used to disintegrate boron and lithium resulting in the production of helium. This was the first experimentally produced transmutation that did not employ radioactive materials.

In collaboration with Edward Teller (1908–   ), Gamow produced in 1936 the Gamow-Teller selection rule for beta decay. This has since been elaborated, but was one of the first formulations to describe beta decay.

Most of Gamow's later work was concerned with the origin of the Universe and the evolution of stars. He contributed to the interpretation of the Hertzsprung-Russell diagram in 1938, supported the model of the expanding Universe in 1939, and examined the origin of nebulae and the production of energy by red giant stars in 1939. During the early 1940s, he published his neutrino theory of supernovae in which he examined neutrino emission during stellar explosions.

In 1948, in collaboration with Ralph Alpher (1921–   ), Gamow examined the state of the Universe prior to the postulated big bang. This work led to the prediction of the existence of residual microwave radiation in the Universe, which was detected and confirmed in 1965 by scientists at Princeton University.

In the entirely different field of molecular biochemistry, Gamow contributed to the solution of the genetic code in which virtually all hereditable biological information is stored. The double helix model for the structure of DNA had been published in 1953 by James Watson (1928–   ) and Francis Crick (1916–   ). The double helix consists of a twisted double chain of four types of nucleotides, sugar residues and phosphates. Gamow realized that if three nucleotides were used at a time, 64 different triplets could be constructed. These could easily code for the different amino acids of which all proteins are constructed. Gamow's theory was found to be correct, and in 1961 the genetic code was cracked and the meanings of the 64 triplets identified.

Gamow was a talented and wide-ranging scientist who, with his fundamental contribution to cosmology, was responsible for the first clear indication of the origin of the Universe.

Gauss, Carl Friedrich (*1777–1855*), was a German mathematician and physicist. Although known mainly for his pioneering work in mathematics, Gauss made important contributions to physics

in the investigation of terrestrial magnetism and the derivation of magnetic units.

Gauss was born into a very poor family in Brunswick on 30 April 1777. He was an infant prodigy, able to calculate even before he could talk. Gauss taught himself to read and must also have worked at arithmetic on his own, for as soon as he was sent to school at the age of eight, he presented a brilliantly simple solution to the problem of adding up any set of whole numbers. Gauss was encouraged to develop his mathematical skills at his first school and then at the Gymnasium, which he entered in 1788. He became so proficient that in 1792, at the age of 14, Gauss was given a stipend by the Duke of Brunswick so that he could devote himself to science. He then spent three years at the Brunswick Collegium Carolinum and then in 1795 went on to the University of Göttingen.

Gauss remained at Göttingen until 1798 and then returned to Brunswick, where he lived alone and immersed himself in his work. In 1806, the duke was killed fighting Napoleon, and in the following year, Gauss obtained the position of Director of the Göttingen Observatory. He retained this position for the rest of his life, and died at Göttingen on 23 February 1855.

In mathematics, Gauss made major contributions to number theory and worked out the basis of non-Euclidean geometry and non-commutative algebra. In 1796 he constructed a seventeen-sided regular polygon using only a ruler and compass, the first construction of a regular figure in modern times. Gauss was also interested in astronomy, and in 1801 he made a remarkable prediction of the position in which the asteroid Ceres could be found. The asteroid, the first to be discovered, had been lost and it was rediscovered exactly where Gauss had computed it to be. This was done with Gauss' theory of least squares.

Gauss' work at Göttingen Observatory involved him in important work in geodesy from 1817 onwards. He developed new and improved surveying methods, inventing the heliotrope in 1821 to reflect an image of the Sun to mark positions over long distances. From 1831, Gauss extended this work into the field of terrestrial magnetism in collaboration with Wilhelm Weber (1804–1891), carrying out a worldwide magnetic survey from which Gauss in 1839 was able to derive a mathematical formula expressing magnetism at any location.

Gauss and Weber also investigated electromagnetism and in 1833 constructed a moving-needle telegraph similar to that later developed by Charles Wheatstone (1802–1875). Gauss did not succeed in gaining support for the development of his telegraph and it was abandoned. He did make a lasting contribution to physics, however, with his insistence in 1833 that all units should be assembled from a few basic or absolute units, specifically length, mass and time. Gauss and Weber also went on to derive units for magnetism, and the CGS unit for magnetic flux density was called the gauss. It has now been replaced by the tesla in the SI system, which does however derive a full consistent set of units from seven basic units in accordance with Gauss' ideas.

Geiger, Hans Wilhelm (*1882-1945*), was a German physicist who invented the geiger counter for detecting radioactivity.

Geiger was born at Neustadt, Rheinland-Pfalz, on 30 September 1882. He studied physics at the Universities of Munich and Erlangen, obtaining his PhD from the latter institution in 1906 with a dissertation on gaseous ionization. In 1906 he became assistant to Arthur Schuster (1851-1934), Professor of Physics at the University of Manchester. Ernest Rutherford (1871-1937) succeeded Schuster in 1907 and Geiger stayed on as his assistant. They were later joined by Ernest Marsden, with whom Geiger collaborated.

In 1912 Geiger became head of the Radioactivity Laboratories at the Physikalische Technische Reichsanstalt in Berlin, after declining the offer of a post at the University of Tübingen. He established a successful research group, which was joined by such eminent scientists as Walther Bothe (1891-1957) and James Chadwick (1891-1974). Geiger served in the German artillery during World War I, and then returned to the Reichsanstalt in Berlin.

In 1925 Geiger accepted a post as Professor of Physics at the University of Kiel. He moved in 1929 to the University of Tübingen, and in 1936 he became head of Physics at the Technical University of Charlottenberg-Berlin as well as the editor of the *Zeitschrift für Physik*. Illness reduced the

pace of his scientific activities during most of World War II and then he lost his home and belongings during the Allied occupation of Germany. Geiger died a few months later on 24 September 1945 at Potsdam.

Geiger's early postdoctoral work in Manchester involved the application of his expertise in gaseous ionization to the field of radioactive decay. One direction which his work took was the development in 1908 of a device that counted alpha particles. The counter consisted of a metal tube containing a gas at low pressure and thin wire in the centre of the tube. The wire and tube were under a high voltage and each alpha particle arriving through a window at one end of the tube caused the gas to ionize, producing a momentary flow of current. The resulting electric signals counted the number of alpha particles entering the tube. With this counter, Geiger was able to show that approximately 3.4×10^{10} alpha particles are emitted per second by a gram of radium, and that each alpha particle has a double charge. Rutherford later demonstrated that the doubly charged alpha particle was in fact a helium nucleus.

In 1909, Marsden and Geiger studied the interactions of alpha particles from radium with metal reflectors. They found that most alpha particles passed straight through the metal, but that a few were deflected at wide angles to the beam. They showed that the amount of deflection depended on the metal that the reflector was made of and that it decreased with a lowering of atomic weight. They used metal reflectors of different thicknesses to demonstrate that the deflection was not caused merely by some surface effect. This work led directly to Rutherford's proposal in 1911 that the atom consists of a central, positively charged nucleus surrounded by electron shells. The observed deflection of the alpha particles was due to the positively charged par-

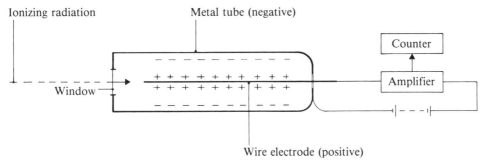

A Geiger-Müller counter has a central wire anode in a metal tube, which acts as the (negative) cathode, containing argon at low pressure. Ionizing radiation enters a "window" made of thin metal foil or mica and ionizes the gas in the tube, giving rise to an electric current which is amplified and made to work a counting device.

ticle interacting with the positively charged nuclei in the metal and being deflected by repulsive forces. Geiger and Marsden later published the mathematical relationship between the amount of alpha scattering and atomic weight.

Other subjects which Geiger studied under Rutherford included the relationship between the range of an alpha particle and its velocity in 1910; the various disintegration products of uranium in 1910 and 1911; and the relationship between the range of an alpha particle and the radioactive constant, which was determined with John Nuttall (1890–1958) in 1911.

In 1912, upon his return to Germany, Geiger began the first of many refinements to his radiation counter enabling it to detect beta particles and other kinds of radiation as well as alpha particles. The modern form of the instrument was finally developed with Walther Müller in 1928, and it is now usually known as the Geiger-Müller counter. It can be operated so that radioactivity causes it to emit audible clicks which can be recorded automatically. Geiger used this instrument to confirm the Compton effect in 1925 and to study cosmic radiation from 1931 onwards. Cosmic rays became a prolonged source of interest which occupied him for most of the rest of his career.

Geiger's contribution to science in discovering a simple and reliable way of detecting radiation not only enabled discoveries to be made in nuclear physics but also afforded an instant method of checking radiation levels and finding radioactive minerals.

Gell-Mann, Murray (*1929–*), is an American theoretical physicist who was awarded the 1969 Nobel Prize in Physics for his work on the classification and interactions of subatomic particles. He is the originator of the quark hypothesis.

Gell-Mann was born in New York City on 15 September 1929. He showed strong scholastic aptitude at an early age and entered Yale University when he was only 15 years old. He received his bachelor's degree in 1948 and proceeded to the Massachusetts Institute of Technology, where he earned his PhD three years later. He spent the next year as a member of the Institute for Advanced Studies at Princeton University. In 1952 he joined the faculty of the University of Chicago as an instructor to work at the Institute for Nuclear Studies under Enrico Fermi (1901–1954), becoming an assistant professor in 1953. In 1955, Gell-Mann moved to the California Institute of Technology at Pasadena as Associate Professor of Theoretical Physics, becoming Professor a year later and in 1966 Robert Andrews

Millikan Professor of Theoretical Physics, a post he still holds.

From the early 1930s, the relatively simple concept of the atom as being composed of only electrons and protons began to give way to more complex models involving neutrons and then other particles. By the 1950s, the field was in a state of complete chaos following the discovery of mesons, which have masses intermediate between a proton and an electron, and then hyperons, which are even more massive than the proton. One of the most puzzling things was that the hyperons and some mesons had much longer lifetimes than was predicted by accepted theory at that time, although still only of the order of 10^{-9} seconds.

In an endeavour to bring order to the subject, Gell-Mann proposed in 1953 that the long-lived particles, and indeed other particles such as the neutron and the proton, should be given a new quantum number called the strangeness number. The strangeness number differed from particle to particle. It could be 0, -1, $+1$, -2 etc. He also proposed the law of conservation of strangeness, which states that the total strangeness must be conserved on both sides of an equation describing a strong or an electromagnetic interaction but *not* a weak interaction. This work was also done independently by Nishijima in Japan.

The law of conservation of strangeness formed an important theoretical basis for the subsequent theory of associated production, which was proposed by Gell-Mann in 1955. This model held that the strong forces which were responsible for the creation of strange particles could create them only in groups of two at a time (i.e. in pairs). As the partners in a pair moved apart, the energy which would be required for them to decay through strong interactions would exceed the energy which had originally gone into their creation. The strange particles therefore survived long enough to decay through weak interactions instead. This model explained their unusually extended lifespan.

Gell-Mann used these rules to group mesons, nucleons (neutrons and protons) and hyperons, and was thereby able to form predictions in the same way that Dmitri Mendeleev (1834–1907) had been able to make predictions about the chemical elements once he had constructed the Periodic Table. Gell-Mann's prediction of a particle which he named xi-zero to complete a doublet with xi-minus was soon rewarded with experimental verification.

The law of conservation of strangeness was also important in the formulation of SU(3) symmetry, a scheme for classifying strongly interacting particles which Gell-Mann proposed in 1961.

This classification system itself formed part of the basis for yet another classification scheme entitled the eightfold way (named after the eight virtues of Buddhism). This model was devised by Y. Ne'emann and Gell-Mann and published in 1962.

The eightfold way was intended to incorporate all the new particles and the new quantum numbers. It postulated the existence of supermultiplets, or groups of eight particles which have the same spin value but different values for charge, isotopic spin, mass and strangeness. The model also predicts the existence of supermultiplets of different sizes. The strongest support for the theory arose from the discovery in 1964 of a particle named omega-minus, which had been predicted by the eightfold way. This model is able to classify all the known elementary particles, even those with lifetimes of less than 10^{-19} second, but it does not yet describe elementary particles as fully as quantum theory describes the atom. There remain to be discovered a number of particles which have been predicted, including the magnetic monopole, the graviton and the intermediate boson.

In 1964 Gell-Mann proposed a model for yet a further level of complexity within the atom. He proposed that particles such as the proton are not themselves fundamental but are composed of quarks. Quarks differ from all previously proposed subatomic particles because they have fractional charges of, for instance, $+2/3$ or $-1/3$. Quarks always occur in pairs or in trios and can never be detected singly, exchanging gluons that bind them together. Gluons are the quanta for interactions between quarks, a process which goes by the exotic name of quantum chromodynamics, and their behaviour is in some ways analogous to the exchange of protons between electrons in electromagnetic interactions (quantum electrodynamics). Six quarks have been predicted, and five have so far been indirectly detected. The names of the quarks are Up, Down, Strange, Charm, Bottom and Top, and they have been ascribed properties of electric charge, strangeness, charm, bottomness, topness, baryon number, and so on.

Gell-Mann's work has been characterized by originality and bold synthesis. His models have been useful not only for their predictive value, but also for the work they have spurred others to do.

Gilbert, William (*1544-1603*), was an English physician and physicist who performed fundamental pioneering research into magnetism and also helped to establish the modern scientific method.

Gilbert was born in Colchester, Essex, on 24 May 1544. He was educated at St John's College, Cambridge, where he graduated in medicine in 1569 and later became a Fellow. In about 1573 he settled in London, where he established a successful medical practice, and in 1599 he was elected President of the Royal College of Physicians. In the following year he was appointed personal physician to Queen Elizabeth I, and was later knighted for his services to the queen. On Elizabeth's death in March 1603 he was appointed physician to her successor, James I, but Gilbert held this position for only a short time because he died on 10 December of that year.

Although successful as a physician, Gilbert's most important contribution to science was his research into magnetism and electrical attraction, which he described in his book *De Magnete, Magneticisque Corporibus, et de Magno Magnete Tellure* (1600; *Concerning Magnetism, Magnetic Bodies, and the Great Magnet Earth*). This work gave a detailed account of years of investigations (on which he is thought to have spent some £5,000 of his own money), which were rigorously performed. The importance of this work was recognized by Galileo, who also considered Gilbert to be the principal founder of the experimental method – before the work of Francis Bacon and Isaac Newton. Not only did Gilbert disprove many popular but erroneous beliefs about magnetism – that lodestone (naturally occurring magnetic iron oxide, the only magnetic material available until Gilbert discovered a method for making metal magnets) cured headaches and rejuvenated the body, for example – but he also discovered many important facts about magnetism, such as the laws of attraction and repulsion and magnetic dip. From his studies of the behaviour of small magnets, Gilbert concluded that the Earth itself acts as a giant bar magnet, with a magnetic pole (a term he introduced) near each geographical pole. He also showed that the strength of a lodestone can be increased by combining it with soft iron, that iron and steel can be magnetized by stroking them with lodestones, and that when an iron magnet is heated to redheat, it loses its magnetism and also cannot be remagnetized while it remains hot. So extensive were Gilbert's investigations of magnetism that not until William Sturgeon made the first electromagnet in 1825 and Michael Faraday began his studies was substantial new knowledge added to the subject.

Gilbert also investigated static electricity. The ancient Greeks had discovered that amber, when rubbed with silk, can attract light objects. Gilbert demonstrated that other substances exhibit the same effect and that the magnitude of the effect is approximately proportional to the area being rubbed. He called these substances "electrics" and clearly differentiated between magnetic attraction and electric attraction (as he called the ability of an electrostatically charged body to attract light objects). This work eventually led to the idea of electrical charge, but it was not until 1745 that it was discovered (by the French physicist Charles Du Fay) that there are two types of electricity, positive and negative.

Gilbert also held remarkably modern views on astronomy. He was the first Englishman to accept Copernicus' idea that the Earth rotates on its axis and revolves around the Sun. He also believed that the stars are at different distances from the Earth and might be orbited by habitable planets, and that the planets were kept in their orbits by magnetic attraction.

Glaser, Donald Arthur (*1926–*), is an American physicist who invented the bubble chamber, an instrument much used in nuclear physics to study short-lived subatomic particles. For this development he was awarded the 1960 Nobel Prize in Physics.

Glaser was born on 21 September 1926 in Cleveland, Ohio, and educated there at the Case Institute of Technology. He graduated in 1946 and then went to the California Institute of Technology, where he gained his PhD three years later. He joined the physics department of the University of Michigan in 1949, and was Professor of Physics there from 1957. Two years later he took up a similar appointment at the University of California, Berkeley, and in 1964 became Professor of Physics and Biology.

In the 1920s, the British physicist C.T.R. Wilson developed the cloud chamber for detecting and recording the presence of elementary particles. It contained a saturated vapour which condensed as a series of liquid droplets along the ionized path left by a particle crossing the chamber. With the advances in particle accelerators in the early 1950s, nuclear physicists began to deal with fast high-energy particles which could be missed by the cloud chamber. In 1952, while he was at the University of Michigan, Glaser built his first bubble chamber. It consisted of a vessel only a few centimetres across containing superheated liquid ether under pressure. When the pressure was released suddenly, particles traversing the chamber left tracks consisting of streams of small bubbles formed when the ether boiled locally; the tracks were photographed using a high-speed camera. In later bubble chambers, liquid hydrogen was substituted for ether and chambers two metres across are now in use. In the early 1960s, Glaser turned his attention from physics to molecular biology, as reflected in his change of appointment at Berkeley.

Goldstein, Eugen (*1850–1930*), was a German physicist who investigated electrical discharges through gases at low pressures. He discovered canal rays and gave cathode rays their name.

Goldstein was born at Gleiwitz in Upper Silesia, now Gliwice in Poland, on 5 September 1850. He went to the University of Breslau in 1869 but after only one year moved to the University of Berlin to work with Hermann Helmholtz (1821–1894), first as his student and then as his assistant. Before obtaining his doctorate he became employed as a physicist at the Berlin Observatory in 1878. Following the award of his doctorate in 1881 for some of his important work on cathode rays, Goldstein continued at the Observatory until 1890, spending the next six years at the Physikalische Technische Reichsanstalt. There then followed some time when he had a laboratory and assistants in his own home, until he was appointed head of the Astrophysical Section of Potsdam Observatory. Goldstein died in Berlin on 25 December 1930.

As Helmholtz's assistant, Goldstein worked on electrical discharges in gases. Goldstein coined the term cathode rays to explain the glow first observed in an evacuated tube by Julius Plücker (1801–1868) in 1858. His first publication, in 1876, demonstrated that cathode rays could cast shadows and that the rays are emitted perpendicular to the cathode surface, enabling a concave cathode to bring them to a focus. There followed investigations by Goldstein and others which showed how cathode rays could be deflected by magnetic fields. This was the period when such phenomena were under investigation throughout Europe, and Goldstein made many contributions which aided the conclusion that cathode rays were fast moving, negative particles or electrons. He himself believed that they were waves not unlike light.

In the course of his investigations, Goldstein studied many different arrangements of anode and cathode discharge circuits. In an experiment in 1886, he perforated the anode and observed glowing yellow streamers behind the anode emanating from the perforations. Since they were connected to the holes or canals, he termed them *Kanalstrahlen* or canal rays. These always moved away from the anode. Wilhem Wien (1864–1928), Goldstein's student, showed in 1898 that they could be deflected by electric and magnetic fields in such a way that they appeared to be positively charged. Earlier, Goldstein had been able to observe only slight deflections. Wien also calculated the charge-to-mass ratio of the rays and found this to be some 10,000 times greater than the corresponding ratio for cathode rays. Later, the rays were called positive rays by J.J. Thompson (1856-1940), who also investigated their nature and led the way to their identification as ionized molecules or atoms of the gaseous contents of the discharge tube. Tubes with different contents formed different positive ions, and the different charge-to-mass ratios were detected by Thomson. Francis Aston (1877-1945) began investigations in this field and developed the mass spectrograph in 1919 to separate positive rays. From these beginnings has developed mass spectrometry, a method extremely useful in chemical analysis.

In 1905 Johannes Stark (1874-1957), another student of Goldstein, used light from canal rays to demonstrate an optical Doppler shift in a terrestrial, rather than a stellar, source of light for the first time.

Goldstein later investigated the wavelengths of light emitted by metals and oxides when canal rays impinge on them, and observed that alkali metals show their characteristic bright spectral lines. He continued his investigation of the complex phenomena and gaseous discharge at the anode for many years, but his subsequent discoveries were interesting and curious rather than of great importance for physics. He compared his work with the natural phenomenon of the aurora borealis, which he believed was caused by cathode rays originating in the Sun. His last paper, published in 1928, gave a new discovery, the importance of which was almost completely missed. In a discharge tube containing nitrogen and hydrogen and possibly other gases, he observed that a trace of ammonia was present after the discharge. It was only much later that investigations along these lines were begun in earnest to see if biologically important molecules, and hence life, could have originated in this way.

Grimaldi, Francesco Maria (*1618-1663*), was an Italian physicist who discovered the diffraction of light and made various observations in physiology.

Grimaldi was born in Bologna on 2 April 1618 and at the age of 14 entered the order of the Society of Jesus, being educated at the Society's houses at Parma, Ferrara and finally, in 1637, back at Bologna. As a Jesuit, his primary studies were in theology, which he finished in 1645. Three years later he became Professor of Mathematics at the Jesuit College in Bologna. There he acted also as assistant to the Professor of Astronomy, Father Giovanni Riccioli (1598-1671), whom he helped with astronomical observations. Grimaldi

remained at the Jesuit College in Bologna, and died there on 28 December 1663.

Grimaldi observed muscle action and was the first to note that minute sounds produced by muscles during contraction. But he is best known for his experiments with light. He let a beam of sunlight enter a darkened room through a small circular aperture and observed that, when the beam passed through a second aperture and onto a screen, the spot of light was slightly larger than the second aperture and had coloured fringes. Grimaldi concluded that the light rays had diverged slightly, becoming bent outwards or diffracted. On placing a narrow obstruction in the light beam, he noticed bright bands at each side of its shadow on the screen. He therefore added diffraction to reflection and refraction, the other known phenomena that "bend" light rays. In modern terms, Grimaldi had observed a phenomenon that can be explained readily only if light is regarded as travelling in waves – contrary to the then accepted corpuscular theory of light. In 1665, two years after Grimaldi's death, a description of the experiments was published in the large work *Physico-mathesis de lumine, coloribus, et iride* (Physicomathematical Thesis of Light, Colours and the Rainbow).

Hahn, Otto (*1879-1968*), was a German radiochemist who discovered nuclear fission. For this achievement he was awarded the 1944 Nobel Prize in Chemistry.

Hahn was born on 8 March 1879 in Frankfurt-am-Main and studied at the University of Marburg, gaining his doctorate at Marburg in 1901. From 1904 to 1905 he worked in London under William Ramsay (1852-1916), who introduced Hahn to radiochemistry. In 1905 he moved to McGill University at Montreal, Canada, to further these studies with Ernest Rutherford (1871-1937). The next year Hahn returned to Germany to work under Emil Fischer (1852-1919) at the University of Berlin. There he was joined in 1907 by Lise Meitner (1878-1968), beginning a collaboration that was to last more than 30 years. In 1912 Hahn was made a member of the Kaiser-Wilhelm Institute for Chemistry in Berlin-Dahlem and in 1928 was appointed its Director. He held this position until 1944, when the Max Planck Institute in Göttingen took over the functions of the Kaiser-Wilhelm Institute and Hahn became President.

Perturbed by the military uses to which nuclear

fission had been put, Hahn was concerned in his later years to warn the world of the great dangers of nuclear weapons. In 1966 he was co-winner of the Enrico Fermi Award with Meitner and Fritz Strassmann (1902–). Hahn died in Göttingen on 28 July 1968.

Hahn's first important piece of research was his discovery of some of the intermediate radioactive isotopes formed in the radioactive breakdown of thorium. These were radiothorium (discovered in 1904) and mesothorium (1907). In 1918 Hahn and Meitner discovered the longest-lived isotope of a new element which they called protactinium, and in 1921 they discovered nuclear isomers – radioisotopes with nuclei containing the same subatomic particles but differing in energy content and half-life.

In the 1930s, Enrico Fermi (1901–1954) and his collaborators showed that nearly every element in the periodic table may undergo a nuclear transformation when bombarded by neutrons. In many cases, radioactive isotopes of the elements are formed and slow neutrons were found to be particularly effective in producing many of these transformations. In 1934 Fermi found that uranium is among the elements in which neutron bombardment induces transformations. The identity of the products was uncertain, but it was suspected that artificial elements higher than uranium had been found.

Hahn, Meitner and Strassmann investigated Fermi's work, believing the formation of radium to have occurred, and treated the bombarded uranium with barium. Radium is chemically very similar to barium and would accompany barium in any chemical reaction, but no radium could be found in the barium-treated fractions. In 1938 Meitner, being Jewish, fled from Germany to escape the Nazis and Hahn and Strassmann carried on the search. Hahn began to wonder if radioactive barium was formed from the uranium when it was bombarded with neutrons, and that this was being carried down by the barium he had added. Barium has such a lower atomic number than uranium, however, that the only way it could possibly have been formed was if the uranium atoms broke in half. The idea of this happening seemed so ridiculous that Hahn hesitated to publish it.

Meitner was now in exile in Copenhagen and with Otto Frisch (1904–1979) quickly confirmed Hahn's explanation, showing the reaction to be an entirely new type of nuclear process and suggesting the name nuclear fission for it. Meitner and Frisch communicated the significance of this discovery to Niels Bohr (1885–1962), who was preparing to visit the United States. Arriving in January 1939, Bohr discussed these results with

Albert Einstein (1879–1955) and others. The presence of barium meant that uranium had been split into two nearly equal fragments, a tremendous jump in transmutation over all previous reactions. Calculations showed that such a reaction should yield 10 to 100 times the energy of less violent nuclear reactions. This was quickly confirmed by experiment, and later the same year it was discovered that neutrons emitted in fission could cause a chain reaction to occur.

Fearing that Nazi Germany would put Hahn's discovery to use and build an atomic bomb, Einstein communicated with the President of the United States and urged that a programme be set up to achieve a nuclear chain reaction. Fermi subsequently built the first atomic reactor in 1942 and the first atomic bomb was exploded in 1945, bringing World War II to a close. Hahn had in fact not worked on the production of nuclear energy for Germany, and the German effort to build a reactor and a bomb had not got anywhere.

Otto Hahn made a discovery of enormous importance for the human race for as well as providing a new and immense source of power, it has given us enormous destructive ability, as he was well aware. He is commemorated in science in the naming of element 105 as hahnium.

Harrison, John (*1693–1776*), was a British horologist and instrument maker who made the first chronometers that were accurate enough to allow the precise determination of longitude at sea, and so permit reliable (and safe) navigation over long distances.

Harrison was born in Foulky, Yorkshire, in March 1693, the son of a carpenter and mechanic. He learned his father's trades and became increasingly interested in and adept at making mechanisms and instruments. In 1726 he made a compensated clock pendulum, which remained the same length at any temperature by making use of the different co-efficients of expansion of two different metals.

In 1714 the British Government's Board of Longitude announced that it would award a series of prizes up to the princely sum of 20,000 to anyone who could make an instrument to determine longitude at sea to an accuracy of 30 minutes (half a degree). By 1728 Harrison had constructed his first marine chronometer. Encouraged by the horologist George Graham (1673–1751) he made various improvements, and in 1735 he submitted one of his instruments for the award. Two other chronometers, smaller and lighter than the first, were finished in 1739 and 1757 and also submitted before the Board had completed trials on the first. Then in about 1760 Harrison perfected his No. 4 Marine Chronometer which was not much larger than a watch of the time and was finally subjected to the ultimate test at sea. On two voyages to the West Indies it kept accurate time to within 5 seconds over the duration of the voyage, equivalent to just over one minute of longitude; after five months on a sea voyage, it was less than one minute (of time) out of true.

A unique feature that contributed to the chronometer's accuracy – and subsequently incorporated into other chronometers – was a device that enabled it to be rewound without temporarily stopping the mechanism. In 1763 the Government awarded Harrison the sum of 5,000, but he did not receive the remainder of the original "prize" of 20,000 until ten years later, by which time the Admiralty had built its own chronometer to Harrison's design. Three years later Harrison died in London on 24 March 1776.

Heaviside, Oliver (*1850–1925*), was a British physicist and electrical engineer who predicted the existence of the ionosphere, which was known for a time as the Kennelly–Heaviside Layer. Heaviside made significant discoveries concerning the passage of electrical waves through the atmosphere and along cables, and added the concepts of inductance, capacitance and impedance to electrical science.

Heaviside was born in Camden Town, London, on 18 May 1850. His uncle was Charles Wheatstone (1802–1875), who was a pioneer of the telegraph and may have stimulated in him an interest in electricity. Heaviside received only an elementary education, and was mainly self-taught. He took up employment with the Great Northern Telegraph Company at Newcastle-upon-Tyne in 1870, when he was 20. This employment lasted only four years, when he was forced to retire because of his deafness. Shortly after he is believed to have visited Denmark to study telegraph apparatus. On his return he was supported first by his parents and later in life he lived with his brother. Heaviside never obtained an academic position but received several honours, including fellowship of the Royal Society in 1891 and the first award of the Faraday Medal by the Institution of Electrical Engineers shortly before he died in Paignton, Devon, on 3 February 1925.

During his early years, Heaviside was absorbed by mathematics. He was familiar with the attempt by Peter Tait (1831–1901) to popularize the quaternions of William Rowan Hamilton (1805–1865), but he rejected the scalar part of the quaternions in his notion of a vector. Heaviside's vectors were of the form $v = ai + bj + ck$, where i, j and k are unit vectors along the Cartesian x-,

y- and z-axes respectively. When Heaviside became involved with work relating to Maxwell's famous theory of electricity, he wrote Maxwell's equations in vector form incorporating some discoveries of his own. Heaviside also used operator techniques in his expression of calculus and made much use of divergent series (those with terms whose sum does not approach a fixed amount). He made great use of these in his electrical calculations when many mathematicians were afraid to venture away from convergent series.

In his twenties and thirties, Heaviside became very interested in electrical science, first carrying out experiments and then developing advanced theoretical discussions. These were, in fact, so advanced that they were eventually dismissed by some mathematicians and scientists, and were classed as too abstract to be published in the electrical journals. He expressed his ideas in the three-volume *Electromagnetic Theory* (1893–1912). Much of this work extended Maxwell's discoveries but he made many valuable discoveries of his own. Heaviside visualized electrical ideas often in mechanical terms and thought of the inertia of machines as being similar to electrical inductance.

When Heaviside became involved with the passage of electricity along conductors, he modified Ohm's law to include inductance and this, together with other electrical properties, resulted in his derivation of the equation of telegraphy. On considering the problem of signal distortion in a telegraph cable, he came to the conclusion that this could be substantially reduced by the addition of small inductance coils throughout its length, and this method has since been used to great effect.

In the third volume of his *Electromagnetic Theory*, Heaviside considered wireless telegraphy and, in drawing attention to the enormous power required to send useful signals long distances, he suggested that they may be guided by hugging the land and sea. He also suggested that part of the atmosphere may act as a good reflector of electrical waves. Arthur Kennelly (1861–1939) in the United States also made a similar suggestion and this layer, which was for some time known as the Kennelly–Heaviside layer, was subsequently shown to exist by Edward Appleton (1892–1965). This part of the atmosphere, about 100 km above the ground, is now known as the ionosphere.

Although from time to time Heaviside had his detractors, perhaps because he was unorthodox in his approach, he was later known and highly valued by the leading physicists and electrical engineers of his day.

Heisenberg, Werner Karl (*1901–1976*), was a German physicist who founded quantum mechanics and the uncertainty principle. In recognition of these achievements, he was awarded the 1932 Nobel Prize in Physics.

Heisenberg was born on 5 December 1901 in Duisberg. He showed an early aptitude for mathematics and when, after leaving school, he came across a book on relativity by Hermann Weyl (1885-1955) entitled *Space, Time And Matter* (1918), he became interested in the mathematical arguments underlying physical concepts. This led Heisenberg to study theoretical physics under Arnold Sommerfeld (1868-1951) at Munich University. There he formed a lasting friendship with Wolfgang Pauli (1900-1958). He obtained his doctor's degree in 1923 and immediately became assistant to Max Born (1882-1970) at Göttingen. From 1924 to 1926, Heisenberg worked with Niels Bohr (1885-1962) in Copenhagen and then in 1927 he was offered the Chair of Theoretical Physics at Leipzig at the age of only 26.

Heisenberg stayed at Leipzig until 1941 and then from 1942 until 1945 was Director of the Max Planck Institute for Physics in Berlin. During World War II he was in charge of atomic research in Germany and it is possible that he may have been able to direct efforts away from military uses of nuclear power. In 1946 Heisenberg was made Director of the Max Planck Institute for Physics in Göttingen, which in 1958 was moved to his home city of Munich. He held the post of Director until 1970, and died in Munich on 1 February 1976.

In the early 1920s, there were burning questions relating to the quantum theory. Bohr had used the quantum concept of Max Planck (1858-1947) to explain the spectral lines of atoms in terms of the energy differences of electron orbits at various quantum states, but there were weaknesses in the results. In 1922 Pauli began to throw doubt on them and Sommerfeld, although an optimist, could see some flaws in Bohr's work.

In 1923 Heisenberg went to Göttingen to work with Born and used a modification of the quantum rules to explain the anomalous Zeeman effect, in which single spectral lines split into groups of closely spaced lines in a strong magnetic field. Information about atomic structure can be deduced from the separation of these lines.

Heisenberg was concerned not to try to picture what happens inside the atom but to find a mathematical system that explained the properties of the atom – in this case, the position of the spectral lines given by hydrogen, the simplest atom. Born helped Heisenberg to develop his ideas, which he presented in 1925 as a system called matrix mech-

anics. By mathematical treatment of values within matrices or arrays, the frequencies of the lines in the hydrogen spectrum were obtained. This was the first precise mathematical description of the workings of the atom and with it Heisenberg is regarded as founding quantum mechanics, which seeks to explain atomic structure in mathematical terms.

The following year, however, Erwin Schrödinger (1887-1961) produced a system of wave mechanics that accounted mathematically for the discovery made in 1923 by Louis De Broglie (1892-) that electrons do not occupy orbits but exist as standing waves around the nucleus. Wave mechanics was a much more convenient system than the matrix mechanics of Heisenberg and Born and rapidly replaced it, though John van Neumann (1903-1957) showed the two systems to be equivalent in 1944.

Nevertheless, Heisenberg was able to predict from studies of the hydrogen spectrum that hydrogen exists in two allotropes - ortho-hydrogen and para-hydrogen - in which the two nuclei of the atoms in a hydrogen molecule spin in the same or opposite directions respectively. The allotropes were discovered in 1929.

In 1927 Heisenberg made the discovery for which he is best known – that of the uncertainty principle. This states that it is impossible to specify precisely both the position and the simultaneous momentum (mass multiplied by velocity) of a particle. There is always a degree of uncertainty in either, and as one is determined with greater precision, the other can only be found less exactly. Multiplying the degrees of uncertainty of the position and momentum yield a value approximately equal to Planck's constant. (This is a consequence of the wave–particle duality discovered by De Broglie.) Heisenberg's uncertainty principle negates cause and effect; it maintains that the result of an action can be expressed only in terms of the probability that a certain effect will occur. The idea was revolutionary and discomforted even Albert Einstein (1879-1955), but it has remained valid.

Another great discovery was made in 1927, when Heisenberg solved the mystery of ferromagnetism. In it he employed the Pauli exclusion principle, which states that no two electrons can have all four quantum numbers the same. Heisenberg used the principle to show that ferromagnetism is caused by electrostatic intereaction between the electrons. This was also a major insight which has stood the test of time.

Heisenberg was a brilliant scientist with a very incisive mind. He will be remembered with gratitude and respect for solving some of the great and complex problems in quantum mechanics which were so crucial at the beginning of this century for our understanding of nuclear physics.

Helmholtz, Hermann Ludwig Ferdinand von (*1821-1894*), was a German physicist and physiologist who made a major contribution to physics with the first precise formulation of the principle of conservation of energy. He also made important advances in physiology, in which he first measured the speed of nerve impulses, invented the ophthalmoscope and revealed the mechanism by which the ear senses tone and pitch. Helmholtz also made important discoveries in physical chemistry.

Helmholtz was born in Potsdam on 31 August 1821. His father was a teacher of philosophy and literature at the Potsdam Gymnasium and his mother was a descendant of William Penn, the founder of the state of Pennsylvania in the United States. Although a delicate child, Helmholtz thrived on scholarship of which his home was not short; his father taught him Latin, Greek, Hebrew, French, Italian and Arabic. He attended the local Gymnasium and showed a talent for physics, but as his father could not afford a university education for him, Helmholtz embarked on the study of medicine, for which financial aid was available in return for a commitment to serve as an army doctor for eight years. In 1838 Helmholtz entered the Friedrich Wilhelm Institute in Berlin, where his time was spent not only on medical and physiological studies but also on chemistry and higher mathematics. He also became an expert pianist.

In 1842 Helmholtz received his MD and became a surgeon with his regiment at Potsdam, where he carried out experiments in a laboratory he set up in the barracks. His ability in science as opposed to medicine was soon recognized, and in 1848 he was released from his military duties. The following year, he took up the post of Associate Professor of Physiology at Königsberg. In 1855 Helmholtz moved to Bonn to become Professor of Anatomy and Physiology, and then in 1858 was appointed Professor of Physiology at the University of Heidelberg. In 1871 he took up the Chair of Physics at the University of Berlin, and in 1887 became Director of the new Physico-Technical Institute of Berlin. His health then began to fail, and Helmholtz died at Berlin on 8 September 1894.

Throughout his life, Helmholtz's phenomenal intellectual capacity and grounding in philosophy were at the basis of his work. While training as a doctor, his supervisor was Johannes Müller (1801-1858), a distinguished physiologist who like Helmholtz was interested in the ideas promoted by philosophers. The abstract nature of the subject was obviously attractive to his superb brain. During his student days, Helmholtz rejected many of the ideas offered by the German philosopher Immanuel Kant (1724-1804). Helmholtz's supervisor subscribed to Kant's Nature philosophy, which assumed that the organism as a whole is greater than the sum of its parts. Helmholtz's scientific work in many fields was guided by an effort to disprove these fundamentals. He was convinced, for example, that living things possess no innate vital force, and that their life processes are driven by the same forces and obey the same principles as non-living systems.

Helmholtz's doctoral submission in 1842 was concerned with the relationship between the nerve fibres and nerve cells of invertebrates, which led to an investigation of the nature and origin of animal heat. In 1850 he measured the velocity of nerve impulses, stimulated by a statement by Müller that vitalism caused the impulses to be instantaneous. Helmholtz measured the impulse velocity by experiments with a frog and found it to be about a tenth of the speed of sound. He went on to investigate muscle action and found in 1848 that animal heat and muscle action are generated by chemical changes in the muscles.

This work led Helmholtz to the idea of the principle of conservation of energy, observing that the energy of life processes is derived entirely from oxidation of food. His deduction was remarkably similar to that made by Julius Mayer (1814-1878) a few years earlier, but Helmholtz was not aware of Mayer's work and when he did arrive at a formulation of the principle in 1847, he expressed it in a more effective way. Helmholtz also had the benefit of the precise experimental determination of the mechanical equivalent of heat published by James Joule (1818-1889) in 1847. He was able to derive a general equation that expressed the kinetic energy of a moving body as being equal to the product of the force and distance through which the force moves to bring about the energy change. This equation could be applied in many fields to show that energy is always conserved and it led to the first law of thermodynamics, which states that the total energy of a system and its surroundings remains constant even if it may be changed from one form of energy to another.

Helmholtz went on to develop thermodynamics in physical chemistry, and in 1882 he derived an expression that relates the total energy of a system to its free energy (which is the proportion that can be converted to forms other than heat) and to its temperature and entropy. It enables chemists to determine the direction of a chemical reaction. In this work, Helmholtz was anticipated independently by Willard Gibbs (1839-1903) and both scientists are usually given credit for it.

Helmholtz's work on nerve impulses led him also to make important discoveries in the physiology of vision and hearing. He invented the ophthalmoscope, which is used to examine the retina, in 1851 and the ophthalmometer, which measures the curvature of the eye, in 1855. He also revived the three-colour theory of vision first proposed in 1801 by Thomas Young (1773-1829), who like Helmholtz was also a physician and physicist. He developed Young's ideas by showing that a single primary colour (red, green or violet) must also affect retinal structures sensitive to the other primary colours. In this way, Helmholtz successfully explained the colour of after-images and the effects of colour blindness. He also extended Young's work on accommodation. In acoustics, Helmholtz's contribution was to produce a comprehensive explanation of how the upper partials in sounds combine to give them a particular tone or timbre, and how resonance may cause this to happen - for example in the mouth cavity to produce vowel sounds. He also formulated a theory of hearing, correctly suggesting that structures within the inner ear resonate at particular frequencies to enable both pitch and tone to be perceived.

Helmholtz also interested himself in hydrodynamics and in 1858 produced an important paper in which he established the mathematical principles that define motion in a vortex. Helmholtz will also be remembered for his electrical double layer theories. First proposed in 1879, they were initially applied to the situation of a solid immersed in a solution. He imagined that a layer of ions is held at a solid surface by an oppositely charged layer of ions in the solution. These ideas were later applied to solids suspended in liquids.

Helmholtz dominated German science during the mid-1800s, his wide-ranging and exact work bringing it to the forefront of world attention, a position Germany was to enjoy well into the following century. He served as a great inspiration to others, not least his many students. Foremost of these was Heinrich Hertz (1857-1894), who as a direct result of Helmholtz's encouragement discovered radio waves. Helmholtz took classical mechanics to its limits in physics, paving the way for the radical departure from tradition that was soon to follow with the quantum theory and relativity. When this revolution did occur, however, it was ushered in mainly by German scientists applying the mathematical and experimental expertise upon which Helmholtz had insisted.

Henry, Joseph (*1797-1878*), was an American physicist who carried out early experiments in electromagnetic induction.

Henry was born in Albany, New York, on 17 December 1797, the son of a labourer. He had little schooling, working his way through Albany Academy to study medicine and then engineering (from 1825). He worked at the academy as a teacher, and in 1826 was made Professor of Mathematics and Physics. He moved to New Jersey College (later Princeton) in 1832 as Professor of Natural Philosophy, in which post he lectured in most of the sciences. He was the Smithsonian Institution's first Director (1846) and first President of the National Academy of Sciences (1868), a position he held until his death, in Washington, on 13 May 1878.

Many of Henry's early experiments were with electromagnetism. By 1830 he had made powerful electromagnets by using many turn of fine insulated wire wound on iron cores. In that year he anticipated Michael Faraday's discovery of electromagnetic induction (although Faraday published first), and two years later he discovered self-induction. He also built a practical electric motor and in 1835 developed the relay (later to be much used in electric telegraphy). In astronomy Henry studied sunspots and solar radiation, and his meteorological studies at the Smithsonian led to the founding of the US Weather Bureau. The unit of inductance was named the henry in 1893.

Hertz, Heinrich Rudolf (*1857-1894*), was a German physicist who discovered radio waves. His name is commemorated in the use of the hertz as a unit of frequency, one hertz being equal to one complete vibration or cycle per second.

Hertz was born in Hamburg on 22 February 1857. As a child he was interested in practical things and equipped his own workshop. At the age of 15 he entered the Johanneum Gymnasium and, on leaving school three years later, went to Frankfurt to gain practical experience as the beginning of a career in engineering. Engineering qualifications were governed by a state examination, and he went to Dresden Polytechnic to work for this in 1876. During a year of compulsory military service from 1876 to 1877, Hertz decided to be a scientist rather than an engineer and on his return he entered Munich University. He began studies in mathematics, but soon switched to practical physics, which greatly interested him.

Hertz moved to Berlin in 1878 and there came into contact with Hermann Helmholtz (1821-1894), who immediately recognized his talents and encouraged him greatly. He gained his PhD in 1880 and remained at Berlin for a further three years to work with Helmholtz as his assistant.

Then in 1883 Hertz moved to Kiel to lecture in physics, but the lack of a proper laboratory there caused him to take up the position of Professor of Physics at Karlsruhe in 1885. He stayed in Karlsruhe for four years, and it was there that he carried out his most important work, discovering radio waves in 1888. In the same year, he began to suffer from toothache, the prelude to a long period of increasingly poor health due to a bone disease. Hertz moved to Bonn in 1889, succeeding Rudolf Clausius (1822-1888) as Professor of Physics. His physical condition steadily deteriorated and he died of blood poisoning on 1 January 1894, at the early age of 36.

In 1879 a prize was offered by the Berlin Academy for the solution of a problem concerned with Maxwell's theory of electricity, which was set by Helmholtz with Hertz particularly in mind. Hertz declined the task believing that it would take up more time and energy than he could then afford. Instead, for his doctorate he carried out a theoretical study of electromagnetic induction in rotating conductors. It was not until five years later on his move to Karlsruhe in 1885 that Hertz found the facilities and the time to work on the problem set by the Berlin Academy. He used large improved induction coils to show that dielectric polarization leads to the same electromagnetic effects as do conduction currents; and he generally confirmed the validity of the famous equations of James Clerk Maxwell concerning the behaviour of electricity. In 1888 he realized that Maxwell's equations implied that electric waves could be produced and would travel through air. Hertz went on to confirm his prediction by constructing an open circuit powered by an induction coil, and an open loop of wire as a receiving circuit. As a spark was produced by the induction coil, so one occurred in the open receiving loop. Electric waves travelled from the coil to the loop, creating a current in the loop and causing a spark to form across the gap. Hertz went on to determine the velocity of these waves (which were later called radio waves), and on showing that it was the same as that of light, devised experiments to show that the waves could be reflected, refracted and diffracted. One particular experiment used prisms made of pitch to demonstrate refraction in the same way that light is refracted by a glass prism.

From about 1890 Hertz gained an interest in mechanics. He developed a system with only one law of motion - that the path of a mechanical system through space is as straight as possible and is travelled with uniform motion. When this law is developed subject to the nature of space and the constraints on matter, it can be shown that the mechanics of Isaac Newton (1642-1727),

Joseph Lagrange (1736-1812) and William Rowan Hamilton (1805-1865), who extended the methods of dealing with mechanical systems considerably, arise as special cases.

Heinrich Hertz made a discovery vital to the progress of technology by demonstrating the generation of radio waves. It is tragic that his early death robbed him of the opportunity to develop his achievements and to see Guglielmo Marconi (1874-1937) and others transform his discovery into a world-wide method of communication.

Herzberg, Gerhard (*1904-*), is a German-born Canadian physicist who is best known for his work in determining - using spectrocopy - the electronic structure and geometry of molecules, especially free radicals (atoms or groups of atoms that possess a free, unbonded electron). He has received many honours for his work, including the 1971 Nobel Prize in Chemistry.

Herzberg was born on 25 December 1904 in Hamburg, where he received his early education. He then studied at the Technische Universität in Darmstadt, from which he gained his doctorate in 1928, and carried out post-doctoral work at the universities of Göttingen (1928 to 1929) and Bristol (1929 to 1930). On returning to Germany in 1930 he became a Privatdozent (an unsalaried lecturer) at the Darmstadt Technische Universität but in 1935, with the rise to power of Adolf Hitler, he fled to Canada, where he became Research Professor of Physics at the University of Saskatchewan, Saskatoon, from 1935 to 1945. He spent the period from 1945 to 1948 in the United States, as Professor of Spectroscopy at the Yerkes Observatory (part of the University of Chicago) in Wisconsin, then returned to Canada. From 1939 until his retirement in 1969 he was Director of the Division of Pure Physics for the National Research Council in Ottawa - a laboratory generally acknowledged as being one of the world's leading centres for molecular spectroscopy.

Herzberg's most important work concerned the application of spectroscopy to elucidate the properties and structure of molecules. Depending on the conditions, molecules absorb or emit electromagnetic radiation (much of it in the visible part of the spectrum) of discrete wavelengths. Moreover, the radiation spectrum is directly dependent on the electronic and geometric structure of an atom or molecule and therefore provides detailed information about molecular energies, rotations, vibrations and electronic configurations. Herzberg, studying common molecules such as hydrogen, oxygen, nitrogen and carbon monoxide, discovered new lines in the spectrum of molecular oxygen; called Herzberg bands, these spectral lines have been useful in analysing the upper atmosphere. He also elucidated the geometric structure of molecular oxygen, carbon monoxide, hydrogen cyanide and acetylene (ethyne); discovered the new molecules phosphorus nitride and phosphorus carbide; proved the existence of the methyl and methylene free radicals; and demonstrated that both neutrons and protons are part of the nucleus. His research in the field of molecular spectroscopy not only provided experimental results of fundamental importance to physical chemistry and quantum mechanics but also helped to stimulate further research into the chemical reactions of gases.

In addition, Herzberg provided much valuable information about certain aspects of astronomy. He interpreted the spectral lines of stars and comets, finding that a rare form of carbon exists in comets. He also showed that hydrogen exists in the atmospheres of some planets, and identified the spectra of certain free radicals in interstellar gas.

Hess, Victor Francis (*1883-1964*), was an Austrian-born American physicist who discovered cosmic rays, for which he was jointly awarded the 1936 Nobel Prize in Physics with Carl Anderson.

Hess was born in Waldstein, Austria, on 24 June 1883, the son of a forester. He was educated in Graz, at the Gymnasium then at the University, obtaining his doctorate from the latter in 1906. From 1906 to 1910 he worked at the Vienna Physical Institute as a member of F. Exner's research group studying radioactivity and atmospheric ionization, then from 1910 to 1920 was an assistant to S. Meyer at the Institute of Radium Research of the Viennese Academy of Sciences. In 1920 Hess was appointed Extraordinary Professor of Experimental Physics at Graz University. From 1921 to 1923, however, he was on a two-year sabbatical in the United States, as Director of the Research Laboratory of the US Radium Corporation in Orange, New Jersey, and also as a consultant to the Department of the Interior (Bureau of Mines). In 1925, two years after his return to Graz University, he became its Professor of Experimental Physics, a post he held until 1931, when he was appointed Professor of Physics at Innsbruck University and Director of its newly established Institute of Radiology; while at Innsbruck he founded a cosmic ray observatory on the Hafelekar mountain, near Innsbruck. After the Nazi occupation of Austria in 1938 Hess – a Roman Catholic himself but with a Jewish wife – emigrated to the United States, where he was Professor of Physics at Fordham University, New York City, until his retirement in 1956 –

having become a naturalized American citizen in 1944. Hess died in Mount Vernon, New York, on 17 December 1964.

In the early 1900s it was found that gases in the atmosphere are always slightly ionized, even samples that had been enclosed in shielded containers. The theories to explain this phenomenon included radioactive contamination by the walls of the containers and the influence of gamma-rays in the soil and air; these theories were later proved incorrect by Hess's findings. In 1910 Theordor Wulf, investigating atmospheric ionization using an electroscope on top of the Eiffel Tower, found that ionization at 300 m above the ground was greater than at ground level, from which he concluded that the ionization was caused by extraterrestrial rays.

Continuing this line of research, Hess – with the help of the Austrian Academy of Sciences and the Austrian Aeroclub – made ten balloon ascents in 1911-12 to collect data about atmospheric ionization. Ascending to altitudes of more than 5,000 m, he established that the intensity of ionization decreased to a minimum at about 1,000 m then increased steadily, being about four times more intense at 5,000 m than at ground level. Moreover, by making ascents at night – and one, on 12 April 1912, during a nearly total solar eclipse – he proved that the ionization was not caused by the Sun. From his findings Hess concluded that radiation of great penetrating power enters the atmosphere from outer space. This discovery of cosmic rays (as this type of radiation was called by Robert Millikan in 1925) led to the study of elementary particles and paved the way for Carl Anderson's discovery of the positron in 1932.

Later in his career Hess investigated the biological effects of exposure to radiation (in 1934 he had a thumb amputated following an accident with radioactive material); the gamma radiation emitted by rocks; dust pollution of the atmosphere; and the refractive indices of liquid mixtures.

Hooke, Robert (*1635-1703*), was a British physicist who was also active in many other branches of science. He is remembered mainly for the derivation of Hooke's law of elasticity, for coining the term cell as used in biology, and for the invention of the hairspring regulator in timepieces and the air pump.

Hooke was born in Freshwater, Isle of Wight, on 18 July 1635. He was sickly as a child, which prevented him from studying for the Church as his father intended. Left on his own, Hooke constructed all kinds of ingenious toys, developing the great mechanical skill that he later applied to instrument making. Upon the death of his father in 1648, Hooke went to London and was educated at Westminster School. There he was introduced to mathematics, mastering Euclid in only a week. In 1653 he went on to Oxford University as a chorister and there became one of a group of brilliant young scientists, among them Robert Boyle (1627-1691), to whom Hooke became an assistant.

Hooke eventually obtained his MA from Oxford in 1663, but the group broke up in 1659 and 1660 and he and most of his colleagues moved to London, where they established the Royal Society in 1662. Hooke was appointed Curator of the Society, a post that entailed the demonstration of several new experiments at every weekly meeting. In 1664 he also became a lecturer in mechanics at the Royal Society, and in the following year he took up the additional post of Professor of Geometry at Gresham College, London. Hooke retained these positions for the rest of his life, and was also Secretary of the Royal Society from 1677 to 1683. He died in London on 3 March 1703.

Hooke's post of curator at the Royal Society required him to provide a continual stream of new ideas to demonstrate before the members, and he consequently examined all fields of experimental science but made no deep or thorough investigations in any of them. His main contributions were in four main areas – mechanics, optics, geology and instrument making.

In mechanics, Hooke was the first to realize that the stress placed upon an elastic body is proportional to the strain produced. This relationship is known as Hooke's law; it was discovered in 1678. But Hooke was active in mechanics long before this, and in 1658 he found that a spiral spring vibrates with a regular period in the same way as a pendulum. He began to develop this discovery to produce a watch with a spring-controlled balance wheel, but it is uncertain whether he made a working model before Christiaan Huygens (1629-1695) did so in 1674. Hooke can thus be credited with the discovery of the principle of the watch if not the invention of the device itself. Hooke himself claimed priority, however, one of many such disputes that were a feature of his life. His main protagonist in this respect was Isaac Newton (1642-1727), with whom Hooke argued credit for the discovery of gravitation. The idea that gravity exists between bodies was prevalent at the time, and in 1664, Hooke suggested that a body is continually pulled into an orbit around a larger body by a force of gravity directed towards the centre of the larger body. This was an important step towards an understanding of gravity, and Hooke also suggested in 1679 that the force of gravity obeys an inverse square law. Both these ideas helped Newton, with his immense analytical powers, to build on Hooke's insight and arrive at his law of universal gravitation in 1687.

Another area of contention between Hooke and Newton was in optics. In 1665 Hooke published a book called *Micrographia*. It contained superb accounts of observations that Hooke had made with the microscope and was the first important work on microscopy. From his description of the empty spaces in the structure of cork as cells came our use of the word cell to mean a living unit of protoplasm. The *Micrographia* also contained Hooke's work on optics. This included the idea that light might consist of waves, which Hooke developed from his observations of spectral colours and patterns in thin films. Newton was again able to build on Hooke's work here, examining the optical effects of thin films in detail.

In geology, Hooke made an important contribution by insisting that fossils are the remains of plants and animals that existed long ago, a daring view in an age dominated by the biblical account of creation. Hooke furthermore held that the history of the Earth would be revealed by a close study of fossils.

As an instrument maker, Hooke made several important inventions and advances. In 1658, while working for Robert Boyle at Oxford, Hooke perfected the air pump, a development that led directly to the derivation of Boyle's law in 1662. He also made considerable advances to the microscope, and invented the wheel barometer, which registered air pressure with a moving pointer; a weather clock, which recorded such factors as air pressure and temperature on a revolving drum; and the universal joint.

Hooke is an unusual figure in the history of science. Although he made no major discoveries himself, his wide-ranging intuition and great experimental prowess sparked off important contributions in others, notably Newton and Huygens.

Huygens, Christiaan (*1629-1695*), was a Dutch physicist and astronomer. He is best known in physics for his explanation of the pendulum and invention of the pendulum clock, and for the first exposition of a wave theory of light. In astronomy, Huygens was the first to recognize the rings of Saturn and discovered its satellite Titan.

Huygens was born on 14 April 1629 at The Hague into a prominent Dutch family with a tradition of diplomatic service to the ruling house of Orange, and a strong inclination towards education and culture. René Descartes (1596-1650) was a frequent guest at the house of Huygens' father, Constantijn, who was a versatile and multi-talented man, a diplomat, a prominent Dutch and Latin poet, and a composer. So it was natural for the young Christiaan to be educated at home to the highest standard. In 1645 he was sent to the University of Leiden to study mathematics and law, followed in 1647 by two years studying law at Breda.

But, eschewing his expected career in diplomacy, Huygens returned to his home to live for sixteen years on an allowance from his father which enabled him to devote himself to his chosen task, the scientific study of nature. This long period of near seclusion was to be the most fruitful period of his career.

In 1666 on the foundation of the Académie Royale des Sciences, Huygens was invited to Paris and lived and worked at the Bibliothèque Royale for fifteen years, until his delicate health and the changing political climate took him back to his home. Here he continued to experiment, only occasionally venturing abroad to meet the other great scientists of the time as in 1689, when he visited London and met Isaac Newton (1642–1727). During his stay in Paris, Huygens twice had to return home for several months because of his health and in 1694 he again fell ill. This time he did not recover, and he died at The Hague on 8 July 1695.

Huygens worked in different areas of science in a way almost impossible in our modern age of vast knowledge and increasing specialization. He made important advances in pure mathematics, applied mathematics and mechanics, which he virtually founded, optics and astronomy, both practical and theoretical, and mechanistic philosophy. He is also credited with the invention of the pendulum clock, enormously important for its use in navigation, since accurate timekeeping is necessary to find longitude at sea. In a seafaring nation such as Holland, this was of particular importance. Typically of Huygens, he developed this work into a thorough study of pendulum systems and harmonic oscillation in general.

At first Huygens concentrated on mathematics. In the age of such revolutionary figures as Descartes, Newton and Gottfried Leibniz (1646–1716), his career may be termed conservative for it contained nothing completely new except the theory of evolutes and Huygens' study of probability including game theory, which originated our modern concept of the expectation of a variable. His suspicion of the new methods may have been partly due to the secrecy of scientists of his time, and partly to Huygens' fastidiousness, which often led him to delay publishing his observations and theories. The importance of his mathematical work is in its improving on avail-able techniques, and Huygens' application of them to find solutions to problems in science.

The first of his many studies in applied mathematics was a paper on hydrostatics, including much mathematical analysis, published in 1650. Fascinating work on impact and collision followed, motivated by Huygens' disbelief in Descartes' laws of impact. Huygens used the idea of relative frames of reference, considering the motion of one body relative to the other. He discovered the law of conservation of momentum, but as yet the vectorial quantity had little intuitive meaning for him and he did not proceed beyond stating the law as the conservation of the centre of gravity of a system of bodies under impact. In *De Motu Corporum* (1656) he was also able to show that the quantity $\frac{1}{2}mv^2$ is conserved in an elastic collision, though again this concept had little intuitive sense for him.

Huygens also studied centrifugal force and showed, in 1659, its similarity to gravitational force, though he lacked the Newtonian concept of acceleration. Both in the early and the later part of his career he considered projectiles and gravity, developing the mathematically primitive ideas of Galileo, and finding in 1659 a remarkably accurate experimental value for the distance covered by a falling body in one second. In fact his gravitational theories successfully deal with several difficult points which Newton carefully avoided. Later, in the 1670s, Huygens studied motion in resisting media, becoming convinced by experiment that the resistance in such media as air is proportional to the square of the velocity. Without calculus, however, he could not find the velocity time curve.

Early in 1657, Huygens developed a clock regulated by a pendulum. The idea was patented and published in the same year, and was a great success; by 1658 major towns in Holland had pendulum tower clocks. Huygens worked at the theory first of the simple pendulum and then of harmonically oscillating systems throughout the rest of his life, publishing the *Horologium Oscillatorium* in 1673. He made many technical and theoretical advances, including the derivation of the relationship of the period T of a simple pendulum to its length l as $T = 2\pi\sqrt{l/g}$. Huygens made use of his previously worked out theory of evolutes in this work.

Huygens is perhaps best known for his wave theory of light. This was the result of much optical work, begun in 1655 when Huygens and his brother began to make telescopes of high technical quality. In that year he discovered Titan, the largest satellite of Saturn. He determined its period of rotation, and also solved the problem of what until then had appeared to be the "arms of

Saturn", showing by subtle analysis that they must be the profile view of a ring surrounding the planet.

The *Traité de la Lumière*, containing Huygen's famous wave or pulse theory of light, was published in 1678. Huygens had been able two years earlier to use his principle of secondary wave fronts to explain reflection and refraction, showing that refraction is related to differing velocities of light in media, and his publication was partly a counter to Newton's particle theory of light. The essence of his theory was that light is transmitted as a pulse with a "tendency to move" through the ether by setting up a whole train of vibrations in the ether in a sort of serial displacement. The thoroughness of Huygens' analysis of this model is impressive, but although he observed the effects due to polarization, he could not yet use his ideas to explain this phenomenon.

The impact of Huygens' work in his own time, and in the eighteenth century was much less than his genius deserved. Essentially a solitary man, he did not attract students or disciples and he was also slow to publish his findings. Nevertheless, after Galileo (1564-1642) and until Newton, he was supreme in mechanics, and his other scientific work has had a significant effect on the development of physics.

J

Jensen, Johannes Hans Daniel (*1907-*   ), is a German physicist who shared the 1963 Nobel Prize in Physics with Maria Goeppert-Mayer (*1906-*   ) and Eugene Wigner (*1902-*   ) for work on the detailed characteristics of atomic nuclei.

Jensen was born in Hamburg on 25 June 1907. He studied at the Universities of Hamburg and Freiburg, gaining a PhD in 1932. From 1932 to 1936 he was an assistant in science at the University of Hamburg, and from 1937 to 1941 in charge of courses at the University. In 1941, he joined the Institute of Technology in Hanover as Ordinary Professor, staying until 1948. Since 1949 he has been Professor at the University of Heidelberg.

With Goeppert-Mayer and Wigner, Jensen proposed the shell theory of nuclear structure in 1949, and explained it in *Elementary Theory Of Nuclear Shell Structure*, written with Goeppert-Mayer in 1955. According to this theory, a nucleus could not be thought of as a random motion of neutrons and protons about a point, but as a structure of shells or spherical layers, each with a different radius and each filled with neutrons and protons.

Careful studies of nuclear energy levels had shown that not only do even numbers of neutrons or protons lead to more stable nuclei than odd numbers, but that nuclei containing certain definite numbers of neutrons or protons, or both, are especially stable (like the electron structures of inert gas atoms). In 1948 Goeppert-Mayer published evidence of the special stability of the following numbers of protons and neutrons: 2, 8, 20, 50, 82 and 126. These are commonly called magic numbers. Similar conclusions were reached by Jensen and Wigner. It is not only the energy levels that show particularly tight binding of nuclei with a magic number of protons or neutrons, or particularly both; the angular momentum also shows properties similar to those observed in closed shells of electrons in atoms. The value of angular momentum is zero for closed shells, but has a value where there are small numbers of neutrons or protons outside the closed shells. It seems likely that what is being dealt with here is something like the periodic table of the elements.

The three Nobel Prize winners have tried to establish what significance the magic numbers have and why they have the values that they do. They have come to the conclusion that the orbital and spin moments of the particles within the nucleus can be treated to a first approximation by methods used for atomic structure. One has to assume that the central field is nothing like that met in an atom, but consists of a square well. In addition, the potential is constant throughout the interior of the sphere but has high barriers at the surface, and the energy levels come in a different order from the order of electronic levels in an atom. For example, the two *l*s levels come lowest and then the six *2p* levels, explaining the magic number 8. If the ten levels of the *3d* orbitals come next followed by two *2s* levels, we add 2 and 10 to 8 and get the next magic number, 20. Jensen and his colleagues then supplemented this theory with a second hypothesis – that there is a very strong spin–orbit interaction between the spin and orbit of a particle and that the lower of two states is always the one with angular momentum parallel rather than antiparallel. In this way, magic numbers seem to fall into place, although research is still going on.

Josephson, Brian David (*1940-*   ), is a British physicist who discovered the Josephson tunnelling effect in superconductivity. He shared the 1973 Nobel Prize in Physics with Leo Esaki (*1925-*   ) and Ivar Giaever (*1929-*   ) for their work on tunnelling in semiconductors and superconductors.

Josephson was born in Cardiff on 4 January 1940. He was educated at Cardiff High School and at Cambridge University where, as an undergraduate, he published an important paper showing that an application of the Mossbauer effect to verify gravitational changes in the energy of photons had failed to take account of Doppler shifts associated with temperature changes.

Josephson became a Fellow of Trinity College, Cambridge, in 1962 and has remained at Cambridge ever since apart from the years 1965 and 1966, when he had an assistant professorship at the University of Illinois. Since 1974 he has been Professor of Physics at Cambridge.

In 1962 Josephson saw some novel connections between solid-state theory and his own experimental problems on superconductivity. He then set out to calculate the current due to quantum mechanical tunnelling across a thin strip of insulator between two superconductors, and the current-voltage characteristics of such junctions are now known as the Josephson effect.

Superconductivity, the property of zero resistivity of some metals below a critical temperature, was discovered by Heike Kamerlingh Onnes (1853-1926) in 1911, and in 1933 it was recognized that superconductors are perfect diamagnets, i.e. they totally repel magnetic field lines. Although the effect could be described by phenomenological macroscopic equations, no clear understanding of the microscopic mechanism emerged until the BCS theory developed by John Bardeen (1908-   ) and co-workers in 1957. This explained the absence of electron scattering by electrons of opposite spin pairing up so that, via the response of the atoms in the metal, the electrons had an attractive rather than repulsive influence on one another.

Josephson's contribution was to solve the problem of how such superconductivity pairs would behave when confronted by an insulating barrier, typically of thickness 1-2 nm. He recognized that the electron pairs could tunnel through barriers in a manner analogous to the behaviour of single particles in alpha decay. One observable prediction is that an alternating current occurs in the barrier when a steady external voltage is applied to a system comprising a superconductor, e.g. lead, with a thin film of oxide at its surface and a superconducting film evaporated on the oxide. The time variation of the phase ϕ of the pair wave functions on the two sides of the barrier is given by $\hbar \, d\phi/dt = 2eV$, where e is the electronic charge, V the applied voltage and $\hbar$ Planck's constant divided by 2π. This results in an AC current of frequency $v = 2eV/\hbar$. The ratio 2e/h is 483.6 MHz 1v, and the effect is known as the AC Josephson effect. Conversely radiation, particularly in the far infrared or microwave region, will excite an extra potential across the junction when absorbed.

In addition, when a steady magnetic field is applied across an insulating barrier, a steady current flows. This is the DC Josephson effect. A circuit containing two such barriers in parallel shows quantum interference, analogous to the two-slit experiment in optics, when a magnetic flux is applied to the system. The current versus magnetic field characteristics of such a system shows oscillations with flux period $\hbar/2e$.

Josephson's predictions were soon verified by J.M. Rowell at the Bell Telephone Laboratories (the DC current-magnetic field characteristic) and by S. Shapiro, who applied an AC voltage to a superconductor-insulator-superconductor junction and observed resonance coupling to the internal AC Josephson supercurrent.

The Josephson effect has the following applications. The frequency of the AC current is very precisely related to fundamental constants of physics, and this has led to the most accurate method of determining h/e, which in turn establishes a voltage standard. The effect may be used as a generator of radiation, particularly in the microwave and far infra-red region. Quantum interference effects are used in squids (superconducting quantum interference devices), which may act as ultra-sensitive magnetometers capable of detecting tiny geophysical anomalies in the Earth's magnetic field or even the anomaly caused by the presence of a submarine. In addition, the fast switching properties of such devices can be exploited in logic elements or binary memories, and this has great potential for future generations of computers. Josephson's discovery may thus have important consequences in the development of artificial intelligence, and he is now absorbed in the mathematical modelling of intelligence.

Joule, James Prescott (*1818-1889*), was a British physicist who verified the principle of conservation of energy by making the first accurate determination of the mechanical equivalent of heat. He also discovered Joule's law, which defines the relation between heat and electricity, and with Lord Kelvin (1824-1907) the Joule-Thomson effect. In recognition of Joule's pioneering work on energy, the SI unit of energy is named the joule.

Joule was born at Salford on 24 December 1818 into a wealthy brewing family. He and his brother were educated at home between 1833 and 1837 in elementary mathematics, natural philosophy and chemistry, partly by John Dalton (1766-1844). Joule was a delicate child and very shy, and apart from his early education he was entirely self-taught in science. He does not seem to have played any part in the family brewing business, although some of his first experiments were done in a laboratory at the brewery.

Joule had great dexterity as an experimenter, and was able to measure temperatures very exactly indeed. At first, other scientists could not credit such accuracy and were disinclined to believe the theories that Joule developed to explain his results. The encouragement of Lord Kelvin from 1847 changed these attitudes, however, and Kelvin subsequently used Joule's practical ability to great advantage. By 1850, Joule was highly thought of among scientists and became a Fellow of the Royal Society. He was awarded the Society's Copley Medal in 1866 and was President of the British Association for the Advancement of Science in 1872 and again in 1887. Joule's own wealth was able to fund his scientific career, and he never took an academic post. His funds eventually ran out, however. He was awarded a pension in 1878 by Queen Victoria, but by that time his mental powers were going. He suffered a long illness and died in Sale, Cheshire, on 11 October 1889.

Joule realized the importance of accurate measurement very early on and exact quantitative data became his hallmark. His most active research period was between 1837 and 1847 and led to the establishment of the principle of conservation of energy and the equivalence of heat and other forms of energy. In a long series of experiments, he studied the quantitative relationship between electrical, mechanical and chemical

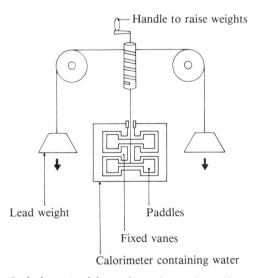

Lead weight   Paddles

Fixed vanes

Calorimeter containing water

Joule determined the mechanical equivalent of heat by measuring the rise in temperature of water agitated by paddles driven by falling weights.

effects and heat, and in 1843 he was able to announce his determination of the amount of work required to produce a unit of heat. This is called the mechanical equivalent of heat (currently accepted value 4.1868 joules/calorie).

Joule's first experiments related the chemical and electrical energy expended to the heat produced in metallic conductors and voltaic and electrolytic cells. These results were published between 1840 and 1843. He proved the relationship, known as Joule's law, that the heat produced in a conductor of resistance r by a current i is proportional to i^2r per second. He went on to discuss the relationship between heat and mechanical power in 1843. Joule first measured the rise in temperature and the current and the mechanical work involved when a small electromagnet rotated in water between the poles of another magnet, his training for these experiments having been provided by early research with William Sturgeon (1783–1850), a pioneer of electromagnetism. Joule then checked the rise in temperature by a more accurate experiment, forcing water through capillary tubes. The third method depended on the compression of air and the fourth produced heat from friction in water using paddles which rotated under the action of a falling weight. This has become the best-known method for the determination of the mechanical equivalent. Joule showed that the results obtained using different liquids (water, mercury and sperm oil) were the same. In the case of water, 772 fl lb of work produced a rise of 1°F in 1 fl lb of water. This value was universally accepted as the mechanical equivalent of heat. It now has no validity, however, because as both heat and work are considered to be forms of energy, they are measured in the same units – in joules. A joule is basically defined as the energy expended when a force of 1 newton moves 1 metre.

The great value of Joule's work in the establishment of the conservation of energy lay in the variety and completeness of his experimental evidence. He showed that the same relationship held in all cases which could be examined experimentally and that the ratio of equivalence of the different forms of energy did not depend on how one form was converted into another or on the materials involved. The principle that Joule had established is in fact the first law of thermodynamics – that energy cannot be created nor destroyed but only transformed.

Because he had not received any formal mathematical training, Joule was unable to keep up with the new science of thermodynamics to which he had made such a fundamental and important contribution. However, the presentation of his final work on the mechanical equivalent of heat in 1847 attracted great interest and support from William Thomson, then only 22 and later to become Lord Kelvin. Much of Joule's later work was carried out with him, for Kelvin had need of Joule's experimental prowess to put his ideas on thermodynamics into practice. This led in 1852 to the discovery of the Joule–Thomson effect, which produces cooling in a gas when the gas expands freely. The effect is caused by the conversion of heat into work done by the molecules in overcoming attractive forces between them as they move apart. It was to prove vital to techniques in the liquefaction of gases and low-temperature physics.

Joule lives on in the use of his name to measure energy, supplanting earlier units such as the erg and calorie. It is an appropriate reflection of his great experimental ability and his tenacity in establishing a basic law of science.

K

Kapitza, Pyotr Leonidovich (*1894–*), is a Russian physicist who is best known for his work on the superfluidity of liquid helium. He also achieved the first high-intensity magnetic fields. For his achievements in low-temperature physics, Kapitza was awarded the 1978 Nobel Prize in Physics. He shared the prize with two Americans, Arno Penzias (1933–) and Robert Wilson (1936–), who discovered the cosmic microwave background radiation, predicted by George Gamow (1904–1968).

Kapitza was born in Kronstadt on 8 July 1894. He graduated in 1919 from Petrograd Polytechnical Institute and then travelled to Britain and worked with Ernest Rutherford (1871–1937) in Cambridge, becoming Deputy Director of Magnetic Research at the Cavendish Laboratory in 1924. In 1930 Kapitza became Director of the Mond Laboratory at Cambridge, which had been built for him. Four years later he went to the Soviet Union for a professional meeting as he had done before, but this time he did not return. His passport was seized and he was held on Stalin's orders. In 1936 he was made Director of the S.I. Vavilov Institute of Physical Problems of the Soviet Academy of Sciences in Moscow. The Mond Laboratory was sold to the Soviet government at cost and transported to the Institute for Kapitza's use. In 1946 he refused to work on the development of nuclear weapons and was put under house arrest until after Stalin's death in 1953. He was restored as Director of the Institute in 1955, a position he has held ever since.

For his graduate work, Kapitza went to Rutherford's laboratory and pioneered the production of strong (though temporary) magnetic fields. In 1924 he designed apparatus that achieved magnetic fields of 500,000 gauss, an intensity that was not surpassed for more than 30 years. In his earliest experiments, Kapitza, using especially constructed accumulator batteries and switch gear, passed currents of up to 8,000 amps through a coil for short intervals of time. In a coil of 1 mm internal diameter, fields of the order of 500,000 gauss for 0.003 second were obtained in this way. By 1927, he had produced stronger currents by short-circuiting an alternating current generator of special construction, and a field of 320,000 gauss in a volume of 2 cm^3 was obtained for 0.01 second.

Kapitza's most renowned work is in connection with liquid helium, which was first produced by Heike Kamerlingh Onnes (1853–1926) in 1908. Kapitza was one of the first to study the unusual properties of helium II – the form of liquid helium that exists below 2.2K. Helium II conducts heat far more rapidly than copper, which is the best conductor at ordinary temperatures, and Kapitza showed that this is because it flows so easily. This property of helium is known as superfluidity, and it has far less viscosity than any other liquid or gas. In 1937 Kapitza persuaded the Soviet physicist Lev Landau (1908–1968) to move to Moscow to head the theory division of his institute. Kapitza published his findings on the superfluidity of helium II in 1941. Landau then continued the work on superfluidity, resulting in the award of the 1962 Nobel Prize in Physics to him for his theory of superfluidity.

In 1939 Kapitza built apparatus for producing large quantities of liquid oxygen. This work and its application was of great importance, particularly to Soviet steel production. He invented a turbine for producing liquid air cheaply in large quantities. His technique for liquefying helium by adiabatic expansion eliminated the presence of liquid hydrogen characteristic of previous methods.

In the 1950s, Kapitza turned his attention partly to ball lightning, a puzzling phenomenon in which high-energy plasma maintains itself for a much longer period than seems likely. His analysis involves the formation of standing waves, and this research turned his interests to controlled thermonuclear fusion, upon which he published a paper in 1969.

Kapitza's award of the Nobel Prize at the age of 84 was a glowing tribute to modern science in the Soviet Union.

Kelvin, Lord (Thomson, William; *1824–1907*),

was a British physicist who first proposed the use of absolute scale of temperature, in which the degree of temperature is now called the kelvin in his honour. Thomson also made other substantial contributions to thermodynamics and the theory of electricity and magnetism, and he was largely responsible for the first successful transatlantic telegraph cable.

Kelvin was born William Thomson in Belfast on 26 June 1824. His father was the Professor of Mathematics at Belfast University and both he and his older brother James Thomson (1822–1892), who also became a prominent physicist, were educated at home by their father. In 1832 Thomson's father took up the post of Professor of Mathematics at Glasgow University, and Thomson himself entered the university two years later at the age of ten to study natural philosophy (science). In 1841, Thomson went on to Cambridge University, graduating in 1845. He then travelled to Paris to work with Henri Regnault (1810–1878) and in 1846 took up the position of Professor of Natural Philosophy at Glasgow, where he created the first physics laboratory in a British university. Among his many honours were a knighthood in 1866, the Royal Society's Copley Medal in 1883, the Presidency of the Royal Society from 1890 to 1894 and a peerage in 1892, when he took the title Baron Kelvin of Largs. Kelvin retired from his chair at Glasgow in 1899 and died at Largs, Ayrshire, on 17 December 1907.

Thomson's early work, begun in 1842 while he was still at Cambridge, was a comparison of the distribution of electrostatic force in a region with the distribution of heat through a solid. He found that they are mathematically equivalent, leading him in 1847 to conclude that electrical and magnetic fields are distributed in a manner analogous to the transfer of energy through an elastic solid. James Clerk Maxwell (1831–1879) later developed this idea into a comprehensive explanation of the electromagnetic field. From 1849 to 1859, Kelvin also developed the discoveries and theories of paramagnetism and diamagnetism made by Michael Faraday (1791–1867) into a full theory of magnetism, developing the terms magnetic permeability and susceptibility, and arriving at an expression for the total energy of a system of magnets. In electricity, Kelvin obtained an expression for the energy possessed by a circuit carrying a current and in 1853 developed a theory of oscillating circuits that was experimentally verified in 1857 and was later used in the production of radio waves.

In Paris in 1845, Kelvin was introduced to the classic work of Sadi Carnot (1796–1832) on the motive power of heat. From a consideration of this theory, which explains that the amount of work produced by an ideal engine is governed only by the temperature at which it operates, Kelvin developed the idea of an absolute temperature scale in which the temperature represents the total energy in a body. He proposed such a scale in 1848 and set absolute zero at $-273°C$, showing that Carnot's theory followed if absolute temperatures were used. However, Kelvin could not accept the idea then still prevalent and accepted by Carnot that heat is a fluid, preferring to see heat as a form of motion. This followed Kelvin's championing of the work of James Joule (1818–1889), whom Kelvin met in 1847, on the determination of the mechanical equivalent of heat. In 1851 Kelvin announced that Carnot's theory and the mechanical theory of heat were compatible provided that it was accepted that heat cannot pass spontaneously from a colder to a hotter body. This is now known as the second law of thermodynamics, which had been advanced independently in 1850 by Rudolf Clausius (1822–1888). In 1852 Kelvin also produced the idea that mechanical energy tends to dissipate as heat, which Clausius later developed into the concept of entropy.

Kelvin and Joule collaborated for several years following their meeting, Joule's experimental prowess matching Kelvin's theoretical ability. In 1852 they discovered the Joule-Thomson effect, which causes gases to undergo a fall in temperature as they expand through a nozzle. The effect is caused by the work done as the gas molecules move apart, and it proved to be great importance in the liquefaction of gases.

Kelvin was also interested in the debate then taking place about the age of the Earth. Hermann Helmholtz (1821–1894) in 1854 gave a value of 25 million years for the Earth's lifetime, assuming that the Sun gained its energy by gravitational contraction. Kelvin came to a similar conclusion in 1862, basing his estimate on the rate of cooling that would have occurred from the time the Earth formed, and reaching an age of 20 million to 400 million years with 100 million years as the most likely figure. Furthermore, the cooling would have produced volcanic upheavals that would have limited the time available for the evolution of life. Although both estimates were far too low, neither scientists knowing of the nuclear processes that fuel the Sun and the radioactivity that warms the Earth, their figures were taken seriously and helped to bring about theories of mutation to explain evolution.

Kelvin's knowledge of electrical theory was applied with great practical value to the laying of the first transatlantic telegraph cable. Kelvin pointed out that a fast rate of signalling could only be achieved by using low voltages, and that these would require very sensitive detection equipment such as the mirror galvanometer that he had invented. The first cable laid in 1857 broke and high voltages were used in the second cable laid a year later as Kelvin's predictions were not believed. The cable did not work, but a third cable laid in 1866 using Kelvin's ideas was successful, and it was for this achievement that he received a knighthood.

Kelvin was also very concerned with the accurate measurement of electricity, and developed an absolute electrometer in 1870. He was instrumental in achieving the international adoption of many of our present-day electrical units in 1881.

Kelvin was one of the greatest physicists of the nineteenth century. His pioneering work on heat consolidated thermodynamics and his understanding of electricity and magnetism paved the way for the explanation of the electromagnetic field later achieved by Maxwell.

Kennelly, Arthur Edwin (*1861–1939*), was a British-born American physicist who first predicted the existence of the ionosphere.

Kennelly was born at Colaba, near Bombay, India, on 17 December 1861. His father was an Irish naval captain and his mother a British colonist. Kennelly was educated at schools in France and England and also at University College, London. In 1876 he became a telegraph operator and from 1878 to 1886 held various jobs as an electrician. In 1887 Kennelly settled in the United States and became principal electrical assistant to Thomas Edison (1847–1931). In 1894 he set up a firm of consulting electrical engineers in Philadelphia. Kennelly took up an academic career in 1902, when he was appointed Professor of Electrical Engineering at Harvard University. He held this position until he retired in 1930, but was also Professor of Electrical Engineering at the Massachusetts Institute of Technology from 1913 to 1924. Kennelly died at Boston, Massachusetts, on 18 June 1939.

Kennelly's main interest as an electrical engineer was the laying of telegraph cables, and he made an important contribution in this field by developing complex mathematical functions to express the distribution and transmission of current and voltage in a cable. Oliver Heaviside (1850–1925) also did valuable work in telegraphy at the same time, and Kennelly's name was more firmly linked with Heaviside when both men in 1902 independently proposed that a layer of electrically charged particles must exist in the upper atmosphere in order to reflect radio waves back to the ground. This followed the epoch-making transmission of radio signals across the

Atlantic Ocean by Guglielmo Marconi (1874–1937) in 1901. The layer was called the Kennelly–Heaviside layer and in 1924 was detected at a height of about 100 km by Edward Appleton (1892–1965). It is now called the ionosphere.

Kennelly also played an important part in the international adoption of standard nomenclature and the MKS system of units, which evolved into the SI system used today.

Kerr, John (*1824–1907*), was a British physicist who discovered the Kerr effect, which produces double refraction in certain media on the application of an electric field.

Kerr was born in Ardrossan, Ayrshire, on 17 December 1824 and received his early education in Skye. He entered Glasgow University in 1941, gaining an MA in physical science in 1849. At Glasgow, Kerr became one of the first research students of Lord Kelvin (1824–1907), and received special prizes for work in magnetism and electricity. He next became a divinity student but, although he completed his course, he did not subsequently pursue a career in the Church. Kerr instead took up the post of lecturer in mathematics at the Free Church Training College for Teachers, in Glasgow, in 1857. He stayed in this post for 44 years, even though research facilities were virtually non-existent. Nevertheless Kerr set up a modest laboratory and although his publications were small in number, his work was of the highest quality. Kelvin must have had Kerr in mind when in a speech many years later he remarked that theology students made some of the best researchers and became all the better clergymen for their scientific experiences. Kerr's election to the Royal Society in 1890 and the award of its Royal Medal in 1898 were fitting recognition from a wider community of a life of modest excellence. He died at Glasgow on 18 August 1907.

Kerr's first important discovery was in 1875 when he demonstrated that birefringence or double refraction occurs in glass and other insulators when subjected to an intense electric field. A 2-inch (5 cm) block of glass had collinear holes drilled from each end until they were separated by $\frac{1}{4}$ inch (6 mm). A beam of polarized light was passed through this narrow band and at the same time an electric field was applied via electrodes inserted into the holes. Nicol prisms were arranged on either side to give extinction of the beam when the glass was free from strain. When the coil producing the field was activated, it was observed that the polarization became elliptical. The effect was strongest when the plane of polarization was 45° to the field, and zero when perpendicular or parallel. Kerr extended the work to other materials including amber and constructed, with great delicacy and manipulative skill, cells in which he could study liquids such as carbon disulphide and paraffin oil. He showed that the extent of the effect, which is more precisely called the electro-optical Kerr effect, is proportional to the square of the field strength.

In 1876 Kerr caused a considerable stir at the Glasgow meeting of the British Association when he demonstrated another remarkable phenomenon of polarized light that we know as the magneto-optical Kerr effect. In this a beam of plane-polarized light was reflected from the polished pole of an electromagnet. When the magnet was switched on the beam became elliptically polarized, the major axis being rotated from the direction of the original plane. The effect depended on the position of the reflecting surface with respect to the direction of magnetization and to the plane of incidence of the light. When both of these were perpendicular, the plane of polarization was turned through a small angle. The mathematical analysis of the effect and its relation to the electromagnetic theory of light was worked out some years later by George Fitzgerald (1851–1901).

The electro-optical Kerr effect is now applied in the Kerr cell, which is an electrically activated optical shutter having no moving parts. The cell contains a tube of liquid and crossed polarizers so that it normally transmits no light. Switching on the cell causes an electric field to produce double refraction in the liquid, allowing light to pass through the polarizers. The effect occurs because the field orientates the molecules of liquid to give double refraction, in which incident light is split into two beams that are polarized at right angles. Very fast shutter speeds are obtainable and Kerr cells have been used to make precise determinations of the speed of light.

Kirchhoff, Gustav Robert (*1824–1887*), was a German physicist who founded the science of spectroscopy. He also discovered laws that govern the flow of electricity in electrical networks and the absorption and emission of radiation in material bodies.

Kirchhoff was born at Königsberg, Germany (now Kaliningrad, USSR) on 12 March 1824. He studied at the University of Königsberg, graduating in 1847. In the following year, he became a lecturer at Berlin and in 1850 was appointed Extraordinary Professor of Physics at Breslau. Robert Bunsen (1811–1899) went to Breslau the following year and began a fruitful collaboration with Kirchhoff. In 1852 Bunsen moved to Heidelberg and Kirchhoff followed him in 1854, becoming Ordinary Professor of Physics there.

Kirchhoff stayed at Heidelberg until 1875, when he moved to Berlin as Professor of Mathematical Physics. Illness forced him to retire in 1886 and he died at Berlin on 17 October 1887.

Kirchhoff made his first important contribution to physics while still a student. In 1845 and 1846 he extended Ohm's law to networks of conductors and derived the laws known as Kirchhoff's laws that determine the value of the current and potential at any point in a network. He went on to consider electrostatic charge and in 1849 showed that electrostatic potential is identical to tension, thus unifying static and current electricity. Kirchhoff made another fundamental discovery in electricity in 1857 by showing theoretically that an oscillating current is propagated in a conductor of zero resistance at the velocity of light. This was important in the development in the 1860s of the electromagnetic theory of light by James Clerk Maxwell (1831–1879) and Ludwig Lorenz (1829–1891).

In the 1850s Bunsen developed his famous gas burner, which gave a colourless flame, and used it to investigate the distinctive colours that metals and their salts produce in a flame. Bunsen used coloured solutions and glass filters to distinguish the colours in a partly successful attempt to identify the substances by the colours they produced. Kirchhoff pointed out to Bunsen that sure identification could be achieved by using a prism to produce spectra of the coloured flames. They developed the spectroscope, and in 1860 discovered that the elements present in the substances each give a characteristic set of spectral lines and set about classifying elements by spectral analysis. In this way, Bunsen discovered two new elements – caesium in 1860 and rubidium in 1861.

Kirchhoff also made another important discovery in 1859 while investigating spectroscopy as an analytical tool. He noticed that certain dark lines in the Sun's spectrum, which had been discovered by Joseph Fraunhofer (1787–1826), were intensified if the sunlight passed through a sodium flame. This observation had in fact been made by Jean Foucault (1819–1868) ten years earlier, but he had not followed it up. Kirchhoff immediately came to the correct conclusion that the sodium flame was absorbing light from the sunlight of the same colour that it emitted, and explained that the Fraunhofer lines are due to the absorption of light by sodium and other elements present in the Sun's atmosphere.

Kirchhoff went on to identify other elements in the Sun's spectrum in this way, and also developed the theoretical aspects of this work. In 1859 he announced another important law which states that the ratio of the emission and absorption powers of all material bodies is the same at a given temperature and a given wavelength of radiation produced. From this, Kirchhoff went on in 1862 to derive the concept of a perfect black body – one that would absorb and emit radiation at all wavelengths. Balfour Stewart (1828–1887) had reached similar conclusions in 1858 by a consideration of the theory of heat exchanges discovered by Pierre Prevost (1751–1830), but Kirchhoff presented the discovery much more cogently.

Kirchhoff's contributions to physics had far-reaching practical and theoretical consequences. The discovery of spectroscopy led to several new elements and to methods of determining the composition of stars and the structure of the atom. The study of black-body radiation led directly to the quantum theory and a radical new view of the nature of matter.

Kundt, August Adolph (*1839–1894*), was a German physicist who is best known for Kundt's tube, a simple device for measuring the velocity of sound in gases and solids.

Kundt was born at Schwerin, Mecklenburg, on 18 November 1839 and educated at the Universities of Leipzig and Berlin, from which he gained his doctorate in 1864. He began his scientific career as a lecturer in 1867, becoming Professor of Physics at the Polytechnic in Zurich the following year. He subsequently took up the chair in physics at the University of Würzburg in 1869, and was one of the founders of the Strasbourg Physical Institute, established in 1872. He ultimately succeeded Hermann Helmholtz (1821–1894) as Professor of Experimental Physics and Director of the Berlin Physical Institute in 1888. Kundt died at Israelsdorf, near Lübeck, on 21 May 1894.

Kundt devised his classic method of determining the velocity of sound in 1866. A Kundt's tube is a glass tube containing some dry powder and closed at one end. Into the open end, a disc attached to a rod is inserted. When the rod is sounded, the vibration of the disc sets up sound waves in the air in the tube and a position is found in which standing waves occur, causing the dust to collect at the nodes of the waves. By measuring the length of the rod and the positions of the nodes in the tube, the velocity of sound in either the rod or air can be found, provided one of these quantities is known. By using rods made of various materials and different gases in the tube, the velocity of sound in a range of solids and gases can be determined. It is also possible using the tube to find the ratio of the molar heat capacities of a gas (and hence the atomicity) and also Young's modulus of elasticity of the material in the rod.

Kundt's later work entailed the demonstration of the dispersion of light in liquids, vapours and metals, and with Wilhelm Röntgen (1845–1923) he experimented with the Faraday effect, showing that the magnetic rotation of the plane of polarizing light occurs in gases. Kundt also published observations on the spectra of lightning and on the electrical properties of crystals.

L

Landé, Alfred (*1888–*), is a German-born American physicist known for the Landé splitting factor in quantum theory.

Landé was born in Elberfeld on 18 December 1888. He studied at the Universities of Marburg, Göttingen and Munich, gaining his DPhil from Munich in 1914. In 1919 he became a lecturer at the University of Frankfurt-am-Main until 1922, when he went to Tübingen as Associate Professor of Theoretical Physics. He visited Columbus, Ohio, in 1929 and again in 1930 and in 1931, because of the rise of the Nazi regime, left Germany for ever to settle in Columbus as Professor of Theoretical Physics at Ohio State University. He has remained there since.

Landé had just gained his doctorate under Arnold Sommerfeld (1868–1951) when World War I began in 1914. He joined the Red Cross and served for a few years in a hospital until Max Born (1882–1970) placed him as his assistant at the Artillerie-Prüfungs-Kommission in Berlin to work on sound detection methods. He collaborated with Born to conclude that Bohr's model of coplanar electronic orbits must be wrong, and that they must be inclined to each other. When they published this paper in 1918, it caused quite a stir in the scientific world. Several more papers were written, and in one of them Landé strongly advocated a tetrahedral arrangement for the four valence electrons of carbon. While at Frankfurt, Landé had the opportunity to visit Niels Bohr (1885–1962) in Copenhagen to discuss the Zeeman effect (the splitting of spectral lines in a magnetic field). Then on moving to Tübingen, he found himself at the most important centre of atomic spectroscopy in Germany. In 1923 Landé published a formula expressing a factor known as the Landé splitting factor for all multiplicities as a function of the quantum numbers of the stationary state of the atom. The Landé "splitting" factor is the ratio of an elementary magnetic moment to its causative angular momentum when the angular momentum is measured in quantized units. It determines fine as well as hyperfine structures of optical and X-ray spectra.

Landé then collaborated with Louis Paschen (1865-1947) and others to analyse in great detail the fine structure of the line spectra and the further splitting of the lines under the action of magnetic fields of increasing strength. He formulated the regularities obeyed by the frequencies and intensities of the lines in terms of the sets of quantum numbers attached to the spectroscopic terms and taking integral or half-integral values.

Langevin, Paul (*1872-1946*), was a French physicist who invented the method of generating ultrasonic waves that is the basis of modern echolocation techniques. He was also the first to explain paramagnetism and diamagnetism, by which substances are either attracted to or repulsed by a magnetic field. Langevin was the leading mathematical physicist of his time in France, and contributed greatly to the dissemination and development of relativity and modern physics in general in his country.

Langevin was born in Paris on 23 January 1872. He attended the École Lavoisier and the École de Physique et de Chimie Industrielles, where he was supervised by Pierre Curie (1859-1906) during his laboratory classes. In 1891 he entered the Sorbonne, but his studies were interrupted for a year in 1893 by the need to discharge his military service. In 1894 Langevin entered the École Normale Superieure, where he studied under Jean Perrin (1870-1942). Langevin won an academic competition which in 1897 enabled him to go to the Cavendish Laboratories at the University of Cambridge for a year. There he studied under J.J. Thomson (1856-1940), and met scientists such as Ernest Rutherford (1871-1937), Charles Wilson (1869-1959) and John Townsend (1868-1957).

Langevin received his PhD in 1902 for work done partly at Cambridge and partly under Curie on gaseous ionization. He spent a great deal of time in Perrin's laboratory, and was caught up in the excitement accompanying the early years of study on radioactivity and ionizing radiation. Langevin joined the faculty of the Collège de France in 1902, and was made Professor of Physics there in 1904, a post he held until 1909 when he was offered a similar position at the Sorbonne.

During World War I Langevin contributed to war research, improving a technique for the accurate detection and location of submarines, which continued to be developed for other purposes after the war. He became a member of the Solvay International Physics Institute in 1921, and was elected President of that organization in 1928. In 1940, after the start of World War II and the German occupation of France, Langevin became Director of the École Municipale de Physique

et de Chimie Industrielles, where he had been teaching since 1902, but he was soon arrested by the Nazis for his outspoken anti-fascist views. He was first imprisoned in Fresnes, and later placed under house arrest in Troyes. The execution of his son-in-law and the deportation of his daughter to Auschwitz (which she survived) forced Langevin to escape to Switzerland in 1944. He returned to Paris later that year and was restored to the Directorship of his old school, but died soon after in Paris on 19 December 1946.

Langevin's early work at the Cavendish Laboratories and at the Sorbonne concerned the analysis of secondary emission of X-rays from metals exposed to radiation, and Langevin discovered the emission of secondary electrons from irradiated metals independently of Georges Sagnac (1869-1928). He also studied the behaviour of ionized gases, being interested in the mobility of positive and negative ions, and in 1903 he published a theory for their recombination at different pressures. He then turned to paramagnetic (weak attractive) and diamagnetic (weak repulsive) phenomena in gases. Curie had demonstrated experimentally in 1895 that the susceptibility of a paramagnetic substance to an external magnetic field varies inversely with temperature. Langevin produced a model based on statistical mechanics to explain this in 1905. He suggested that the alignment of molecular moments in a paramagnetic substance would be random in the absence of an externally applied magnetic field, but would be non-random in its presence. The greater the temperature, however, the greater the thermal motion of the molecules and thus the greater the disturbance to their alignment by the magnetic field.

Langevin further postulated that the magnetic properties of a substance are determined by the valence electrons, a suggestion which influenced Niels Bohr (1885-1962) in the construction of his classic model describing the structure of the atom. He was able to extend his description of magnetism in terms of electron theory to account for diamagnetism. He showed how a magnetic field would affect the motion of electrons in the molecules to produce a moment that is opposed to the field. This enabled predictions to be made concerning the temperature-independence of this phenomenon and furthermore to allow estimates to be made of the size of electron orbits.

Langevin became increasingly involved with the study of Einstein's work on Brownian motion and on space and time. He was a firm supporter of the theory of the equivalence of energy and mass. Einstein later wrote that Langevin had all the tools for the development of the special theory of relativity at his disposal before Einstein proposed it himself and that if he had not proposed the theory, Langevin would have done so.

During World War I, Langevin took up the suggestion which had been made by several scientists that the reflection of ultrasonic waves from objects could be used to locate them. He used high-frequency radio circuitry to oscillate piezoelectric crystals and thus obtain ultrasonic waves at high intensity, and within a few years had a practical system for the echo-location of submarines. This method has become the basis of modern sonar and is used for scientific as well as military purposes.

Laue, Max Theodor Felix von (*1879-1960*), was a German physicist who established that X-rays are electromagnetic waves by producing X-ray diffraction in crystals. In recognition of this achievement he was awarded the 1914 Nobel Prize in Physics.

Laue was born at Pfaffendorf, near Koblenz, on 9 October 1879. He entered the University of Strasbourg in 1899, but soon transferred to the University of Göttingen, where he chose to specialize in theoretical physics. He then attended the University of Berlin, where he obtained his DPhil for a dissertation supervised by Max Planck (1858-1947) on interference theory. In 1903 Laue returned to Göttingen, where he spent two years studying art and obtained a teaching certificate. He then became an assistant to Planck at the Institute of Theoretical Physics in Berlin, cementing a long and fruitful partnership between the two scientists. Laue remained in Berlin for four years, during which time he qualified as a lecturer at the University, and became an early adherent of Einstein's special theory of relativity. He published the first monograph on the subject in 1909, which was expanded in 1919 to include the general theory of relativity and subsequently ran to several editions.

In 1909 Laue moved to the University of Munich, and became a lecturer at the Institute of Theoretical Physics, which was directed by Arnold Sommerfeld (1868-1951). It was here that he began his work on the nature of X-rays and crystal structure for which he was awarded the Nobel Prize in 1914, only two years after the research was carried out, a remarkable testimony to the importance of the work.

Laue became a full Professor at the University of Frankfurt in 1914, but spent the years of World War I at the University of Würzburg, working on the development of amplifying equipment to improve communications for the military. After the end of the war he exchanged teaching posts with Max Born (1882-1970) and went to Berlin, where he became Professor of Theoretical Physics and

Director of the Institute of Theoretical Physics.

In the 1920s and early 1930s, through the German Research Association, Laue directed the provision of financial resources for physics in Germany, thus helping to bring about the important discoveries in theoretical physics with which Germany led the world at that time. In 1932 he was awarded the Max Planck Medal by the German Physical Society. But the rise to power of Adolf Hitler in 1933 and the consequent persecution of Jewish scientists (such as Einstein) and manipulation of German science by the National Socialist Party was intolerable to Laue. His protests led to a gradual trimming of his influence and he lost his position in the German Research Association. He did, however, continue to act as Professor at the University of Berlin until 1943, when he resigned in protest. Although Laue refused to participate in the German atomic energy project, he was nevertheless interned in Britain by the allies after the war, along with other German atomic physicists.

In 1946 Laue returned to Germany where he helped to rebuild German science. He served as Deputy Director of the Kaiser Wilhelm Institute for Physics, and in 1951 became the Director of the Max Planck Institute for Research in Physical Chemistry. He died on 23 April 1960 as a result of a car accident.

Laue's early work in Berlin under Max Planck was chiefly concerned with interference phenomena. He also worked on the entropy of beams of rays, and developed a proof for Einstein's special theory of relativity based on optics. This used the verification in 1851 by Armand Fizeau (1819-1896) of a theory developed even earlier by Augustin Fresnel (1788-1827) that the velocity of light is affected by the motion of water. This seemed to be at odds with special relativity, but Laue was able to show that Fresnel's theory could be derived from the conclusions of relativity.

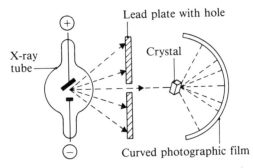

Laue laid the foundations of X-ray crystallography by demonstrating that a narrow beam of X-rays is diffracted by the regular array of atoms in a crystal lattice.

Fizeau's verification thus also became an experimental confirmation of relativity, contributing greatly to its rapid acceptance.

At the time of Laue's move to Munich in 1909, the subjects of crystal structure and the nature of X-radiation were ill-defined. It had been proposed that crystals consist of orderly arrays of atoms, and that X-rays are a type of electromagnetic radiation like light, but with very short wavelengths. The wavelength of normal monochromatic light was determined by the use of man-made diffraction gratings, but if X-rays did in fact have such short wavelengths, no grating sufficiently fine could possibly be produced with which to diffract them. Laue realized that if crystals are indeed such orderly atomic arrays, then they could be used as superfine gratings.

To test Laue's ideas, Sommerfeld's assistant Walter Friedrich and Paul Knipping, a postgraduate student, began experiments on 21 April 1912 using copper sulphate. They bombarded the crystal with X-rays and produced a photographic plate with a dark central patch representing X-rays that had penetrated straight through the crystal surrounded by a multilayered halo of regularly spaced spots representing diffracted X-rays. The results were announced to the Bavarian Academy of Science less than two weeks later along with Laue's mathematical formulation called the "theory of diffraction in a three-dimensional grating". The experimental demonstration of the nature of crystal structure and of X-rays at one strike was widely acclaimed.

Following World War I, Laue expanded his original theory of X-ray diffraction. He had initially considered only the interaction between the atoms in the crystal and the radiation waves, but he now included a correction for the forces acting between the atoms. This correction accounted for the slight deviations which had already been noticed. Laue did not participate in the development of quantum theory, however, being rather cautious in his approach to it, but he did incorporate the discovery of electron interference into his diffraction theory. He also did some important work on superconductivity, including the effect of magnetic fields on this phenomenon, publishing papers on the subject between 1937 and 1947.

Laue's achievement proved to be one of the most significant discoveries of the twentieth century. Einstein described it as one of the most beautiful discoveries in physics, and it has had a profound influence on physics, chemistry and biology. Two entirely new branches of science arose out of Laue's prize-winning work, although he had no more than passing interest in them. These were X-ray crystallography, which was developed by William Henry Bragg (1862-1942) and William Lawrence Bragg (1890-1971) and led to the determination of the structure of DNA in 1953, and X-ray spectroscopy, which was developed by Maurice De Broglie (1875-1960) and others for the exact measurement of the wavelength of X-rays and for advances in atomic theory.

Lawrence, Ernest Orlando (*1901-1958*), was an American physicist who was responsible for the concept of and the development of the cyclotron. For this achievement he was awarded the 1939 Nobel Prize in Physics. As Director of the Radiation Laboratories at Berkeley, California, he and his co-workers then produced a remarkable sequence of discoveries which included the creation of radioactive isotopes and the synthesis of new transuranic elements.

Lawrence was born in Canton, South Dakota, on 8 August 1901. He went to the University of South Dakota, where he was awarded a BS degree in 1922, and then continued his studies at the University of Minnesota, specializing in physics and gaining an MA the following year. After a further two years spent at the University of Chicago, he went to Yale University where he carried out research on photoelectricity and gained his PhD in 1925. He continued at Yale as a National Research Fellow and later as Assistant Professor of Physics until 1928. During this period he made a precise determination of the ionization potential (the energy required to remove an electron) of the mercury atom, developed methods for spark discharges of minute duration (3×10^{-9} sec), and discovered a new method of measuring the charge-to-mass ratio of the electron (e/m). Lawrence then returned to the University of California as Associate Professor of Physics and in 1930 he became, at 29, the youngest full professor (of physics) at Berkeley. Lawrence retained this position until the end of his life together with the directorship of the Radiation Laboratories, which he commenced in 1936.

During World War II, Lawrence was involved with the separation of uranium-235 and plutonium for the development of the atomic bomb, and he organized the Los Alamos Scientific Laboratories at which much of the work on this project was carried out. After the war, he continued as a believer in nuclear weapons and advocated the acceleration of their development. He died at Palo Alto, California, on 27 August 1958.

In 1929 Lawrence was pondering methods of attacking the atomic nucleus with particles at high energies. The methods then developed involved the generation of very high voltages of electricity. To Lawrence, these seemed to be very limited in the long run as the electrical engineering necessary seemed likely to be technically very difficult, and their cost would eventually prove to be prohibitive. Early that same year, he came across an article in a German periodical which described a linear device for the acceleration of ions, and Lawrence realized the potential of the design for producing high-energy particles which could be directed at atomic nuclei. On carrying out the calculation to produce a machine that would produce protons with the energy of one million electron volts, he discovered that the device would be too long for the laboratory space he had available. He therefore considered bending the accelerator so that the particles would travel in a spiral.

This idea led to the cyclotron, which had two electrodes that were hollow and semicircular in shape mounted in a vacuum between the poles of a magnet. In between the two electrodes was the source of the particles. To the electrodes was connected a source of electricity whose polarity could be oscillated, positive and negative, from one electrode to the other at very high frequency. The negative field caused the particles to turn in a circular path in each electrode and each time they crossed between the electrodes they received an impetus which accelerated them further, giving them more and more energy without involving very high voltages. As this happened, the increased velocity carried the particles farther from the centre of the apparatus, producing a spiral path.

The first cyclotrons were made in 1930 and were only a few centimetres in diameter and of very crude design. They were made by Nels Edlefsen, one of Lawrence's research students, and

one of them showed some indication of working. Later the same year M. Stanley Livingston, another of Lawrence's research students, constructed a further small, but improved device which accelerated protons to 80,000 electron volts with 1,000 volts used on the electrodes. Once the principle had been seen to work well, larger and improved devices were made. Each new design produced particles of higher energy than its predecessor and new results were obtained from the use of the accelerated particles in nuclear transformations. One of these was the disintegration of the lithium nucleus to produce helium nuclei, confirming the first artificial transformation made by John Cockcroft (1897–1962) and Ernest Walton (1903–   ) in 1932, and a 68 cm model was used to produce artificial radioactivity. With increasing size, the engineering problems associated with power supplies and the production of large magnetic fields increased, and in 1936 the Radiation Laboratory with the necessary engineering and administrative facilities was opened to house the new equipment.

From his laboratory, a multitude of discoveries in chemistry, physics and biology were made under Lawrence's direction. Hundreds of radioactive isotopes were produced, including carbon-14, iodine-131 and uranium-233. Furthermore, over the years, most of the transuranium elements were synthesized. Mesons, which were then little known particles, were produced and studied within a laboratory for the first time at the Radiation Laboratory, and anti-particles were also found. Many of these discoveries owe their origin to other famous scientists who worked within the laboratory, but Lawrence worked tirelessly advising researchers and in making the experiments possible. Fairly early in the development of the cyclotron it became apparent that as particles were accelerated to high speeds their masses increased, as predicted by the special theory of relativity. This increase in mass caused them to lose synchronization with the oscillating electric field. The solution of this problem by Vladimir Veksler (1907–1966) and Edwin McMillan (1907–   ) independently led to the development of the synchrotron and particles of even higher energies.

Lawrence made an important contribution to physics with the invention of cyclotron, for the subsequent development of high-energy physics and the elucidation of the subatomic structure of matter was highly dependent on this machine and its successors. These have also provided radio-isotopes of great value in medicine. Appropriately, Lawrence's name is remembered in the naming of element 103 as lawrencium, for it was discovered in his laboratory at Berkeley.

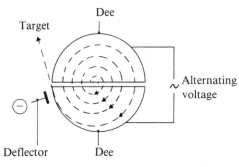

Lawrence's original cyclotron consisted of two D-shaped chambers maintained in a vacuum. Positive ions were accelerated across the gap between them by a high-frequency alternating voltage and deflected into a spiral path by powerful magnets above and below the dees.

Lebedev, Pyotr Nikolayevich (*1866-1912*), was a Russian physicist whose most important contribution to science was the detection and measurement of the pressure that light exerts on bodies, an effect that had been predicted by James Clerk Maxwell in his electromagnetic theory of light.

Lebedev was born in Moscow on 8 March 1866. He initially received training in business and engineering in Moscow but decided that he would rather be a physicist and so went to the University of Strasbourg to study physics under August Kundt. His teacher moved to Berlin in 1888 and Lebedev tried to follow him but found that he did not possess the qualifications necessary to enrol in Berlin University, and so he returned to Russia in 1891. On his return he joined the physics department of Moscow Univeristy - at the invitation of the head of the department, A.G. Stoletov - and became Professor of Physics there in the following year, although he did not obtain his PhD until 1900. In 1911 government interference in university affairs caused a storm of protest, which led to the resignation of many of the university's staff, including Lebedev. Although he was subsequently offered numerous prestigious positions at other universities, both in Russia and elsewhere, the shock of the upheaval precipitated a collapse of his health and he died shortly afterwards, on 14 March 1912 (in Moscow).

Lebedev began studying light pressure (now called radiation pressure) in the late 1890s but did not complete his investigations until 1910. Working first with solid bodies and later with gases, he not only observed the minute physical effects caused by the infinitesimal pressure exerted by light on matter but also measured this pressure using extremely lightweight apparatus in an evacuated chamber. His findings provided substantial supportive evidence for Maxwell's theory of electromagnetic radiation, which had predicted the phenomenon of light pressure. Also, Lebedev suggested that the force of the light pressure emanating from the Sun could balance the gravitational force attracting cosmic dust particles towards it, and that this was the reason why comets' tails point away from the Sun. Later, however, it was discovered that comets' tails point away from the Sun because of the much greater effect of the solar wind. The Swedish chemist Svante Arrhenius (1859-1927) took up the idea of light pressure to explain how primordial spores might have travelled through space in his theory of the extraterrestrial origin of life. This model has not become widely accepted because it does not explain how the spores themselves originated nor how the travelling spores could endure the intense cosmic radiation in outer space.

Lebedev also investigated (while working for his doctorate) the effects of electromagnetic, acoustic and hydrodynamic waves on resonators; demonstrated the behavioural similarities between light and (as they are now known to be) other electromagnetic radiations; detected electromagnetic waves of higher frequency than the radio waves that had been studied by Heinrich Hertz and Augusto Righi; and researched into the Earth's magnetic field.

Leclanché, Georges (*1839-1882*), was a French engineer who invented the Leclanché battery or dry cell in 1866. This is the kind of battery used today in torches, calculators, portable radios, and so on.

Leclanché was born in Paris in 1839. Educated at the École Centrale des Arts et Manufactures, he joined the Compagnie du Chemin de l'Est as an engineer in 1860. Six years later, he developed his electric cell, which consisted of a zinc anode and a carbon cathode separated by a solution of ammonium chloride. The following year, in 1867, he gave up his job as a railway engineer to devote all his time to the improvement of the cell's design. He was successful in having it adopted by the Belgian Telegraphic Service in 1868.

The Leclanché cell rapidly came into general use whenever an intermittent supply of electricity was needed and it was later developed into the familiar dry battery in use today. Towards the end of his life, Leclanché diversified his researches and worked for a while on electrical methods of time measurement. He died in Paris on 14 September 1882.

Almost any electrolytic cell with electrodes of different materials can act as a battery. The first cells to be invented were wet cells made by Alessandro Volta (1745-1827) in 1800. They were made of tin or copper and zinc or silver separated by pasteboard or hide soaked in water, vinegar or salt solution. These first electric batteries, although cumbersome, caused a revolution by making comparatively large amounts of electric current available for the first time. The revolution was carried even further when Leclanché produced the first dry cell, which facilitated both handling and mobility. Leclanché's investigations into new kinds of electrodes and electrolyte enabled him to make the advance that he did. Volta's cell prompted several other types of cell, among them a design by Robert Bunsen (1811-1899) for a battery containing carbon and zinc electrodes and an acid such as chromic acid as the electrolyte. Leclanché produced the most useful design of all by having zinc for the negative pole,

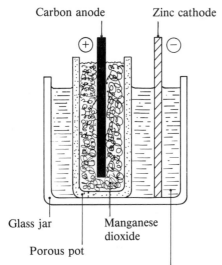

Carbon anode   Zinc cathode

Glass jar   Manganese dioxide

Porous pot

Ammonium chloride solution

The wet Leclanché cell has a zinc cathode immersed in an ammonium chloride electrolyte, and a carbon anode in a depolarizer of manganese dioxide and carbon granules contained in a porous pot.

carbon for the positive pole and a solution of ammonium chloride as the electrolyte. This first cell was the forerunner of all subsequent dry cells in that it was sealed so that the outside stayed dry.

Although there are other types of dry cells in existence today, such as those using mercury, the Leclanché cell is still the only one produced on a large scale. In the modern dry Leclanché cell, zinc serves both as the container and anode, the cathode is formed from graphite, and the electrolyte is a paste of ammonium chloride, zinc chloride, manganese dioxide and carbon particles. The cell produces 1.5 volts.

Lenard, Philipp Eduard Anton (*1862-1947*), was a Hungarian-born German physicist who devised a way of producing beams of cathode rays (electrons) in air, enabling electrons to be studied. This led him to the first conclusion that an atom is mostly empty space, and Lenard was awarded the 1905 Nobel Prize in Physics as a result. He also did pioneering research on the photoelectric effect.

Lenard was born on 7 June 1862 at Pozsony, Hungary (now Bratislava, Czechoslovakia), but spent most of his life in Germany. He studied physics at Heidelberg under Robert Bunsen (1811-1899) and at Berlin under Hermann Helmholtz (1821-1894), receiving a doctorate in 1886 from Heidelberg. He spent a further three years as an assistant at Heidelberg and in 1891 became assistant to Heinrich Hertz (1857-1894) at Bonn,

assuming command of Hertz's laboratory on his early death in 1894. He then took an associate professorship at Breslau the same year, then moved in turn to Aachen in 1895, Heidelberg in 1896 and Kiel, where he was appointed Professor of Experimental Physics in 1898. He then held the same post at Heidelberg from 1907 to 1931. Lenard became a follower of Hitler, the only eminent scientist to do so, in 1924 and spent his later years reviling Jewish scientists such as Albert Einstein (1879-1955). He was antagonistic by nature and in his book *Great Men of Science* (1934), he omitted Wilhelm Röntgen (1845-1923) and several other eminent modern scientists who had had priority disputes with him, who had criticized Lenard's work or whose work Lenard considered inferior to his own. Lenard died in Messelhausen, Germany, on 20 May 1947.

Lenard's initial studies were in mechanics investigating the oscillation of precipitated water drops, work no doubt stimulated by his regard for the studies of Hertz. In his youth Lenard had been fascinated by the phenomena of luminescence and later with his knowledge of science he returned to the topic. He studied the luminosity of pyrogallic acid in the presence of alkali and sodium hydrogen sulphite, establishing that the crucial factor was the oxidation of the acid. He continued to look at luminescent compounds for 20 years along with his main field of study.

Lenard's principal contribution to physics can be traced back to work begun in 1892. Inspired by William Crookes (1832-1919), who in 1879 had published a paper on the movement of cathode rays in discharge tubes, Lenard conceived an experiment to examine these rays outside the tube. He was then assistant to Hertz, who had shown that a piece of uranium glass covered with aluminium foil and put inside the discharge tube became luminescent when struck by cathode rays. Lenard developed a technique using aluminium foil as a window in a discharge tube, and showed that the cathode rays could move about 8 cm through the air after passing through the thin aluminium window. Since the cathode rays were able to pass through the foil, he suggested that the atoms in the metal must consist of a large proportion of empty space. A further conclusion of greater significance to later work was that the part of the atom where the mass was concentrated consisted of neutral doublets or "dynamids" of negative and positive electricity. This proposal preceded by ten years the classic model of the atom proposed by Ernest Rutherford (1871-1937) in 1911.

Lenard had at his fingertips a great knowledge of electricity. He devised the grid in the thermionic valve that controls electron flow. He also showed that an electron must have a certain minimum energy before it can produce ionization in a gas. From 1902 onwards, Lenard studied photoelectricity and discovered several fundamental effects. He showed that negative electricity can be released from metals by exposure to ultraviolet light and later found that this electricity was identical in properties to cathode rays (electrons). He also discovered that the energy of the electrons produced depends on the wavelength of the light incident on the metal. He explained that the release of electrons was caused by a resonance effect intensified by vibrations induced by the ultraviolet light. Einstein in 1905 provided a correct explanation of photoelectricity by using the quantum theory, which Lenard rejected.

Philipp Lenard was a gifted experimental physicist who was able to build on the earlier work of other scientists, enabling theoretical physicists to use his results to delve deeper into the structure of matter. Many of his discoveries are fundamental to our understanding of atomic physics.

Lenz, Heinrich Friedrich Emil (*1804–1865*), was a Russian physicist who is known for Lenz's law, which is a fundamental law of electromagnetism.

Lenz was born in Dorpat, now Tartu in the Estonian Soviet Socialist Republic, on 12 February 1804. He graduated from secondary education in 1820 and entered the University of Dorpat, where he studied chemistry and physics. His physics teacher recommended Lenz for the post of geophysical scientist to accompany Otto von Kotzebue (1787–1846) on his third expedition around the world, which lasted from 1823 to 1826. Upon his return, Lenz was appointed scientific assistant at the St Petersburg Academy of Science, later becoming Associate Academician in 1830 and Full Academician in 1834. From 1840 to 1863, Lenz was Dean of Mathematics and Physics at the University of St Petersburg, where he was also elected Rector. He was also the author of a number of very successful books which ran to many editions. Lenz died after suffering a stroke while on holiday in Rome on 10 February 1865.

Lenz's major fields of study were geophysics and electromagnetism. While on his voyage with Kotzebue, he studied climatic conditions such as barometric pressure, finding the areas of maximum and minimum pressure that exist in the tropics and determine the overall climatic pattern. Lenz also made a careful investigation of water salinity, discovering areas of maximum salinity either side of the equator in the Atlantic and Pacific Oceans and establishing the differences in salinity between these oceans and the Indian Ocean. Lenz also made extremely accurate measurements of the temperature and specific gravity of sea water. His geophysical observations of the oceans were not bettered until the following century.

In 1829 Lenz went on a mountaineering expedition to the Caucasus in southern Russia, where he made a study of some of the natural resources of the area as well as making measurements of mountain heights and of the level of the Caspian Sea.

Lenz's studies of electromagnetism date from 1831, following the discovery in that year of electromagnetic induction by Michael Faraday (1791–1867) and Joseph Henry (1797–1878). Lenz's first major discovery was that the direction of a current which is induced by an electromagnetic force always opposes the direction of the electromagnetic force that produces it. This law was published in 1833 and it is known as Lenz's law. When a moving magnet or coil produces a current by induction in a conductor, the induced current flows in such a direction that it in turn produces a magnetic field that opposes the motion of the magnet or coil inducing the current. This means that work has to be done by the magnet or coil to produce current, and Lenz's law is in fact a special case of the law of conservation of energy. If the induced current were to flow in the opposite direction, it would assist the motion of the magnet or coil and a perpetual-motion machine would result because energy would increase without any work being done, which is impossible. Lenz's law later helped Hermann Helmholtz (1821–1894) to formulate the law of conservation of energy, and it is applied today in electrical machines such as generators and electric motors.

Around the same time, Lenz also began to study the relationship between heat and current and discovered, independently of James Joule (1818–1889), the law now known as Joule's law which describes the proportional relationship between the production of heat and the square of the current. Lenz also found that the strength of a magnetic field is proportional to the strength of the magnetic induction. He also worked on the application of certain theoretical principles to engineering design, on formulating programs for geographical expeditions, and on establishing the unit for the measurement of electrical resistance. A final major area of study was electrochemistry where in the 1840s, he made a series of investigations into additivity laws.

Lindemann, Frederick Alexander (*1886–1957*), was a British physicist who was involved with Hermann Nernst (1864–1941) in advancing the quantum theory. He later became Lord Cherwell and played an important role in the administration of British science during and after World War II.

Lindemann was born in Baden-Baden, Germany, on 5 April 1886. He went to school in Scotland and Germany, and attended the University of Berlin where he gained his PhD in 1910. Lindemann remained at Berlin until 1914, when he returned to Britain and during World War I became Director of the RAF Physical Laboratory, where he was concerned with aircraft stability. In 1919, Lindemann became Professor of Experimental Philosophy at Oxford, building up the Clarendon Laboratory into an important scientific institution. In 1941, he was granted a peerage and took the title of Lord Cherwell. Lindemann was Paymaster-General from 1942 to 1945 and again from 1951 to 1953. In this position he gave valuable advice to the British government, helping to direct scientific research during World War II and to create the Atomic Energy Authority afterwards. Lindemann returned to Oxford from 1945 to 1951 and from 1953 to 1956, when he retired. He was then instrumental in founding Churchill College, Cambridge, to promote the study of technology. Lindemann was awarded the Hughes Medal of the Royal Society in 1956, and died at Oxford on 3 July 1957.

Lindemann's main contributions to physics were made in his early years at Berlin, where he studied with and later assisted Nernst. Nernst and Lindemann together made an important advance in quantum theory in 1911 by constructing a special calorimeter and measuring specific heats at very low temperatures. They confirmed the specific heat equation proposed by Albert Einstein (1879-1955) in 1907, in which he used the quantum theory to predict that the specific heats of solids would become zero at absolute zero. Lindemann also derived a formula which relates the melting point of a crystalline solid to the amplitude of vibration of its atoms.

In World War I, Lindemann developed a theory to explain why the aircraft of that time were liable to spin out of control. He then worked out a way of recovering from a spin and successfully tested it himself.

Lissajous, Jules Antoine (*1822-1880*), was a French physicist who developed Lissajous figures for demonstrating wave motion.

Lissajous was born at Versailles on 4 March 1822. He was educated at the École Normale Supérieure from 1841 to 1847, when he became Professor of Physics at the Lycée Saint-Louis. He became Rector of the Academy of Chambéry in 1874, and then took up the same position at Besançon in 1875. In 1879 Lissajous was elected a member of the Paris Academy, and he died at Plombières on 24 June 1880.

Lissajous was interested in acoustics and from 1855 developed Lissajous figures as a means of visually demonstrating the vibrations that produce sound waves. He first reflected a light beam from a mirror attached to a vibrating object such as a tuning fork to another mirror that rotated. The light was then reflected onto a screen, where the spot traced out a curve whose shape depended on the amplitude and frequency of the vibration. Lissajous then refined this method by using two mirrors mounted on vibrating tuning forks at right angles, and produced a wider variety of figures. By making one of the forks a standard, the acoustic characteristics of the other fork could be determined by the shape of the Lissajous figure produced.

Lissajous figures can now be demonstrated on the screen of an oscilloscope by applying alternating currents of different frequencies to the deflection plates. The curves produced depend on the ratio of the frequencies, enabling signals to be compared with each other.

Lizhi, Fang (*1936-*), is a Chinese astrophysicist who has researched into various aspects of cosmology, laser emission and nuclear physics but who is probably best known in the West for the important part he has played in helping to free Chinese science from political restrictions.

Lizhi was born in 1936, one of six children of a railway mechanic. A talented child, he entered Peking University when he was only 16 years old to study science, and graduated in theoretical physics four years later, in 1956. After graduating he joined the Academia Sinica's Institute of Modern Physics, working on an experimental nuclear reactor, then in 1958 became an assistant lecturer at Peking University, working in the field of solid state physics. In 1962 he published (with the President of the Institute of Physics) the first paper on the line width of laser emission.

In the mid-1960s the political situation in China became increasingly unstable, and in 1966 the university was effectively closed and turned over to political discussion. Lizhi, like most other academics, had to spend six months of the year working in the fields with the peasants for "re-education". From 1967 to 1971 the situation remained bad and Lizhi, with other outspoken critics of the regime, was, in effect, interned in an isolated part of the university campus, allowed neither to work nor to go home. The only scientific book to which he had access was a work on general relativity, and it was his reading of this that turned his attention towards astrophysics.

In 1972, after the death of the ultra left-wing

political leader Lin Piao, life for Lizhi and other scientists improved markedly and he published a paper on cosmology. But this paper was severely – and pseudonymously – criticized and although the President of Peking University prevented further attacks, Lizhi himself was not allowed to reply to his critics. Faced with such restrictions, he continued to advocate greater freedom of expression and the exclusion of politics from science. As a result of his and others' efforts, attitudes to science in China gradually improved and the Chinese scientific community became freer to exchange ideas with foreign scientists, by such means as foreign exchange visits, for example. Lizhi himself has visited many universities in the United States and for a short period was a Senior Visiting Fellow at Cambridge University. He is now Professor of Physics at the Peking University of Science and Technology, working in the field of astrophysics.

Lodge, Oliver Joseph (*1851–1940*), was a British physicist who was among the pioneers of radio. He also proved that the ether does not exist, a discovery that proved fundamental to the development of relativity.

Lodge was born at Penkhull, Staffordshire, on 12 June 1851, where his father supplied clay and other materials for the pottery industry. As the eldest son, Lodge entered his father's firm at the age of 14 and worked there for six years. In 1871, he began to study science at London University, at first while still working part-time for his father. He obtained his BSc in 1873 followed by a DSc on electrical topics in 1877.

Lodge became the first Professor of Physics at the University of Liverpool on its founding in 1881, and there carried out his most important experimental work. In 1900 he moved to the University of Birmingham to become its first Principal. Among many subsequent honours were a knighthood in 1902 and the presidency of the British Association for the Advancement of Science in 1913. Lodge retired in 1919. Following the death of his son in World War I, he became interested in psychic phenomena and devoted much of his later life to psychical research. Lodge died at Lake near Salisbury on 22 August 1940.

Lodge's first significant paper concerned the shape of lines of force and equipotential lines between two electrodes applied to conducting surfaces. He also proposed how a Daniell Cell could be modified in order that it might be used as a standard for e.m.f. measurements. During the 1880s, Lodge devoted a great deal of time to experiments involving the discharge of electricity from Leyden jars. Two of his sons extended this work, which was then used as the basis of the

high-tension electric ignition system used in early internal combustion engines.

Lodge also began work on the production of electromagnetic waves, following the prediction by James Clerk Maxwell (1831–1879) that such waves must exist. He came close to achieving Maxwell's prediction, but was just anticipated by Heinrich Hertz (1857–1894) in 1888. Lodge then turned to methods of detecting the waves and invented a coherer, a device consisting of a container packed with metal granules whose electrical resistance varies with the passage of electromagnetic radiation. This was developed into a detector of radio waves in the early investigations of radio communication, with which Lodge was closely involved.

Lodge's other major contribution to science was made in 1893 following the classic Michelson-Morley experiments of 1881 and 1887. These had failed to detect the ether that was postulated as a medium for the propagation of light waves. This result could be explained by the ether moving with the Earth, but Lodge disproved this unlikely cause in a clever experiment in which light rays were passed between two rotating disks. The resulting interference effects showed the ether does not exist, providing one of postulates – that all motion is relative – on which Albert Einstein (1879–1955) built the special theory of relativity.

Lorentz, Hendrik Antoon (*1853–1928*), was a Dutch physicist who helped to develop the theory of electromagnetism, which was recognized by the award (jointly with his pupil Pieter Zeeman) of the 1902 Nobel Prize in Physics.

Lorentz was born in Arnhem, Holland, on 18 July 1853. He was educated at local schools and at the University of Leyden, which he left at the age of 19 to return to Arnhem as a teacher while writing his PhD thesis on the theory of light reflection and refraction. By the time he was 24 he was Professor of Theoretical Physics at Leyden. He remained there for 39 years, before taking up the Directorship of the Teyler Institute in Haarlem where he was able to use the museum's laboratory facilities. He died in Haarlem on 4 February 1928.

Much of Lorentz's work was concerned with James Clerk Maxwell's theory of electromagnetism and his development of it became fundamental to Albert Einstein's Special Theory of Relativity. Lorentz attributed the generation of light by atoms to oscillations of charged particles (electrons) within them. This theory was confirmed in 1896 by the discovery of the Zeeman effect, in which a magnetic field splits spectral lines.

In 1904 Lorentz extended the work of George

FitzGerald to account for the negative result of the Michelson-Morley experiment and produced the so-called Lorentz transformations, which mathematically predict the changes to mass, length and time for an object travelling at near the speed of light.

Lorenz, Ludwig Valentin (*1829–1891*), was a Danish mathematician and physicist who made important contributions to our knowledge of heat, electricity and optics. He is, however, relatively little known, partly because he published most of his work in Danish and partly because of his idiosyncratic mathematical style.

Lorenz was born in Elsinore on 18 January 1829. He graduated in civil engineering from the Technical University in Copenhagen. He then taught at a teacher-training college and at the Military Academy in Copenhagen, becoming Professor of Physics at the latter in 1876. After 1887, however, he received sufficient financial support from the Carlsberg Foundation to be able to devote himself entirely to research. He died in Copenhagen on 9 June 1891.

Lorenz is perhaps best known for his work on optics and electromagnetic theory. Early in his investigations he found that the theoretical models describing the nature of light were contradictory and incompatible, and he therefore concentrated his efforts on studying the transmission of light rather than its nature. He investigated the mathematical description for light propagation through a single homogeneous medium and also described the passage of light between different mediums. His most famous discovery was the mathematical relationship between the refractive index and the density of a medium. This formula was published by Lorenz in 1869 and by Hendrick Lorentz (who discovered it independently) in 1870 and is therefore called the Lorentz-Lorenz formula. Today it is usually given as

$$R = \frac{n^2 - 1}{n^2 + 1} \cdot \frac{M}{\rho}$$

where R is the molecular refractivity, n is the refractive index, M is the molecular weight and ρ is the density. Also in 1869 Lorenz published an experimental verification (for water) of the formula. In addition, he studied birefringence (double refraction) and wrote a paper on the electromagnetic theory of light in 1867 – after James Clerk Maxwell's theory had been published in Britain but at a time when it was almost unknown elsewhere in Europe. Lorenz's approach was different from that of Maxwell and he was able to derive a correct value for the velocity of light using his theories.

Lorenz's other main major contribution to science was his discovery of what is now called Lorenz's law. Relating a metal's thermal conductivity (λ) and its electrical conductivity (σ) to its absolute temperature (T), the law is usually stated mathematically as (λ/σ) α T. A believer in combining theory and experiment, he performed a series of experiments to test his law and thereby confirmed its validity.

Lorenz also did basic work on the development of the continuous loading method for reducing current losses along cables, and helped to establish the ohm as the internationally accepted unit of electrical resistance. His work in pure mathematics included studies of prime numbers and Bessel functions, which are widely used in mathematical physics.

Lummer, Otto Richard (*1860–1925*), was a German physicist who specialized in optics and is particularly remembered for his work on thermal radiation. His investigations led directly to the radiation formula of Max Planck (1858–1947), which marked the beginning of quantum theory.

Lummer was born in Jena, Saxony, on 17 July 1860. He attended a number of different German universities, which was a common practice at the time, and in 1884 wrote his doctoral dissertation at Berlin on work conducted in the department of Hermann Helmholtz (1821–1894). Lummer then became an assistant to Helmholtz and moved with him to the newly established Physikalische Technische Reichsanstalt in Berlin in 1887. Lummer became a member of this research institute in his own right in 1889, and in 1894 was made professor there. In 1904, he was appointed Professor of Physics at Breslau (now Wroclaw, Poland), and he died there on 5 July 1925.

Lummer's early research was on interference fringes produced by internal reflection in mica plates. These fringes had in fact been noted before, but were nevertheless named Lummer fringes. His next area of study concerned the establishment of an international standard of luminosity. This work was done in collaboration with Eugen Brodhun, and they designed a photometer named the Lummer–Brodhun cube. This represented a considerable improvement on the grease-spot photometer which Robert Bunsen (1811–1899) had originated.

The study of radiant heat then attracted Lummer's attention. As a black body is a perfect heat absorber, a black-body radiator was believed to be the most efficient transmitter of thermal radiation. However, until that time, it was considered to be merely a theoretical object. Lummer and Wilhelm Wien (1864–1928) made a practical black-body radiator by making a small aperture in a hollow sphere. When heated to a particular temperature, it behaved like an ideal black body.

In 1898 Lummer and Ernst Pringsheim (1859-1917) began a quantitative study on emission from black bodies. They were able to confirm Wien's displacement law, which is used to determine the temperature of a black body spectroscopically and has been applied to stellar temperature determinations, but found an anomaly in Wien's radiation law. Their result was confirmed by another research group headed by Heinrich Rubens (1865-1922) and Ferdinand Kurlbaum (1857-1927), who extended the work. These studies were of critical significance in the development of Planck's radiation formula, which was presented to the Berlin Physical Society on 19 October 1900 and marks the beginning of quantum theory.

Lummer's early work on interference fringes led him in 1902 to the design of a high-resolution spectroscope. Ernst Gehrcke improved it by adding a prism, and the Lummer-Gehrcke interference spectroscope was a great advance on its predecessor, the interferometer designed by Charles Fabry (1867-1945) and Alfred Perot (1863-1925).

Other areas which interested Lummer were the subject of solar radiation and the problem of obtaining a source of monochromatic illumination. In the former area, he managed to obtain an estimate for the temperature of the Sun, and in the latter he designed a mercury vapour lamp, which is still used when monochromatic light is required, for instance in fluorescence microscopy.

Lyman, Theodore (*1874-1954*), was an American physicist famous for his spectroscopic work in the ultraviolet region.

Lyman was born in Boston on 23 November 1874. His father was a marine biologist devoted to the interests of Harvard College, where Lyman also spent his scientific career. Lyman came from a wealthy family and after 1885 lived at the ancestral mansion built by his grandfather at Brookline, Massachusetts. Lyman entered Harvard in 1893 with tastes leaning towards physical sciences. In his first year, he took and passed a course in physics. In his second and third years, he worked hard at electrical engineering and might well have gone on to make a career of it had it not been for the influence of Wallace Sabine (1868-1919), who lectured to Lyman in optics. Lyman was offered an assistantship in physics and gained a BA in 1897 followed by a PhD in 1900. During the winter of 1901-1902 he studied under J.J. Thomson (1856-1940) at Cambridge and then spent the summer of 1902 in Göttingen. On his return to Harvard, he became an instructor, progressing to assistant professor in 1907. In

1921, he became Hollis Professor of Mathematics and Natural Philosophy. He held this position for five years and then retired Emeritus in 1925, fifteen years before the official retiring age. It was generally thought that he retired to have more freedom. From 1910 to 1947, he also held the position of Director of the Jefferson Physical Laboratory. Lyman received many honours, among them the presidencies of the American Physical Society from 1921 to 1922 and the American Academy of Arts and Sciences from 1924 to 1927. He died after a long illness at Brookline on 11 October 1954.

Lyman's scientific work was confined to the spectroscopy of the extreme ultraviolet region. When he was commencing his research, the observable spectrum had been extended into the ultraviolet as far as 1260 Å by Victor Schumann (1841-1913), who enclosed the entire spectroscope in an evacuated chamber to eliminate absorption by air and by using fluorite for windows, lenses and prisms. Although Schumann had obtained a wealth of new spectroscopic lines beyond 2000 Å, the wavelengths could not be exactly determined without knowledge of the index of refraction of the fluorite of his prism.

Sabine suggested that Lyman should try a concave ruled grating instead of a fluorite prism. Success took seven years. False lines of a new kind were found in the Schumann range due to light in the visible region. These came to be called Lyman ghosts and gave Lyman the subject for his PhD thesis. By 1906, he had published reports of more than 300 lines due to hydrogen in the 1675-1228 Å region and another 50 probably due to hydrogen in the 1228-1030 Å region. He established the limit of transparency of fluorite to be 1260 Å and looked at the absorbency of other suitable solids but found none better. He also examined the absorption of various gases.

At the beginning of the century, spectroscopic analysis had received an enormous boost because of the discovery of the mathematical regularities shown by many spectra. This was very important in substantiating the quantum theory of atomic structure proposed by Niels Bohr (1885-1962) in 1913. Two series of hydrogen spectra had been found, the Paschen series and the Balmer series. The wave number v of each line in these series is given by the expression $v = R(l/m^2 - 1/n^2)$ where R is the Rydberg constant and n is an integer greater than m, which has the value 3 for the Paschen series and 2 for the Balmer series. Johann Balmer (1825-1898), who discovered this relationship, had predicted the existence of a series of lines in the ultraviolet in which m would be equal to 1. Lyman announced the discovery of the first three members of this series in 1914, and it was named the Lyman series. He predicted that the first line, the Lyman alpha, would be present in the Sun's spectrum but absorption by the Earth's atmosphere prevented Lyman from observing it. The line was eventually photographed by a rocket five years after Lyman's death, and ultraviolet observation of the Sun by satellite has since become very important in solar research.

By 1917, Lyman had extended the spectrum to 500 Å. War service and then college administration subsequently reduced his scientific output, and others continued to extend the spectrum further. Lyman turned to spectroscopic examination of elements other than hydrogen, the first being helium. In 1924, seven lines were tabulated in the principal series of helium and Lyman made the rare observation of the continuous spectra beyond the limit of this series due to the recapture of free electrons of different kinetic energies. Papers followed on a series of spectra in the ultraviolet region of aluminium, magnesium and neon. Lyman's last paper was published in 1935 on the transparency of air between 1100 and 1300 Å. Towards the end of his life, Lyman suffered a very sore hand from excess exposure to ultraviolet radiation, and impaired eyesight.

Lyman was also a keen traveller and collector. His most important trip was to the Altai mountains of China and Mongolia. He brought back the first specimen of a gazelle which became named *Procapra altaica* and also 13 previously unknown smaller mammalian species. A stoat became known as Lyman's stoat, *Mustela lymani*.

M

Mach, Ernst (*1838–1916*), was an Austrian physicist whose name was given to the Mach number, the velocity of a body in a medium relative to the speed of sound in that medium. Mach also made an important contribution to science in a fundamental reappraisal of scientific thought. He sought to understand knowledge in the context of the physiological, sensory and psychological processes that govern and limit its acquisition. This led him to question mechanical explanations of matter and the Universe that could not be adequately observed, and to favour more conceptual or mathematical explanations. This approach to science had a profound influence on Albert Einstein (1879–1955) in the formulation of the general theory of relativity.

Mach was born in Chirlitz-Turas, then in Austria-Hungary but now in Czechoslovakia, on 18 February 1838. His family moved to Unter Siebenbrunn near Vienna in 1840. He was almost entirely educated at home by his parents until the age of 15, when he entered the local Gymnasium. He was most impressed by the study of natural science and, in particular, enjoyed the lessons of his teacher of natural history, a man named F.X. Wessely. Mach began his studies at the University of Vienna in 1855 and was awarded his PhD in 1860 for a thesis on electricity. While in Vienna he was influenced by Gustav Fechner (1801–1887), who worked on "psychophysics" or the physiology of perception.

Mach lectured at the University, and also earned extra money by giving popular lectures on a variety of scientific topics. He published two books in 1863, one on physics for medical students and the other on psychophysics. He moved to Graz in 1864 where he became Professor of Mathematics and, in 1866, Professor of Physics. He then went to the University of Prague in 1867, where he was appointed Professor of Experimental Physics.

Mach remained in Prague for 28 years, conducting many research projects and publishing many books and lectures. He served as Rector to the University from 1882 to 1884. In 1895 he became Professor of History and Theory of Inductive Sciences at the University of Vienna. He suffered a stroke in 1897, which caused paralysis of his right side and from which he made only a slow recovery. He retired from the University in 1901, and was appointed to the upper chamber of the Austrian parliament, a post he held for 12 years. In 1913, Mach moved to his son's home in Vaterstetten, near Munich, Germany. He continued to write books and died there on 19 February 1916.

Mach's early work in Vienna was in the department of Andreas von Ettingshausen, who had succeeded Johann Doppler (1803–1853) as Professor of Experimental Physics. Accordingly, Mach's research was aimed at investigating Doppler's then controversial law which described the relationship between the perceived frequency of sound and light and the motion of the observer relative to that of the source. Mach also investigated vibration and resonance. His interest in subjects which his colleagues saw as being only of peripheral interest, such as perception, was active even in these early days. His book on psychophysics, published in 1863, examined the complex physiological problems associated with vision and Mach concluded that the reductionist mechanistic approach had not given satisfactory explanations of phenomena.

At Graz, Mach was forced to fund his research out of his own pocket and lacking equipment for investigations into physics, he continued to study subjects like vision, hearing and our sense of time. He investigated stimulation of the retinal field with spatial patterns and discovered a strange visual effect called Mach bands. This was subsequently forgotten, and was rediscovered in the 1950s.

In Prague, Mach was able to turn to issues of a more physical nature. He made a long theoretical study of mechanics and thermodynamics. He did not, however, abandon his other interests. Among his projects were a study of the kinesthetic sense and how it responds to body movements, more work on Mach bands, investigations of hearing and vision, various aspects of optics, and wave phenomena of mechanical, electrical and optical kinds. One of Mach's most important contributions arose from his work, published in 1887, on the photography of projectiles in flight, which showed the shock wave produced by the gas around the tip of the projectile. The Mach angle describes the angle between the direction of motion and the shock wave, and Mach found that it varies with the speed of the projectile, the flow of gas changing its character when the projectile reaches the speed of sound. This came to be very important in aerodynamics and particularly in supersonic flight, and in 1929 the term Mach number came into use to describe the ratio of the velocity of an object to the speed of sound in the medium in which the object is moving. An aircraft flying at Mach 2 is therefore flying at twice the speed of sound in air at that particular height.

Mach's philosophy of science – although he would never have described it in those terms, feeling himself to be a scientist and not a philosopher – included an investigation of modern science based on an analysis of the sequence of previous developments. He felt that the very order in which discoveries had been made altered their content and that this was an important factor to bear in mind when assessing their value and meaning. Mach was very suspicious of any model which could not be tested in at least an indirect fashion. Because they could not be observed, he was forced to reject the theory of atoms (which was in his day quite inaccurate, but became less crude towards the end of his life) as being merely a hypothesis which had got out of hand. He was considered quite eccentric by many of his colleagues for whom atomism was an exciting development. However in that it subsequently became increasingly difficult to explain atoms as concrete objects and theoretical physicists turned to mathematical and statistical treatments of the energies and positions of atomic particles to obtain more valid descriptions of the atom, Mach can be said to be vindicated in his approach and

his views did in fact aid the development of quantum mechanics.

One of Mach's most important books was *Die Mechanik* which appeared in 1863. This gave rise to an enduring debate on Mach's principle, which states that a body could have no inertia in a Universe devoid of all other mass as inertia depends on the reciprocal interaction of bodies, however distant. This principle influenced Einstein who tried to find a mathematical formulation to describe it, playing a role in Einstein's thinking which culminated in his explanation of gravity in the general theory of relativity.

Mach was greatly displeased to find that he was being hailed as a predecessor of relativity, a model which he rejected. He intended to write a book criticizing Einstein's theory, but died before this was possible.

Mach postulated that all knowledge is mediated by perception, and believed that the greatest scientific advances would only arise through a deeper understanding of this process. His stubborn scepticism forced him into a somewhat isolated position, but he was subsequently respected by scientists as great as Einstein. Mach is remembered as a scientist skilled not only at experimental design, execution and interpretation but also at thinking about the wider implications of his work – a rare quality.

Maiman, Theodore Harold (*1927-*), is an American physicist who is best known for constructing (in 1960) the first working laser.

Maiman was born in Los Angeles on 11 July 1927, the son of an electrical engineer. After a period of military service (1945 to 1946) in the United States Navy, he studied engineering and physics at Columbia University, obtaining his BS degree in 1949. He then moved to Stanford University to do postgraduate work, gaining his MS in electrical engineering in 1951 and his PhD in physics in 1955. From 1955 to 1961 – the period in which he built the first laser – he worked at the Hughes Research Laboratories. In 1962 he founded his first company, the Korad Corporation (of which he was the President until 1968), which became a leading developer and manufacturer of lasers. In 1968 he founded Maiman Associates, a laser and optics consultancy, and four years later he co-founded the Laser Video Corporation, of which he was Vice-President until 1975. In that year he joined the TRW Electronics Company, Los Angeles, as Director of Advanced Technology.

On moving to the Hughes Research Laboratories in 1955, Maiman began working on the maser, the first working model of which had been built in 1953 by Charles Townes. Maiman made a number of design improvements that increased the practicability of the solid-state maser, then set out to develop an optical maser, or laser (an acronym for *Light Amplification by Stimulated Emission of Radiation*). Although Townes and A.L. Schawlow published a paper in which they demonstrated the theoretical possibility of constructing a laser and started to build one themselves, it was Maiman who actually constructed the first working laser in 1960. His laser consisted of a cylindrical, synthetic ruby crystal with parallel, mirror-coated ends, the mirror coating at one end being semi-transparent to allow the emission of the laser beam. A "flash lamp" provided a burst of intense white light, part of which was absorbed by the chromium atoms in the ruby which, as a result, were stimulated to emit non-coherent red light. This red light was then reflected back and forth by the mirrored ends of the ruby until eventually some of the light emerged through the semi-transparent end as an intense beam of coherent, monochromatic red light – laser light. Maiman's apparatus produced pulses of laser light; the first continuous-beam laser was made in 1961 by Ali Javan at the Bell Telephone Laboratories.

Since its original development, numerous improvements have been made to the laser and, using materials other than synthetic ruby (gases, for example), it is now possible to generate laser light of almost any frequency; even tunable lasers have been constructed. Moreover, the laser has found many practical applications – as a "light scalpel" in microsurgery, in astronomy, spectroscopy, chemistry and physics, in holography (a type of three-dimensional photography) and in communications, to give but a few examples.

Malus, Étienne Louis (*1775–1812*), was a French physicist who discovered polarized light. He found that light is not only polarized on passing through a double-refracting crystal but also on reflection from a surface.

Malus was born in Paris on 23 June 1775. He received private instruction in the classics and mathematics until the age of 18. After a year in military service, he became one of the first students to enter the École Polytechnique in Paris. He studied there for only two years without receiving any diplomas, and then became a sublieutenant in the engineers' corps in 1796. Malus sent on Napoleon's campaign in Egypt and Syria in 1798, but contracted a serious infection and was sent home to Marseilles in 1801. He then undertook postings to Lille in 1802, Anvers in 1804, and Strasbourg in 1806. During this period, Malus was able to resume his scientific activities. He became an examiner for the École Polytech-

nique in geometry, analysis and physics, which caused him to make frequent visits to Paris. This allowed him to renew his contacts with many other scientists.

Malus was recalled to Paris permanently in 1808, and in 1810 was elevated to the rank of major. His scientific career reached its peak in the same year with the award of a prize from the French Institute and his election to its first class. In addition Malus was awarded the Rumford Medal by the Royal Society in 1811. However, his health had been seriously undermined by the illness he suffered abroad and he died of tuberculosis in Paris on 23 February 1812 at the early age of 37.

Malus' research in the field of optics may be traced as far back as his period in Egypt under Napoleon, when he found the time to work on the nature of light. His first important publication appeared in 1807. It was entitled *Traité d'Optique*, and was notable for its mathematical style. In it he put forward the equation which was later known as the Malus theorem, which described some of the differences in the properties of light following a second reflection or refraction as distinct from its properties following the first reflection or refraction. This theorem was given a full mathematical proof by William Rowan Hamilton (1805–1865) in 1824, who also extended the work.

Malus began doing experiments on double refraction in 1807. This phenomenon, which was first found in 1669 by Erasmus Bartholin (1625–1698), causes a light beam to split into two beams on passing through Iceland spar and certain other crystals. The French Institute offered a prize in 1808 for an experimental and theoretical explanation of double refraction, and this encouraged Malus to continue his work in this area. Christiaan Huygens (1629–1695) had found empirical laws to describe double refraction, but they were based on the assumption that light is wave-like in character, a theory that was not popular with those scientists who held with Newton's belief in its particulate nature. However, Malus' results confirmed Huygens' laws, and in 1810 he was awarded the French Institute's prize for his experiments and also for his theoretical deduction of the laws. The method he used in his analysis was the same as that which Pierre Laplace (1749–1827) had applied to the same problem a year previously.

A more important result of Malus' investigations was announced soon after its discovery in 1808. Malus held a piece of Iceland spar up to some light reflecting off the windows of the Luxembourg Palace in Paris. To his surprise, the light beam emanating from the crystal was single, not double. He further noted that of the two beams that normally emerge from the crystal, only one was reflected from a water surface if the crystal was held at a certain angle. The other passed into the water and was refracted. If the crystal was turned perpendicular, the second beam was reflected and the first refracted. The effect was most intense at an angle of reflection that varied from one medium to another. Malus concluded that light reflected from a surface behaves in the same way as the beams of light emerging after double refraction in a crystal. Although he had confirmed Huygens' laws of double refraction, Malus still believed that light consisted of particles which have sides or poles, and he thought that in the two refracted beams, the particles were lined up in planes perpendicular to each other. He described the light as being "polarized" in perpendicular directions and thus concluded that light is also polarized on reflection from surfaces. He found too that the reflected ray is polarized in one plane while the refracted ray that passes into the surface is polarized in the perpendicular plane. Malus also discovered the law of polarization that relates the intensity of the polarized beam to the angle of reflection.

Malus' work on polarization was continued by David Brewster (1781–1868), Jean Biot (1774–1862) and François Arago (1786–1853) after his untimely death. His explanation of polarization was rationalized by Augustin Fresnel (1788–1827) who, in 1821, concluded that light exists as transverse waves.

Malus was a talented scientist who made a major discovery but whose research was curbed by his devotion to his military duties and by his poor health and early death.

Maxwell, James Clerk (*1831–1879*), was a British physicist who discovered that light consists of electromagnetic waves and established the kinetic theory of gases. He also proved the nature of Saturn's rings and demonstrated the principles governing colour vision.

Maxwell was born at Edinburgh on 13 November 1831. He was educated at Edinburgh Academy from 1841 to 1847, when he entered the University of Edinburgh. He then went on to study at Cambridge in 1850, graduating in 1854. He became Professor of Natural Philosophy at Marischal College, Aberdeen, in 1856 and moved to London in 1860 to take up the post of Professor of Natural Philosophy and Astronomy at King's College. On the death of his father in 1865, Maxwell returned to his family home in Scotland and devoted himself to research. However in 1871 he was persuaded to move to Cambridge, where he became the first Professor of Experimental Physics and set up the Cavendish Laboratory, which

opened in 1874. Maxwell continued in this position until 1879, when he contracted cancer. He died at Cambridge on 5 November 1879, at the early age of 48.

Maxwell demonstrated his great analytical ability at the age of 15, when he discovered an original method for drawing a perfect oval. His first important contribution to science was made from 1849 onwards, when Maxwell applied himself to colour vision. He revived the three-colour theory of Thomas Young (1773–1829) and extended the work of Hermann Helmholtz (1821–1894) on colour vision. Maxwell showed how colours could be built up from mixtures of the primary colours red, green and blue, by spinning discs containing sectors of these colours in various sizes. In the 1850s, he refined this approach by inventing a colour box in which the three primary colours could be selected from the Sun's spectrum and combined together. Maxwell confirmed Young's theory that the eye has three kinds of receptors sensitive to the primary colours and showed that colour blindness is due to defects in the receptors. He also explained fully how the addition and subtraction of primary colours produces all other colours, and crowned this achievement in 1861 by producing the first colour photograph to use a three-colour process. This picture, the ancestor of all colour photography, printing and television, was taken of a tartan ribbon by using red, green and blue filters to photograph the tartan and to project a coloured image.

Maxwell worked on several areas of enquiry at the same time, and from 1855 to 1859 took up the problem of Saturn's rings. No-one could give a satisfactory explanation for the rings that would result in a stable structure. Maxwell proved that a solid ring would collapse and a fluid ring would break up, but found that a ring composed of concentric circles of satellites could achieve stability, arriving at the correct conclusion that the rings are composed of many small bodies in orbit around Saturn.

Maxwell's development of the electromagnetic theory of light took many years. It began with the paper *On Faraday's Lines Of Force* (1855–1856), in which Maxwell built on the views of Michael Faraday (1791–1867) that electric and magnetic effects result from fields of lines of force that surround conductors and magnets. Maxwell drew an analogy between the behaviour of the lines of force and the flow of an incompressible liquid, thereby deriving equations that represented known electric and magnetic effects. The next step towards the electromagnetic theory took place with the publication of the paper *On Physical Lines Of Force* (1861–1862). Here Maxwell developed a model for the medium in which electric and magnetic effects could occur. This could throw some light on the nature of lines of force. He devised a hypothetical medium consisting of an incompressible fluid containing rotating vortices responding to magnetic intensity separated by cells responding to electric current.

By considering how the motion of the vortices and cells could produce magnetic and electric effects, Maxwell was successful in explaining all known effects of electromagnetism, showing that the lines of force must behave in a similar way. However Maxwell went further, and considered what effects would be caused if the medium were elastic. It turned out that the movement of a charge would set up a disturbance in the medium, forming transverse waves that would be propagated through the medium. The velocity of these waves would be equal to the ratio of the value for a current when measured in electrostatic units and electromagnetic units. This had been determined by Friedrich Kohlrausch (1840-1910) and Wilhelm Weber (1804-1891), and it was equal to the velocity of light. Maxwell thus inferred that light consists of transverse waves in the same medium that causes electric and magnetic phenomena.

Maxwell was reinforced in this opinion by work undertaken to make basic definitions of electric and magnetic quantities in terms of mass, length and time. In *On The Elementary Regulations Of Electric Quantities* (1863), he found that the ratio of the two definitions of any quantity based on electric and magnetic forces is always equal to the velocity of light. He considered that light must consist of electromagnetic waves, but first needed to prove this by abandoning the vortex analogy and arriving at an explanation based purely on dynamic principles. This he achieved in *A Dynamical Theory Of The Electromagnetic Field* (1864), in which he developed the fundamental equations that describe the electromagnetic field. These showed that light is propagated in two waves, one magnetic and the other electric, which vibrate perpendicular to each other and to the direction of propagation. This was confirmed in Maxwell's *Note On The Electromagnetic Theory of Light* (1868), which used an electrical derivation of the theory instead of the dynamical formulation, and Maxwell's whole work on the subject was summed up in *Treatise On Electricity And Magnetism* in 1873.

The treatise also established that light has a radiation pressure, and suggested that a whole family of electromagnetic radiations must exist of which light was only one. This was confirmed in 1888 with the sensational discovery of radio waves by Heinrich Hertz (1857-1894). Sadly,

Maxwell did not live long enough to see this triumphant vindication of his work. He also did not live to see the ether (the medium in which light waves were said to be propagated) disproved with the classic experiments of Albert Michelson (1852-1931) and Edward Morley (1838-1923) in 1881 and 1887, which Maxwell himself suggested in the last year of his life. However this did not discredit Maxwell as his equations and description of electromagnetic waves remain valid even though the waves require no medium.

Maxwell's other major contribution to physics was to provide a mathematical basis for the kinetic theory of gases. Here he built on the achievements of Rudolf Clausius (1822-1888), who in 1857 to 1858 had shown that a gas must consist of molecules in constant motion colliding with each other and the walls of the container. Clausius developed the idea of the mean free path, which is the average distance that a molecule travels between collisions. As the molecules have a high velocity, the mean free path must be very small, otherwise gases would diffuse much faster than they do and have greater thermal conductivities.

Maxwell's development of the kinetic theory was stimulated by his success in the similar problem of Saturn's rings. It dates from 1860, when he used a statistical treatment to express the wide range of velocities that the molecules in a quantity of gas must inevitably possess. He arrived at a formula to express the distribution of velocity in gas molecules, relating it to temperature and thus finally showing that heat resides in the motion of molecules - a view that had been suspected for some time. Maxwell then applied it with some success to viscosity, diffusion and other properties of gases that depend on the nature of the motion of their molecules.

However, in 1865, Maxwell and his wife carried out exacting experiments to measure the viscosity of gases over a wide range of pressure and temperature. They found that the viscosity is independent of the pressure and that it is very nearly proportional to the absolute temperature. This later finding conflicted with the previous distribution law and Maxwell modified his conception of the kinetic theory by assuming that molecules do not undergo elastic collisions as had been thought but are subject to a repulsive force that varies inversely with the fifth power of the distance between them. This led to new equations that satisfied the viscosity-temperature relationship, as well as the laws of partial pressures and diffusion.

However, Maxwell's kinetic theory did not fully explain heat conduction, and it was modified by Ludwig Boltzmann (1844-1906) in 1868, resulting in the Maxwell–Boltzmann distribution law. Both men thereafter contributed to successive refinements of the kinetic theory and it proved fully applicable to all properties of gases. It also led Maxwell to an accurate estimate of the size of molecules and to a method of separating gases in a centrifuge. The kinetic theory, being a statistical derivation, also revised opinions on the validity of the second law of thermodynamics, which states that heat cannot of its own accord flow from a colder to a hotter body. In the case of two connected containers of gases at the same temperature, it is statistically possible for the molecules to diffuse so that the faster-moving molecules all concentrate in one container while the slower molecules gather in the other, making the first container hotter and the second colder. Maxwell conceived this hypothesis, which is known as Maxwell's demon. Even though this is very unlikely, it is not impossible and the second law can therefore be considered to be not absolute but only highly probable.

Maxwell is generally considered to be the greatest theoretical physicist of the 1800s, as his forebear Faraday was the greatest experimental physicist. His rigorous mathematical ability was combined with great insight to enable him to achieve brilliant syntheses of knowledge in the two most important areas of physics at that time. In building on Faraday's work to discover the electromagnetic nature of light, Maxwell not only explained electromagnetism but paved the way for the discovery and application of the whole spectrum of electromagnetic radiation that has characterized modern physics. In developing the kinetic theory of gases, Maxwell gave the final proof that the nature of heat resides in the motion of molecules.

Mayer, Julius Robert (*1814–1878*), was a German physicist who was the first to formulate the principle of conservation of energy and determine the mechanical equivalent of heat.

Mayer was born in Heilbronn on 25 November 1814 and received a classical and theological education there. In 1832 he went to the University of Tübingen to study and in spite of being expelled in 1837 for membership of a student secret society, he managed to qualify as a doctor with distinction in the following year. In 1840, he took a position as a ship's physician and sailed to East Indies for a year. He then settled in his native city and built up a prosperous medical practice. In 1842, Justus Liebig (1803–1873) published Mayer's classic paper on the conservation of energy in his *Annalen der Chemie*. This was followed by two papers that Mayer himself published. In 1845, he extended his ideas into the world of living things and in 1848 to the Sun, Moon and Earth. Disappointed at the lack of recognition and despairing because others were making the same discoveries independently and gaining priority, Mayer tried to kill himself in 1850. He was then confined to mental institutions during the 1850s, but from 1858 he at last began to gain the credit he deserved, principally by the efforts of Hermann Helmholtz (1821–1894), Rudolf Clausius (1822–1888) and John Tyndall (1820–1893). As a result, Mayer was recognized by the scientific world, receiving the Royal Society's Copley Medal in 1871. Mayer died in Heilbronn on 20 March 1878.

Mayer's conviction that the various forms of energy are interconvertible arose from an observation made during his voyage to the East. He found while blood letting that the venous blood of the European sailors was much redder in the tropics than at home. Mayer put this down to a greater concentration of oxygen in the blood caused by the body using less oxygen, as less heat was required in the tropics to keep the body warm. From this, Mayer made a conceptual leap to the idea that work such as muscular force, heat such as body heat and other forms of energy such as chemical energy produced by the oxidation of food in the body are all interconvertible. The amount of work or heat produced by the body must be balanced by the oxidation of a certain amount of food, and therefore work or energy is not created but only transformed from one form to another.

This in essence is the principle of conservation of energy, which Mayer conceived as an idea but without any evidence to prove it in 1840. On returning to his home, he set about learning physics in order to prove his conviction. In fact, other scientists had been working towards the same conclusions but no-one had yet formulated them so widely as Mayer. In 1839, Marc Seguin (1786–1875) had made a rough estimate of the mechanical equivalent of heat, assuming that the loss of heat represented by the fall of temperature of steam on expanding was equivalent to the mechanical work produced by the expansion. He also remarked that it was absurd to suppose that "a finite quantity of heat could produce an indefinite quantity of mechanical action and that it was more natural to assume that a certain quantity of heat disappeared in the very act of producing motive power".

In 1842, Mayer stated the equivalence of heat and work more definitely. He published an attempt to determine the mechanical equivalent of heat from the heat produced when air is compressed. He made the assumption that the whole of the work done in compressing the air was converted into heat, and by using the specific heats of air at constant volume and constant pressure, he was able to reach a value for the mechanical equivalent solely on theoretical grounds. He concluded that the heat required to raise the temperature of 1 kg of water by 1°C would be equivalent to the work done by a mass of 1 kg in falling 365 m. This result is about 15 per cent too low, but this was mainly due to the inaccuracy of the values for specific heats that Mayer had to use. James Joule (1818–1889) made the first accurate derivation experimentally in 1847, and credit for the determination of the mechanical equivalent of heat goes to him. But Mayer had clearly demonstrated the validity of the principle of conservation of energy and is generally regarded as its founder, though Helmholtz expressed it in a much clearer and more specific way in 1847.

In 1845, Mayer extended the principle of the interconvertibility and conservation of energy to magnetism, electricity, chemical energy and to the living world. He described the energy conversions that take place in living organisms, realizing that plants convert the Sun's energy into food that is consumed by animals to provide a source of energy to power their muscles and provide body heat. By insisting that living things are powered solely by physical processes utilizing solar energy and not by any kind of innate vital force, Mayer took a daring step forward and laid the foundations of modern physiology.

Mayer's paper of 1848 was concerned with astronomy. He realized correctly that chemical reactions could not provide enough energy to power the Sun, and proposed incorrectly that the Sun produces heat by meteoric bombardment. But he also calculated that tidal friction caused by the Moon's gravitation gradually slows the Earth's rotation, an effect now known to exist. However, like most of Mayer's ideas, this was later proposed independently by others.

Mayer was a very bold thinker and it is unfortunate that his lack of experimental ability and his position outside the scientific community prevented him from securing the proofs and immediate recognition that his ideas deserved. However in conceiving the principle of conservation of energy and applying it to all processes in the Universe both living and non-living, he made a discovery of fundamental importance to science.

Meitner, Lise (*1878–1968*), was an Austrian-born Swedish physicist who was one of the first scientists to study radioactive decay and the radiations emitted during this process. Her most famous work was done in 1938 in collaboration with Otto Frisch (1904–1979), her nephew, on describing

for the first time the splitting or fission of the uranium nucleus under neutron bombardment. This publication provoked a flurry of research activity and was of pivotal importance in the development of nuclear physics.

Meitner was born in Vienna on 7 November 1878. She became interested in science at an early age, but before studying physics, her parents insisted that she should first qualify as a French teacher in order to be certain of supporting herself. She passed the examination in French and then entered the University of Vienna in 1901. She obtained her PhD from that University, becoming only the second woman to do so, in 1905, her thesis work on thermal conduction having been supervised by Ludwig Boltzmann (1844–1906).

In 1907, Meitner entered the University of Berlin to continue her studies under Max Planck (1858–1947). She met Otto Hahn (1875–1966) soon after arriving in Berlin. He was seeking a physicist to work with him on radioactivity at the Kaiser-Wilhelm Institute for Chemistry. Meitner joined Hahn, but their supervisor Emil Fischer (1852–1919) would not allow Meitner to work in his laboratory because she was a woman, and they had to set up a small laboratory in a carpenter's work room. Despite this inauspicious start, Meitner became a member of the Kaiser-Wilhelm Institute in 1912, and in 1917 was made joint Director of the Institute with Hahn and was also appointed head of the Physics Department.

In 1912 Meitner had also become an assistant to Planck at the Berlin Institute of Theoretical Physics. She was appointed Docent at the University of Berlin in 1922, and then made extraordinary Professor of Physics in 1926. Meitner, who was Jewish, remained in Berlin when the Nazis came to power in 1933 because she was protected by her Austrian citizenship. However the German annexation of Austria in 1938 deprived her of this citizenship and placed her life in danger. With the aid of Dutch scientists, she escaped to Holland and soon moved to Denmark as the guest of Niels Bohr (1885–1962). She was then offered a post at the Nobel Physical Institute in Stockholm, where a cyclotron was being built, and Meitner accepted. It was shortly after her arrival in Sweden that Meitner and Frisch, who was working at Bohr's Institute in Copenhagen, made the discovery of nuclear fission.

During World War II, Meitner was invited to participate in the development program for the construction of the nuclear bomb, but she refused in the hope that such a weapon would not be feasible. In 1947, a laboratory was established for her by the Swedish Atomic Energy Commission at the Royal Institute of Technology, and she later moved to the Royal Swedish Academy of Engineering Science to work on an experimental nuclear reactor. In 1949, she became a Swedish citizen. In 1960 she retired from her post in Sweden and settled in Cambridge, England. The Fermi Award was given jointly to Meitner, Hahn and Fritz Strassmann (1902–) in 1966, Meitner being the first woman to be so honoured. She died in Cambridge on 27 October 1968.

Meitner's early work in Berlin with Hahn concerned the analysis of physical properties of radioactive substances. Hahn's primary interest lay in the discovery of new elements, but Meitner's work was concerned with examining radiation emissions. They were able to determine the beta line spectra of numerous isotopes, leading to the discovery of protactinium in 1918. During the 1920s, Meitner studied the relationship between beta and gamma irradiation. She examined the basis for the continuous beta spectrum, her results leading Wolfgang Pauli (1900–1958) to postulate the existance of the neutrino. She was the first to describe the emission of Auger electrons, which occurs when an electron rather than a photon is emitted after one electron drops from a higher to a lower electron shell in the atom.

The rapid developments in physics during the 1930s, such as the discovery of the neutron, artificial radioactivity and the positron, did not leave Meitner behind. In 1933 she used a Wilson cloud chamber to photograph positron production by gamma radiation and in the following year, she began to study the effects of neutron bombardment on uranium with Hahn. They were interested in confirming results of Enrico Fermi (1901–1954) that suggested the production of transuranic elements, i.e. elements with atomic numbers higher than that of uranium (92). In 1935 Meitner and Hahn used a hydrogen sulphide precipitation method to remove elements with atomic numbers between 84 and 92 from their neutron-irradiated sample of uranium. They thought that they had found evidence for elements with atomic numbers of 93, 94, 95 and 96. Then in 1938, after Meitner was forced to flee from Germany, Hahn and Strassmann found that the radioactive elements produced by neutron bombardment of uranium had properties like radium. From Sweden, Meitner requested firm chemical evidence for the identities of the products. Hahn and Strassmann were surprised to find that the neutron bombardment had produced not transuranic elements but three isotopes of barium, which has an atomic number of 56.

Meitner and Frisch realized that these results indicated that the uranium nucleus had been split into smaller fragments. They predicted correctly that krypton would also be found among the products of this splitting process, which they named fission. A paper describing their analysis appeared in January 1939, and immediately set in motion a series of discoveries leading to the first nuclear reactor in 1942 and the first atomic bomb in 1945.

Meitner had also found evidence for the production of uranium-239 by the capture of a neutron by uranium-238. Beta decay of this new, heavy isotope would yield a transuranic element with the atomic number 93. This element was found by Edwin McMillan (1907–) and Philip Abelson (1913–) in 1940 and named neptunium.

Meitner continued to study the nature of fission products and contributed to the design of an experiment whereby fission products of uranium could be collected. Her later research concerned the production of new radioactive species using the cyclotron, and also the development of the shell model of the nucleus.

Meitner was a distinguished scientist who made important contributions to nuclear physics despite having to overcome both sexual and racial discrimination.

Michelson, Albert Abraham (*1852–1931*), was a German-born American physicist who, in association with Edward Morley (1838–1923), performed the classic Michelson–Morley experiment for light waves. Michelson also made very precise determinations of the velocity of light. This work entailed the development of extremely sensitive optical equipment, and in recognition of his achievements in optics and measurement, Michelson was awarded the 1907 Nobel Prize in Physics, becoming the first American to gain a Nobel Prize.

Michelson was born in Strelno in Germany, now Strzelno in Poland, on 19 December 1852. His family emigrated to the United States while he was a young child and eventually settled in Nevada. Michelson went to school in San Francisco and then tried unsuccessfully to enter the US Naval Academy at Annapolis. However, he was allowed to plead his case with the President of the United States, Ulysses S. Grant, who directed that Michelson be admitted in 1869. After graduating in 1873, Michelson spent two years at sea and was then appointed as an instructor in physics and chemistry at the Academy. From 1880 to 1882, Michelson undertook postgraduate study at Berlin under Hermann Helmholtz (1821–1894) and at Paris. On returning to the United States, he left the navy and was appointed Professor of Physics at the Case School of Applied Science in Cleveland, Ohio. In 1889 Michelson moved to Clark University at Worcester, Massachusetts, and then in 1892 became Professor of Physics at the University of Chicago, a position he held until 1929. Among his honours were the presidency of the American Physical Society from 1901 to 1903 and the award of the Royal Society's Copley Medal in 1907. Michelson died on 9 May 1931.

Michelson began his scientific career in 1878, when he improved the rotating-mirror method of Jean Foucault (1819–1868) to determine the velocity of light. This led to the construction of an interferometer to detect any difference in the velocity of light in two directions at right angles. In this instrument, a beam was split into two beams at right angles. Each was sent to a mirror and the reflected beams were made to interfere with each other. The interference pattern produced was recorded and the interferometer turned through a right angle. If there was any difference in the velocity of light, it would cause the light to take different times to traverse the

same paths and a change would occur in the interference pattern produced. Michelson built the interferometer to make an experiment suggested by James Clerk Maxwell (1831–1879) to detect the motion of the Earth through the ether, which was believed to exist as the medium in which light waves were propagated. If the Earth were moving through the ether, light would travel slower in the direction of the Earth's motion than at right angles to it. The amount of change in the interference pattern produced in the interferometer would indicate how fast the Earth was moving through the ether.

Michelson first undertook this experiment at Berlin in 1881. He could detect no change in the interference pattern and so later set about constructing a much more sensitive interferometer in collaboration with Morley, with whom Michelson began to work in 1885. The experiment was repeated in 1887 and still no effect due to the ether was found. This was a disappointment to Mich-

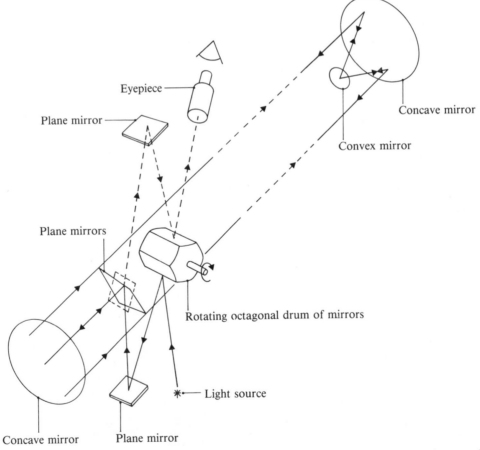

Eyepiece

Plane mirror

Concave mirror

Convex mirror

Plane mirrors

Rotating octagonal drum of mirrors

Light source

Concave mirror

Plane mirror

Michelson determined the velocity of light by using a rotating drum faced with eight or more mirrors to time a light beam over a distance of more than 70 km.

elson, and he set about finding other uses for the interferometer. However the experiment, which is now known as the Michelson-Morley experiment, marked a turning point in theoretical physics, for its negative result demonstrated that the velocity of light is constant whatever the motion of the observer. Two explanations could account for this. One was that the ether does exist but moves with the Earth; this was disproved by Oliver Lodge (1851-1940) in 1893. The other was that the ether does not exist but that moving objects contract slightly in the direction of their motion. This was put forward by George Fitz-Gerald (1851-1901) and became part of the special theory of relativity proposed by Albert Einstein (1879-1955) in 1905. Thus the Michelson-Morley experiment was of crucial importance in the formulation of relativity, though Michelson himself remained sceptical.

Michelson's other achievements were concerned with extremely precise measurement. In 1892 and 1893, he and Morley redefined the length of the standard metre kept at Paris in terms of a certain number of wavelengths of monochromatic light, using a red line in the cadmium spectrum. This method of defining the standard unit of length was finally adopted in 1960, and a krypton line is now used.

Michelson also developed his interferometer into a precision instrument for measuring the diameters of heavenly bodies and in 1920 announced the size of the giant star Betelgeuse, the first star to be measured. Michelson then undertook extremely precise determinations of the velocity of light, measuring it over a 35-km path between two mountain peaks in California. In 1926, he obtained the value $299,796 \pm 4$ km per sec., the range including the present value of $299,792.5$ km per sec.

Michelson later returned to the Michelson-Morley experiment and repeated it yet again to try and produce a positive result. He did not succeed a third time, and this helped to verify Einstein. No one else has succeeded since.

Michelson's gift for extremely precise experimental work enabled him to make one of the most important discoveries in physics. It is ironic that only such ability could yield the negative result that was required for a new understanding of the nature of the Universe.

Millikan, Robert Andrews (*1868-1953*), was an American physicist who made the first determination of the charge of the electron and of Planck's constant. For these achievements, he was awarded the 1923 Nobel Prize in Physics.

Millikan was born at Morrison, Illinois, on 22 March 1868. He showed no interest in science as

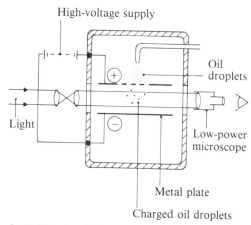

In Millikan's oil-drop experiment, oil droplets fell through fine holes in the upper of two charged metal plates, and by measuring the velocity of the charged droplets he determined the charge on them – a multiple of the charge on the electron.

a child and became interested in physics only after entering Oberlin College in 1886, where he obtained his BA in 1891 and MA in 1893. Millikan then went to Columbia University to continue his studies in physics, gaining his PhD in 1895. He then went to Germany to study with Max Planck (1858-1947) at Berlin and Hermann Nernst (1864-1941) at Göttingen before taking up an assistantship in physics at the University of Chicago in 1896.

Millikan remained at Chicago until 1921. At first he concentrated on teaching but from 1907, when he became Associate Professor of Physics, he took more interest in research and began his experiments to find the electronic charge, completing this work in 1913. In 1910, Millikan became Professor of Physics at Chicago and during World War I was director of research for the National Research Council, which was concerned with defence research. In 1921, Millikan moved to Pasadena to become Director of the Norman Bridge Laboratory at the California Institute of Technology. He retained this position until 1945, when he retired. In addition to the 1923 Nobel Prize in Physics, Millikan received many honours, including the award of the Royal Society's Hughes Medal in 1923 and the Presidency of the American Physical Society from 1916 to 1918. Millikan died at Pasadena on 19 December 1953.

Millikan employed a method to determine the electronic charge that was simple in concept but difficult in practice, and a satisfactory result took him the five years from 1908 to 1913 to achieve. He began by studying the rate of fall of water droplets under the influence of an electric field.

Millikan conjectured correctly that the droplets would take up integral multiples of the electronic charge, which he would be able to compute from the strength of field required to counteract the gravitational force on the droplets. By 1909, Millikan had arrived at an approximate value for the electronic charge. However, the droplets evaporated too quickly to make precise determination possible and Millikan switched to oil droplets. These were far less volatile and furthermore Millikan was able to irradicate the suspended droplets to vary their charge. In 1913, Millikan finally announced a highly accurate value for the electronic charge that was not bettered for many years.

Millikan also worked on a study of the photoelectric effect during this period, investigating the interpretation of Albert Einstein (1879–1955) that the kinetic energy of an electron emitted by incident radiation is proportional to the frequency of the radiation multiplied by Planck's constant. Millikan took great pains to improve the sensitivity of his apparatus and announced in 1916 that Einstein's equation was valid, thereby obtaining an accurate value for Planck's constant.

After World War I, Millikan moved into two new areas of research. In the 1920s, he investigated the ultraviolet spectra of many elements, extending the frequency range and identifying many new lines. Millikan also undertook a thorough programme of research into cosmic rays, a term that he coined in 1925, when he proved that the rays do come from space. Millikan did this by comparing the intensity of ionization in two lakes at different altitudes. He found that the intensity was the same at different depths, the absorptive power of the difference in the depth of water being equal to the absorptive power of the depth of atmosphere between the two altitudes. This proved that the rays producing the ionization must have passed through the atmosphere from above and could not have a terrestrial origin.

Millikan went on to assert that cosmic rays were electromagnetic waves, a theory disproved by Arthur Compton (1892–1962) in 1934, when he demonstrated that they consist of charged particles. However, in the course of his research, Millikan directed Carl Anderson (1905–) to study cosmic rays in a cloud chamber and, as a result, Anderson discovered the positron.

Millikan's achievements are of fundamental value in the history of science. His determination of the charge on the electron was very important because it proved experimentally that electrons are particles of electricity, while the determination of Planck's constant was vital to the development of quantum theory.

Morley, Edward Williams (*1838–1923*), was an American physicist and chemist who is best known for his collaboration with Albert Michelson (1852–1931) in the classic Michelson–Morley experiment that disproved the existence of the ether as a medium that propagates light waves.

Morley was born in Newark, New Jersey, on 29 January 1838. He was taught at home by his parents until 1857, when he entered Williams College. He obtained a bachelor's degree from there in 1860, and then began theological training at the Andover Seminary, intending to become a Congregational minister like his father. At the same time he continued his studies at Williams College, which awarded him a master's degree in 1863. Morley completed his theological training in 1864, and worked for a year with the Sanitary Commission in Fort Monroe in Virginia, before returning to the Andover Academy for another year of study. In 1866 he got a teaching job at the South Berkshire Academy in Marlboro, Massachusetts.

In 1868 Morley was offered a ministry in Twinsburg, Ohio, and a teaching post in the chemistry department of Western Reserve College in Hudson, Ohio. He accepted the latter, but only on the condition that he be permitted to preach at the University chapel. Morley remained at Western Reserve College, later called Adelbert College when the college moved to Cleveland, Ohio, for the rest of his career. He became Professor of Chemistry there in 1869 and retired in 1906. From 1873 to 1888, he simultaneously held the post of Professor of Chemistry and Toxicology at Cleveland Medical College. Morley's contributions to the fields of physics and chemistry were recognized with the award of several distinguished honours, including the Davy Medal of the Royal Society in 1907, and the presidency of the American Association for the Advancement of Sciences from 1895 to 1896. Morley died in West Hartford, Connecticut, on 24 February 1923.

All of Morley's research involved the use of precision instruments. During the early part of his scientific career, he was involved with the design of such equipment. One of his instruments was an eudiometer, which he applied to test a theory concerning the origin of cold waves of air. Using the eudiometer, which was accurate to within 0.0025%, Morley was able to confirm on the basis of the oxygen content of the air and meteorological data that, under certain conditions, cold air derives from the downward movement of air from high altitudes rather than from the southward movement of northerly cold air.

Morley's most important contribution to science came with his collaboration with Michelson, which began in 1885. Michelson too was concerned with precision measurement, and the two men improved the interferometer that Michelson had first used in 1881 in an unsuccessful attempt to detect the motion of the Earth through the aether. The confirmation of this negative result in 1887 by Michelson and Morley led to the conclusion that the velocity of light is constant irrespective of the motion of the observer, which is one of the postulates of the special theory of relativity.

Morley also achieved wide recognition with the publication in 1895 of his accurate determinations of the densities of hydrogen and oxygen, and the ratios for their combination. Morley also investigated a controversial and long-standing theory known as Prout's hypothesis (proposed by William Prout (1785-1850) in 1815), which suggested that all the elements of the periodic table are multiples of the hydrogen atom. Morley decided to test this theory by taking the atomic weight of hydrogen to equal one, and then determining the relative atomic weight of oxygen by chemical means. He found that the ratio of their atomic weights was 1:15.879, not 16 as expected if oxygen was an integral multiple of hydrogen. Morley felt that he had finally disproved Prout's hypothesis. However the discovery of isotopes later led scientists to realize that chemical methods of determining atomic weight provide only an average result for the weights of all the different isotopes present in the sample. Prout's idea was essentially correct and he was honoured in 1920 when Ernest Rutherford (1871-1937) suggested that the subatomic particle which forms the hydrogen nucleus be named the *pro*ton.

Morley continued doing analytical research after his retirement. His constant preoccupation with precision and accuracy produced a rich yield of results during the course of his career, and their importance was quickly recognized.

Moseley, Henry Gwyn Jeffreys (*1887-1915*), was a British physicist who first established the atomic numbers of the elements by studying their X-ray spectra. This led to a complete classification of the elements, and also provided an experimental basis for an understanding of the structure of the atom.

Moseley was born at Weymouth on 23 November 1887. He came from a family of prestigious scientists, his father being Professor of Anatomy at Oxford and a member of the great *Challenger* expedition that surveyed the world's oceans from 1872 to 1876. Moseley was educated at Eton and in 1906 entered Trinity College, Oxford, where he obtained a degree in physics in 1910. Immediately after graduation, he was appointed lecturer in physics in the laboratory of Ernest Rutherford

(1871-1937) at Manchester, becoming a research fellow in 1912. Moseley remained with Rutherford until 1913. He then worked privately at Oxford with a view to obtaining a professorship there, and in 1914 he visited Australia. On the outbreak of World War I, he returned home and immediately enlisted in the army. Fearing for his safety, Rutherford endeavoured unsuccessfully to secure him scientific duties. Mosely was sent to the Dardanelles and was killed at Gallipolli on 10 August 1915.

Moseley was a researcher only from 1910 until 1914, and yet he made discoveries which were of fundamental importance to the development of both physics and chemistry. When he joined Rutherford's group in 1910, Rutherford was researching the phenomena associated with natural radioactivity. Moseley at first helped Rutherford in this work, but when reports of the diffraction of X-rays by Max von Laue (1879-1960) reached him in 1912, Moseley persuaded Rutherford to allow him to study X-ray spectra. He received instruction in X-ray diffraction from Lawrence Bragg (1890-1971) and in 1913 Moseley introduced X-ray spectroscopy to determine the X-ray spectra of the elements.

In a series of brilliant investigations, Moseley allowed the X-rays produced from various substances used as a target in an X-ray tube to be diffracted by a crystal of potassium ferrocyanide. The glancing angles were measured accurately and the position of the diffracted beams determined to obtain the wavelengths and frequencies of the X-rays emitted. Moseley examined metals from aluminium to gold and he found that their X-ray spectra were similar but with a deviation that changed regularly through the series. He found that a graph of the square root of the frequency of each radiation against the number representing the element's position in the periodic table gave a straight line. He called this number the atomic number of the element, which has since been shown to be the positive charge on the nucleus and thus the number of protons in the nucleus. Since the atom is electrically neutral, the atomic number is also the number of electrons surrounding the nucleus.

It was as a direct result of this work that atomic numbers were placed on a sound experimental foundation. Moseley found that when the elements are arranged in the periodic table according to their atomic numbers, all irregularity caused in the older system of grouping elements by their atomic weight disappeared. Now that the elements were numbered, the rare earth elements could be sorted out, a process that Moseley began at Oxford towards the end of his life. The numbering system also enabled Moseley to predict that several more elements would be discovered, namely those with atomic numbers of 43, 61, 72, 75, 87 and 91. These were all found in due course.

Although the number of elements which Moseley was able to examine was limited, the equation relating the square root of the frequency to the atomic number has been found to hold in all cases. The equation is known as Moseley's Law. It has enabled scientists to identify a total of 105 elements in a continuous series of atomic numbers. Any further elements that might be produced by nuclear reactions can only have greater atomic numbers.

In 1913 and 1914, the young physicist published his findings in two remarkable papers in the *Philosophical Magazine* and entitled them *The High-Frequency Spectra of the Elements*. Moseley's discovery told how many electrons were present in any element, and tied in nicely with the quantum theory of the hydrogen atom which was published in 1913 by Niels Bohr (1885-1962).

Moseley's fundamental discovery was a milestone in our knowledge of the constitution of the atom, and we are left to ponder on what this great brain might have discovered had he not been so tragically killed at so young an age.

Mössbauer, Rudolf Ludwig (*1929-*), is a German physicist who was awarded (with Robert Hofstadter) the 1961 Nobel Prize in Physics for his discovery of the Mössbauer effect. The effect, which involves the recoil-free absorption of gamma radiation by an atomic nucleus, provided experimental verification for Albert Einstein's theory of relativity.

Mössbauer was born in Munich on 31 January 1929, and was educated there. He graduated from the Munich Institute of Technology in 1952 and was awarded his PhD in 1958, the same year that he announced the Mössbauer effect, which he discovered during his post-graduate research in Heidelberg at the Max-Planck Institute for Medical Research. In 1960 he went to the United States and a year later became Professor of Physics at the California Institute of Technology, Pasadena. He remained in this position while simultaneously holding a professorship at Munich.

Mössbauer began research into the effects of gamma rays on matter in 1953. The absorption of a gamma ray by an atomic nucleus usually causes it to recoil, so affecting the wavelength of the re-emitted ray. Mössbauer found that at low temperatures crystals will absorb gamma rays of a specific wavelength and resonate, so that the crystal as a whole recoils while the nuclei do not. This recoil-less nuclear resonance absorption became known as the Mössbauer effect. A lengthen-

ing of the gamma-ray wavelength in a gravitational field, as predicted by the general theory of relativity, was observed experimentally in 1960.

Mott, Nevill Francis (*1905-*), is a British physicist whose work on semiconductors won him the 1977 Nobel Prize in Physics. He shared the prize with Philip Anderson (1923-), who has also worked on crystalline materials, and John Van Vleck (1899-1980), who played a central role in the development of the laser.

Mott was born on 30 September 1905. He was educated at Clifton College and then at St John's College, Cambridge. He became a lecturer at Manchester University in 1929 and at Gonville and Caius College, Cambridge, in 1930. In 1933, he moved to Bristol to become Melville Wills Professor of Theoretical Physics and held this position until 1948, when he became Director of the Henry Herbert Wills Physical Laboratories at Bristol. From 1954 to 1971, he was Cavendish Professor of Physics at Cambridge University and then Senior Research Fellow at Imperial College, London, from 1971 to 1973. He is now Emeritus Professor at Cambridge and has retired to Milton Keynes. His honours include a knighthood in 1972 and the award of the Royal Society's Copley Medal also in 1972.

Mott is a leading authority on solid state physics, particularly on the theory of electrons in metals and on dislocations and other defects in the crystalline structure. He was the first, with R.W. Gurney, to put forward a comprehensive theory of the process involved when a photographic film is exposed to light. They postulated that the incident light produces free electrons and holes which wander about the crystal. The electrons become trapped at imperfections, which might be dislocations or possibly foreign atoms, and attract interstitial silver ions to form silver atoms and make the latent image. When a developer is present, the entire grain may be catalysed into free silver by the initially formed specks of silver.

Mott's work on semiconductors, which won him the Nobel Prize, has shown how a cheap and reliable material can be used to improve the performance of electronic circuits, increasing the memory capacity of computers by several times. More efficient photovoltaic cells can now be produced which are capable of converting solar energy into electricity. The use of carefully prepared crystalline materials as semiconductors has led to a revolution in the transistor industry. Mott and his colleagues have discovered special electrical characteristics in glassy semiconductors and have laid down fundamental laws of behaviour for their materials. Their subject has been described as the last frontier of solid state physics and their and Anderson's research opens the way for a wide range of new developments in electronics, including cheaper methods of solar heating.

Mottelson, Ben Roy (*1926–*). *See* Bohr, Aage Niels.

N

Newton, Isaac (*1642-1727*), was a British physicist and mathematician who is regarded as one of the greatest scientists ever to have lived. In physics, he discovered the three laws of motion that bear his name and was the first to explain gravitation, clearly defining the nature of mass, weight, force, inertia and acceleration. In his honour, the SI unit of force is called the newton. Newton also made fundamental discoveries in optics, finding that white light is composed of a spectrum of colours and inventing the reflecting telescope. In mathematics, Newton's principal contribution was to formulate the calculus and the binomial theorem.

Newton was born at Woolsthorpe, Lincolnshire, on 25 December 1642 by the old Julian calendar, but on 4 January 1643 by modern reckoning. His birthplace, Woolsthorpe Manor, is now preserved. Newton's was an inauspicious beginning for he was a premature, sickly baby born after his father's death, and his survival was not expected. When he was three, his mother remarried and the young Newton was left in his grandmother's care. He soon began to take refuge in things mechanical, reputedly making waterclocks, kites bearing fiery lanterns aloft, and a model mill powered by a mouse, as well as innumerable drawings and diagrams. When Newton was 12, he began to attend the King's School, Grantham, but his schooling was not to last. His mother, widowed again, returned to Woolsthorpe in 1658 and withdrew him from school with the intention of making him into a farmer. Fortunately, his uncle recognized Newton's ability and managed to get him back to school to prepare for university entrance. This Newton achieved in 1661, when he went to Trinity College, Cambridge, and began to delve widely and deeply into the scholarship of the day.

In 1665, the year that he became a Bachelor of Arts, the university was closed because of the plague and Newton spent eighteen months at Woolsthorpe, with only the occasional visit to Cambridge. Such seclusion was a prominent feature of Newton's creative life and, during this period, he laid the foundations of his work in mathematics, optics, dynamics and celestial mechanics, performing his first prism experiments and reflecting on motion and gravitation.

Newton returned to Cambridge in 1666 and became a minor Fellow of Trinity in 1667 and a major Fellow the following year. He also received his Master of Arts degree in 1668 and became Lucasian Professor of Mathematics – at the age of only 26. It is said that the previous incumbent, Isaac Barrow (1630-1677), resigned the post to make way for Newton. Newton remained at Cambridge almost 30 years, studying alone for the most part, though in frequent contact with other leading scientists by letter and through the Royal Society in London, which elected him a Fellow in 1672. These were Newton's most fertile years. He laboured day and night in his chemical laboratory, at his calculations, or immersed in theological and mystical speculations. In Cambridge, he completed what may be described as his greatest single work, the *Philosophae Naturalis Principia Mathematica* (*Mathematical Principles of Natural Philosophy*). This was presented to the Royal Society in 1686, who subsequently withdrew from publishing it through shortage of funds. The astronomer Edmund Halley (1656-1742), a wealthy man and friend of Newton, paid for the publication of the *Principia* in 1687. In it, Newton revealed his laws of motion and the law of universal gravitation.

After the *Principia* appeared, Newton appeared to become bored with Cambridge and his scientific professorship. In 1689, he was elected a member of Parliament for the university and in London he encountered many other eminent minds, notably Christiaan Huygens (1629-1695). The excessive strain of Newton's studies and the attendant disputes caused him to suffer severe depression in 1692, when he was described as having "lost his reason". Four years later, he accepted the appointment of Warden of the London Mint, becoming Master in 1699. He took these new, well-paid duties very seriously, revising the coinage and taking severe measures against forgers. Although his scientific work continued, it was greatly diminished.

Newton was elected President of the Royal Society in 1703, an office he held until his death, and in 1704 he summed up his life's work on light in *Opticks*. The following year, Newton was knighted by Queen Anne. Although he had turned grey at 30, Newton's constitution remained strong and it is said he had sharp sight and hearing, as well as all his teeth, at the age of 80. His later years were given to revisions of the *Principia*, and he died on 20 March 1727. Newton was accorded a state funeral and buried in Westminster Abbey, an occasion that prompted Voltaire to remark that England honoured a mathematician as other nations honoured a king.

Any consideration of Newton must take account of the imperfections of his character, for the size of his genius was matched by his ambition. A hypersensitivity to criticism and possessiveness about his work made conflicts with other scientists a prominent feature of his later life. This negative side of Newton's nature may be well illustrated by his dispute with Gottfried Leibniz (1646-1716). These two great mathematicians worked independently on the development of a differential calculus, both making significant advances. No-one today would seriously question Leibniz's originality and true mathematical genius, but Newton branded him a plagiarist and claimed sole invention of the calculus. When Leibniz appealed to the Royal Society for a fair hearing, Newton appointed a committee of his own supporters and even wrote their, supposedly impartial, report himself. He then further proceeded to review this report anonymously, later remarking that "he had broken Leibniz's heart with his reply to him". The partisan and "patriotic" views that resulted from this controversy served to isolate English mathematics and to set it back many years, for it was Leibniz' terminology that came to be used.

A similar dispute arose between Newton and Robert Hooke (1635-1703), one of the more brilliant and versatile members of the Royal Society, who supported Huygens' wave theory of light. Although, in the past, he had collaborated with Hooke, Newton published results without giving credit to their originator. Hooke, however, was notably disputatious and better able to stand up for himself than Leibniz. On the other hand, Newton remained faithful to those he regarded as friends, appointing several to positions in the Mint after he took charge, and part of his quarrel with the Astronomer Royal, John Flamsteed (1646-1719), was that Flamsteed had fallen out with Newton's friend Halley.

Newton's work itself must be considered in many parts: he was a brilliant mathematician and an equally exceptional optical physicist, he revolutionized our understanding of gravity and, throughout his life, studied chemistry, alchemy, and wrote millions of words on theological speculation and mysticism.

As a mathematician, Newton developed unusually late, being well through his university career when he studied Pierre de Fermat (1601-1665), René Descartes (1596-1650) and others, before returning to Euclid (fl.300s BC), whom he had previously dismissed. However, in those two plague years of 1665 and 1666, Newton more than made up for this delay, and much of his later work can be seen as a revision and extension of the creativity of that period. To quote one of his own notebooks: "In the beginning of the year 1665 I found the method for approximating series and the binomial theorem. The same year I found the method of tangents of Gregory and in November had the direct method of fluxions (differential calculus) and in January (1666) had the theory of colours (of light) and in May following I had entrance into the inverse method of fluxions (integral calculus) and in the same year I began to think of gravity extending to the orb of the moon . . ."

The zenith of his mathematics was the *Principia*, and after this Newton did little mathematics, though his genius remained sharp and when Bernouilli and Leibniz composed problems with the specific intention of defeating him, Newton solved each one the first day he saw it. Both in his own day and afterwards, Newton influenced mathematics "following his own wish" by "his creation of the fluxional calculus and the theory of infinite series", which together made up his analytic technique. But he was also active in algebra and number theory, classical and analytical geometry, computation and approximation and even probability. For three centuries, most of his papers lay buried in the Portsmouth Collection of his manuscripts and only now are scholars examining his complete mathematics for the first time.

Newton's work in dynamics also began in those two years of enforced isolation at Woolsthorpe. He had already considered the motion of colliding bodies and circular motion, and had arrived at ideas of how force and inertia affect motion and of centrifugal force. Newton was now inspired to consider the problem of gravity by seeing an apple fall from a tree – a story that, according to Newton himself, is true. He wondered if the force that pulled the apple to the ground could also extend into space and pull the Moon into an orbit around the Earth. Newton assumed that the rate of fall is proportional to the force of gravity and that this force is inversely proportional to the square of the distance from the centre of the Earth. He then worked out what the motion of the Moon should be if these assumptions were correct, but obtained a figure that was too low. Disappointed, Newton set aside his considerations on gravity and did not return to them until 1679.

Newton was then able to satisfy himself that his assumptions were indeed true and he also had a better radius of the Earth than was available in the plague years. He then set to recalculating the Moon's motion on the basis of his theory of gravity and obtained a correct result. Newton also found that his theory explained the laws of planetary motion that had been derived earlier that century by Johannes Kepler (1571-1630) on the basis of observations of the planets.

Newton presented his conclusions on dynamics in the *Principia*. Although he had already developed the calculus, he did not use it in the *Principia*, preferring to prove all his results geometrically. In this great work, Newton's plan was first to develop the subject of general dynamics from a mathematical point of view and then to apply the results in the solution of important astronomical and physical problems. It included a synthesis of Kepler's laws of planetary motion and Galileo's laws of falling bodies, developing the system of mechanics we know today, including the three famous laws of motion. The first law states that every body remains at rest or in constant motion in a straight line unless it is acted upon by a force. This defines inertia, finally disproving the idea which had been prevalent since Aristotle (384-322 BC) had mooted it, that force is required to keep anything moving. The second law states that a force accelerates a body by an amount proportional to its mass. This was the first clear definition of force and it also distinguished mass from weight. The third law states that action and reaction are equal and opposite, which showed how things could be made to move.

Newton also developed his general theory of gravitation as a universal law of attraction between any two objects, stating that the force of gravity is proportional to the masses of the objects and decreases in proportion to the square of the distance between the two bodies. Though, in the years before, there had been considerable correspondence between Newton, Hooke, Halley and Kepler on the mathematical formulation of these laws, Newton did not complete the work until the writing of the *Principia*.

"I was in the prime of my age for invention" said Newton of those two years 1665 and 1666, and it was in that period that he performed his fundamental work in optics. Again it should be pointed out that the study of Newton's optics has been limited to his published letters and the *Opticks* of 1704, its publication delayed until after Hooke's death to avoid yet another controversy over originality. No adequate edition or full translation of the voluminous *Lectiones Opticae* exists. Newton began those first, crucial experiments by passing sunlight through a prism, finding that it dispersed the white light into a spectrum of colours. He then took a second prism and showed that it could combine the colours in the spectrum and form white light again. In this way, Newton proved that the colours are a prop-

erty of light and not of the prism. An interesting byproduct of these early speculations was the development of the reflecting telescope. Newton held the erroneous opinion that optical dispersion was independent of the medium through which the light was refracted and, therefore, that nothing could be done to correct the chromatic aberration caused by lenses. He therefore set about building a telescope in which the objective lens is replaced by a curved mirror, in which aberration could not occur. In 1668 Newton succeeded in making the first reflecting telescope, a tiny instrument only 15 cm long, but the direct ancestor of today's huge astronomical reflecting telescopes. In this invention, Newton was anticipated to some degree by James Gregory (1638-1675) who had produced a design for a reflecting telescope five years earlier but had not succeeded in constructing one.

Other scientists, Hooke especially, were critical of Newton's early reports, seeing too little connection between experimental result and theory, so that, in the course of a debate lasting several years, Newton was forced to refine his theories with considerable subtlety. He performed further experiments in which he investigated many other optical phenomena, including thin film interference effects, one of which, "Newton's rings", is named after him.

The *Opticks* presented a highly systematized and organized account of Newton's work and his theory of the nature of light and the effects that light produces. In fact, although he held that light rays were corpuscular in nature, he integrated into his ideas the concept of periodicity, holding that "ether waves" were associated with light corpuscles, a remarkable conceptual leap, for Hooke and Huygens, the founder of the wave theory, both denied periodicity to light waves. The corpuscle concept lent itself to an analysis by forces and established an analogy between the action of gross bodies and that of light, reinforcing the universalizing tendency of the *Principia*. However, Newton's prestige was such that the corpuscular theory held sway for much longer than it deserved, not being finally overthrown until early in the 1800s. Ironically, it was the investigation of interference effects by Thomas Young (1773-1829) that led to the establishment of the wave theory of light.

Although comparatively little is known of the bulk of Newton's complete writings in chemistry and physics, we know even less about his chemistry and alchemy, chronology prophecy and theology. The vast number of documents he wrote on these matters have never yet been properly analysed, but what is certain is that he took great interest in alchemy, performing many chemical experiments in his own laboratory and being in contact with Robert Boyle (1627–1691). He also wrote much on ancient chronology and the authenticity of certain biblical texts.

Newton's greatest achievement was to demonstrate that scientific principles are of universal application. In the *Principia Mathematica*, he built logically and analytically from mathematical premises and the evidence of experiment and observation to develop a model of the Universe that is still of general validity. "If I have seen further than other men," he once said with perhaps assumed modesty, "it is because I have stood on the shoulders of giants"; and Newton was certainly able to bring together the knowledge of his forebears in a brilliant synthesis. Newton's life marked the first great flowering of the scientific method, which had been evolving in fits and starts since the time of the ancient Greeks. But Newton really established it, completing a scientific revolution in Europe that had begun with Nicolaus Copernicus (1473–1543) and ushering in the Age of Reason, in which the scientific method was expected to yield complete knowledge by the elucidation of the basic laws that govern the Universe. No knowledge can ever be total, but Newton's example brought about an explosion of investigation and discovery that has never really abated. He perhaps foresaw this when he remarked "To myself, I seem to have been only like a boy playing on the seashore, and diverting myself in now and then finding a smoother pebble or a prettier shell than ordinary, whilst the great ocean of truth lay all undiscovered before me".

With his extraordinary insight into the workings of nature and rare tenacity in wresting its secrets and revealing them in as fundamental and concise a way as possible, Newton stands as a colossus of science. In physics, only Archimedes (287–212 BC) and Albert Einstein (1879–1955), who also possessed these qualities, may be compared to him.

Nicol, William (*1768–1851*), was a British physicist and geologist who is best known for inventing the first device for obtaining plane-polarized light – the Nicol prism.

Very little is known of Nicol's life. He was born in Scotland in 1768 and seems to have spent most of his career lecturing at the University of Edinburgh, where James Clerk Maxwell may have been one of his students. Nicol did not publish any of his research findings until 1826, when he was 58 years old, with the result that his work made relatively little impact during his lifetime. He died in Edinburgh on 2 September 1851.

Nicol invented the Nicol prism, as it is now called, in 1828. Consisting of Iceland spar (a naturally occurring, transparent crystalline form of calcium carbonate), it utilized the phenomenon of double refraction discovered by Erasmus Bartholin in 1699. Nicol made his prism by bisecting a parallelepiped of Iceland spar along its shortest diagonal then cementing the two halves back in their original position with Canada balsam, which has a refractive index between the two indices of the double-refracting Iceland spar. Light entering the prism is refracted into two rays, one of which is reflected by the Canada balsam (an example of total internal reflection) out of the side of the prism, the other ray being transmitted, with very little deviation, through the prism and emerging as plane-polarized light. This second, plane-polarized ray can then be passed through another Nicol prism aligned parallel to the first. Rotating the second prism causes the amount of light transmitted through it to decrease, reaching a minimum (with no light transmitted) when the second prism has been rotated through 90°, then increasing again to a maximum when the second prism has been rotated through 180Z. Furthermore, if a solution of an organic substance is placed between the two prisms, the second prism must be turned through a specific angle to allow maximum light transmis-

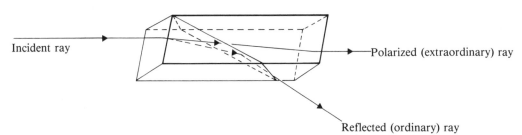

Incident ray

Polarized (extraordinary) ray

Reflected (ordinary) ray

A Nicol prism acts as a polarizer. It consists of a rhomboidal calcite crystal sliced diagonally and cemented together with Canada balsam. An incident ray is doubly refracted on entering the end face of the prism. The extraordinary ray crosses the junction unaffected and emerges as a plane polarized ray; the ordinary ray is internally reflected and merges from the side of the prism to be absorbed by its mount.

sion; this angle represents the degree of refraction of the polarized light. Nicol prisms greatly facilitated the study of refraction and polarization, and later played an essential part in the development of polarimetry, especially in the use of this technique to investigate molecular structures and optical activity of organic compounds.

In 1815 Nicol, who was primarily a geologist, developed a method of preparing extremely thin sections of crystals and rocks for microscopical study. His technique (which involved cementing the specimen to a glass slide and then carefully grinding until it was extremely thin) made it possible to view mineral samples by transmitted rather than reflected light and therefore enabled the minerals' internal structures to be seen. Nicol also used this technique to examine the cell structure of fossil woods, and the information he obtained from these studies was later used as a basis for identification and classification. But because of his reluctance to publish his work, Nicol's slide-preparation technique did not become widely used until after 1853, when Henry Sorby demonstrated its usefulness for studying mineral structures.

Nobili, Leopoldo (*1784-1835*), was an Italian physicist who carried out early research into electrochemistry and thermoelectricity.

Nobili was born in Trassilico in 1784. After leaving university he joined the artillery as a Captain, and then became Professor of Physics at the Florence Museum. He died in Florence on 5 August 1835.

In 1828 Nobili published the results of his electrochemical research, in which he made simple cells by immersing platinum electrodes in various solutions of mixed salts and alkalis. Later (1825) he measured the currents produced by them using a moving-magnet astatic galvanometer of his own invention. Four years later he made use of the Seebeck effect to construct a thermocouple for measuring radiant heat (by calibrating the current it generated), employing a series of six antimony-bismuth bimetallic junctions.

Oersted, Hans Christian (*1777-1851*), was a Danish physicist who discovered that an electric current produces a magnetic field.

Oersted was born at Rudkøbing, Langeland, on 14 August 1777. He had little formal education as a child but on moving to Copenhagen in 1794, Oersted entered the university and gained a

degree in pharmacy in 1797, proceeding to a doctorate in 1799. He then worked as a pharmacist before making a tour of Europe from 1801 to 1803 to complete his studies in science. On his return, Oersted gave public lectures with great success, for he was a very good teacher, and then in 1806 became Professor of Physics at Copenhagen. He retained this position until 1829, when he became director of the Polytechnic Institute in Copenhagen. As a teacher and writer, Oersted was instrumental in raising science in Denmark to an international standard, founding the Danish Society for the Promotion of Natural Science in 1824. Oersted remained at the Polytechnic Institute until his death, which occurred at Copenhagen on 9 March 1851.

Oersted made his historic discovery of electromagnetism in 1820, but he had been seeking the effect since 1813 when he predicted that an electric current would produce magnetism when it flowed through a wire just as it produced heat and light. Oersted made this prediction on philosophical grounds, believing that all forces must be interconvertible. Others were also seeking the electromagnetic effect, but considered that the magnetic field would lie in the direction of the current and had not been able to detect it. Oersted reasoned that the effect must be a lateral one and early in 1820, he set up an experiment with a compass needle placed beneath a wire connected to a battery. A lecture intervened before he could perform the experiment and, unable to wait, Oersted decided to try it out before his students. The needle moved feebly, making no great impression on the audience but thrilling Oersted. Because the effect was so small, Oersted delayed publication and investigated it more fully, finding that a circular magnetic field is produced around a wire carrying a current. He communicated this momentous discovery to the major scientific journals of Europe in July 1820.

In 1822, Oersted turned to the compressibility of gases and liquids, devising a useful apparatus to determine compressibility. He also investigated thermoelectricity, in 1823. Oersted may have wanted to continue work on electromagnetism, but his sensational discovery resulted in an explosion of activity by other scientists and Oersted possibly felt unable to compete. Major theoretical and practical advances were made by André Ampère (1775-1836) and Michael Faraday (1791-1867) soon afterwards, Oersted thereby providing the basis for the main thrust of physics in the 1800s.

Ohm, Georg Simon (*1789-1854*), was a German physicist who is remembered for Ohm's law, which relates the current flowing through a conductor to the potential difference and the resistance.

Ohm was born at Erlangen, Bavaria, on 16 March 1789. He received a basic education in science from his father, who was a master locksmith, and in 1805 he entered the University of Erlangen. However, he left after a year and until 1811 was a school teacher and private tutor in Switzerland. He then returned to Erlangen and gained his PhD in the same year. Ohm then became a privatdozent (unpaid lecturer) in mathematics at Erlangen, but after a year was forced to take up a post as a schoolteacher in Bamberg. In 1817, Ohm moved to Cologne to teach at the Jesuit Gymnasium and in 1825 he decided to pursue original research in physics. He obtained leave in 1826 and went to Berlin, where he produced his great work on electricity, *Die Galvanische Kette*, in 1827.

Ohm hoped to obtain an academic post on the strength of his achievements, but found that his work was little appreciated, mainly because of its mathematical rigour which few German physicists understood at that time. He stayed in Berlin as a schoolteacher, and then in 1833 moved to Nuremberg where he became Professor of Physics at the Polytechnic Institute, which was not the prestigious university appointment that Ohm both desired and deserved. However, Ohm's work began to achieve recognition, especially in Britain where he was awarded the Royal Society's Copley Medal in 1841. His ability eventually also made its mark in Germany and in 1849 he became Extraordinary Professor of Physics at Munich, acceding to the chair of physics proper in 1852. Ohm thus achieved his ambition but had little time left to savour his success. He died at Munich on 6 July 1854.

Ohm began the work that led him to his law of electricity in 1825. He investigated the amount of electromagnetic force produced in a wire carrying a current, expecting it to decrease with the length of the wire in the circuit. He used a voltaic pile to produce a current and connected varying lengths of wire to it, measuring the electromagnetic force with the magnetic needle of a galvanometer. Ohm found that a longer wire produced a greater loss in electromagnetic force.

Ohm continued these investigations in 1826 using a thermocouple as the source of current because it produced a constant electric current unlike the voltaic pile, which fluctuated. He found that the electromagnetic force, which is in fact a measure of the current, was equal to the electromotive force produced by the thermocouple divided by the length of the conductor being tested plus a quantity that Ohm called the resistance of the remainder of the circuit, including the thermocouple itself. From this, Ohm reached the more general statement that the current is equal to the tension (e.m.f. or potential difference) divided by the overall resistance of the circuit, thus expressing the law in the form known as Ohm's law.

Ohm went on to use an electroscope to measure how the tension varied at different points along a conductor to verify his law, and presented his arguments in mathematical form in his great work of 1827. He made a useful analogy with the flow of heat through a conductor, pointing out that an electric current flows through a conductor of varying resistance from one tension or potential to another to produce a potential difference, just as heat flows through a conductor of varying conductivity from one temperature to another to produce a temperature difference. Ohm used the analytical theory of heat published by Jean Fourier (1768-1830) in 1822 to justify this approach, believing partly from his use of thermocouples that there was an intimate link between heat and electricity.

Ohm's derivation of a basic law of nature from experiment was a classic piece of scientific deduction. Together with the laws of electrodynamics discovered by André Ampère (1775-1836) at about the same time, Ohm's law marks the first theoretical investigation of electricity. It is fitting that his name is remembered in both the unit of resistance, the ohm, and the unit of conductivity, the mho (ohm spelt backwards).

Onnes, Heike Kamerlingh (*1853-1926*), was a Dutch physicist who is particularly remembered for the contributions he made to the study of the properties of matter at low temperatures. He first liquefied helium and later discovered superconductivity, gaining the 1913 Nobel Prize in Physics in recognition of his work.

Onnes was born in Groningen on 21 September 1853 and attended local schools. In 1870 he entered the University of Groningen to study physics and mathematics. He won two prizes at the university during his early years there for his studies on the nature of the chemical bond. In 1871, Onnes travelled to Heidelberg to study under Gustav Kirchhoff (1824-1887) and Robert Bunsen (1811-1899). He then returned to Groningen and in 1876 completed the research for his PhD, on new proofs for the Earth's rotation, but the degree was not awarded until 1879. In the meantime, Onnes served as an assistant at the Polytechnic in Delft and later lectured there. In 1882, he was appointed Professor of Experimental Physics at the University of Leiden, a post he held for 42 years. In 1894, he founded the famous cryogenic laboratories at Leiden, which became a world centre of low-temperature physics. Onnes died in Leiden on 21 February 1926.

During his years at Delft, Onnes met Johannes van der Waals (1837-1923), who was then Professor of Physics in Amsterdam. Their discussions led Onnes to become interested in the properties of matter over a wide temperature range, and in particular at the lower end of the scale. Onnes felt that he might thereby be able to obtain experimental evidence to support van der Waals' theories concerning the equations of state for gases.

Onnes applied the cascade method for cooling gases that had been developed by James Dewar (1842-1923), and in 1908 succeeded in liquefying helium, a feat which had eluded Dewar. He was not content merely to report the technical achievements involved in these processes, he also wanted to investigate how matter behaves at very low temperatures. In 1910, Onnes succeeded in lowering the temperature of liquid helium to 0.8K. Lord Kelvin (1824-1907) had postulated in 1902 that as the temperature approached absolute zero, electrical resistance would increase. In 1911, Onnes found the reverse to be the case, showing that the electrical resistance of a conductor tends to decrease and vanish as temperature approaches absolute zero. He called this phenomenon supraconductivity, later renamed superconductivity.

Onnes made a particular study of the effects of low temperature on the conductivity of mercury, lead, nickel and manganese/iron alloys. He found that the imposition of a magnetic field eliminated superconductivity even at low temperatures. Special alloys have now been produced which do not behave in this manner.

Onnes was also interested in the magneto-optical properties of metals at low temperature, and in the technical application of low-temperature physics to the industrial and commercial uses of refrigeration.

Oppenheimer, Julius Robert (*1904-1967*), was an American physicist who contributed significantly to the growth of quantum mechanics and played a critical role in the rapid development of the first atomic bombs. In his later years, he was a prominent advocate of international control of nuclear technology and of a cautious approach to the escalation of the military applications of that knowledge.

Oppenheimer was born in New York on 22 April 1904. He attended the Ethical Culture School and was a very serious, studious child. His interest in minerals and geology led to his admission to the Minerological Club of New York at the mere age of 11. In 1922, he went to Harvard University, graduating after only three of the usual four years in 1925. He spent the next year in Cambridge with Ernest Rutherford (1871-1937), Werner Heisenberg (1901-1976) and Paul Dirac (1902-   ), and in 1926 at the invitation of Max Born (1882-1970) went to Göttingen where he worked on quantum theory of molecules and *bremsstrahlung* (continuous radiation emission). He received his PhD from Göttingen in 1927. Oppenheimer then returned to the United States and became a National Research Fellow, and in 1929 he was appointed Assistant Professor at both the California Institute of Technology (CalTech) and the University of California at Berkeley. He spent the next thirteen years commuting between these two campuses, becoming Associate Professor in 1931 and Professor in 1936.

During World War II from 1943 to 1945, Oppenheimer was Director of the Los Alamos Scientific Laboratories in New Mexico, where he headed the research team that produced the first atomic bombs. After the war, he returned briefly to California and then in 1947 was made Director of the Institute of Advanced Study at Princeton University. Oppenheimer also served as Chairman of the General Advisory Committee to the Atomic Energy Commission from 1946 to 1952. He retired as Director of the Institute of Advanced Study in 1966, but continued as Professor there until his death at Princeton on 18 February 1967.

Oppenheimer's most important research was to investigate the equations describing the energy states of the atom that Dirac had formulated in 1928. In 1930, Oppenheimer was instrumental in showing that the equations indicated that a positively charged particle with the mass of an electron could exist. This particle was detected in 1932 and called the positron.

During the 1930s at California, Oppenheimer built up a formidable research group around him. Theoretical physics had never before been studied with such intensity in the United States. When World War II broke out in 1939 in Europe, it was immediately apparent to Oppenheimer that the newly discovered phenomenon of nuclear fission could have great military significance. Work on the various aspects of bomb construction began in many places, one of them being Berkeley. The Manhattan Project, the code name for the programme aimed at the production of the atomic bomb, was formally initiated in 1942. Oppenheimer suggested that the work on the various related projects be brought together to one site and proposed a remote location in the Pecos Valley, New Mexico. The Los Alamos research centre was set up there in 1943 with Oppenheimer as Director.

Oppenheimer did not take on personal responsibility for the development of any single aspect of the bomb programme, but concentrated first on gathering together the finest scientists he could find and secondly on instilling in the whole team a sense of urgency and intense excitement. The success of the Los Alamos project in so quickly overcoming the enormous number of new problems is in no small measure attributable to his efforts. Oppenheimer also served as one of the four scientists consulted on the decision of how to deploy the bomb, the scientists recommending that a populated "military target" be selected.

Oppenheimer was also involved in the decision to develop the hydrogen bomb after the war. The majority of the AEC Advisory Committee, of which Oppenheimer was chairman, was opposed to this but the unexpected explosion of a nuclear device by the Soviet Union in the summer of 1949 led to President Truman overriding this advice. Oppenheimer's offer of resignation from the committee was not accepted, but in 1953, at the height of the McCarthy era, Oppenheimer was informed that President Eisenhower had ordered that his security clearance (permission for access to secret information) was to be withdrawn on the basis of suspicions concerning his loyalty. Oppenheimer opposed this and underwent a gruelling quasi-judicial procedure which did not lead to his clearance being restored. There is little doubt that those who had disagreed with Oppenheimer's position regarding the H-bomb were at least partly responsible for this.

In 1963 President Johnson publicly awarded Oppenheimer the Enrico Fermi Prize, the highest award the AEC can confer, as an attempt to make amends for the unjust treatment he had received.

P

Pascal, Blaise (*1623–1662*), was a French mathematician and physicist. His main achievements in physics were to show that the pressure of the atmosphere varies with height and to formulate the principle known as Pascal's principle that governs hydraulics. He also invented the first mechanical calculating machine.

Pascal was born at Clermont-Ferrand on 19 June 1623. His mother died when he was a few years old and Pascal's father, who was a mathematician, devoted himself to the raising of his children. In 1631, the family moved to Paris and Pascal began to study mathematics at about the age of 12, producing original work in geometry by the time he was 16. In 1641, the family went to Rouen. There Pascal developed and manufactured his calculating machine, but then his health began to decline and he started to interest himself in religion. He returned to Paris in 1647 and began his work in physics. This culminated in his classic treatise on hydrostatics, which was completed in 1654 but not published until the year after his death. Pascal then concerned himself with mathematics, particularly with probability theory and the development of calculus, for the next five years. In 1659, he became very ill and subsequently devoted himself almost entirely to religious speculation, though in 1662 Pascal did involve himself in the establishment of the first city transport system in the world. This consisted of a fleet of horse-drawn carriages, plying fixed routes in Paris at regular intervals. Pascal died shortly after on 19 August 1662.

Pascal designed his calculating machine in 1642 at the age of only 19. It mechanized addition and subtraction by the operation of rotating gears. Pascal took three years to produce a satisfactory working model and then organized the manufacture and sale of the machine himself. It was not a great success, possibly because its high price did not make it an economic proposition. Seven models of the calculator still exist.

Pascal's work in hydrostatics was inspired by the experiment of Evangelista Torricelli (1608–1647) in 1643, which demonstrated that air pressure supports a column of mercury only about 76 cm high. In 1647, Pascal succeeded in repeating Torricelli's experiment, but this time using wine and water in tubes 12 m high fixed to the masts of ships. He confirmed that a vacuum must exist in the space at the top of the tube, and set out to prove that the column of mercury, wine or water is held up by the weight of air exerted on the container of liquid at the base of the tube. Pascal suggested that at high altitudes there would be less air above the tube and that the column would be lower. Unable through poor health to undertake the experiment himself, he entrusted it to his brother-in-law who obtained the expected results using a mercury column in the mountains of the Puy de Dôme in 1648.

Pascal's proof that the height of a column of mercury does depend on air pressure led rapidly to investigations of the use of the mercury barometer in weather forecasting. Pascal however turned to a study of pressure in liquids and gases, and found that it is transmitted equally in all directions throughout a fluid and is always exerted perpendicular to any surface in or containing the fluid. This is known as Pascal's principle and it was propounded in the treatise on hydrostatics that Pascal completed in 1654. This principle is fundamental to applications of hydrostatics and governs the operation of hydraulic machines.

Pascal's pioneering work on fluid pressure laid the foundations for both hydraulics and meteorology. In his honour, the SI unit for pressure is called the pascal. It is equal to one newton per square metre.

Pauli, Wolfgang (*1900–1958*), was an Austrian-born Swiss physicist who made a substantial contribution to quantum theory with the Pauli exclusion principle. For this achievement, Pauli was awarded the 1945 Nobel Prize in Physics. He also postulated the existence of the neutrino.

Pauli was born in Vienna on 25 April 1900. His father was Professor of Colloid Chemistry at the University of Vienna and his godfather was Ernst Mach (1837–1916). Pauli made rapid progress in science while at school in Vienna and by the time he entered the University of Munich to study under Arnold Sommerfeld (1868–1951), he had already mastered both the special and general theories of relativity proposed by Albert Einstein (1879–1955). Recognizing his ability, Sommerfeld gave Pauli the task of preparing a comprehensive exposition of relativity, as Einstein had not done so. Pauli produced a monograph of extraordinary clarity, an amazing achievement for a student of 19.

Pauli obtained his doctorate in 1922 and then went to Göttingen as an assistant to Max Born (1882–1970). He soon moved to Copenhagen to study with Niels Bohr (1885–1962) and then in 1923 went to Hamburg as a privatdozent (unpaid lecturer). In 1928, Pauli was appointed Professor of Experimental Physics at the Eidgenössische Technical University, Zurich. He retained this position until the end of his life, but spent World War II in the United States at the Institute for Advanced Study, Princeton. Pauli became a Swiss citizen on his return, and died at Zurich on 15 December 1958.

In the early 1920s, the quantum model of the atom proposed by Bohr in 1913 and elaborated by Sommerfeld in 1916 was in some disarray. Observations of the magnetic anomaly in alkali metals and of the fine spectra of alkaline earth metals did not accord with the Bohr-Sommerfeld model and it was suggested that the quantum numbers used to describe the energy levels of electrons in atoms in this model would have to be abandoned. Pauli realized that the situation could be explained if a fourth quantum number were added to the three already used (n, l and m). This number, s, would represent the spin of the electron and would have two possible values. He further proposed that no two electrons in the same atom can have the same values for their four quantum numbers. This is the Pauli exclusion principle, which was announced in 1925.

The exclusion principle means that the energy state of each electron in an atom can be defined by giving a unique set of values to the four quantum numbers. It not only accounted for the unusual properties of the elements that had been observed, but also gave a means of determining the arrangement of electrons into shells around the nucleus that explained the classification of elements into related groups. The successive shells could contain a maximum of 2, 8, 18, 32 and 50 electrons, with most elements containing outer valence electrons and inner complete shells. This discovery was of great importance, for it gave an explanation of the similarities in the properties of elements and revealed the significance of ordering elements by their atomic number.

Pauli's other main contribution to physics was made in 1930. The production of beta radiation in a continuous spectrum had puzzled physicists as theory demanded that the spectrum should be discontinuous. It appeared to be caused by a loss of energy when beta particles (electrons) were emitted from atoms, but no explanation could be found for such a loss. It was suggested that the theory of conservation of energy would have to be abandoned, but Pauli proposed that the emission of an electron in beta decay is accompanied by the production of an unknown particle. This particle would have unusual properties, having no charge and zero mass at rest - hence the fact that it had not been observed. Pauli persisted in this opinion, and in 1934 Enrico Fermi (1901–1954) confirmed Pauli's view and called the particle the neutrino. It was eventually detected in 1956.

Pauli made substantial advances in our understanding of the nature of the atom by adhering to accepted theories that he felt he could not abandon. He demonstrated exceptional insight, for such an approach usually blinds scientists to progress. Pauli summed up his life in a characteristically succinct fashion when he declared "In my youth I believed myself to be a revolutionary; now I see that I was a classicist."

Peierls, Rudolf Ernst (*1907–*), is a German-born British physicist who made contributions to quantum theory and to nuclear physics.

Peierls was born in Berlin, Germany, on 5 June 1907. He was educated at the Humboldt School, Oberschöneweide, Berlin and then at the University of Berlin. He studied with Arnold Sommerfeld (1868–1951) in Munich, with Werner Heisenberg (1901–1976) in Leipzig, and with Wolfgang Pauli (1900–1958) in Zurich. From 1929 to 1932, he worked as Pauli's research assistant at the Federal Institute of Technology in Zurich. He held a Rockefeller Fellowship in Rome and Cambridge between 1932 and 1933, and was an Honorary Research Fellow at Manchester University from 1933 to 1935. He then became an Assistant in Research for the Royal Society at the Mond Laboratory in Cambridge in 1935 and in 1937, he was appointed Professor of Mathematical Physics (formerly called Applied Mathematics) at the University of Birmingham. Peierls worked on the Atomic Project in Birmingham from 1940 to 1943 and in the United States from 1943 to 1946. He then returned to Birmingham until 1963, when he became Wykeham Professor of Physics at the University of Oxford. From 1974 to 1977, he was Professor of Physics at the University of Washington, Seattle. Peierls is now an Honorary Fellow of New College, Oxford. His many honours include a knighthood in 1968 and the award of the Royal Medal from the Royal Society in 1959, the Max Planck Medal of the Association of German Physical Societies in 1963, and the Enrico Fermi Award of the US Department of Energy in 1980.

Peierls began his research in 1928, a very exciting time in the development of quantum theory. The laws of quantum mechanics had been formulated consistently and now was the time to begin to apply them to the many unexplained phenomena in the fields of atomic, molecular and solid-state physics. His first work was on the theory of solids and concerned a phenomenon called the Hall effect. Then, in 1929, he developed the theory of heat conduction in non-metallic crystals, concluding that the thermal conductivity of a large perfect crystal should grow exponentially at low temperatures. This was not verified experimentally until 1951. Peierls also proposed a general theory of the diamagnetism of metals.

In nuclear physics, Peierls contributed to the early theory of the neutron-proton system and, in 1938, gave the first complete treatment of resonances in nuclear collisions. During World War II, he was concerned with atomic energy. Uranium fission and the emission of secondary neutrons had been discovered and the possibility of releasing nuclear energy was of wide interest. In 1940, Otto Frisch (1904–1979) and Peierls showed that a simple estimate of the energy released in a chain reaction indicated that a fission bomb would make a weapon of fantastic power. They drew the attention of the British government to this in 1940, and Peierls was placed in charge of a small theoretical group concerned with isotope separation by more precise methods for evaluating the chain reaction and its efficiency. In 1943, when Britain decided not to continue its work on nuclear energy, Peierls moved

to the United States to help in the work of the Manhattan Project, first in New York in consultation with designers of the isotope separation plans and then at Los Alamos.

Peregrinus, Petrus (*born c. 1220*), was a medieval French scientist and scholar about whom little is known except for his seminal work – based largely on experiment – on magnetism. His real name was Peregrinus de Maricourt and he may have been given the name "Peter the Pilgrim" because he was a crusader. He was an engineer in the French army under Louis IX and was active in Paris in the middle of the thirteenth century, where he advised Roger Bacon. He took part in the siege of Lucera in Italy in 1269 and in that year published his findings about magnets in *Epistola de Magnete*. In it he described a simple compass (a piece of magnetized iron on a wooden disc floating in water) and outlined the laws of magnetic attraction and repulsion. His ideas were taken up 250 years later by William Gilbert.

Perrin, Jean Baptiste (*1870–1942*), was a French physicist who made the first demonstration of the existence of atoms. He did this by quantitative observation of Brownian motion. In recognition of this achievement, Perrin was awarded the 1926 Nobel Prize in Physics. He also made an important contribution to the discovery that cathode rays are electrons.

Perrin was born in Lille on 30 September 1870. He was educated in Lyons and Paris and in 1891 entered the École Normale Supérieure, gaining his doctorate six years later. He was then appointed to a readership in physical chemistry at the Sorbonne in 1897 and in 1910 he became Professor of Physical Chemistry there. Perrin retained this position until 1940, when his outspoken antifascism caused him to flee the German occupation. He went to New York, where he died on 17 April 1942.

Perrin's first work of significance was done in 1895 on the nature of cathode rays. The cathode rays generated in discharge tubes were allowed to penetrate thin sheets of glass or aluminium and collected in a hollow cylinder. In this way the rays were shown to carry a negative charge, an indication that they consisted of negatively charged particles. The rays could thus be retarded by an electric field, and Perrin carried out further experiments which included imposing a negative charge on a fluorescent screen onto which various rays were focused. As the negative charge was increased, the intensity of fluorescence fell. He was able in this way to establish crude values for e/m, the charge-to-mass ratio of an electron, which were improved upon by the classic studies

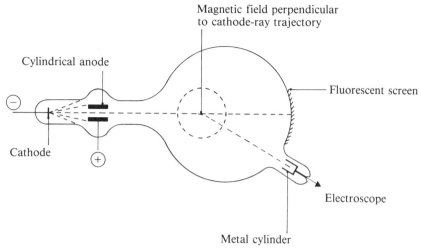

Magnetic field perpendicular
to cathode-ray trajectory

Cylindrical anode

Fluorescent screen

Cathode

Electroscope

Metal cylinder

Perrin demonstrated that cathode rays carry a negative charge, using a specially modified cathode-ray tube in which the rays (electrons) were "collected" in a metal cylinder and their accumulated charge registered by an electrometer.

of J.J. Thomson (1856–1940) in 1897, which established the existence of the electron.

Perrin's more important contribution to scientific knowledge was in papers published in 1909 on atomic theory. Perrin extended the work of Robert Brown (1773–1858), who in 1827 had reported that pollen grains suspended in water and observed by microscope appeared to be in rapid random motion. It was believed that Brownian motion occurs because the tiny pollen grains are jostled by moving water molecules. Perrin suggested that, this being the case, the principles of the kinetic theory of gases were applicable as the grains and water molecules would both behave like gas molecules even though the pollen grains were much greater in size than water molecules.

The experiments that Perrin performed to measure Brownian motion are classics. One system involved gamboge particles obtained from vegetable sap, and required the isolation of 0.1 g of particles of the necessary size from a sample weighing a kilogram; the isolation took several months. In the experiment, the distribution of suspended particles in a container was analysed by depth. It was found that their number decreases exponentially with height and, using principles proposed by Albert Einstein (1879–1955), Perrin was able to deduce a definite value for Avogadro's number which agreed substantially with experimental values obtained in other ways. This showed that Perrin's assumption was correct and that Brownian motion is due to molecular bombardment. Perrin's work on Brownian motion came as close as was possible then to detecting atoms without actually seeing them and it was accepted as a final proof of the existence of atoms.

Pippard, (Alfred) Brian (*1920–   *), is a British physicist who has carried out important work in superconductivity.

Pippard was born on 7 September 1920 in London. He was educated at Clifton College, Bristol and then at Clare College, Cambridge, obtaining his BA in 1941. He then worked as a Scientific Officer at the Radar Research and Development Establishment at Great Malvern until 1945, when he returned to Cambridge. He gained his PhD in 1949, then became a Lecturer in Physics in 1950 and a Reader in 1959. He was then appointed John Humphrey Plummer Professor of Physics at Cambridge in 1960 and since 1971, he has been Cavendish Professor of Physics there. Pippard's honours include a knighthood in 1975, and the award of the Hughes Medal of the Royal Society in 1958.

Pippard is the son of an eminent professor of engineering, and as a boy he was attracted by the fascination of low-temperature physics. He was deterred from this though, thinking his mathematical ability was inadequate. He intended to become a chemist but after graduating in 1941, his work on the design of radar aerials during the war deflected him towards physics. After the war, he became involved in low-temperature work and decided to concentrate his efforts on the task of applying microwaves to the study of superconductors. He worked especially on the way in which electric currents flow without resistance in a thin layer at the surface of the metal. He measured the thickness (about 1000 Å) of this penetration layer and examined variations with temperature and purity. He found that when he tried to change the properties at one point by applying a disturbance, he influenced the metal over a distance which in pure metals is usually greater than the penetration layer thickness. Because of this, he said that the electrons of superconductors possess a property which he called coherence. From this starting point, he worked out an equation relating current to magnetic field. Similar work was being done at the same time in Russia by Lev Landau (1908–1968) and others. In 1957, a definitive theory of superconductivity was derived by John Bardeen (1908–   ), Leon Cooper (1930–   ) and John Schrieffer (1931–   ) and it was found to provide a consistent explanation for both Pippard's and Landau's work. Soon after this, Pippard's guess that impurities in the metal could shorten the coherence length was confirmed, and "dirty" superconductors were produced with the important technological property of carrying currents and generating extremely strong magnetic fields without their resistance reappearing.

Pippard also discovered that absorption of microwaves at the surface of a given metal at low temperatures is governed by one particular characteristic of the conduction electrons – the shape of the Fermi surface. This initiated experiments and theoretical work in many laboratories, which transformed understanding of the dynamical laws governing the motion of electrons in metals. It also clarified the understanding of the way in which one metal differs from another in the details of this motion.

Pixii, Hippolyte (*1808–1835*), was a French inventor who made the first practical electricity generator.

Following Michael Faraday's announcement to the Royal Society (on 24 November 1831) of his discovery of electromagnetic induction and his suggestions for making a simple dynamo, Pixii (an instrument maker, who had learned the craft from his father) set out to construct a practical electricity generator. Shortly afterwards he made a device that consisted of a permanent horseshoe magnet, rotated by means of a treadle, and a coil of copper wire above each of the magnet's poles. The two coils were linked and the free ends of the wires connected to terminals, from which a small alternating current was obtained when the magnet rotated. This device was first publicly exhibited at the French Academy of Sciences in Paris on 3 September 1832. Later, at the suggestion of André-Marie Ampère, a commutator (a simple switching device for reversing the connections to

the terminals as the magnet is rotated) was fitted so that Pixii's generator could produce direct-current electricity. This revised generator was taken to England in November 1833 by Count de Predevalli and exhibited in London. Pixii himself died two years later, only 27 years old, in 1835.

Although Pixii's machine generated only a small current, it was nevertheless the first practical electricity generator and the forerunner of all modern generators.

Planck, Max Karl Ernst Ludwig (*1858–1947*), was a German physicist who discovered that energy consists of fundamental indivisible units that he called quanta. This discovery, made in 1900, marked the foundation of the quantum theory that revolutionized physics in the early 1900s. For this achievement, Planck gained the 1918 Nobel Prize in Physics.

Planck was born at Kiel on 23 April 1858. In 1867, his family moved to Munich, where Planck studied at the Maximilian Gymnasium before entering the University of Munich in 1874. Planck studied mathematics and physics, spending some time in 1877 and 1878 with Gustav Kirchhoff (1824–1887) and Hermann Helmholtz (1821–1894) at the University of Berlin. Planck gained his PhD at Munich with a dissertation on thermodynamics in 1879 and became a lecturer there in the following year. In 1885, he was appointed Extraordinary Professor of Physics at Kiel and then in 1888 moved to Berlin, where he became Assistant Professor of Physics and Director of the newly founded Institute for Theoretical Physics. Planck rose to become Professor of Physics at Berlin in 1892, a position he retained until 1926. In 1930, he was appointed President of the Kaiser Wilhelm Institute but resigned in 1937 in protest at the Nazi's treatment of Jewish scientists. In 1945, the Institute was renamed the Max Planck Institute and moved to Göttingen. Planck was reappointed its President, a position he retained until he died at Göttingen on 4 October 1947.

In 1862, Kirchhoff had introduced the idea of a perfect black body that would absorb and emit radiation at all frequencies, reaching an equilibrium that depended on temperature and not the nature of the surface of the body. A series of investigations were then undertaken into the nature of the thermal radiation emitted by black bodies following the discovery by Josef Stefan (1835–1893) in 1879 that the total energy emitted is proportional to the fourth power of the absolute temperature. Measurements of the frequency distribution of black body radiation by Wilhelm Wien (1864–1928) in 1893 produced the result that the distribution is a function of the frequency and the temperature. A plot of the energy of the radiation against the frequency resulted in a series of curves at different temperatures, the peak value of energy occurring at a higher frequency with greater temperature. This may be observed in the varying colour produced by a glowing object. At low temperatures, it glows red but as the temperature rises the peak energy is emitted at a greater frequency, and the colour become yellow and then white.

Wien found an expression to relate peak frequency and temperature in his displacement law, and then attempted to derive a radiation law that would relate the energy to frequency and temperature. He discovered a radiation law in 1896 that was valid at high frequencies only, while Lord Rayleigh (1842-1919) later found a similar equation that held for radiation emitted at low frequencies. Planck was able to combine these two radiation laws to arrive at a formula that represented the observed energy of the radiation at any given frequency and temperature. This entailed making the assumption that the energy consists of the sum of a finite number of discrete units of energy that he called quanta, and that the energy ε of each quantum is given by the equation $\varepsilon = h\nu$, where ν is the frequency of the radiation and h is a constant now recognized to be a fundamental constant of nature and called Planck's constant. By thus directly relating the energy of a radiation to its frequency, an explanation was found for the observation that radiation of greater energy has a higher frequency distribution.

Classical physics had been unable to account for the distribution of radiation, for Planck's idea that energy must consist of indivisible particles was revolutionary, totally contravening the accepted belief that radiation consisted of waves. But it found rapid acceptance because an explanation for photoelectricity was provided by Albert Einstein (1879-1955) in 1905 using Planck's quantum theory, and in 1913, Niels Bohr (1885-1962) applied the quantum theory to the atom and evidence was at last obtained of the behaviour of electrons in the atom. This was later developed into a full system of quantum mechanics in the 1920s, when it also became clear that energy and matter have both a particle and wave nature. Thus the year 1900 marked not only the beginning of a new century but, with the discovery of the quantum theory, the end of the era of classical physics and the founding of modern physics.

Plücker, Julius (*1801-1868*), was a German mathematician and a physicist. He made fundamental contributions to the field of analytical geometry and was a pioneer of the investigations of cathode rays that led eventually to the discovery of the electron.

Plücker was born in Elberfeld on 16 June 1801. He attended the Gymnasium in Düsseldorf, and studied at the universities of Bonn, Heidelberg, Berlin and Paris. He was awarded his PhD from the University of Warburg in 1824, and he then took up a lectureship at the University of Bonn, where he became a Professor of Mathematics in 1828. In 1833 he moved to Berlin where he held simultaneous posts as extraordinary Professor at the University of Berlin, and as a teacher at the Friedrich Wilhelm Gymnasium. A personality conflict with one of his colleagues prompted him to move to the University of Halle in 1834, where he held the chair of Mathematics for two years. In 1836 Plücker became Professor of Mathematics at the University of Bonn, a post he held until 1847, when he became Professor of Physics at the same institution. He held this post until his death.

Plücker was the author of a number of books on advanced mathematics, and he also published many papers on his work in experimental physics. He did not gain much standing at home among other German physicists, but his talents were quickly recognized abroad. He was elected Fellow of the Royal Society of London in 1855, and was awarded the Copley Medal by that body in 1868. He was also made a Member of the French Academy of Sciences in 1867. Plücker died in Bonn on 22 May 1868.

The first half of Plücker's career was devoted to the study of mathematics. He found a valuable vehicle for the dissemination of his ideas in a newly founded German mathematical journal. He published books on analytical geometry in 1828, 1831, 1835 and 1839. He resumed the study of geometry shortly before his death, and his latest studies were published in 1868. His mathematics was characterized by elegance and clarity. He was able to correct some errors in work published by Leonhard Euler (1707-1783) in 1748. The work he did towards the end of his life was completed by his assistant Felix Klein (1849-1925). During these years Plücker introduced six equations of higher plane curves which have been named Plückers coordinates. His work led to the foundation of line geometry.

When Plücker became Professor of Physics at Bonn in 1847, he turned away from his studies on geometry and plunged into theoretical and experimental physics. He studied optics and gas spectroscopy, recognizing early the potential of the latter technique in analysis. He found the first three hydrogen lines well before Robert Bunsen (1811-1899) and Gustav Kirchhoff (1824-1887) had begun their experiments in this field.

Plücker was strongly influenced by Michael Faraday (1791–1867), who had experimented with electrical discharge in gases at very low pressures. Plücker took up this work and, unlike Faraday, had the advantage of being able to use high-vacuum tubes, which were developed by Heinrich Geissler (1814–1879) in 1855. He found in 1858 that the discharge causes a fluorescent glow to form on the glass walls of the tube, and that the glass could be made to shift by applying an electromagnet to the tube. Johann Hittorf (1824–1914), Plücker's student, continued this work and showed in 1869 that the glow was produced by cathode rays formed in the tube, and in 1897 J.J. Thomson (1856–1940) demonstrated that the rays consist of electrons.

Poisson, Siméon Denis (*1781–1840*), was a French mathematician and physicist. He is mainly remembered for Poisson's ratio in elasticity, which is the ratio of the lateral contraction of a body to its longitudinal extension. The ratio is constant for a given material.

Poisson was born at Pithiviers, Loiret, on 21 June 1781. He went to school at Fontainebleau and entered the École Polytechnique in 1798, where he studied under Joseph Lagrange (1736–1813) and Pierre Laplace (1749–1827). Poisson graduated from the École Polytechnique in 1800 and then became a demonstrator there, rising to deputy professor in 1802 and full professor in 1806. In 1808, he became an astronomer at the Bureau des Longitudes and in the following year was appointed Professor of the Faculty of Sciences at Paris. From 1820, he was closely involved with the administration of education in France, insisting on a proper scientific policy. Poisson died at Paris on 25 April 1840.

Poisson's main contribution to physics was to develop mathematical explanations of phenomena. He was particularly active in electricity and magnetism, in which he derived expressions for the potential and force acting at various points in a system. He was also interested in heat and developed the idea of quantity of heat as well as formulas for the propagation of heat. Poisson summed up his work in several books towards the end of his life. They include *Treatise on Mechanics* (1833) and *Mathematical Theory of Heat* (1835). Poisson also published *Researches on the Movement of Projectiles in Air* (1835), which builds on the work of Gaspard Coriolis (1792–1834) and was the first account of the effects of the Earth's rotation on motion. It inspired the famous pendulum experiment carried out in 1850 by Jean Foucault (1819–1868) that first demonstrated the Earth's rotation.

Poisson also made contributions to mathematics, especially in probability theory, and to

astronomy, in which he investigated planetary and lunar motion.

Powell, Cecil Frank (*1903–1969*), was a British physicist who developed photographic techniques for studying subatomic particles and who discovered the pi-meson (pion). For this discovery he was awarded the 1950 Nobel Prize in Physics.

Powell was born in Tonbridge, Kent, on 5 December 1903, the son of a gunsmith. He won a scholarship to Cambridge University in 1921 and graduated four years later. He then went to the Cavendish Laboratory to do research under Ernest Rutherford and C.T.R. Wilson, working on methods of taking improved photographs of particle tracks in a cloud chamber. Powell gained his PhD in 1928 and moved to the Wills Physics Laboratory at Bristol University as research assistant to A.M. Tyndall (1881–1961). He remained at Bristol, becoming Professor of Physics in 1948 and Director of the laboratory in 1964.

In the early 1930s Tyndall and Powell studied the mobility of ions in gases and the way water droplets condense on ions in a cloud chamber. Then in 1938, instead of photographing the cloud-chamber tracks, Powell made the ionizing particles trace paths in the emulsions of a stack of photographic plates. The technique received a boost with the development of more sensitive emulsions during World War II and in 1947 Powell used it in his discovery of the pi-meson (predicted by Hideki Yukawa in 1935). Powell collaborated with the Italian physicist Giuseppe Occhislini, and together they published *Nuclear Physics in Photographs* (1947), which became a standard text on the subject.

Poynting, John Henry (*1852–1914*), was a British physicist, mathematician and inventor whose various contributions to science included an equation by which the rate of flow of electromagnetic energy (now called the Poynting vector) can be determined, and the measurement of Newton's gravitational constant. He received many honours for his work, including the Royal Society's Royal Medal in 1905.

Poynting was born in Monton, Lancashire, on 9 September 1852. He attended his father's school until 1867, when he entered Owens College in Manchester (later Manchester University), where he gained an external BSc from London University in 1872. He then studied at Trinity College, Cambridge, from 1872 to 1876. After graduation he served as a physics demonstrator - under Balfour Stewart (1828–1887) - at Owens College until 1878, when he was appointed a Research

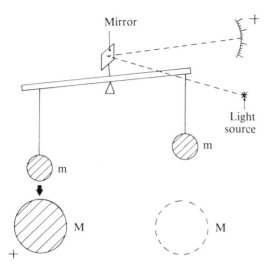

Poynting determined the gravitational constant, G, using a robust but sensitive balance. The beam was counterpoised by two lead alloy balls of mass m (about 22 kg) and its deflection noted after the introduction of the massive sphere M (about 150 kg), first under one end and then under the other end of the beam.

Fellow at Trinity College where he researched in the Cavendish Laboratories under James Clerk Maxwell. In 1880 he became Professor of Physics at Mason College, Birmingham (which became Birmingham University in 1900), a post he held until his death - caused by a diabetic attack - on 30 March 1914 (in Birmingham).

Poynting's first publications, of the late 1870s, were in the field of mathematics and included such subjects as statistical studies of alcoholism in England. After moving to the Cavendish Laboratories in 1878 he began a long series of experiments to determine Newton's gravitational constant (from which can be calculated the Earth's mean density) which was the subject of a competition at Cambridge. He published his most accurate results in 1891, having obtained them using an ordinary beam balance; his figures differ only slightly from those now generally accepted. His experimental method was refined in 1895 by Charles Boys, who used a quartz fibre torsion balance. Poynting recognized the value of Boys' apparatus and used it for several later studies of his own, such as the measurement of radiation pressure.

Poynting's best-known work concerned the transmission of energy in electromagnetic fields. In *On the Transfer of Energy in the Electromagnetic Field* (1884) he published an equation (which he worked out using Maxwell's electro-magnetic field theory) by which the magnitude and direction of the flow of electromagnetic energy - the Poynting vector - can be determined. This equation is usually expressed as:

$$S = (1/\mu)EB \sin \theta$$

where S is the Poynting vector, μ is the permeability of the medium, E is the strength of the electric field, B is the strength of the magnetic field, and θ is the angle between the vectors representing the electric and magnetic fields.

Poynting, in collaboration with W. Barlow, also did important work on radiation. In 1903 he suggested the existence of an effect of the Sun's radiation that causes small particles orbiting the Sun to gradually approach it and eventually plunge in. This idea was later developed by the American physicist Howard Robertson - who related it to the theory of relativity - and is now known as the Poynting-Robertson effect. Poynting also devised a method for measuring the radiation pressure from a body; his method can be used to determine the absolute temperature of celestial objects.

Poynting's other work included a theoretical analysis of the solid to liquid phase change (1881); a statistical analysis of changes in commodity prices on the Stock Exchange (1884); a study of osmotic pressure; and the construction of a saccharometer and a double-image micrometer.

Prandtl, Ludwig (*1875–1953*), was a German physicist who put fluid mechanics on a sound theoretical basis. In particular, he originated the boundary layer theory and did pioneering work in aerodynamics.

Prandtl was born in Freising on 4 February 1875, and entered the Technische Hochschule at Munich in 1894. He specialized in engineering, obtaining his first degree in 1898 and a doctorate in 1900 with a thesis on the lateral instability of beams in bending. In the same year, Prandtl went to work in the Maschinenfabrik Augsburg-Nürnberg, where he became interested in fluid flow. In 1901, he gained a professorship at the Technische Hochschule in Hanover, and then became Professor of Applied Mechanics at Göttingen in 1904. There he constructed the first German wind tunnel in 1909 and built up an important centre for aerodynamics. Prandtl continued to work at Göttingen until his death. An American investigation team arriving there after World War II found that Prandtl, though still active, had not contributed greatly to the German effort. Prandtl died at Göttingen on 15 August 1953.

Prandtl's interest in fluid flow was triggered by his first task in industry, which was to improve a device for the removal of shavings. His studies revealed many weaknesses in the understanding of fluid mechanics. The current theory was unable to explain the observation that in a pipe a fluid would separate from the wall in a sharply divergent section instead of completely filling the pipe. In 1904, Prandtl published a very important paper which proposed that no matter how small the viscosity of a fluid, it is always stationary at the walls of the pipe. This thin static region or boundary layer has a profound influence on the flow of the fluid, and an understanding of the effects of boundary layers was developed to explain the action of lift and drag on aerofoils during the following half century.

In 1906, Prandtl was joined at Göttingen by Theodore von Karman (1881-1963), who arrived as a student and subsequently became Prandtl's collaborator. In 1907, Prandtl investigated supersonic flow, extending the pioneering work of Ernst Mach (1838-1916) to slender bodies. From 1909, Prandtl's aerodynamic studies developed apace as the world became interested in flight. He turned to the problem of drag, which could not be fully explained by the skin friction produced by the boundary layer on a wing. In 1911 and 1912, Karman and Prandtl discovered how vortices cause drag. Prandtl's major contribution being an explanation of induced drag, which he showed was caused by lift inducing a trailing vortex. Much of this work was published after World War I and resulted in major changes in wing design and streamlining of aircraft.

The efforts of Prandtl and Karman in the 1920s led to a greater understanding of turbulent flow. In 1926 Prandtl developed the concept of mixing length - the average distance that a swirling fluid element travels before it dissipates its motion - and was able to produce a plausible theory of turbulence. The concept of mixing length can be thought of as being similar to the mean free path in the kinetic theory of gases. Prandtl's work on turbulence is still the basis of present day theory.

Modern-day aircraft with their high degree of streamlining and swept-back wings all owe their shapes to the work of Prandtl and Karman.

Prévost, Pierre (*1751-1839*), was a Swiss physicist who first showed that all bodies radiate heat, no matter how hot or cold they are.

Prévost was born in Geneva on 3 March 1751. His father, a Calvinist minister, was very keen that his son should have the best possible education and Prévost was sent to study classics, science and theology, but ultimately he turned to the study of law and gained his degree in 1773. After graduating he became a teacher and held various positions in Holland, Lyons and Paris. On the death of his father he returned to Geneva and for a time was Professor of Literature there, but after a year he eventually decided to go back to Paris and work on the translation of a Greek drama.

In 1786 Prevost left Paris once more for Geneva, where he became active in politics. It was at this time that his interest in science re-emerged and he devoted much of his research to the problems of magnetism and then to heat. He was appointed Professor of Philosophy and General Physics at Geneva in 1793 and remained in this post until his retirement in 1823. In his later years, Prévost chose to abandon the earlier research in which he had won such a reputation in favour of studying the ageing process of man. He used himself for his observations, noting down in detail every sign of advancement which his mind, body and mirror showed. A man of many talents, he used his ability for experimental research to the very end. He died in Geneva on 8 April 1839.

Prévost made his classic analysis of heat radiation in 1791. He conducted experiments to determine the heat properties of different kinds of objects under identical conditions. He found that dark, rough-textured objects give out more radiation than smooth, light-coloured bodies, given that both are at the same temperature. He also found that the reverse is true - that dark rough objects absorb more heat radiation than light smooth ones. From these experiments, Prévost conceived of heat as being a fluid composed of particles and that during radiation, the particles streamed out in the form of rays between radiating bodies.

This led to Prévost's theory of heat exchanges. If several objects at different temperatures are placed together, they exchange heat by radiation until all achieve the same temperature. All the objects can then remain at this temperature, however, only if they are receiving as much heat from their surroundings as they radiate away.

Even though Prévost's idea of heat being a fluid, which was the caloric theory current at that time, was erroneous, it did not prevent his basic ideas on heat radiation from being correct. In challenging the notion then prevalent that heat and cold are separate, cold being produced by the entry of cold into an object rather than by an outflow of heat, Prévost made a basic advance in our knowledge of energy. Further consideration of the subject a century later led to the quantum theory of Max Planck (1858-1947) and to the idea that heat and other forms of energy are in fact particulate in nature.

Pringsheim, Ernst (*1859-1917*), was German physicist whose experimental work on the nature of thermal radiation led directly to the quantum theory.

Pringsheim was born in Breslau, Germany (now Wroclaw, Poland) on 11 June 1859. He studied at gymnasia in Breslau and in 1877 entered the University of Heidelberg, moving on to Breslau in 1878 and Berlin in 1879. He gained his PhD at Berlin in 1882 and became a lecturer there in 1886. Pringsheim became Professor of Physics at Berlin in 1896 and in 1905 moved to Breslau to take up the post of Professor of Experimental Physics. He died at Breslau on 28 June 1917.

In 1881, Pringsheim developed an infrared spectrometer that made the first accurate measurements of wavelengths in the infrared region. He put the instrument to its most important use from 1896 onwards when he began to collaborate with Otto Lummer (1860–1925) on a study of black-body radiation. This led to a verification of the Stefan–Boltzmann law that relates the energy radiated by a body to its absolute temperature. Pringsheim and Lummer then proceeded to make careful measurements of the distribution of energy with frequency at various temperatures. They confirmed Wien's displacement law, which relates the peak frequency of maximum energy to the temperature, but in 1899 found anomalies in radiation laws that had been devised to express the energy of the radiation in terms of its frequency and temperature. The results encouraged Max Planck (1858–1947) to find a new radiation law that would account for the experimental results and in 1900, Planck arrived at such a law by assuming that the energy of the radiation consists of indivisible units that he called quanta. This marked the founding of the quantum theory.

R

Rainwater, Leo James (*1917–   *). *See* Bohr, Aage Niels.

Raman, Chandrasekhara Venkata (*1888–1970*), was an Indian physicist who discovered that light is scattered by the molecules in a gas, liquid or solid so as to cause a change in its wavelength. This effect is known as Raman scattering and the Raman spectra produced are used to obtain information on the structure of molecules. For its discovery, Raman was awarded the 1930 Nobel Prize in Physics.

Raman was born in Trichinopoly, Madras, on 7 November 1888. He studied at the A.V.N. College in Vizagapatam, where his father was Professor of Mathematics and Physics, and at the Presidency College of the University of Madras where he obtained a BA in 1904 and an MA in 1907. Although aged only 16 and 19 respectively, Raman gained first class degrees of great distinction. However, he was unable to continue his scientific education as this would have entailed leaving India, and because there were no opportunities for a scientific career in India, Raman entered the financial division of the civil service in 1907, working as an accountant in Calcutta for ten years.

During this time, Raman pursued his studies privately, using the facilities at the laboratories of the Indian Association for the Cultivation of Science in Calcutta. He concentrated his efforts on investigations into vibration in sound and the theory of musical instruments, an interest that continued throughout his life. His work on these subjects and on diffraction prompted an offer of the professorship of physics at the University of Calcutta, which Raman took up in 1917.

Raman remained at Calcutta until 1933, and it was during this period of his life that he made his most important contributions to physics. In 1926 he established the *Indian Journal of Physics* and in 1928 was made President of the Indian Science Congress. Further honours came with the award of a knighthood by the British government in 1929 and the Hughes Medal of the Royal Society in 1930, in addition to the Nobel Prize in Physics in the same year.

In 1934, Raman became head of the physics department at the Indian Institute of Science, a post he held until 1948, also serving as President of the Institute from 1933 to 1937. The Indian government then built the Raman Research Institute for him at Bangalore and he became its first Director in 1948. Raman took his duties as an educator very seriously and trained a great number of young scientists who later rose to positions of responsibility in science. Among his colleagues at the Institute was Homi Bhabha (1909–1966). Raman remained Director of his Institute until he died at Bangalore on 21 November 1970.

Raman was inspired to work on the scattering of light in 1921, when returning to India by sea from a conference in Britain. He was struck by the intense blue colour of the Mediterranean Sea, which he could not reconcile with the explanation put forward by Lord Rayleigh (1842–1919) that attributed the blue colour to the scattering of light by particles suspended in the water. Raman began to investigate this phenomenon upon his arrival in Calcutta. He showed that the blue colour of the sea is produced by the scattering of light by water molecules.

In 1923, Arthur Compton (1892-1923) discovered the Compton effect, in which X-rays are scattered on passing through matter and emerge with a longer wavelength. This was explained by assuming that X-ray particles or photons had collided with electrons and lost some energy. In 1925, Werner Heisenberg (1901-1976) predicted that this effect should be observed with visible light. Raman had independently already come to the same conclusion and had in fact made a preliminary observation of this light scattering effect in 1923. He then refined his experiments and in 1928 was able to report the existence of the scattering effect for monochromatic light in dust-free air and pure liquids. The Raman spectra produced show lines displaced to either side of the normal line in a gas and a continuous band in dense liquids. The effect is caused by the internal motion of the molecules encountered, which may impart energy to the light photons or absorb energy in the resulting collisions. Raman scattering therefore gives precise information on the motion and shape of molecules.

Raman's other research included the effects of sound waves on the scattering of light in 1935 and 1936, the vibration of atoms in crystals in the 1940s, the optics of gemstones, particularly diamonds, and of minerals in the 1950s, and the physiology of human colour vision in the 1960s.

Raman's discovery is important not only because it affords a method for the analysis of molecular structure but also because in demonstrating conclusively that light may behave as particles (photons), it confirms the quantum theory. However Raman is also to be remembered as the father of Indian science.

Rayleigh, Lord (John William Strutt; *1842-1919*), was a British physicist who, with William Ramsay (1852-1916), discovered the element argon. For this achievement Rayleigh was awarded the 1904

Nobel Prize in Physics while Ramsay gained the 1904 Nobel Prize in Chemistry. However, Rayleigh possessed a remarkable grasp of all the fundamental areas of classical physics (electromagnetic theory, thermodynamics, statistical mechanics), producing important contributions in all of these fields.

Rayleigh was born John William Strutt at Langford Grove, Essex, on 12 November 1842. He received private tutoring until 1861 when he entered Trinity College, Cambridge, to study mathematics, graduating in 1865. He was then elected to a Fellowship of Trinity College, which he held until his marriage in 1871. After graduating from Cambridge he travelled to the United States until 1868, and then set up a laboratory in the family home at Terling Place. On the death of his father in 1873, Strutt inherited his title and became Lord Rayleigh. He continued his scientific research, which was considered rather eccentric for a person in his privileged position.

The same year marked Rayleigh's election to the Fellowship of the Royal Society, which he later served as Secretary from 1885 to 1896 and President from 1905 to 1908, and which awarded him the Rumford and Copley Medals. In 1879, he succeeded James Clerk Maxwell (1831-1879) as Cavendish Professor of Experimental Physics at the University of Cambridge, a post he held until his return from the Montreal meeting of the British Association for the Advancement of Science in 1884, at which Rayleigh had held the Presidency.

After 1884, Rayleigh confined most of his research activities to his personal laboratory and study at home. He did serve as Professor of Natural Philosophy at the Royal Institution in London from 1887 to 1905, but his duties there did not require him often to leave home. In 1900, he contributed to the foundation of the National Physical Laboratories at Teddington, Middlesex.

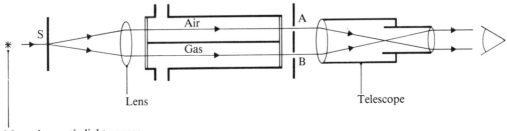

In Rayleigh's refractometer, light from a monochromatic light source passes through a narrow slit at the focus of a lens and then through glass-ended tubes containing air and the gas being studied. Slits A and B at the exit ends of the tubes give rise to two sets of interference bands, which are made to coincide by adjusting the pressure of the gas, from which its refractive index can be found.

In 1908, Rayleigh was appointed Chancellor of Cambridge University, a post he held until his death at Terling Place on 30 June 1919.

Rayleigh's early researches at home during the late 1860s and early 1870s were largely concerned with the properties of waves in the fields of optics and acoustics. He did work on resonance, extending the studies of Hermann Helmholtz (1821–1894), and on vibration. Rayleigh also studied light and colour. In 1871, he explained that the blue colour of the sky arises from the scattering of light by dust particles in the air, and was able to relate the degree of scattering to the wavelength of the light. Rayleigh was also interested in diffraction gratings, and made the first accurate definition of the resolving power of diffraction gratings. This led to improvements in the spectroscope, which in the 1870s was becoming an important tool in the study of solar and chemical spectra. Rayleigh was also responsible for the invention of the optical zone plate.

At Cambridge, Rayleigh's professorial responsibilities enabled him to improve the teaching of experimental physics, causing an explosion in the popularity of the subject which had far-reaching consequences for physics in Britain. In 1884, he completed the project initiated by his predecessor Maxwell that sought the accurate standardization of the three basic electrical units, the ohm, ampere and volt. His insistence on accuracy led to the designing of more precise electrical instruments.

After leaving Cambridge, Rayleigh continued to do research in a broad range of subjects including light and sound radiation, thermodynamics, electromagnetism and mechanics. He was very conscientious at keeping up with developments as they appeared in the scientific literature, and having a keen critical eye, he was often able to devise new experiments to rectify weaknesses he found in the work of others.

The work which most caught the public eye began with Rayleigh's careful study of the measurement of the density of different gases. He originally became interested in this problem because of the old theory known as Prout's hypothesis that all the elements are multiples of hydrogen and would have atomic weights in integers. Rayleigh's results did not support this theory, as others had found, but he made the incidental observation that whenever he measured the density of nitrogen in air it was 0.5 per cent greater than the density of nitrogen from any other source. He immediately eliminated all the possible suggestions for the source of the impurity causing the increase, but could not solve the problem. In desperation he published a short note in *Nature* in 1892, asking for suggestions. Over the next three years, Rayleigh and Ramsay both studied the problem and in the end jointly announced the discovery of a new element: argon. The gas had escaped detection by chemists because of its extreme inertness, which renders it virtually devoid of any chemical properties. Argon might have been discovered a century earlier if Henry Cavendish (1731–1810) had followed up his observation of a residual quantity of gas in air that he simply could not oxidize.

The discovery of argon was followed by one of Rayleigh's most important contributions to physics. This was the Rayleigh–Jeans equation, published in 1900, which described the distribution of wavelengths in black-body radiation. This equation could only account for the longer wavelengths, and Wilhelm Wien (1864–1928) later produced an equation to describe the shorter wavelength radiation.

This inconsistency led to the formulation shortly after of the quantum theory by Max Planck (1858–1947), which accounted for the distribution of all wavelengths by assuming that energy exists in indivisible units called quanta. Rayleigh was not enthusiastic about such a revolutionary solution, which overturned classical ideas of radiation. He was likewise unable to agree with the explanation of the hydrogen spectrum produced by Niels Bohr (1885–1962) in 1913, which developed from the quantum theory, and he also found the special theory of relativity proposed by Albert Einstein (1879–1955) in 1905 to his distaste because it dispensed with the ether as a medium for light waves. He had in fact made an attempt to detect the ether in 1901, and his negative result only added to the evidence for relativity.

However, such conservatism should not blind us to Rayleigh's achievements in advancing and consolidating the branches of classical physics that remained valid. And in bringing about the discovery of argon, he initiated the uncovering of a whole family of elements (the rare gases) that are of great importance in themselves and to an understanding of chemical bonding.

Ritter, Johann Wilhelm (*1776–1810*), was a German physicist who carried out early work on electrolytic cells and who discovered ultraviolet radiation.

Ritter was born in Samnitz, Silesia (now in Poland), on 16 December 1776. He worked first as a pharmacist's apprentice and then after four years, in 1795, went to Jena to study medicine. Until 1804 he also taught at the University of Jena and at Gotha, before moving to Munich as a member of the Bavarian Academy of Science.

He died in Munich six years later on 23 January 1810.

In 1800 Ritter electrolysed water to produce hydrogen and oxygen and two years later developed a dry battery, both of which phenomena convinced him that electrical forces were involved in chemical bonding. He also compiled an electro-chemical series. At about the same time he was studying the effect of light on chemical reactions, and from the darkening of silver chloride in light he discovered ultraviolet radiation.

Röntgen, Wilhelm Konrad (*1845-1923*), was a German physicist who discovered X-rays. For this achievement, he was awarded the first Nobel Prize in Physics in 1901.

Röntgen was born in Lennep, Prussia, on 27 March 1845. He received his early education in Holland and then entered the Polytechnic in Zurich, Switzerland, in 1866 to study mechanical engineering. Röntgen received a diploma in this subject in 1868 and a PhD in 1869. He then became an assistant to August Kundt (1839-1894), who was Professor of Physics at Zurich, and changed direction towards pure science. Under Kundt's guidance, Röntgen made rapid progress in physics. In 1871, he moved to Würzburg and then in 1872 to Strasbourg both times in order to remain with Kundt. He then obtained the position of Professor of Physics and Mathematics at the Agricultural Academy of Hohenheim in 1875, but returned to Strasbourg the following year to teach physics. He was then Professor of Physics at Giessen from 1879 to 1888, when he was appointed to the same position at Würzburg, also becoming Director of the Physical Institute there. Finally in 1900, Röntgen became Professor of Physics and Director of the Physical Institute at Munich. He retired in 1920, and died in poverty on 10 February 1923 at Munich, following runaway inflation in Germany.

During Röntgen's career, he worked on such diverse topics as elasticity, heat conduction in crystals, specific heat capacities of gases and the rotation of plane-polarized light. In 1888, Röntgen made an important contribution to electricity when he confirmed that magnetic effects are produced by the motion of electrostatic charges, following a demonstration of the effect made by Henry Rowland (1848-1901) in 1875, but not since repeated.

It was during his period in Würzburg that Röntgen made his most momentous discovery. In November 1895 he was investigating the properties of cathode rays emitted by a high-vacuum discharge tube, particularly the luminescence produced when such rays impinged on certain chemicals. One of the substances with which he was experimenting was barium platinocyanide. Surprisingly, he found that it glowed even when the tube was encased in black cardboard. He then removed the chemical to an adjacent room; as before it glowed whenever the tube was activated. Such high penetrating power led Röntgen to the conclusion that the radiation was entirely different from cathode rays. Unable to establish the nature of the radiation, which in fact came from the glass walls of the tube when struck by the cathode rays, he coined the term "X-rays". Röntgen was not in doubt that his discovery was unique and therefore decided to look more closely at the nature of his X-rays before publicly announcing their existence. He established that they pass unchanged through cardboard and thin plates of metal, travel in straight lines and are not deflected by electric or magnetic fields.

By January 1896, Röntgen was ready to reveal his work to the general public. As X-rays are absorbed by bone, he illustrated one lecture with an X-ray photograph of a man's hand. The impact was tremendous. Soon the use of X-ray equipment and photography in medical work developed both in Europe and America. The discovery also served as an impetus to other scientists. In France it led Antoine Becquerel (1852-1908) to the discovery of radioactivity the same year, which in turn caused a revolution in ideas of the atom, while the demonstration of X-ray diffraction in 1912 by Max von Laue (1879-1960) brought about methods of investigating atomic and molecular structure.

It is likely that X-rays had been produced by others before Röntgen, because experiments with cathode rays had been going on ever since Julius Plücker (1801-1868) first produced them in 1858. William Crookes (1832-1919) had noticed that photographic plates kept near cathode-ray tubes became fogged, an effect almost certainly due to X-rays. However it was Röntgen who first realized the existence of X-rays and first investigated their properties. It was only right that he was acclaimed by the world for a discovery that has brought immense benefits both in medicine and science. It is perhaps fitting that it was made by a man of total integrity who refused to make any financial gain out of his good fortune, believing that the products of scientific research should be made freely available to all.

Rowland, Henry Augustus (*1848-1901*), was an American physicist who is best known for the development of the concave diffraction grating, which heralded a new era in the analysis of spectra.

Rowland was born in Honesdale, Pennsylvania, on 27 November 1848. As a child he displayed a clear interest in science, and entered the Rensselaer Polytechnic Institute at Troy, New York, in 1865, graduating with a degree in civil engineering in 1870. Rowland spent the next year working on surveys as a railway engineer. In 1871, he became a teacher of natural science at Wooster College in Ohio, but returned to the Rensselaer Polytechnic in 1872 to serve first as an Instructor, and from 1874 as Assistant Professor.

The newly established Johns Hopkins University in Baltimore, Maryland, offered Rowland the Chair of Physics in 1876. He accepted, and spent the next year travelling in Europe meeting scientists such as James Clerk Maxwell (1831-1879) and Hermann Helmholtz (1821-1894), conducting some research and purchasing equipment to make the physics laboratories at Johns Hopkins among the best equipped in the world. Rowland remained as Professor of Physics there until his death at Baltimore on 16 April 1901. He was also the founder and first President of the American Physical Society.

Rowland felt that he did not comfortably fit into the category of either experimental or theoretical physicist. He designed his experiments so that their results might shed light on questions of theoretical interest, but he was also extremely talented at the practical design of experimental apparatus.

His earliest research, in 1873 and 1874, concerned the measurement of the magnetic permeability of nickel, iron and steel, and the demonstration of its variation with the strength of the magnetizing force. This led to one of his most noteworthy experiments, which was conducted while on a brief visit to Helmholtz's laboratory in Berlin in 1875. The question of whether a moving electrically charged body would demonstrate certain properties of an electric current, such as the ability to create a magnetic field, had arisen from the work of Michael Faraday and Maxwell. If it did, then an electric current could be regarded as a sequence of electric charges in motion. Rowland was able to provide the first demonstration that this is in fact so by showing that a rapidly rotating charged body was able to deflect a magnet. Such was the delicacy of this experiment that it was not confirmed until Wilhelm Röntgen (1845-1923) succeeded in repeating it in 1888.

Upon his return to the United States, Rowland began a series of studies aimed at the accurate determination of certain physical constants. He first investigated the value for the ohm, the unit of electrical resistance. The value which he published in 1878 is very close to that accepted today. He then repeated Joule's determination of the mechanical equivalent of heat in 1879, and was able to improve the accuracy of the result.

The development of the concave diffraction grating in 1882 stands as Rowland's major contribution to physics. The science of spectroscopy was well-advanced from the days when prisms had been relied upon for the production of spectra, due particularly to the introduction by Joseph Fraunhofer (1787-1826) of ruled gratings in place of prisms. The quality of the results obtainable depended on the accuracy and density of the scratched rulings on the diffraction gratings. Rowland saw that a critical limiting factor in the ability to produce these lines was the availability of a perfect screw for the ruling machine. He tackled the problem using his engineering expertise, and was eventually able to produce lines at a density of more than 16,000 per cm (40,000 per inch) of grating. This gave a much greater revolving power, but Rowland went on to improve spectroscopy even further by the introduction of a concave metal or glass grating. This had the advantage of being self-focusing and thus eliminated the need for lenses, which absorbed some wavelengths of the spectrum.

Rowland's concave diffraction gratings were a sensational success. He sold over a hundred of the devices, which enabled scientists to accomplish in a few hours what had previously taken days to achieve. Rowland then put his invention to use in the years 1886 to 1895 by remapping the solar spectrum, publishing the wavelengths for 14,000 lines with an accuracy ten times better than his predecessors had managed.

Rumford, Count (Benjamin Thompson; *1753-1814*), was an American physicist who first demonstrated conclusively that heat is not a fluid but a form of motion.

Thompson was born of a farming family at Woburn, Massachusetts, on 26 March 1753. At the age of 19, he became a schoolmaster as a result of much self instruction and some help from local clergy. He moved to Rumford (now Concord, New Hampshire) and almost immediately married a wealthy widow many years his senior. Thompson's first activities seem to have been political. When the War of Independence broke out he remained loyal to the Crown and acted as some sort of secret agent. Obliged to flee to London in 1776 (having separated from his wife the year before), he was rewarded with government work and the appointment as Lt Colonel of a regiment in New York. After the war, he retired from the army and lived permanently in exile in Europe. Thompson moved to Bavaria and spent the next few years with the civil administration there, becoming war and police minister as well as grand chamberlain to the Elector.

In 1781 Thompson was made a Fellow of the Royal Society on the basis of a paper on gunpowder and cannon vents. He had studied the relationship between various gunpowders and the apparent force with which the cannon balls were shot forth. This was a topic, part of a basic interest in guns and other weapons, to which he frequently returned, and in 1797 he produced a gunpowder standard.

In 1791 Thompson was made a Count of the Holy Roman Empire in recognition of all his work in Bavaria. He took the title from Rumford in his homeland, and it is by this name that we know him today.

Rumford was greatly concerned with the promotion of science and in 1796, established the Rumford medals in the Royal Society and in the Academy of Arts and Science, Boston. These were the best endowed prizes of the time, and they still exist today.

In 1799, Rumford returned to England and with Joseph Banks (1743-1820) founded the Royal Institution, choosing Humphry Davy (1778-1829) as lecturer. Its aim was the popularization of science and technology, a tradition that still continues there.

Two years later Rumford resumed his travels. He settled in Paris and married the widow of Antoine Lavoisier (1743-1794), who had produced the caloric theory of heat that Rumford overthrew. However, this was a second unsuccessful match and after separating from his wife, Rumford lived at Auteuil near Paris until his death on 21 August 1814. In his will he endowed the Rumford chair at Harvard, still occupied by a succession of distinguished scientists.

Rumford's early work in Bavaria shows him at his most versatile and innovative. He combined social experiments with his lifelong interests concerning heat in all its aspects. When he employed beggars from the streets to manufacture military uniforms, he was faced with a feeding problem. A study of nutrition led to the recognition of the importance of water and vegetables and Rumford decided that soups would fit the requirements. He devised many recipes and developed cheap food emphasizing the potato. Meanwhile soldiers were being employed in gardening to produce the vegetables, Rumford's interest in gardens and landscape giving Munich its huge Englischer Garten, which he planned and which remains an important feature of the city today. The uniform enterprise led to a study of insulation and to the conclusion that heat was lost mainly through convection; thus clothing should be designed to inhibit this.

No application of heat technology was too humble for Rumford's scrutiny. He devised the domestic range - the "fire in a box" - and special utensils to go with it. In the interests of fuel efficiency, he devised a calorimeter to compare the heats of combustion of various fuels. Smoky fireplaces also drew his attention, and after a study of the various air movements, he produced designs incorporating all the features now considered essential in open fires and chimneys such as the smoke shelf and damper.

His search for an alternative to alcoholic drinks led to the promotion of coffee and the design of the first percolator.

The work for which Rumford is best remembered took place in 1798. As military commander for the Elector of Bavaria, he was concerned with the manufacture of cannon. These were bored from blocks of iron with drills, and it was believed that the cannons became hot because as the drills cut into the cannon, heat was escaping in the form of a fluid called caloric. However, Rumford noticed that heat production increased as the drills became blunter and cut less into the metal. If a very blunt drill was used, no metal was removed yet the heat output appeared to be limitless. Clearly heat could not be a fluid in the metal, but must be related to the work done in turning the drill. Rumford also studied the expansion of liquids of different densities and different specific heats and showed by careful weighings that the expansion was not due to caloric taking up the extra space.

Although the majority of Rumford's scientific work related to heat and its applications, he had an important subsidiary interest in light. He invented the Rumford shadow photometer and established the standard candle, which was the international unit of luminous intensity right up to the 1900s. Transmission of light and shadows cast by coloured sources interested him, and he also looked into concepts of complementary colours. Photosynthesis drew his passing glance and he was probably one of the first to try to relate heat and light in their effects on chemical reaction - the beginnings of the science of photochemistry.

Rumford's contribution to science in demolishing the caloric theory of heat was very important because it paved the way for the realization of the fact that heat is a form of energy and that all forms of energy are interconvertible. However it took several decades to establish the view that caloric does not exist, as the caloric theory readily explained the important conclusions on heat radiation made by Pierre Prévost (1751-1839) in 1791 and on the motive power of heat made by Sadi Carnot (1796-1832) in 1824.

Rutherford, Ernest (*1871-1937*), was a British

physicist who first explained that radioactivity is produced by the disintegration of atoms and discovered that alpha particles consist of helium nuclei. For these achievements, Rutherford was awarded the 1908 Nobel Prize in Chemistry. Rutherford went on to make two more discoveries of fundamental importance to nuclear physics. He was the first to determine the basic structure of the atom and show that it consists of a central nucleus surrounded by electrons, and he also produced the first artificial transformation, thereby changing one element into another.

Rutherford was born near Nelson, New Zealand, on 30 August 1871. His father was a wheelwright and farmer who, like his mother, had emigrated from Britain to New Zealand when a child. Rutherford did not show any great aptitude for science as a child and when he entered Nelson College in 1887, he exhibited an all-round ability. He went on to Canterbury College, Christchurch, in 1889, receiving a BA degree in 1892. He then embarked on a study of mathematics and physics, gaining his MA in 1893 and then a BSc in 1894. Rutherford investigated the magnetic properties of iron by high-frequency electric discharges for his science degree, and constructed a very sensitive detector of radio waves as a result of his research. This was only six years after Heinrich Hertz (1857-1894) had discovered radio waves, and the same year that Guglielmo Marconi (1874-1937) began his radio experiments.

In 1895, Rutherford went to Britain to study at the Cavendish Laboratory, Cambridge. There he became the first research student to work under J.J. Thomson (1856-1940). Armed with his radio detector, Rutherford made a big impact on Cambridge, but under Thomson's guidance, he soon turned to the work in atomic physics that was to become his career. In 1898, helped by Thomson, Rutherford obtained his first academic position with a Professorship in Physics at McGill University, Montreal, Canada, which then boasted the best-equipped laboratory in the world. He was attracted back to Britain in 1907, when he succeeded Arthur Schuster (1851-1934) at Manchester, Schuster declaring that he would resign his chair only for Rutherford. Rutherford built up a renowned laboratory at Manchester, and it was there that he made his momentous discoveries of the nuclear atom and artificial transformation.

During World War I, Rutherford worked for the Admiralty on methods of locating submarines and then in 1919 moved to Cambridge to become Professor of Physics and Director of the Cavendish Laboratory in succession to Thomson. He retained this position for the rest of his life, and was also Professor of Natural Philosophy at the Royal Institution from 1921 onwards. Many honours were accorded to Rutherford in addition to the 1908 Nobel Prize in Chemistry. They included the Royal Society's Copley Medal in 1922, the Presidency of the Royal Society from 1925 to 1930, a knighthood in 1914, the Order of Merit in 1925, and a peerage in 1921, Rutherford taking the title Baron Rutherford of Nelson. In his last years, Rutherford was active in helping refugee scientists who had escaped from Nazi Germany. Rutherford died at Cambridge on 19 October 1937 and is buried in Westminster Abbey.

When Rutherford first came to the Cavendish Laboratory, Thomson put him to work to study the effect that X-rays have on the discharge of electricity in gases. This was early in 1896, only a few weeks after Wilhelm Röntgen (1845-1923) had discovered X-rays. Rutherford found that positive and negative ions are formed, and measured the mobility of the ions produced. In 1897 he went on to make a similar study of the effects of ultraviolet light and the radioactivity produced by uranium minerals, which had been discovered by Antoine Becquerel (1852-1908) the year before. Rutherford then became fascinated by radioactivity and began a series of investigations to explore its nature. In 1898, he found that there are two kinds of radioactivity with different penetrating power. The less penetrating he called alpha rays and the more penetrating beta rays. In 1900, Rutherford discovered a third type of radioactivity with great penetrating power, which he called gamma rays. (Alpha and beta rays were later found to consist of streams of particles and so are now known as alpha particles and beta particles. Gamma rays were found to be electromagnetic waves of very high frequency and so are called gamma rays or gamma radiation.)

When Rutherford moved to Montreal in 1898, he began to use thorium as a source of radioactivity instead of uranium. He found that thorium produces an intensely radioactive gas, which

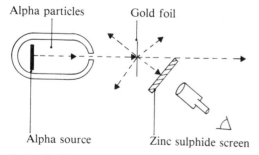

Alpha particles   Gold foil

Alpha source   Zinc sulphide screen

Rutherford postulated the existence of the atomic nucleus by observing wide-angle scattering of (positively charged) alpha particles by gold atoms.

he called emanation. This was a decay product of thorium and Rutherford discovered several more, including thorium X. To identify these products, Rutherford enlisted the aid of Frederick Soddy (1877-1956), who was later to discover isotopes. Analysis of the decay products enabled Rutherford and Soddy in 1903 to explain that radioactivity is an atomic phenomenon, caused by the breakdown of the atoms in the radioactive element to produce a new element. Rutherford found that the intensity of the radioactivity produced decreases at a rate governed by the element's half-life. The idea that atoms could change their identity was revolutionary, yet so compelling was Rutherford's explanation of radioactivity that it was accepted immediately with very little opposition.

Rutherford was now concerned to identify alpha rays, which he was sure consisted of positively charged particles and specifically either hydrogen or helium ions. Deflection of the rays in electric and magnetic fields proved in 1903 that they are positive particles, but Rutherford was unable to determine the amount of charge because his apparatus was not sensitive enough.

In 1904, with Bertram Boltwood (1870-1927), Rutherford worked out the series of transformations that radioactive elements undergo and showed that they end as lead. They were able to estimate the rates of change involved and in 1907 Boltwood calculated the ages of mineral samples, arriving at figures of more than a thousand million years. This was the first proof of the age of rocks, and the method of radioactive dating has since been developed into a precise way of finding the age of rocks, fossils and ancient artefacts.

On returning to Britain in 1907, Rutherford continued to explore alpha particles. In conjunction with Hans Geiger (1882-1945), he developed ionization chambers and scintillation screens to count the particles produced by a source of radioactivity, and by dividing the total charge produced by the number of particles counted, arrived at the conclusion that each particle has two positive charges. The final proof that alpha particles are helium ions came in the same year, when Rutherford and Thomas Royds succeeded in trapping alpha particles in a glass tube and by sparking the gas produced showed from its spectrum that it was helium.

Rutherford's next major discovery came only a year later in 1909. He suggested to Geiger and a gifted student named Ernest Marsden that they investigate the scattering of alpha particles by gold foil. They used a scintillation counter that could be moved around the foil, which was struck by a beam of alpha particles from a radon source. Geiger and Marsden found that a few particles were deflected through angles of more than 90° by the foil. Rutherford was convinced that the explanation lay in the nature of the gold atoms in the foil, believing that each contained a positively charged nucleus surrounded by electrons. Only such nuclei could repulse the positively charged alpha particles that happened to strike them to produce such enormous deflections. But Rutherford needed proof of this theory. He worked out that the nucleus must have a diameter of about 10^{-13} cm - 100,000 times smaller than the atom - and calculated the numbers of particles that would be scattered at different angles. These predictions were confirmed experimentally by Geiger and Marsden, and Rutherford announced the nuclear structure of the atom in 1911.

Few were convinced that the atom could be almost entirely empty space as Rutherford contended. However, among those who agreed with Rutherford was Niels Bohr (1885-1962). He came to Manchester to work in 1912 and in 1913 produced his quantum model of the atom which assumed a central positive nucleus surrounded by electrons orbiting at various energy levels. Also in 1913, another of Rutherford's co-workers, Henry Moseley (1887-1915), announced his discovery of the atomic number, which identifies elements, and showed that it could only be given by the number of positive charges on the nucleus, and thus the number of electrons around it. Rutherford's view of the nuclear atom was thereby vindicated, and universally accepted.

Several more important discoveries were made at Manchester. In 1914, Rutherford found that positive rays consist of hydrogen nuclei. Also in 1914, Rutherford and Edward Andrade showed that gamma rays are electromagnetic waves by diffracting them with a crystal. They measured the wavelengths of the rays and found that they lie beyond X-rays in the electromagnetic spectrum. Becquerel in 1900 had identified beta rays with cathode rays, which were shown to be electrons, and so the nature of radioactivity was now revealed in full.

Rutherford's work was now interrupted by war and he did not return to physics until 1917, when he made his last great discovery. He made it unaided, unlike most of his earlier discoveries, because all his colleagues and students were still engaged in war work. Rutherford followed up earlier work by Marsden in which scintillations were noticed in hydrogen bombarded by alpha particles well beyond their range in the gas. These were due to hydrogen nuclei knocked on by the alpha particles, which was not unexpected. However Rutherford now carried out the same experiment using nitrogen instead of hydrogen, and he found that hydrogen nuclei were still produced and not nitrogen nuclei. Rutherford announced his interpretation of this result in 1919, stating that the alpha particles had caused the nitrogen nuclei to disintegrate, forming hydrogen and oxygen nuclei. This was the first artificial transformation of one element into another. Rutherford found similar results with other elements and announced that the nucleus of any atom must be composed of hydrogen nuclei. At Rutherford's suggestion, the name proton was given to the hydrogen nucleus in 1920. He also speculated in the same year that uncharged particles, which were later called neutrons, must also exist in the nucleus.

Rutherford continued work on artificial transformation in the 1920s. Under his direction, Patrick Blackett (1897–1974) in 1925 used a Wilson cloud chamber to record the tracks of disintegrated nuclei, showing that the bombarding alpha particles combines with the nucleus before disintegration and does not break the nucleus apart like a bullet. Bombardment with alpha particles had its limits as large nuclei repelled them without disintegrating, and Rutherford directed the construction of an accelerator to produce particles of the required energy. The first one was built by John Cockcroft (1897–1967) and Ernest Walton (1903–   ), and went into operation at the Cavendish Laboratory in 1932. In the same year, another of Rutherford's colleagues, James Chadwick (1891–1974), discovered the neutron at the Cavendish Laboratory.

Rutherford was to make one final discovery of great significance. In 1934, using some of the heavy water recently discovered in the United States, Rutherford, Marcus Oliphant and Paul Harteck bombarded deuterium with deuterons and produced tritium. This may be considered the first nuclear fusion reaction.

Rutherford may be considered the father of nuclear physics, both for the fundamental discoveries that he made and for the encouragement and direction he gave to so many important physicists involved in the development of this science.

Rydberg, Johannes Robert (*1854–1919*), was a Swedish physicist who discovered a mathematical expression that gives the frequencies of spectral lines for elements. It includes a constant named the Rydberg constant after him.

Rydberg was born in Halmstad on 8 November 1854. He was educated at the Gymnasium in Halmstad and in 1873 entered the University of Lund, graduating in mathematics in 1875 and gaining a doctorate in this subject in 1879. He then remained at Lund for the rest of his life,

beginning work as a lecturer in mathematics in 1880. He became a lecturer in physics in 1882 and was appointed Professor of Physics provisionally in 1897 and permanently in 1901. He retained this position until a month before his death, which occurred at Lund on 28 December 1919.

Rydberg worked in the field of spectroscopy. He did not do a great amount of experimental investigation, but was concerned to organize the mass of observations of spectral lines into some kind of order. Rydberg began by classifying the lines into three types: principal (strong, persistent lines), sharp (weaker but well-defined lines) and diffuse (broader lines). Each spectrum of an element consists of several series of these lines superimposed over each other. He then sought to find a mathematical relationship that would relate the frequencies of the lines in a particular series. In 1890, he achieved this by using a quantity called the wave number, which is the reciprocal of the wavelength. The formula expresses the wave number in terms of a constant common to all series (the Rydberg constant), two constants that are characteristic of the particular series, and an integer. The lines are then given by changing the value of the integer.

Rydberg then found that Johann Balmer (1825–1898) had already developed a formula for a series of lines of the hydrogen spectrum in 1885. However, it turned out to be a special case of his own more general formula. Rydberg then went on to produce another formula which he believed would express the frequency of every line in every series of an element. This formula is

$$N = R[1/(n+a)^2 - 1/(m+b)^2]$$

where N is the wave number, R is the Rydberg constant, n and m are integers, m being greater than n, and a and b are constants for a particular series.

Rydberg's intuition proved to be correct and five more series of hydrogen lines were subsequently discovered that fitted the formula. Although it was an empirical discovery and Rydberg was unable to explain why his formula expressed the spectral lines, Niels Bohr (1885–1962) was able to show that it gave the energy states required for the theory of atomic structure that he presented in 1913.

In 1897 Rydberg put forward the idea of atomic number and the importance of this in revising the periodic table. His views were vindicated in the brilliant research conducted into X-ray spectra by Henry Moseley (1887–1915) in 1913. The Rydberg formula also proved to be of use in determining the electronic shell structure of elements, which provided a proper basis for the classification of the elements.

143

S

Sabine, Edward (*1788-1883*), was a British geophysicist who made important studies of terrestrial magnetism.

Sabine was born in Dublin, Ireland, on 14 October 1788. He received a military education at the Royal Military Academy at Woolwich, and never attended any university courses in science. In 1803 Sabine was commissioned in the Royal Artillery, with which he served his military career, rising to the rank of Major General in 1859. In 1818, he was elected to the Royal Society, serving in a variety of positions and ultimately becoming President from 1861 to 1871.

In 1818 Sabine accompanied the expedition headed by Sir John Ross (1777-1856) to explore the North-West Passage as official astronomer. The following year he went with William Parry (1790-1855) to the Arctic. While on this voyage he planned a trip in the southern hemisphere which he undertook at the behest of the Royal Society from 1821 to 1822. Sabine then collaborated with Charles Babbage (1792-1871) in 1826 on a survey of magnetism in Britain, a project which was not completed until the 1830s and which was repeated by Sabine himself in the late 1850s. Sabine was also active in the British Association, serving as Secretary to the organization from 1838 to 1859, with the exception of the year 1852, when he was President. From 1849 to 1871, he was deeply involved with the administration of the King's Observatory at Kew. Sabine was awarded several honours, including the Copley Medal of the Royal Society, and was knighted in 1869. He died in Richmond, Surrey, on 26 June 1883.

During the 1820s, one of Sabine's major concerns was the use of the pendulum apparatus designed by Henry Kater (1777-1835) to determine the shape of the Earth. It was for these studies, which involved analysing data from 17 field stations around the globe, that Sabine was awarded the Copley Medal. His conclusions have since been somewhat modified because he failed to consider the fact that the density of the crust is not uniform and so obtained an erroneous result for the shape of the Earth.

Sabine's greatest scientific interest was the study of terrestrial magnetism, and he used his considerable influence to instigate a British "magnetic crusade". An expedition to establish observatories in the southern hemisphere was sent out in 1839 and Sabine managed to extend its duration for two three-year periods beyond its original duration, and thereby accumulated an enormous bulk of data. With this, Sabine in 1851 discovered a 10-11 year periodic fluctuation in the number of magnetic storms. He then brilliantly correlated this magnetic cycle with data Samuel Schwabe (1789-1875) had collected on a similar variation in solar activity. Sabine was thereby able to link the incidence of magnetic storms with the sunspot cycle. This work was also done independently by Johann von Lamont (1805-1879) about the same time. Other results also grew out of Sabine's huge mass of data and in 1851, he was able to demonstrate that the daily variation in magnetic activity comprised two different components.

Sabine's enthusiasm for the subject of terrestrial magnetism yielded important new findings in that field, but it is considered that he caused too great a proportion of the available funding for research to be diverted to fields relevant to that subject and may have compromised other more important fields of research.

Sakharov, Andrei Dmitriyevich (*1921-*), is a Russian physicist who was closely involved with the development of Soviet thermonuclear weapons. He later repudiated this work and became an active campaigner for nuclear disarmament and human rights. This resulted in the award of the 1975 Nobel Peace Prize and in his banishment in 1980.

Sakharov was born in Moscow on 21 May 1921 and followed in his father's footsteps to become a physicist. He showed exceptional scientific ability early on in his education and studied at Moscow State University, graduating in 1942. In 1945, Sakharov joined the staff of the P.N. Lebedev Institute of Physics in Moscow as a physicist and spent his research life there. In 1953, at the age of 32, he became the youngest man ever to be made a Full Member of the Soviet Academy of Sciences. Sakharov's other Soviet honours include the Hero of Socialist Labour, the Order of Lenin, and Laureate of the USSR. In addition to the 1975 Nobel Peace Prize, his foreign honours include Membership of the American Academy of Arts and Sciences in 1969 and the National Academy of Sciences in 1972, the Eleanor Roosevelt Peace Award in 1973, and the Cino del Duca Prize and the Reinhold Niebuhr Prize from Chicago University in 1974.

In 1980, Sakharov was stripped of his Soviet honours and banished to Gorky, where he has since lived on a pension from the Academy of Sciences. He has continued to be given honours abroad, receiving the Fritt Ord Prize in 1980 and becoming a Foreign Associate of the French Academy of Science in 1981.

At the P.N. Lebedev Institute of Physics, Sakharov worked with Igor Tamm (1895-1971), who was to win the 1958 Nobel Prize in Physics with Pavel Cherenkov (1904-   ) and Ilia Frank (1908-   ) for their work on Cherenkov radiation. In 1948, Sakharov and Tamm published a paper in which they outlined a principle for the magnetic isolation of high temperature plasma, and in so doing significantly altered the course of Soviet research into thermonuclear reactions. From 1948 to 1956, their work was solely on research connected with nuclear weapons and was top secret. It led directly to the explosion of the first Soviet hydrogen bomb in 1953 but by 1950, Sakharov and Tamm had also formulated the theoretical basis for controlled thermonuclear fusion - the means by which thermonuclear power could be used for the generation of electricity and other peaceful ends.

By the end of the 1950s, Sakharov was becoming interested in wider issues and in 1958, with Yakov B. Zeldovich, he published an article in *Pravda* advocating educational reforms which contradicted official pronouncements. Sakharov pointed out that mathematicians and physicists are most creative early on in their careers and proposed early entry into university. Many of Sakharov's ideas were incorporated. In the early 1960s, he joined the controversy between the genetics of Gregor Mendel (1822-1884) and that of Trofim Lysenko (1898-1976) and was instrumental in breaking Lysenko's hold over Soviet science and in giving science some political immunity. His scientific papers in the 1960s concerned the structure of the Universe. In 1965 he wrote on the initial stages of an expanding Universe and the appearance of non-uniformity in the distribution of matter, and in the following year on quarks, which are thought by some physicists to be the basic components of protons.

After the mid-1960s, Sakharov's activities showed a shift of interest. In 1968, he published a famous essay entitled *Progress, Peaceful Coexistence and Intellectual Freedom*, which argued for a reduction of nuclear arms by all nuclear powers, an increase in international cooperation and the establishment of civil liberties in Russia. This was followed in 1970 by the founding of a Committee for Human Rights by Sakharov and other Soviet physicists to promote the principles expressed in the Universal Declaration of Human Rights. Sakharov's subsequent publications on this theme included *Sakharov Speaks* (1974), *My Country and the World* (1975) and *Alarm and Hope* (1979) and made him an international figure. But his fame also brought increasing harassment from the Soviet authorities, and Sakharov was not allowed to go to Norway to collect his Nobel Prize. Finally, in 1980, he was removed from Moscow and banished to Gorky, ending both his work and his influence.

Sakharov's fundamental work on controlled thermonuclear fusion may one day result in the production of cheap energy. His bravery in resisting oppression and calling for the peaceful use of science demonstrate a rare strength of character.

Schrödinger, Erwin (*1887-1961*), was an Austrian physicist who founded wave mechanics with the formulation of the Schrödinger wave equation to describe the behaviour of electrons in atoms. For this achievement, he was awarded the 1933 Nobel Peace Prize with Paul Dirac (1902-   ) and Werner Heisenberg (1901-1976), who also made important advances in the theory of atomic structure.

Schrödinger was born in Vienna on 12 August 1887. His father was an oilcloth manufacturer who had studied chemistry and his mother the daughter of a chemistry professor. Apart from a few weeks when he attended an elementary school in Innsbruck, Schrödinger received his early education from a private tutor. In 1898 he entered the Gymnasium in Vienna where he enjoyed mathematics, physics and ancient languages. He then attended the University of Vienna, specializing in physics. Schrödinger obtained his doctorate in 1910 and a year later he became an assistant in the University's Second Physics Institute. His early research ranged over many topics in experimental and theoretical physics.

During World War I, Schrödinger served as an artillery officer and then returned to his previous post at Vienna. Conditions were difficult in Austria after the war and Schrödinger decided to go to Germany in 1920. After a series of short-lived posts at Jena, Stuttgart and Breslau, he became Professor of Physics at Zurich in 1921.

Schrödinger's most productive work was done at Zurich and it resulted in his succeeding Max Planck (1858-1947) as Professor of Theoretical Physics at Berlin in 1927. He remained there until the rise of the Nazis in 1933, when Schrödinger went to Oxford, England, where he became a fellow of Magdalen College. Homesick, he returned to Austria in 1936 to take up a post at Graz, but the Nazi takeover of Austria in 1938 placed Schrödinger in danger. The intervention of the Prime Minister of Ireland, Eamon de Valera (1882-1975), led to his appointment in 1939 to a post at the Institute for Advanced Studies in Dublin. Schrödinger continued work in theoretical physics there until 1956, when he returned to Austria to a chair at the University of Vienna. In the following year, a severe illness occurred from which Schrödinger never fully recovered. He died in Vienna on 4 January 1961.

The origin of Schrödinger's great discovery of wave mechanics began with the work of Louis De Broglie (1892-   ) who, in 1924, using ideas from Einstein's special theory of relativity, showed that an electron or any other particle has a wave associated with it. The fundamental result was that $\lambda = h/p$ where λ is the wavelength of the associated wave, h is Planck's constant and p is the momentum of the particle. An immediate deduction from this discovery was that if particles, and particularly electrons, have waves then their behaviour should be capable of description by a particular type of partial differential equation known as a wave equation in the same way as sound and other kinds of waves. These ideas were taken up by both De Broglie and Schrödinger and in 1926 each published the same wave equation which, when written in relativistic terms, is:

$$\frac{1}{c^2} \cdot \frac{\delta^2 \psi}{\delta t^2} = \frac{\delta^2 \psi}{\delta x^2} - \frac{\delta^2 \psi}{\delta y^2} + \frac{\delta^2 \psi}{\delta z^2} - \frac{4\pi^2 m^2 c^2}{h^2} \cdot \psi$$

where ψ is the wave function, t is the time, m the mass of the electron, c is the velocity of light, h is Planck's constant and x,y and z represent the position of the electron in Cartesian co-ordinates. Unfortunately, while the equation is true, it was very little help in developing further facts and explanations.

Later the same year, however, Schrödinger used a new approach. After spending some time studying the mathematics of partial differential equations and using the Hamiltonian function, a powerful idea in mechanics due to William Rowan Hamilton (1805-1865), he formulated an equation in terms of the energies of the electron and the field in which it was situated. His new equation was:

$$\frac{\delta^2 \psi}{\delta x^2} + \frac{\delta^2 \psi}{\delta y^2} + \frac{\delta^2 \psi}{\delta z^2} + \frac{8\pi^2 m}{h^2}(E - V)\psi = 0$$

where E is the total energy of the electron and V is the potential of the field in which the electron is moving. This equation neglects the small effects of special relativity. Partial differential equations have many solutions and very stringent conditions had to be fulfilled by the individual solutions of this equation in order for it to be useful in describing the electron. Among other things, they had to be finite and possess only one value. These solutions were associated with special values of E, known as proper values or eigenvalues. Schrödinger solved the equation for the hydrogen atom, where $V = -e^2/r$, e being the electron's charge and r is its distance from the nucleus, and found that the values of E corresponded with those of the energy levels given in the older theory

of Niels Bohr (1885-1962). Also, to each value of E there corresponded a finite number of particular solutions for the wave function ψ, and these could be associated with lines in the spectrum of atomic hydrogen. In the hydrogen atom the wave function describes where we can expect to find the electron, and it turns out that while it is most likely to be where Bohr predicted it to be, it does not follow a circular orbit but is described by the more complicated notion of an orbital, a region in space where the electron can be found with varying degrees of probability.

Atoms other than hydrogen and also molecules and ions can be described by Schrödinger's wave equation but such cases are very difficult to solve. In certain cases approximations have been used, usually with the numerical work being carried out on a computer.

Schrödinger's mathematical description of electron waves found immediate acceptance because these waves could be visualized as standing waves around the nucleus. In 1925, a year before Schrödinger published his results, a mathematical system called matrix mechanics developed by Max Born (1882-1970) and Werner Heisenberg (1901-1976) had also succeeded in describing the structure of the atom but it was totally theoretical and gave no picture of the atom. Schrödinger's vindication of De Broglie's picture of electron waves immediately overturned matrix mechanics, though it was later shown that wave mechanics is equivalent to matrix mechanics.

During his later years, Schrödinger became increasingly worried by the way quantum mechanics, of which wave mechanics is a part, was interpreted, in particular with the probabilistic nature of the wave function. Schrödinger believed he had given a great description to the atom in the same way that Newton's laws described mechanics and Maxwell's equations described electrodynamics, only to find that the structure of the atom became increasingly more difficult to describe explicitly with each new discovery. Much of his later work was concerned with philosophy, particularly as applied to physics and the atom.

Schrödinger made a fundamental contribution to physics in finally producing a solid mathematical explanation of the quantum theory first advanced by Planck in 1900, and the subsequent structures of the atom formulated by Bohr and De Broglie.

Shaw, William Napier (*1854-1945*), was a British meteorologist who, in the late 1800s and early 1900s, did much to establish the then young science of meteorology. He is probably best known, however, for introducing in 1909 the millibar as the meteorological unit of atmospheric pressure (not used internationally until 1929) and for inventing the tephigram, a thermodynamic diagram widely used in meteorology, in about 1915. He received numerous honours for his work, including the 1910 Symons Gold Medal (the Royal Meteorological Society's highest award) and a knighthood in 1915.

Shaw was born in Birmingham on 4 March 1854, the third son of a manufacturing goldsmith and jeweller. He was educated at King Edward VI School, Birmingham, then won a scholarship to Emmanuel College, Cambridge, from which he graduated in 1876. In the following year he was elected a Fellow of Emmanuel College and was also appointed a lecturer in experimental physics at the Cavendish Laboratory (part of Cambridge University); he became Assistant Director of the Cavendish Laboratory in 1898. In 1900 he was appointed Secretary of the Meteorological Council which, because of the large workload involved, necessitated his resigning from the Cavendish Laboratory; he retained his fellowship until 1906, however. In 1905 he was made Director of the Meteorological Office, a post he held until his official retirement in 1920; under his directorship the Meteorological Office was transferred to the Air Ministry. From 1907 until 1920 he was also Reader in Meteorology then, on retiring in 1920, was appointed the first Professor of Meteorology at the Royal College of Science of the Imperial College of Science and Technology (part of London University), where he remained until 1924. In 1923 he married Sarah Dugdale, a lecturer at Newnham College, Cambridge. Even after retiring (for the second time), Shaw continued his meteorological writings. He died in London on 23 March 1945.

In addition to his introduction of the millibar and invention of the tephigram - both of which are still used in meteorology - Shaw made several other important contributions to the science. While at the Meteorological Office he pioneered the study of the upper atmosphere by using instruments carried by kites and high-altitude balloons. In 1906, working with R. Lempfert, he measured the rate of descent of air in two anticyclones (arriving at figures of 350 m and 450 m per day) and, in the case of one particular depression, calculated that two million million tonnes of air must have moved to account for the pressure drop. From these studies - described in *Life History of Surface Air Currents* (1906) - Shaw came near to proposing the polar front theory of cyclones later put forward by Jacob Bjerknes. Again in collaboration with Lempfert, Shaw wrote *Weather Forecasting* (1911) and *The Air and its Ways* (1923), in which they described their work in determining the paths of air (by means of

synoptic charts) in and around the North Atlantic pressure system. This work on pressure fronts formed the basis of a great deal of later work in the field. As a successor to *Forecasting Weather*, Shaw wrote the four-volume *Manual of Meteorology* (1926-1931), his most important book and still a valuable standard reference work. He also studied hygrometry, evaporation, and ventilation, and (with J.S. Owens), wrote *The Smoke Problem of Great Cities* (1925), an early work on atmospheric pollution.

Shockley, William Bradford (*1910-*). *See* Bardeen, John.

Simon, Franz Eugen (*1893-1956*), was a German-born British physicist who developed methods of achieving extremely low temperatures and who also established the validity of the third law of thermodynamics.

Simon was born in Berlin on 2 July 1893. In 1903, he entered the Kaiser Friedrich Reform Gymnasium, Berlin, and received a classical education. However, Simon's interest in science enabled him in 1912 to enter the University of Munich to read physics, chemistry and mathematics. He spent a year in Munich under Arnold Sommerfeld (1868-1951) and then a term at Göttingen before he was called up for military service in 1913. Simon was wounded twice and became one of the first poison gas casualties, but was awarded the Iron Cross first class. In 1919, he resumed his studies at Berlin, obtaining his DPhil in 1921 under Hermann Nernst (1864-1941). In 1922, Simon became Assistant to Nernst at the Physical Chemical Institute of the University of Berlin and remained there for ten years, becoming a privatdozent (unpaid lecturer) in 1924 and Associate Professor in 1927.

In 1931, Simon took over the Chair of Physical Chemistry at the Technical University in Breslau. With the rise to power of Hitler in 1933, Simon could foresee trouble brewing because he was Jewish. He resigned his post in that year, and accepted an invitation from Frederick Lindemann (Lord Cherwell; 1886-1957) to work at the Clarendon Laboratory, Oxford. In 1936, Simon became a Reader in Thermodynamics there. He then decided to stay in Britain and became a British citizen in 1938. During World War II, Simon worked on the atomic bomb project, being concerned with the separation of uranium isotopes by gaseous diffusion.

After the war, Simon became Professor of Thermodynamics at Oxford in 1945 and held this post until 1956, when he was appointed Dr Lee's Professor of Experimental Philosophy at Oxford, succeeding Lindemann. He held this position for only a few weeks and then died at Oxford on 31 October 1956. Among the honours Simon received were the Rumford Medal of the Royal Society in 1948 and a knighthood in 1955.

Simon's first scientific work was his PhD thesis under Nernst on the study of specific heats at low temperatures. While he was at the Physical Chemistry Institute at Berlin University, he built up the low temperature department. He worked on the solidification of helium and other gases by the use of high pressure, and discovered the specific heat anomaly in solid orthohydrogen. In 1930, he installed a new hydrogen liquefier into his laboratory to his own design and this design was adopted by many other laboratories. In 1932, Simon worked out a method for generating liquid helium by single-stroke adiabatic expansion, and this too came to be used widely for its simplicity and cheapness.

From 1933, when Simon went to Britain, his work was concerned with magnetic cooling and investigations below 1K, the properties of liquid helium and specific heats. He made a major contribution to physics by showing that the third law of thermodynamics is obeyed at very low temperatures. This law was proposed by Nernst in 1905 and it states that the entropy of a substance approaches zero as its temperature approaches absolute zero. There were subsequently doubts that this is a universal law applicable in all cases, but Simon's low temperature work dispelled them and the expression of the third law in this form is largely due to his efforts.

Simon also did a lot of work on helium. Helium is the only substance which, under its vapour pressure, remains liquid down to absolute zero. Liquid helium is unique too in that at low temperatures, its internal energy is smaller than that of the solid in equilibrium with it. Simon succeeded in establishing the helium vapour pressure scale below 1.7K and heat transport in liquid helium below 1K. He worked on the properties of fluids at high pressure and low temperature, and showed that helium could be solidified at a temperature ten times as high as its liquid/gas critical point. He also worked on heat conductivity in connection with radiation damage.

In the magnetic field, Simon is most noted for his lead in using magnetic cooling to open up a new range of very low temperatures for a wide variety of physical experiments. In Britain in the 1930s, he developed adiabatic demagnetization to investigate properties of substances below 1K. He then went on to investigate nuclear cooling, showing that the cooling effect is limited by interaction energies and that if, instead of a paramagnetic salt, a substance is chosen whose para-

magnetism is due to nuclear spins, then lower temperatures can be reached as the interaction energies for nuclear magnetic moments are smaller than for electron moments. In this way, Simon finally achieved temperatures nearly one millionth of a degree above absolute zero.

Simpson, George Clark (*1878–1965*), was a British meteorologist whose numerous contributions to meteorology included studies of atmospheric electricity and of the effect of radiation on the polar ice, and standardization of the Beaufort Scale of wind speed. Among the many honours he received for his work were the Symons Gold Medal from the Royal Meteorological Society in 1930 and a knighthood in 1935.

Simpson was born in Derby on 2 September 1878, the son of a successful tradesman. In about 1887 he was sent to the Diocesan School, Derby, a small school (with a limited curriculum) for educating the sons of tradesmen and artisans. He left school in 1894 and entered his father's business. After reading popular science books, however, he became interested in optics and began to attend evening classes. On his father's suggestion, he then decided to try to further his education at Owens College, Manchester (later Manchester University) and, after private coaching, passed the entrance examination and began studying at the college in 1897. Because of his lack of higher education, he was initially advised to study for an ordinary degree but, at the instigation of Arthur Schuster (1851–1934), changed to an honours degree course. He gained a first class honours degree in 1900 and became an unsalaried tutor at Owens College. In 1902 he won a travelling scholarship and went to Göttingen University to study under Emil Wiechert (1861–1928), after which he visited Lapland to investigate atmospheric electricity before returning to England. In 1905 Schuster set up a small meteorology department at Manchester University (as Owens College had become) and placed Simpson in charge; this position was the first lectureship in meteorology at a British University. In the same year Simpson also accepted an invitation to assist William Shaw, the newly appointed Director of the British Meteorological Office. While holding these posts Simpson travelled widely, spending a period (from 1906) with the Indian Meteorological Office inspecting meteorological stations throughout India and Burma, travelling to the Antarctic in 1910 as a meteorologist on Robert Scott's last expedition, and visiting Mesopotamia (from 1916) as a meteorological adviser to the British Expeditionary Force. In 1920, when in Egypt as a member of the Egyptian government's Nile Project Commission, he was summoned back to England to succeed Shaw as Director of the Meteorological Office in London, a post he held until officially retiring in 1938. In the following year, however, with the outbreak of World War II, he returned from retirement to take charge of Kew Observatory, continuing research into the electrical structure of thunderstorms until 1947. Simpson spent his last years in Westbury-on-Trym, near Bristol, and died in Bristol on 1 January 1965.

Simpson's early work – carried out while at Owens College – concerned magnetism and electricity. At Göttingen University, however, his interest turned to meteorology and he demonstrated that the Earth's permanent negative charge cannot be maintained by the absorption of negative ions from the atmosphere. Continuing this line of research in Lapland, he measured dissipation of atmospheric electricity and ionization and radioactivity in the atmosphere; he described the results of these studies in *Atmospheric Electricity in High Altitudes* (1905). He also investigated ionization, radioactivity and potential gradients while on the Antarctic expedition.

When Simpson became Shaw's assistant at the Meteorological Office, he began working on the Beaufort Scale. This scale, which was devised in 1805 by the British Admiral and hydrographer Francis Beaufort (1774-1857), described and classified wind force at sea but made no reference to actual wind speeds (as originally formulated it was based on the effect of the wind on a fully rigged man-o'-war sailing ship). Simpson devised a revised form of the Beaufort Scale in which the numbers of the original scale were assigned wind speeds measured by freely exposed anemometer at a height of 36 feet (11 m) above ground level. In 1921 he was asked by the International Meteorological Committee to reconcile international differences between sets of Beaufort Scale equivalent wind speeds, and in 1926 the Committee accepted the scale Simpson himself had devised earlier. In 1939, however, the Committee adopted a new scale based on wind speed measurements from an anemometer at 6 m (19.5 feet) above ground level, although for some time the United States and British weather services continued to use Simpson's 11 m elevation scale.

As Director of the Meteorological Office, Simpson investigated the effects of solar radiation on the polar ice caps. He concluded that excessive solar radiation would increase the amount of cloud and that the resultant increase in precipitation would lead to enlargement of the ice caps. He then investigated the possibility that this conclusion might explain the Ice Ages. In a series of papers on this subject he showed that, in glaciated regions, the initial effect of increased radiation is greater precipitation (in the form of snow) which, in turn, leads to enlargement of the ice sheet, followed by recession of the ice as the radiation increases further. Then, when the radiation decreases, the resultant drop in temperature causes the precipitation to fall as snow again, which leads to a second advance of the ice.

Snell, Willebrord (*1580-1626*), was a Dutch physicist who discovered the law of refraction. He also founded the method of determining distances by triangulation.

Snell was born in Leiden in 1580. His father was Professor of Mathematics at the University of Leiden, and Snell studied law there. From 1600 to 1604 he travelled throughout Europe, working with and meeting such scientists as Tycho Brahe (1546-1601) and Johannes Kepler (1571-1630). In 1613, Snell succeeded to his father's position at the University of Leiden and there taught mathematics, physics and optics. He died at Leiden on 30 October 1626.

Snell developed the method of triangulation in 1615, starting with his house and the spires of nearby churches as reference points. He used a large quadrant over 2 m long to determine angles, and by building up a network of triangles, was able to obtain a value for the distance between two towns on the same meridian. From this, Snell made an accurate determination of the radius of the Earth.

Snell is best known for Snell's law of refraction in optics, which states that the ratio of the sines of the angles of the incident and refracted rays to the normal is a constant. This constant is now called the refractive index of the two media involved. Snell discovered this law after much experimental work in 1621, and he formulated it in terms of the lengths of the paths traversed by the rays rather than the sines of the angles. Snell did not publish his law, and it first appeared in *Dioptrique* (1637) by René Descartes (1596-1650). There Descartes expressed the law using the sines of the angles, which could easily be derived from Snell's original formulation. Whether Descartes knew of Snell's work or discovered the law independently is not known.

Sommerfeld, Arnold (Johannes Wilhelm) (*1868-1951*), was a German physicist who made an important contribution to the development of the quantum theory of atomic structure. He was also a gifted teacher of science.

Sommerfeld was born in Königsberg, Prussia (now Kaliningrad in Russia) on 5 December 1868. After attending the local Gymnasium, he entered Königsberg University in 1886 and opted for mathematics. He received his PhD in 1891 and then obtained an assistantship at the Mineralogical Institute in Göttingen from 1893 to 1894. In 1895, he became a privatdozent (unpaid lecturer) in mathematics at Göttingen University and in 1897, was appointed Professor of Mathematics at the Mining Academy in Clausthal. In 1900, Sommerfeld became Professor of Technical Mechanics at the Technical Institute in Aachen and in 1906 moved to Munich University as Director of the Institute of Theoretical Physics, which was established there for him. Sommerfeld built his institute into a leading centre of physics and attracted many gifted scientists as students, notably Peter Debye (1884-1966), Wolfgang Pauli (1900-1958), Werner Heisenberg (1901-1976) and Hans Bethe (1906-   ). It was also under Sommerfeld's direction that Max von Laue and his colleagues made the famous discovery of X-ray diffraction in 1912. Sommerfeld also helped to spread and advance physics by publishing several important books that summed up current knowledge in several fields. The most influential of these were *Atombau Und Spektrallinien* (*Atomic Structure and Spectral Lines*; 1919) and *Wellenmechanischer Ergänzungsband* (*Wave Mechanics*; 1929).

Sommerfeld remained at Munich until 1940, when he retired. He courageously defended Albert Einstein (1879-1955) and other Jewish scientists in the Weimar and Nazi periods when anti-semitism was prevalent in Germany. Sommerfeld returned to his post at the Institute of Theoretical Physics in Munich after World War II. He died in Munich on 26 April 1951 after being struck by a car.

Sommerfeld was active as a theoretician in several fields both in physics and engineering, and he produced a four-volume work on the theory of gyroscopes from 1897 to 1910 in association with Felix Klein (1849-1925). However, his principal contribution to science was in the development of quantum theory. Sommerfeld promoted the theory as a fundamental law of nature, and inspired Niels Bohr (1885-1962) to apply the theory to the structure of the atom. Sommerfeld took the quantum model of the atom that Bohr proposed in 1913 and worked out in 1915 that electrons must move in elliptical and not circular orbits around the nucleus. This led him in 1916 to predict a series of spectral lines based on the relativistic effects that would occur with elliptical orbits. Friedrich Paschen (1865-1945) immediately undertook the spectroscopic work required and confirmed Sommerfeld's predictions. This evidence for Bohr's ideas led to a rapid acceptance of the quantum theory of the atom.

Stark, Johannes (*1874-1957*), was a German physicist who is known for his discovery of the phenomenon (now called the Stark effect) of the division of spectral lines in an electric field, and for his discovery of the Doppler effect in canal rays (positively charged ions produced by an electric discharge in a rarefied gas; impelled towards the cathode, the particles pass through it – if it is perforated – to form a beam). For this work he received the 1919 Nobel Prize in Physics.

Stark was born in Schickenhof, Bavaria, on 15 April 1874. He studied chemistry, physics, mathematics and crystallography at the University of Munich, from which he graduated in 1898 and where he spent the following two years working at the Physical Institute. In 1900 he became a lecturer at the University of Göttingen, then in 1906 was appointed Extraordinary Professor at the Technische Hochschule in Hanover. In 1909 he moved to the Technische Hochschule in Aachen, where he held a professorship until 1917. From 1917 to 1922 he was Professor of Physics at the University of Greifswald; between 1920 and 1922 he also lectured at the University of Würzburg. He then attempted to set up a porcelain factory in northern Germany but this scheme failed, largely because of the depressed state of the German economy, and so he tried – unsuccessfully – to return to academic life. A vehement antisemite, Stark was attracted to the rising Nazi movement and joined the Nazi party in 1930. Three years later he became President of the Reich Physical-Technical Institute and also President of the German Research Association. But his attempts to become an important influence in German physics brought him into conflict with the authorities and he was forced to resign in 1939. Nor did his decline end there: because of his Nazi background, in 1947 he was sentenced to four years internment in a labour camp by a German denazification court. Stark died on 21 June 1957 in Traunstein, West Germany.

In 1902 Stark predicted that the high-velocity canal rays produced in a cathode-ray tube should exhibit the Doppler effect (the change in the observed frequency of a wave resulting from movement of the wave's source or the observer or both). Three years later he proved his prediction correct by demonstrating the frequency shift in hydrogen canal rays.

His next major work was his discovery (announced in 1913) of the spectral phenomenon now called the Stark effect. Following Pieter Zeeman's demonstration in 1896 of the division of spectral lines caused by the influence of a magnetic field, Stark succeeded in showing (by photographing the spectrum emitted by canal rays – consisting of hydrogen and helium atoms – as they passed through a strong electric field) that an electric field produces a similar splitting effect on the spectral lines. The Stark effect is produced because the electric field causes the radiating atom's electron cloud to alter its position with respect to the nucleus, which distorts the electron orbitals. Light is emitted when an excited electron moves from a high to a lower energy orbital, so distortion of the orbitals also distorts the emitted light, this effect being manifested as splitting of the spectral lines.

Stark is also known for his modification (in 1913) of the photo-equivalence law proposed by Albert Einstein in 1906. Now called the Stark-Einstein law, it states that each molecule involved in a photochemical reaction absorbs only one quantum of the radiation that causes the reaction.

Stefan, Josef (*1835-1893*), was an Austrian physicist who first determined the relation between the amount of energy radiated by a body and its temperature. This expression is usually known as the Stefan-Boltzmann radiation law because Ludwig Boltzmann (1844-1906) gave a theoretical explanation of it.

Stefan was born at Klagenfurt on 24 March 1835. He studied at the Gymnasium there and entered the University of Vienna in 1853. After completing his studies, Stefan became a lecturer at the University in 1858, rising to Professor of Higher Mathematics and Physics in 1863. He retained this position for the rest of his life, and was also Director of the Institute for Experimental Physics at Vienna from 1866. From 1885 to his death, Stefan served as Vice-President of the Imperial Academy of Sciences. He died at Vienna on 7 January 1893.

Stefan's discovery of his radiation law was made in 1879. For a long time, it had been known that Newton's law of cooling, which held that the rate of cooling of a hot body is proportional to the difference in temperature between the body and its surroundings, is incorrect for large temperature differences. Many people had found that the amount of heat given out by a very hot body is far greater than expected by Newton's law.

Stephan followed up experimental work by John Tyndall (1820-1893), who had measured the amount of radiant heat produced by a platinum wire heated to varying degrees of incandescence by an electric current. He found that over the greatest range, from about 525°C up to about 1200°C, the intensity of radiation increased by 11.7 times. Stefan realized that this increase in intensity was equal to the ratio of the absolute temperatures raised to the fourth power, and from this deduced his radiation law. This states that the total energy radiated in a given time by a given area of a body, E, is equal to σT^4, where

T is the absolute temperature and σ is a constant known as the Stefan constant. Stefan confirmed the validity of his law over wide temperature ranges.

In 1884, Boltzmann, a former student of Stefan, gave a theoretical explanation of Stefan's law based on thermodynamic principles and the kinetic theory developed by James Clerk Maxwell (1831-1879). Boltzmann pointed out that it held only for perfect black bodies, and Stefan had in fact been able to derive the law because platinum approximates to a black body. However, from his law, Stefan was able to make the first accurate determination of the surface temperature of the Sun, obtaining a value of approximately 6000°C.

Stefan also made several other contributions to physics. He was an able experimental physicist, and produced accurate measurements of the conductivities of gases that helped to confirm Maxwell's kinetic theory. He also investigated diffusion in gases, making theoretical derivations that confirmed experimental results.

Stern, Otto (*1888-1969*), was a German-born American physicist who showed that beams of atoms and molecules have wave properties. He also determined the magnetic moment of the proton. For these achievements, Stern gained the 1943 Nobel Prize in Physics.

Stern was born in Sohrau, Upper Silesia, then in Germany but now Zory in Poland, on 17 February 1888. His family moved to Breslau in 1892. Stern entered the Johannes Gymnasium in Breslau in 1897, and obtained his Arbitur in 1906. Following the custom of the time, Stern then attended a number of German universities. He went to Freiburg im Breisgau, Munich and Breslau, giving him the opportunity to attend lectures by such prominent scientists as Arnold Sommerfeld (1868-1951), Otto Lummer (1860-1925) and Ernst Pringsheim (1859-1917). Stern received his PhD from Breslau in 1912 for a dissertation on the kinetic theory of osmotic pressure in concentrated solutions with special reference to solutions of carbon dioxide.

Although Stern's thesis work had been in the field of physical chemistry, he was fascinated by theoretical physics. He arranged to join Albert Einstein (1879-1955) in Prague as a postdoctoral associate. When Einstein moved to Zurich in 1913, Stern followed him and took up a post as privatdozent (unpaid lecturer) in physical chemistry at the Technical High School in Zurich.

Stern served in the army in World War I and was assigned to meteorological work on the Russian front. He was able to work on theoretical physics in his spare time, and was then transferred to more congenial laboratory work in Berlin towards the end of the war. In 1918, he took up the position of privatdozent in the department of theoretical physics at the University of Frankfurt. Stern obtained his first professional position in 1921, when he was made Associate Professor of Theoretical Physics at the University of Rostock, but he soon moved to the University of Hamburg where, in 1923, he became Professor of Physical Chemistry and Director of the Institute of Physical Chemistry.

The next ten years marked the peak of Stern's career. He made important contributions to the understanding of quantum theory, and built up a thriving research group. Many of his associates were Jewish as indeed was Stern himself, and things became increasingly difficult during the early 1930s as the Nazis rose to power. The sacking of Stern's longtime associate Immanuel Estermann and an order to remove a portrait of Einstein from the laboratory were the last straws. Stern resigned his post in 1933 and went to the Carnegie Technical Institute in Pittsburg in the United States, where he was given the post of Research Professor and set up a new department for the study of molecular beams.

Stern was granted American citizenship in 1939 and worked as a consultant to the US War Department during World War II. After the war he retired and moved to Berkeley, California, where he maintained contact with the scientific community on a private basis only. He died in Berkeley of a heart attack on 17 August 1969.

The first phase of Stern's scientific career covers the period from 1912 until 1918. During these years he was absorbed in purely theoretical work and in learning how to choose the really central issues for study in an experimental context. His theoretical work was partly in the field of statistical thermodynamics, in which he proposed an elegant derivation of the entropy constant.

After World War I, Stern began to concentrate on the molecular beam method, which had been discovered by Louis Dunoyer (1880-1963) in 1911. This method consisted of opening a tiny hole in a heated container held inside a region of high vacuum. The vapour molecules inside the heated container flowed out to form a straight beam of moving particles suffering virtually no collisions in the vacuum. The beam could be narrowed still further by the use of slits, and a system of rotating slits could be used to select only those particles travelling at particular velocities. This was a powerful tool in the study of the magnetic and other properties of particles, atoms and molecules.

Stern's first experiments with this device were completed in 1919. They dealt with the measurement of molecular velocities and confirmed the Maxwellian distribution of velocities. He then began an experiment with Walther Gerlach (1899-   ) that was intended to measure the magnetic moment of metal atoms and also to investigate the question of spatial quantization.

Developing the quantum model of the atom proposed by Niels Bohr (1885-1962) in 1913, Sommerfeld had derived a formula for the magnetic moment of the silver atom and predicted that silver atoms in a magnetic field could orient in only two directions with respect to that field. This latter idea was not compatible with classical theory. The Stern-Gerlach experiment would determine which of these theories was correct.

The experiment consisted of passing a narrow beam of silver atoms through a strong magnetic field. Classical theory predicted that this field would cause the beam to broaden, but spatial quantization predicted that the beam would split into two distinct separate beams. The result, showing a split beam, was the first clear evidence for space quantization. Stern and Gerlach also obtained a measurement of the magnetic moment of the silver atom.

Stern then went on to improve this molecular beam technique and in 1931 was able to detect the wave nature of particles in the beams. This was an important confirmation of wave-particle duality, which had been proposed in 1924 by Louis De Broglie (1892-   ) for the electron and extended to all particles.

In 1933 Stern measured the magnetic moment of the proton and the deuteron. The magnetic moment of the proton had been predicted by Paul Dirac (1902-   ) to be one nuclear magneton. Stern's group, despite much advice not to attempt the difficult experiment whose result was in any case already "known", caused much astonishment when they demonstrated that the proton's magnetic moment was 2.5 times greater than expected. The explanation for this discrepancy lies partly in parallel proton movements.

Stern's experiments with molecular beams came at a critical time in the development of quantum theory and nuclear physics as they provided the firm experimental evidence that was needed for theories in quantum mechanics that were hitherto highly controversial. Stern's great talent lay in his experimental foresight, which was based on a solid theoretical grounding, coupled with an almost fanatical obsession with experimental and technical detail.

Stevinus, Simon (*c.1548-1620*), was a Flemish scientist who, in physics, developed statics and hydrodynamics and who introduced decimal notation into mathematics.

Stevinus was born in Bruges (now in Belgium)

in about 1548. He began work in Antwerp as a clerk and then entered Dutch Government service, using his engineering skills to become Quartermaster-General to the army. (For Prince Maurice of Nassau he designed sluices that could be used to flood parts of Holland to defend it from attack.) He married very late in life and died in The Hague in the early part of 1620.

Stevinus' interests were wide-ranging. In statics he made use of the parallelogram of forces and in dynamics he made a scientific study of pulley systems. In hydrostatics Stevinus noted that the pressure exerted by a liquid depends only on its height and is independent of the shape of the vessel containing it. He is supposed to have anticipated Galileo in an experiment in which he dropped two unequal weights from a tall building to demonstrate that they fell at the same rate.

Stevinus wrote in the vernacular (a principle he advocated for all scientists). Even so his book on mechanics *De Beghinselen der Weeghcoust* (1586), written in Flemish, was 20 years later translated into Latin (as *Hypomnemata Mathematica*) by Willebrord Snell (1591-1626).

Stokes, George Gabriel (*1819-1903*), was a British physicist who is mainly remembered for Stokes' law, which relates the force moving a body through a fluid to the velocity and size of the body and the viscosity of the fluid. He also made important contributions in optics, particularly in the field of fluorescence, a term that he coined.

Stokes was born at Skreen, Sligo, in Ireland on 13 August 1819 and went to school in Dublin and to college in Bristol, England, before entering Cambridge University in 1837. He graduated in mathematics in 1841, and became a fellow of Pembroke College. In 1849, Stokes was appointed Lucasian Professor of Mathematics at Cambridge, a position he retained until his death. Among the honours accorded to him were the Presidency of the Royal Society from 1885 to 1890, a knighthood in 1889, and the Royal Society's Copley Medal in 1893. He died at Cambridge on 1 February 1903.

Much of Stokes's extensive reputation was gained through the work he carried out on the theory of viscous fluids from 1845 to 1850. He derived the equation later known as Stokes's law, which determines the movement of a small sphere through viscous fluids of various density. The equation can be stated as $F = 6\pi\eta rv$, where F is the force acting on the sphere, η the coefficient of viscosity, r the radius of the sphere and v its velocity. Stokes' law enables the resistance of fluids to motion to be assessed and the terminal velocity of a body to be calculated. It was to be of enormous importance to science as the basis of the famous oil-drop experiments to determine the charge on the electron performed by Robert Millikan (1868-1953) from 1909 to 1913.

Stokes' investigation into fluid dynamics led him to consider the problem of the ether, the hypothetical medium that was believed to exist as a medium for the propagation of light waves. In 1848, Stokes showed that the laws of optics held if the Earth pulled the ether with it in its motion through space and from this assumed the ether to be an elastic substance that flowed with the Earth. The classic Michelson-Morley experiments of 1881 and 1887 did not totally negate this contention; it was shown to be untrue by Oliver Lodge (1851-1940) in 1893 and the existence of the ether was finally disproved.

Stokes made another important contribution with the first explanation of fluorescence in 1852. He had examined the blue light that is emitted in certain circumstances by a solution of quinine sulphate that is normally colourless. Stokes showed that ultraviolet light was being absorbed by the solution and then re-emitted as visible light. He was then able to use fluorescence as a method to study ultraviolet spectra. Stokes went on in 1854 to realize that the Sun's spectrum is made up of spectra of the elements it contains and concluded that the dark Fraunhofer lines are the spectral lines of elements absorbing light in the Sun's outer layers. He did not, however, develop this important idea. It was left to Robert Bunsen (1811-1899) and Gustav Kirchhoff (1824-1887) to propose the method of spectrum analysis in 1860.

Another field in which Stokes made his mark was geodesy and in 1849 he published an important study of the variation of gravity at the surface of the Earth. Stokes was also a gifted mathematician and helped to develop Fourier series.

Stoney, George Johnstone (*1826-1911*), was an Irish physicist who is best known for introducing the term electron (although he used it in a sense different from that in which it is used today). He was the first to receive the Boyle Medal of the Royal Dublin Society, of which he was honorary secretary for 20 years, and was elected a Fellow of the Royal Society of London in 1861.

Stoney was born at Oakley Park, King's County (now in the Republic of Ireland) on 15 February 1826; his brother, Bindon Blood Stoney, was a well-known civil engineer. The son of an impoverished landowner, Stoney had to finance his own education at Trinity College, Dublin, by private teaching. After graduating in 1848, he became an assistant to the astronomer Lord Rosse (William Parsons), through whose influence Stoney was appointed Professor of Natural

Philosophy at Queen's College, Galway, in 1852. He returned to Dublin in 1857 to become Secretary of the Queen's University, a position he held until the university was absorbed into the Royal Irish University in 1882. He was then superintendent of Civil Service examinations until his retirement in 1893, after which he moved to London so that his daughters could receive a university education. Stoney died in London on 5 July 1911.

In 1874 Stoney, speaking at a British Association Meeting in Belfast, is reported to have mentioned "an absolute unit of electricity", but his first published use of the word "electron" was in 1891 when he used the term to define minimum electric charge. Although electron passed into general scientific usage, it came to refer to the negatively charged particles of small mass that orbit the atomic nucleus and conduct electric current in solids.

In addition, Stoney researched into molecular physics and the kinetic theory of gases: he estimated the number of molecules in a specific volume of gas under standard conditions but arrived at an incorrect result because of basic errors in his initial calculations. He also proposed explanations for the escape of hydrogen and helium from the Earth's atmosphere and for the lack of atmospheres on moons.

Strutt, John William (*1842-1919*). *See* Rayleigh, Lord.

Sutherland, Gordon (*1907-1980*), was a British physicist who is best known for his work in infrared spectroscopy, particularly the use of this technique for studying molecular structure. He received many honours for his work, including a knighthood in 1960.

Sutherland was born in Caithness, Scotland, on 8 April 1907. He was educated at the Morgan Academy, Dundee, and graduated from St Andrew's University, then did postdoctoral work at Trinity College, Cambridge, where he joined one of Eric Rideal's research groups working on infrared spectroscopy. From 1931 to 1933 he was in the United States as a Commonwealth Fund Fellow at the University of Michigan, Ann Arbor (one of the leading centres for spectroscopy studies), working with D. Dennison. After returning to Britain he was elected to the Stokes Studentship at Pembroke College, Cambridge, in 1934 and was made a Fellow of the College in the following year. During his fellowship - which he held until 1949 - he spent a year as an assistant to the Director of Production of the Ministry of Supply, was a Proctor of the University from 1943 to 1944, and served on the Council of the University Senate from 1946 to 1949; he was also

appointed University Reader in Spectroscopy in 1947. While at Cambridge he established a successful research group, first in the Department of Physical Chemistry and later in the newly founded Department of Colloid Science. In 1949 he left Cambridge to take up the position of Professor of Physics at the University of Michigan, a post he held until 1956, when he returned to Britain to become Director of the National Physical Laboratory at Teddington. In 1962 he visited China with one of the first post-war delegations from the Royal Society. From 1964 until his retirement in 1977 Sutherland was Master of Emanual College, Cambridge. He died in Cambridge on 27 June 1980.

Sutherland spent most of his career using infrared spectroscopy to elucidate molecular structure. Working with William Penney (1909-), he showed that the four atoms of hydrogen peroxide (H_2O_2) do not lie in the same plane but that the molecule's structure resembles a partly opened book, with the oxygen atoms aligned along the spine and the O–H bonds lying across each cover. Later, during World War II, Sutherland and his research group at Cambridge analysed fuel from crashed German aircraft in order to discover their sources of oil. At Michigan University he was one of the first to use spectroscopy to study biophysical problems; he also continued his investigations into simpler molecules and crystals.

As Director of the National Physical Laboratory, Sutherland reorganized the institution along similar lines to that of the US National Bureau of Standards and established departments of pure physics, applied physics and standards. The scientific reputation of the laboratory was greatly enhanced under Sutherland's management and, while there, he also researched into the structure of a wide range of substances from proteins to the different forms of diamonds. After his appointment as Master of Emmanuel College, he became less active in fundamental research and turned his attention to educational issues.

T

Tabor, David (*1913-*), is a British physicist who has worked mainly in tribology, the study of the effects between solid surfaces.

Tabor was born in London on 23 October 1913. He was educated at Regent Street Polytechnic, London, from 1925 to 1931 and then he went to read physics at the Royal College of Science, London, obtaining his BSc in 1934. From 1934 to

1936, he researched under George Thomson (1892-1975) and then from 1936 to 1939 under Frank Bowden (1903-1968) at Cambridge. He gained his PhD in 1939, and then went to Australia in 1940 to work in tribophysics at a Division of the Commonwealth Scientific Research Organization in Melbourne. In 1946, he returned to Cambridge, and worked in the section of the Cavendish Laboratory concerned with the physics and chemistry of solids. He was Assistant Director of Research until 1961, when he was made a Lecturer in Physics. He subsequently became a Reader in Physics in 1964 and Professor of Physics in 1973, a position he held until 1981. He is now Emeritus Professor. Among his many awards is the Guthrie Medal of the Institute of Physics in 1974.

Tabor's research interests have been very wide. Early investigations were into the friction and lubrication of metals, low-energy and high-energy electron diffraction techniques and high vacuum methods for studying clean surfaces, the adsorption of vapours and the first stages of conversion of a chemisorbed film to a chemically formed film. Bowden introduced the idea of using mica to study the contact between two surfaces since the cleavage faces are molecularly smooth. Tabor extended this to a study of forces between two curved mica surfaces and has shown that normal Van der Waals forces operate for separations less than 100 Å, and retarded Van der Waals forces for separations larger than 500 Å.

As a byproduct of an investigation of the action of windscreen wiper blades, Tabor has been able to study directly the repulsive forces between electrically charged double-layers. These and the attractive Van der Waals forces are of basic importance in colloid stability.

Tabor has also looked at the friction and transfer of polymers. This work includes the effect of speed and temperature and he has attempted to correlate the behaviour with visco-elastic properties. He has shown that the low friction of teflon is not due to poor adhesion but to molecular structure, and has worked on the self-lubrication of polymers by incorporating surface materials into the polymer itself. A study of the friction of rubber led to the introduction of high-hysteresis rubber into automobile tyres as means of increasing their skid-resistance. Tabor has also examined the effect of hydrostatic pressure on the visco-elastic properties of polymers and has shown that by decreasing the free volume, hydrostatic pressure increases the glass transition temperature.

Tabor has researched into the shear properties of molecular films of long-chain organic molecules as an extension of earlier work on the mechanism of boundary lubrication, and has shown that the shear strength of these materials rises sharply when they are subjected to high pressure. This sheds light on the mechanism of thin film lubrication.

Tabor's work on the hardness of solids includes an explanation of the indentation hardness of metals in terms of their basic yield properties, the first account of plastic indentation and elastic recovery which explains rebound in terms of plastic and elastic properties (rebound hardness), the effect of temperature and loading time on indentation hardness and the first correlation of the hardness behaviour with the creep properties of the material (hot-hardness), a study of scratch hardness and a simple physical explanation of the Mohs scale used in the testing of minerals.

He has also carried out a broad study of the creep of polycrystalline ice over a wide range of temperatures and strain rates, and has explained the behaviour in terms of various dislocation and grain-boundary properties. These results have a bearing on the flow of glaciers.

Tabor has looked at diffusion in polymers, studying the diffusion of suitably tagged organic molecules through a polymer matrix. By increasing the length of the diffusant, he has provided experimental evidence for the first time for the process of reptation, whereby the diffusant worms its way through the free volume of the polymer. He has also examined the effect of hydrostatic pressure on diffusion since this shows how the polymer matrix restricts the movement of the diffusant.

Tabor has also studied the machining of tools using a transparent tool so that the sliding of the chip over the tool face can be directly observed. Finally, he has studied the adhesion of steel to cement and has demonstrated the important role of shear stresses in compacting the cement.

Tesla, Nikola (*1856-1943*), was a Croatian-born American physicist and electrical engineer who was one of the great pioneers of the use of alternating current electricity. In particular, he invented the alternating current induction motor and the high-frequency coil which bears his name.

Tesla was born at midnight between 9 and 10 July 1856 in Smiljan, Croatia (then part of Austria-Hungary but now in Yugoslavia). His father was a priest of the local Serbian Orthodox Church. Tesla was very clever as a child and grew up with a liking for writing poetry and experimentation. It was intended that he should follow his father and become a priest, but Tesla developed an interest in scientific pursuits while he was at the Real Gymnasium in Karlovac. On leaving school he studied engineering at the Technical University at Graz, Austria. In 1880 he went

155

to the University of Prague to continue his studies but the death of his father caused him to leave without graduating.

In 1881, Tesla went to Budapest as an engineer for a telephone company and a year later took up a similar position in Paris. He went to the United States in 1884, and worked for Thomas Edison (1847-1931) for a year before setting up on his own. From 1888, Tesla was associated with George Westinghouse (1846-1914), who bought and successfully exploited Tesla's patents, leading to the introduction of alternating current for power transmission. Tesla became an American citizen in 1889 and after 1892, when his mother died, he became increasingly withdrawn and eccentric. In 1912 both he and Edison were proposed for the Nobel Prize in Physics but Tesla refused to be associated with Edison, who had conducted an unscrupulous campaign for the adoption of direct current. In the event, neither received the prize. Tesla neglected to patent many of his discoveries and made little profit from them. He lived his last years as a recluse and died in New York on 7 January 1943.

In 1878, during his student days at Graz, Tesla saw a direct current electric dynamo and motor demonstrated and felt that the machine could be improved by eliminating the commutator and sparking brushes, which were sources of wear. His idea for the induction motor came to him in Budapest four years later. He had the notion of an iron rotor spinning between stationary coils which were electrified by two out-of-phase alternating currents producing a rotating magnetic field. Like many of his other ideas, Tesla mentally developed his motor for all kinds of practical applications before ever a model was built.

Tesla built his first working induction motor while he was on assignment in Strasbourg in 1883. However, he found that he could raise little interest in his inventions in Europe so he set off for New York, where he eventually set up his own laboratory and workshop in 1887 to develop his motor in a practical way. Only months later he applied for and was granted a complicated set of patents covering the generation, transmission and use of alternating current electricity. At about the same time he lectured to the American Institute of Electrical Engineers on his polyphase alternating current system. After learning about the talk, Westinghouse quickly bought Tesla's patents.

Westinghouse was able to back Tesla's ideas and as a demonstration, employed his system for lighting at the 1893 World Columbian Exposition in Chicago. Months later Westinghouse won the contract to generate electricity at Niagara Falls, using Tesla's system to supply local industries and deliver polyphase alternating current to the town of Buffalo 22 miles (35 km) distant.

After 1888 Tesla's interests turned to alternating currents at very high frequencies, which he felt might be useful for lighting and for communication. After first using high-frequency alternators for these purposes, he designed what has come to be known as the Tesla coil. This is an air core transformer with the primary and secondary windings tuned in resonance to produce high-frequency, high-voltage electricity. Using this device, Tesla produced an electric spark 135 feet (40 m) long in 1899. He also lit more than 200 lamps over a distance of 25 miles (40 km) without the use of intervening wires. Gas-filled tubes are readily energized by high-frequency currents and so lights of this type were easily operated within the field of a large Tesla coil. Characteristic of his way of working, Tesla soon developed all manner of coils which have since found numerous applications in electrical and electronic devices.

Tesla was very interested in the possibility of radio communication and as early as 1897 he demonstrated remote control of two model boats on the lake in Madison Square Gardens in New York. He extended this to guided weapons, in particular a remote control torpedo. In 1900 he began to construct a broadcasting station on Long Island in the hope of developing "World Wireless"; this eventually proved too expensive for his backers and was abandoned. However, many of his ideas have come to fruition at the hands of others. Tesla also outlined a scheme for detecting ships at sea which was later developed as radar. One of his most ambitious ideas was to transmit alternating current electricity to anywhere in the world without wires by·using the Earth itself as an enormous oscillator. There were many other inventions, including electrical clocks and turbines, but often they remained in his head, there being no money to put them into practice.

Tesla has given the world one of the most practical devices of all time, the alternating current induction motor. This, coupled with the distinct advantage that alternating current can be transmitted over much greater distances than direct current, has given the motive power for most of our present day machines.

Thomson, Benjamin (*1753-1814*). *See* Rumford, Count.

Thomson, George Paget (*1892-1975*), was a British physicist who in 1927 first demonstrated electron diffraction, a confirmation of the wave nature of the electron. Clinton Davisson (1881-1958) also made the same discovery independently using a different method and in recognition of their achievement, Thomson and Davisson shared the 1937 Nobel Prize in Physics.

Thomson was born in Cambridge on 3 May 1892, the son of J.J. Thomson (1856–1940). He was educated at Perse School, Cambridge, and then at Trinity College, Cambridge, where he took a first-class honours degrees in mathematics and in physics in 1913. For a year he joined his father's research team but on the outbreak of World War I joined the infantry and saw active service in France. Thomson then transferred to the Royal Air Force and spent the rest of the war investigating the stability of aeroplanes. In 1919, he returned to Cambridge to become a fellow and lecturer at Corpus Christi College. Then in 1922 he became Professor of Natural Philosophy at the University of Aberdeen, holding the post until 1930, when he moved to Imperial College, London, as Professor of Physics.

During World War II, Thomson headed many government committees, including the British Committee on Atomic Energy which investigated the possibility of atomic weapons. For part of 1942 he was Scientific Liaison Officer at Ottawa, where he built up close contact with the United States atomic bomb project, and later in the war he became Scientific Adviser to the Air Ministry. Thomson returned to Imperial College after the war, interesting himself in thermonuclear fusion and undertaking vital research in this field. He retained his professorship there until 1952, when he became master of Corpus Christi College, Cambridge. Among the many honours he received were a knighthood in 1943 and Presidency of the Institute of Physics from 1958 to 1960 and of the British Association for the Advancement of Science in 1960. Thomson retired in 1962 and died at Cambridge on 10 September 1975.

During the mid-1920s, Thomson carried out a series of experiments hoping to verify a hypothesis initially presented in 1924 by Louis De Broglie (1892–) that electrons possess a duality, acting both as particles and as waves. The basis of the experiment involved the bombardment of very thin metal (aluminium, gold and platinum) and celluloid foils with a narrow beam of electrons. The beam was scattered into a series of rings in a similar manner to the rings associated with X-ray diffraction in metals. Applying mathematical formulae to measurements of the rings together with a knowledge of the crystal lattice, Thomson showed in 1927 that all the readings were in complete agreement with De Broglie's theory. Electrons were therefore shown to possess wave-particle duality. Several modifications to the initial experiments proved that the scattering effects were not the result of X-rays which had been produced by the impact of electrons on the metal foil.

George Thomson's achievements parallel those of his father to an extraordinary degree. Both made fundamental discoveries concerning the electron, J.J. Thomson proving the existence of the electron as a particle in 1897 and his son demonstrating its wave nature 30 years later. Both men also became professors by the age of 30, both gained knighthoods and both were awarded the Nobel Prize.

Thomson, James (*1822–1892*) was a British physicist and engineer who discovered that the melting point of ice decreases with pressure. He was also an authority on hydrodynamics and invented the vortex water wheel.

Thomson was born on 16 February 1822 at Belfast into a family of scientists. His father was Professor of Mathematics at Belfast and his younger brother was William Thomson, later Lord Kelvin (1824–1907). Thomson received his early education from his father and then at the age of only ten began to attend Glasgow University, obtaining an MA in 1839. He subsequently held a succession of engineering posts, and then settled in Belfast in 1851 as a civil engineer. In 1857, Thomson became Professor of Civil Engineering at Belfast and in 1873 moved to Glasgow to take up the same position there. He resigned his chair in 1889 and died in Glasgow on 8 May 1892.

As a young man Thomson was most interested in engineering projects, especially those involving paddles and water wheels, and while still a student he invented a device for feathering paddles. In 1850, Thomson invented the vortex water wheel, which was a smaller and more efficient turbine than those in use at the time, and it came into wide use. On moving to Belfast, Thomson continued his investigations into whirling fluids, making improvements to pumps, fans and turbines.

Thomson's most important discovery was made in 1849, when he determined the lowering of melting point caused by pressure on ice. This led him to reach an understanding of the way in which glaciers flow. Thomson also carried out painstaking studies of the phase relationships of solids, liquids and gases, and was involved in both geology and meteorology, producing scientific papers on currents and winds.

Thomson, Joseph John (J.J.) (*1856–1940*), was a British physicist who is famous for discovering the electron and for his research into the conduction of electricity through gases, for which he was awarded the 1906 Nobel Prize in Physics. He also received several other honours, including a

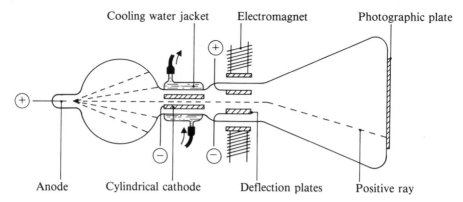

Thomson deflected positive ions using electric and magnetic fields, and so calculated their charge-to-mass ratio, giving a method for determining atomic masses.

knighthood in 1908 and the Order of Merit in 1912.

Thomson was born at Cheetham Hill, near Manchester, on 18 December 1856, the son of an antiquarian bookseller. At the age of 14 he went to Owens College, Manchester (later Manchester University), to study engineering. When his father died two years later, however, his family could not afford the premium for engineering training and so, with the help of a scholarship, Thomson studied physics, chemistry and mathematics. In 1876 he won a scholarship to Trinity College, Cambridge, where he remained – except for visiting lectureships to Princeton University in 1896 and to Yale University in 1904 – for the rest of his life.

After graduating in mathematics in 1880, he worked at the Cavendish Laboratory under Lord Rayleigh, succeeding him as Cavendish Professor of Experimental Physics in 1884. In 1919 he resigned the Cavendish professorship (being suc-

ceeded in turn by his student Ernest Rutherford), having been elected Master of Trinity College the previous year. He held this post until his death (in Cambridge) on 30 August 1940.

Thomson's first important research concerned vortex rings, which won him the Adam's Prize in 1883. It was then thought that atoms may be in the form of vortex rings in the "ether", an idea which although untrue, led Thomson to begin his investigations into cathode rays and these, in turn, led to his famous discovery of the electron in 1897. At the end of the 19th century there was considerable debate as to whether cathode rays were charged particles or whether they were some undefined process in the ether. Hertz had apparently shown that cathode rays were not deflected by an electric field (a finding which indicated that they were not particulate) but Thomson proved this to be incorrect in 1897, and demonstrated that Hertz's failure to obtain a deflection was caused by his use of an insufficiently

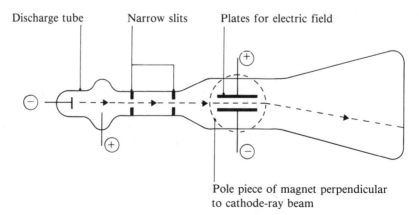

Thomson determined e/m, the ratio of the charge to the mass of an electron, by subjecting a collimated beam of cathode rays to simultaneous deflection by electric and magnetic fields.

evacuated cathode-ray tube. Having proved the particulate nature of cathode rays, Thomson went on to determine their charge-to-mass ratio, finding it to be constant – irrespective of the gas in the cathode ray tube – and with a value nearly 1,000 times smaller than that obtained for hydrogen ions in liquid electrolysis. He also measured the charge of the cathode-ray particles and found it to be the same in the gaseous discharge as in electrolysis. Thus he demonstrated that cathode rays are fundamental, negatively charged particles with a mass much less than the lightest atom known. He announced these findings during a lecture at the Royal Institution on 30 April 1897, calling the cathode-ray particles "corpuscles". The Dutch physicist Hendrik Lorentz later named them "electrons" (a term first used – with a slightly different meaning – by the Irish physicist George Stoney), which became generally accepted.

Thomson then spent several years investigating the nature and properties of electrons, after which he began researching into "canal rays", streams of positively charged ions, which Thomson named positive rays. Using magnetic and electric fields to deflect these rays, he found (in 1912) that ions of neon gas are deflected by different amounts, indicating that they consist of a mixture of ions with different charge-to-mass ratios. The British chemist Frederick Soddy had earlier proposed the existence of isotopes and Thomson proved this idea correct when he identified – also in 1912 – the isotope neon-22. This work was later continued by Francis Aston (one of Thomson's students and, later, the developer of the mass spectrograph), A.J. Dempster and other scientists, and led to the discovery of many other isotopes.

In addition to his pioneering research, Thomson wrote several notable works that were widely used in British universities, including *Notes on Recent Researches in Electricity and Magnetism* (1893), *Elements of the Mathematical Theory of Electricity and Magnetism* (1895) and, with John Poynting, the four-volume *Textbook of Physics*. Equally important, Thomson developed the Cavendish Laboratory into the world's leading centre for subatomic physics in the early 20th century. Furthermore, he trained a generation of scientists who subsequently made fundamental contributions to physics: seven of his research assistants – including his only son, George Thomson – later won Nobel Prizes.

Thomson, William (*1824–1907*). *See* Kelvin, Lord.

Tolansky, Samuel (*1907–1973*), was a British phy-

sicist who made important contributions to the fields of spectroscopy and interferometry.

Tolansky was born in Newcastle-upon-Tyne on 17 November 1907. He attended Snow Street School and Rutherford College and then in 1925 went to Armstrong College, part of Durham University, where he was awarded his BSc in 1928. He undertook scientific research at Armstrong College from 1929 to 1931, when he spent a year at the Physikalische Technische Reichsanstalt in Berlin under Friedrich Paschen (1865–1947).

On his return to England, Tolansky went to London to spend two years doing research at Imperial College and received his PhD in 1934. He then moved to the physics department of Manchester University, where he served as an assistant lecturer under Lawrence Bragg (1890–1971). In 1936 Tolansky was awarded a DSc by Manchester University, and he subsequently became a lecturer in 1937 and senior lecturer in 1945, and in 1946 was given the post of reader in physics. In the following year, Tolansky moved to the Royal Holloway College, part of London University, to take up the chair of physics. He retained this position until he died in London on 4 March 1973.

Tolansky's early research centred on the study of line and band spectra and at Paschen's department in Berlin, Tolansky was exposed to studies in virtually all areas of spectroscopy. His main interest until his move to London in 1947 was the analysis of hyperfine structures in atomic spectra. He made a particular study of the spectrum of mercury, but the occurrence of multiple isotopes in his samples complicated the analysis. He also studied the hyperfine structure of the spectra of halogen gases such as chlorine and bromine, and of arsenic, iron, copper and platinum. He used the analysis of spectra to investigate nuclear spin, and magnetic and quadruple moments.

During World War II, Tolansky was requested by Tube Alloys (a euphemistic name for the body which was co-ordinating British research into the possibilities of constructing an atomic bomb) to obtain information on the spin of uranium-235, which is the isotope capable of fission in a nuclear chain reaction. Tolansky was unable to obtain any material in which the proportion of uranium-235 was enriched, so he had to use samples in which the proportion was only 0.7%. He was nevertheless able to demonstrate that the spin is in excess of $\frac{1}{2}$, and suggested that it was most likely to be $\frac{5}{2}$ or $\frac{7}{2}$. The latter figure is the value which is currently accepted.

After the war, Tolansky concentrated on the applications of multiple beam interferometry. He used it to investigate the fine details of surface structure as the method is able to resolve structure as small as 15 Å in height. He examined the vibration patterns in oscillating quartz crystals and the microtopography of many different crystals, particularly diamonds. He was especially interested in the growth features of crystals such as growth spirals. A quantitative means of assessing the hardness of materials grew out of Tolansky's work on interferometry as the depths of indentations made by the impact of a standard hardness tester could be accurately assessed by using interferometry. Another application for the technique lay in the measurement of the thickness of thin film.

Torricelli, Evangelista (*1608-1647*), was an Italian physicist and mathematician who is best known for his invention of the barometer.

Torricelli was born on 15 October 1608 in Faenza and was educated, mainly in mathematics, at the Sapienza College, Rome. He was impressed by the works of Galileo and the respect became mutual when Galileo read Torricelli's *De motu* (1641), which dealt with movement. In that same year Galileo invited him to Florence, and after Galileo's death the following year became Professor of Mathematics at Florence, where he remained for the rest of his life. He died there on 25 October 1647.

Galileo had been puzzled why a lift pump could not lift a column of water more than about 9 m – current explanations were based on Nature's supposed abhorrence of a vacuum. Torricelli realized that the atmosphere must have weight, and the height of the water column is limited by atmospheric pressure. In 1643 he filled a long glass tube, closed at one end, with mercury and inverted it in a dish of mercury. Atmospheric pressure supported a column of mercury about 76 cm long; the space above the mercury was a vacuum. Mercury is nearly 14 times as dense as water, and the mercury column was only about one-fourteenth the height of the maximum water column.

Torricelli also noticed that the height of the mercury column varied slightly from day to day and finally came to the conclusion that this was a reflection of variations in atmospheric pressure. Thus by 1644 he had developed the mercury barometer.

Townes, Charles Hard (*1915-*), is an American physicist who is best known for his investigations into the theory, and subsequent invention, of the maser (1953). He has received numerous honours for this work, including the 1964 Nobel Prize in Physics, which he shared with Nikolay Basov and Aleksandr Prokhorov, two Soviet scientists who independently invented the maser in 1955.

Townes, the son of a lawyer, was born in Greenville, South Carolina, on 28 July 1915. He was educated at Furman University, Greenville, from which he graduated in 1935, studied for his master's degree at Duke University and then moved to the California Institute of Technology to work for a PhD, which he gained in 1939. From 1939 to 1947 he worked at the Bell Telephone Laboratories designing radar bomb-aiming systems, after which he joined the physics department of the University of Columbia, becoming Professor of Physics in 1950. Next, he worked at the Massachusetts Institute of Technology from 1961 until 1967, when he was appointed Professor of Physics at the University of California, Berkeley.

In about 1950 Townes became interested in the possibility of constructing a device that could generate high-intensity microwaves, and by 1951 he had concluded that it might be possible to build such a device based on the principle that molecules emit radiation when they move from one energy level to a lower one. Ammonia molecules can occupy only two energy levels and, Townes argued, if a molecule in the high energy level can be made to absorb a photon of a specific frequency, then the molecule should fall to the lower energy level, emitting two photons of the same frequency and producing a coherent beam of single frequency radiation.

Using ammonia molecules, the radiation emitted would have a wavelength of 1.25 cm and would therefore be in the microwave region of the electromagnetic spectrum. But in constructing a device using this principle of the amplification by stimulated emission of radiation Townes had to develop a method (now called population inversion) for separating the relatively scarce high-energy molecules from the more common lower energy ones. He succeeded by using an electric field that focused the high-energy ammonia molecules into a resonator, and by 1953 he had constructed the first working maser (an acronym for *M*icrowave *A*mplification by *S*timulated *E*mission of *R*adiation).

Masers quickly found numerous applications – in atomic clocks (still the most accurate timepieces available) and radiotelescope receivers, for example. In the late 1950s solid-state masers (in which molecules of a solid were used instead of gaseous ammonia) were made and were used to amplify weak signals reflected from the Echo I passive communications satellite and radar reflections from Venus.

In 1958 Townes published a paper that demonstrated the theoretical possibility of producing an optical maser to produce a coherent beam of single-frequency visible light, rather than a microwave beam. But the first working optical maser (or laser, from *L*ight *A*mplification by *S*timulated *E*mission of *R*adiation) was built by Theodore Maiman in 1960.

Townsend, John Sealy Edward (*1868-1957*), was an Irish mathematical physicist who was responsible for the development of the study of the kinetics of electrons and ions in gases. He was the first to obtain a value for the charge on the electron and to explain how electric discharges pass through gases.

Townsend was born in Galway on 7 June 1868. He attended Corrig School and in 1885 entered Trinity College, Dublin. There he studied mathematics, physics and experimental science, graduating in 1890. He spent the next four years teaching and lecturing, especially on mathematics, and in 1895 Townsend went to England, where he remained for the rest of his life. He gained entry to Cambridge University as a research student, and he and Ernest Rutherford (1871-1937) became the first such students to work under J.J. Thomson (1856-1940). Townsend was soon recognized as a scientist of rare quality, and when Oxford University established a new chair of experimental physics in 1900 with the intention of improving the standard of instruction in the fields of electricity and magnetism, Townsend was invited to become the first Wykeham Professor. He accepted, and most of the rest of his professional career was spent in Oxford.

During his early years at Oxford, Townsend was deeply involved with the construction of a permanent Electrical Laboratory. This was completed in 1910, but Townsend's research was then disrupted by the outbreak of World War I. He spent the war years at Woolwich, researching into radio telegraphy for the Royal Naval Air Service. Townsend resumed his work on gaseous ionization at Oxford after the war and continued there until 1941, when he was knighted and retired from his university duties. He did not, however, cease working. He spent a period teaching at Winchester School, and then returned to Oxford where he wrote a number of monographs. Townsend died at Oxford on 16 February 1957.

Townsend's earliest research at Cambridge was in the field of magnetism, but he soon turned to the subject which would occupy him for the rest of his career, namely the properties of ionized gases. He studied the conductivity of gases ionized by the newly discovered X-rays and in 1897 developed a method for producing ionized gases using electrolysis. This method enabled Townsend to obtain the first estimate for the electron charge in 1898. It was later modified by J.J. Thomson and Charles Wilson (1869-1959), and

formed part of the basis for the famous oil drop experiments performed by Robert Millikan (1868-1953) from 1909 to 1912.

In 1898 Townsend began the first study of ionic diffusion in gases. He studied diffusion in gases which had been ionized (or electrified) by means of the so-called Townsend discharge. This involved the passage of a weak current through low-pressure gases. He found that the coefficient of diffusion of an ion was only a quarter of that of a neutral molecule, indicating a smaller mean free path for ions.

Around the time of Townsend's move to Oxford, he began to develop his collision theory of ionization. He based this theory on results he had himself obtained and those of Aleksandr Stoletov (1839-1896), which indicated that the ionization potential of molecules was tenfold less than was generally accepted. This meant that collisions by negative ions (electrons) could induce the formation of secondary ions, thus carrying an electric charge through a gas.

The study of the multiplication of charges in a gas was Townsend's major preoccupation for the next few years. He determined the coefficient of multiplication, also called Townsend's first ionization coefficient, which describes the number of pairs of ions produced by the movement of one electron through 1 cm in the direction of an electric field.

Townsend also studied the electrical conditions which lead to the production of a spark in a gas, and on the confusing role played in this by the positive ions that are produced simultaneously with the electrons.

During the 1920s, Townsend was involved with the measurement of the average fraction of energy lost by an electron in a single collision. He discovered in 1924 that this fraction was very small when the electrons were passed through a monatomic gas such as helium or argon. Carl Ramsauer (1879-1955) was independently engaged in a similar study and their results, which are called the Ramsauer-Townsend effect, were later found to be analogous to electron diffraction and were important in understanding the wave-like nature of the electron.

Tyndall, John (*1820-1893*), was an Irish physicist who is mainly remembered for the Tyndall effect, which is the scattering of light by very small particles suspended in a medium. The discovery of this effect enabled Tyndall to explain the blue colour of the sky.

Tyndall was born at Leighlinbridge, Carlow, on 2 August 1820. He went to school in Carlow and then held a succession of surveying and engineering jobs in Ireland and England. In 1847, he became a teacher of mathematics at Queenswood College, Hampshire, where he was a colleague of the chemist Edward Frankland (1825–1899). Drawn to the study of science by Frankland, Tyndall left with him in 1848 to enter the University of Marburg, Germany. There Tyndall studied physics and mathematics, and also chemistry under Robert Bunsen (1811–1899). Obtaining his doctorate in 1850, he returned to Queenwood in 1851 and in 1853 became Professor of Natural Philosophy at the Royal Institution. From 1859 to 1868, Tyndall was also Professor of Physics at the Royal School of Mines.

In 1867, Tyndall became Superintendent of the Royal Institution, succeeding Michael Faraday (1791–1867). In his position as lecturer at the Royal Institution and as a journalist and writer, he did much to popularize science in Britain and also in the United States, where he toured from 1872 to 1873. Tyndall also championed those he believed had been wrongly treated, and was responsible for the recognition of Britain of the pioneering work done on the conservation of energy by Julius Mayer (1814–1878). In 1886, Tyndall became seriously ill and he retired from the Royal Institution in the following year. He died from an accidental overdose of drugs at Hindhead, Surrey, on 4 December 1893.

The discovery of the Tyndall effect was made in 1869 when Tyndall was investigating the passage of light through liquids. He found that light passes unimpeded through a pure solvent or an ordinary solution, but that the beam becomes visible in a colloidal solution. Tyndall realized that the colloidal particles although invisible to the eye were big enough to scatter the light, and reasoned that a similar suspension of dust particles in the atmosphere causes the blue light in the sunlight passing through the atmosphere to be scattered more than the red, producing a blue sky. This explanation was confirmed by Lord Rayleigh (1842–1919) in 1871, who showed that the scattering is inversely proportional to the fourth power of the wavelength.

This work led Tyndall to consider the likelihood that the air contains minute living microorganisms, and he was able to show that pure air devoid of any suspended particles as indicated by the absence of the Tyndall effect did not produce putrefaction in foods. The air must therefore contain bacteria. This result was important in confirming the work of Louis Pasteur (1822–1895) that rejected the spontaneous generation of life, and it also inspired Tyndall to develop methods of sterilizing by heat treatment.

Tyndall also carried out experimental work on the absorption and transmission of heat by gases, especially water vapour and atmospheric gases, which was important in the development of meteorology.

V

Van Allen, James Alfred (*1914–*), is an American physicist who was closely involved with the early development of the United States space program and discovered the magnetosphere, the zone of high levels of radiation around the Earth caused by the presence of trapped charged particles. This region is popularly known as the Van Allen belt.

Van Allen was born in Mount Pleasant, Iowa, on 7 September 1914. He grew up there and then went to the Iowa Wesleyan College, where he received his BS degree in 1935. He then went to the University of Iowa, where he earned his MS in 1936 and his PhD in 1939. From 1939 to 1942, Van Allen worked as a research fellow at the Carnegie Institute in Washington DC in the department of terrestrial magnetism. During World War II, from 1942 to 1946, Van Allen served as an Ordnance and Gunnery Officer with the US Navy. He participated in the development of the proximity fuse, which was a device attached to a missile such as an anti-aircraft shell so that it detonated when it neared the target and the radio waves it emitted were reflected back to it with sufficient intensity from the target. This meant that detonation could occur even when the missile had not been aimed sufficiently accurately for a direct hit, and this greatly increased the effectiveness of anti-aircraft weapons.

Van Allen's wartime work gave him experience with the miniaturization of sophisticated equipment, and it was put to good use in his next post from 1946 to 1950 as Supervisor of the High Altitude Research Group and Proximity Fuse Unit in the Applied Physics Department at Johns Hopkins University. During the period from 1949 to 1957, Van Allen organized and led scientific expeditions to Peru (1949), the Gulf of Alaska (1950), Greenland (1952 and 1957) and Antarctica (1957) to study cosmic radiation.

In 1951, Van Allen became Professor of Physics and Head of the Physics Department at the University of Iowa. From 1953 to 1954 he participated in Project Matterhorn, which was concerned with the study of controlled thermonuclear reactions, and he also served as a research associate at Princeton University. Van Allen was then closely involved with the organization of International Geophysical Year, which took place from July 1957 to December 1958. In

1959 he was also made Professor of Astronomy at Iowa, and since 1972, Van Allen has been Carver Professor of Physics there. He lives in Iowa City.

Van Allen's work immediately after the end of World War II involved utilization of the unused German stock of V-2 rockets and of Aerobee rockets for research purposes. Devices for the measurement of the levels of cosmic radiation were sent to the outer regions of the atmosphere in these rockets, and the data were radioed back to Earth. In 1949 Van Allen conceived of rocket-balloons (rockoons) which began to be used in 1952. They consisted of a small rocket which was lifted by means of a balloon into the stratosphere and then fired off, thus being able to reach heights attainable otherwise only by a much larger rocket. Van Allen's experience in the miniaturization of electronic equipment enabled him to include a maximum amount of instrumentation in the limited payload of these rockets, and this was to be crucial to the early stages of the US space program.

The possibility of sending a rocket into orbit around the Earth, thereby creating an artificial satellite, was finally given serious consideration by the US government in the mid-1950s. President Eisenhower announced the Vanguard Program in 1955, which promised to put an artificial satellite into orbit within two years to coincide with the scheduled International Geophysical Year, which was itself timed to coincide with a peak in solar activity. Van Allen was given the responsibility for the instrumentation of the proposed satellites.

Van Allen was on a scientific expedition to the Antarctic when the news of the world's first artificial satellite, the Russian Sputnik 1, broke on 4 October 1957. This precipitated great activity in the American camp, and the first US satellite, Explorer 1, was launched on 31 January 1958. Part of Explorer's payload was a geiger counter which Van Allen had intended to measure the levels of cosmic radiation, but at a height of about 500 miles (800 km), the counters registered a radiation level of zero. This was an absurd reading, and instrument failure was suspected. When the same result was recorded by Explorer 3, which was launched on 26 March 1958, Van Allen realized that the zero reading could have resulted from the counters being swamped with very high counts of radiation. The counter which was sent up with Explorer 4 on 26 July 1958 was shielded with lead in order to allow less radiation to penetrate, and this showed clearly that parts of space contained much higher levels of radiation than had previously been suspected.

Van Allen studied the size and distribution of the high radiation zones. He found that it consists of two toroidal belts around the Earth, which arise by the trapping of charged particles in the Earth's magnetic field. They were named the Van Allen belts, but are now more usually known as the magnetosphere.

Van de Graaff, Robert Jemison (*1901–1967*), was an American physicist who designed and built the electrostatic high-voltage generator named after him.

Van de Graaff was born in Tuscaloosa, Alabama, on 20 December 1901. He studied to be an engineer, obtaining a BS degree from the University of Alabama in 1922 and an MS a year later. He worked for a short while for the Alabama Power Company, but left in 1924 to travel to the Sorbonne in Paris for further study. There Van de Graaff was deeply impressed by lectures given by Marie Curie (1867–1934), which focused his attentions on the exciting developments in atomic physics. In 1925, he went to study at Oxford under John Townsend (1868–1957), receiving a BSc in 1926 and a PhD in 1928. Van de Graaff conceived the idea of his generator at this time and returned to the United States in 1929 to de-

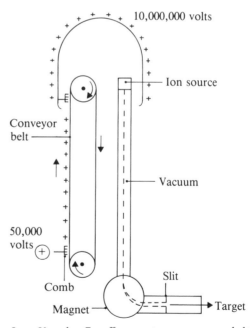

In a Van der Graaff generator, a conveyor belt carries charge from a high-voltage supply to a hollow domed terminal, where it accumulates on the outside. Ions from a discharge tube are accelerated down an evacuated tube, bent through 90° by a magnetic field perpendicular to their path, and collimated by a narrow slit.

velop it. He built a working model at Princeton University, where he served as a National Research Fellow from 1929 to 1931. He then undertook further development at the Massachusetts Institute of Technology, where he was appointed Research Associate in 1931. Van de Graaff then became Associate Professor of Physics at MIT in 1934, and retained his position until 1960, when he resigned to devote all his time to the High Voltage Engineering Corporation (HVEC), a company he had set up in 1946 with John Trump. Van de Graaff died in Boston on 16 January 1967.

Van de Graaff's main work at Oxford concerned the mobility of ions in the gaseous state, but he saw the need for beams of high-energy subatomic particles in the study of the properties of atoms. He realized that a high potential could be built up by storing electrostatic charge within a hollow sphere and that this could be achieved by depositing charges on to a moving belt that carries the charges into the sphere, where a collector transfers them to the outer surface of the sphere. Van de Graaff's first working model, constructed in 1929, operated at 80,000 volts and he soon upgraded this to 2 million volts, and eventually to 5 million volts. At MIT, the generator was developed so that it could be used to accelerate subatomic particles to very high velocities, and this technology was then immediately applied to nuclear investigations and also to clinical research. Trump and Van de Graaff collaborated to modify the generator so that it could be used in the generation of hard X-rays for use in radiotherapy in treating internal tumours and the first machine, a 1-MeV X-ray generator, was installed in a Boston hospital in 1937.

During World War II, the US Navy commissioned the production of five generators with 2-MeV capacity for use in the X-ray examination of munitions. The experience gained during these years enabled Van de Graaff to set up HVEC for the commercial production of generators. The company developed the Van de Graaff generator for the wide variety of scientific, medical and industrial research purposes in which it is employed today. The tandem principle of particle acceleration and a new insulating core transformer invented by Van de Graaff contributed to these advances.

Van Vleck, John Hasbrouck (*1899–1980*), was an American physicist who made important contributions to our knowledge of magnetism, as a result of which he is widely considered to be one of the fathers of modern magnetic theory. He received many honours for his work, including the 1977 Nobel Prize in Physics, which he was awarded jointly with Philip Anderson and Nevill Mott.

Van Vleck was born in Middletown, Connecticut, on 13 March 1899, the son of a mathematics professor. He was educated at the University of Wisconsin, from which he graduated in 1920, and at Harvard University, from which he gained his master's degree in 1921 and his doctorate in 1922. He then stayed at Harvard as an instructor in physics until 1923, when he went to the University of Minnesota as an assistant professor. In 1927 he married Abigail Pearson, and was promoted to full Professor of Physics at Minnesota. He was Professor of Physics at Wisconsin University from 1928 to 1934 – during which period he was a Guggenheim Foundation Fellow (1930) – then returned to Harvard. He remained at Harvard until formally retiring in 1969, having been Hollis Professor of Mathematics and Natural Philosophy since 1951; on retiring he was made an Emeritus Professor. While at Harvard he held various other positions in addition to the Hollis professorship: Dean of Engineering and Applied Physics from 1951 to 1957, Lorentz Professor at Leiden University, Holland, in 1960; and Eastman Professor at Oxford University from 1962 to 1963. Van Vleck died in Cambridge, Massachusetts, on 27 October 1980.

Van Vleck devoted most of his career to studying magnetism, particularly its relationship to atomic structure. With the coming of quantum wave mechanics in the early 1930s he began investigating its implications for magnetism and devised a theory – using wave mechanics – that gives an accurate explanation of the magnetic properties of individual atoms in a series of chemical elements. He also introduced the idea of temperature-independent susceptibility in paramagnetic materials – a phenomenon now called Van Vleck paramagnetism – and drew attention to the importance of electron correlation (the interaction between the movements of electrons) in the appearance of localized magnetic moments in metals. His most important work, however, was probably his formulation of the ligand field theory, which is still one of the most useful tools for interpreting the patterns of chemical bonds in complex compounds. This theory explains the magnetic, electrical and optical properties of many elements and compounds by considering the influences exerted on the electrons in particular atoms by other atoms nearby.

Van Vleck also worked on radar during World War II. He found that water molecules in the atmosphere absorb radar waves with a wavelength of about 1.25 cm, and that oxygen molecules have a similar effect on 0.5 cm radar waves. This finding was important for the development of effective radar systems and, later, in microwave communications and radio-astronomy.

Vening Meinesz, Felix Andries (*1887–1966*), was a Dutch geophysicist who originated the method of making very precise gravity measurements in the stable environment of a submarine. The results he obtained were important in the fields of geophysics and geodesy.

Vening Meinesz was born at The Hague on 30 July 1887, and took a degree in civil engineering at the Technical University of Delft in 1910. He was first employed by the government to take part in a gravimetric survey of Holland. Over the next decade he took measurements at over 50 sites, and was particularly concerned with overcoming the problem of inaccuracies caused by unstable support for his apparatus. His PhD thesis, submitted to the Technical University of Delft in 1915, dealt with this problem. Vening Meinesz developed a device which required the measurement of the mean periods of two pendulums which swung from the same apparatus. The mean of the two periods is not affected by disturbances in the horizontal plane, and so can be used to determine the local gravitational force accurately.

From 1923 to 1939, Vening Meinesz undertook 11 scientific expeditions at sea in submarines. He was fortunate in receiving the cooperation of the Royal Netherlands Navy. The outbreak of World War II put a temporary stop to such peaceful uses of submarines, but expeditions were resumed in the late 1940s. By then it was Vening Meinesz's younger associates who actually put out to sea, but his pendulum apparatus was the only one suited to marine gravimetric measurement until the end of the 1950s. Spring gravimetric devices have since been developed which can be mounted on stable platforms in surface vessels, but Vening Meinesz's method has been applied in thousands of measurements around the world.

Vening Meinesz became Professor of Cartography at the University of Utrecht in 1927, and in 1935 was also made Professor of Geophysics at the same university. He held both these posts until 1957, and from 1938 to 1957 he also held the simultaneous post of Professor of Physical Geodesy at the University of Delft. Vening Meinesz died in Amersfort, Holland, on 10 August 1966.

During the course of his early research, Vening Meinesz realized that measurements of the Earth's gravitational field could yield important indications of the nature of the internal features of the Earth itself. A prerequisite of such study would be the ability to make accurate measurements of the Earth's gravitational field in as many different places as possible. Values could be obtained on land with relative ease, although they might be subject to large distortions by the presence of local features such as mountains. Measurement at sea was made impossible by turbulence caused by waves and wind, but was most desirable because so much of the Earth's surface is covered by ocean and because there are fewer problems with local geographic features as the sea bed is the nearest source of distortion.

It was suggested to Vening Meinesz that gravimetric experiments could be conducted below the sea's surface in submarines because disruption from waves decreases exponentially with the depth of the submarine. On his first voyage, Vening Meinesz found that once he had modified the design of his apparatus to compensate for the craft's rolling, he was indeed able to make very accurate measurements.

One of the earliest important findings to arise from these studies was the discovery of low gravity belts in the Indonesian Archipelago running from Sumatra to the Mindanao Deep. Vening Meinesz proposed this to have arisen as a result of a downward buckling of the crust causing light sediments to fill the resulting depressions. This is the origin of the concept of the geosyncline. Vening Meinesz later returned to the question of crustal deformation and suggested it to be a consequence of convection currents arising from the cooling of the Earth at its surface. He elaborated this into a short-lived hypothesis that denied the existence of continental drift, but abundant evidence was soon amassed to support the view that continental drift does occur and is driven by convection currents in the mantle.

The results Vening Meinesz obtained on his expeditions at sea were also applied in the field of geodesy, which is concerned with the analysis of the Earth's shape. He showed that the equilibrium shape of a rotating ellipsoid is disrupted by irregularly distributed masses, but that the height of these anomalous masses does not exceed 40 km. He was able to discount the model of the Earth's shape which proposed a flattening at the equator.

Volta, Alessandro (*1745–1827*), was an Italian physicist who discovered how to produce electric current and built the first electric battery. He also invented the electrophorus as a ready means of producing charges of static electricity.

Volta was born at Como on 18 February 1745. He received his early education at various religious institutions but showed a flair for science, particularly the study of electricity which had been brought to the forefront of attention by the experiments and theories of Benjamin Franklin (1706–1790). Volta began to experiment with static electricity in 1765 and soon gained a reputation as a scientist, leading to his appointment as Principal of the Gymnasium at Como in 1774 and, a year later, as Professor of Experimental Physics there. In 1778, Volta took up the same position at Pavia and remained there until 1819. In 1799, the conflict between Austria and France over the region caused him to lose his post but he was reinstated following the French victory in 1800. Volta then travelled to Paris in 1801 to demonstrate his discoveries in electricity to Napoleon, who made him a count and awarded him a pension. Volta retained his academic post when Austria returned to power in 1814 and retired in 1819. He died at Como on 5 March 1827.

Volta's first major contribution to physics was the invention of the electrophorus in 1775. He had researched thoroughly into the nature and quantity of electrostatic charge generated by various materials, and he used this knowledge to develop a simple practical device for the production of charges. His electrophorus consisted of a disc made of turpentine, resin and wax, which was rubbed to give it a negative charge. A plate covered in tin foil was lowered by an insulated handle on to the disc, which induced a positive charge on the lower side of the foil. The negative charge that was likewise induced on the upper surface was removed by touching it to ground the charge, leaving a positive charge on the foil. This process could then be repeated to build up a greater and greater charge. Volta went on to realize from his electrostatic experiments that the quantity of charge produced is proportional to the product of its tension and the capacity of the conductor. He developed a simple electrometer similar to the gold-leaf electroscope but using straws so that it was much cheaper to make. This instrument was very sensitive and Volta was able to use it to measure tension, proposing a unit that was equivalent to about 13,500 volts.

Volta's next important work did not concern electricity but the air and gases. In 1776, he discovered methane by isolating and examining the properties of marsh gas found in Lake Maggiore. He then made the first accurate estimate of the proportion of oxygen in the air by exploding air with hydrogen to remove the oxygen. Later, in about 1795 to 1796, Volta recognized that the vapour pressure of a liquid is independent of the pressure of the atmosphere and depends only on temperature. This anticipated the law of partial pressures put forward by John Dalton (1766–1844) in 1801.

Volta's greatest contribution to science began with the discovery by Luigi Galvani (1737–1798) in 1791 that the muscles in dead frogs contract when two dissimilar metals (brass and iron) are brought into contact with the muscle and each other. Volta successfully repeated Galvani's experiments using different metals and different animals, and he also found that placing the two metals on his tongue produced an unpleasant sensation. The effects were due to electricity and in 1792, Volta concluded that the source of the electricity was in the junction of the metals and not, as Galvani thought, in the animals. Volta even succeeded in producing a list of metals in order of their electricity production based on the strength of the sensation they made on his tongue, thereby deriving the electromotive series.

Volta's tongue and Galvani's frogs proved to be highly sensitive detectors of electricity – much more so than Volta's electrometer. In 1796, Volta set out to measure the electricity produced by different metals, but to register any deflection in the electrometer he had to increase the tension by multiplying that given by a single junction. He soon hit upon the idea of piling discs of metals on top of each other and found that they had to be separated by a moist conductor to produce a current. The political upheavals of this period prevented Volta from proceeding immediately to construct a battery but he had undoubtedly achieved the "voltaic pile", as it came to be called, by 1800. In that year, he wrote to the President of the Royal Society, Joseph Banks (1743–1820), and described two arrangements of conductors that produced an electric current. One was a pile of silver and zinc discs separated by cardboard moistened with brine, and the other a series of glasses of salty or alkaline water in which bimetallic curved electrodes were dipped.

Volta's discovery was a sensation, for it enabled high electric currents to be produced for the first time. It was quickly applied to produce electrolysis, resulting in the discovery of several new chemical elements, and then led throughout the 1800s to the great discoveries in electromagnetism and electronics which culminated in the invention of the electrical machines and electronic devices that we enjoy today. Volta's genius lay in an ability to construct simple devices and in his tenacity to follow through his convictions. He was not a great theoretician and did not attempt to explain his discovery. However, he did see the need for establishing proper measurement of electricity, and it is fitting that the unit of electric potential, tension or electromotive force is named the volt in his honour.

Von Guericke, Otto (*1602–1686*), was a German physicist who invented the air pump and carried out the classic experiment of the Magdeburg hemispheres that demonstrated the pressure of the atmosphere. He also constructed the first machine for generating static electricity.

Von Guericke was born at Magdeburg on 20 November 1602 into a wealthy family, which afforded him wide educational opportunities. He attended several universities, going to Leipzig from 1617 to 1620, Helmstedt in 1620, Jena in 1621 and 1622 and Leiden from 1622 to 1625. He studied law, science and engineering, and on his return to Magdeburg was made an alderman of the city.

In 1631 Magdeburg sustained tremendous war damage, most of the population of 40,000 being butchered, and he moved to Brunswick and Erfurt where he worked as engineer to the Swedish government and later for that of Saxony as well. He was able to serve Magdeburg as envoy to various occupying powers, for as the fortunes of war swayed back and forth, French, Hapsburg and Swedish forces gained control. Guericke, as he then was, represented Madgeburg at various conferences and diets which marked at least a lessening of hostilities in that part of Europe.

In 1646, Guericke became mayor of Magdeburg and his scientific achievements were made from this time onwards into the 1650s. He was ennobled and became von Guericke in 1666 and remained mayor until 1676. In 1681 he retired and went to live with his son in Hamburg, where he remained for the rest of his life. Von Guericke died at Hamburg on 11 May 1686.

It is remarkable that, amidst all the political turmoil surrounding him, von Guericke found time for deep philosophical speculation about the nature of space. At the time, Aristotle's idea that "nature abhors a vacuum" - that a vacuum could not exist - was being hotly debated. The phrase had been taken up by René Descartes (1596–1650) and had great currency, but in 1643 Evangelista Torricelli (1608–1647) had demonstrated that a vacuum could exist in the space above an enclosed column of mercury. His experiment could be explained by the atmosphere possessing weight, and von Guericke decided to resolve matters by experiment. He set about constructing an air pump in an attempt to pump the air from a vessel and produce a vacuum. He postulated that if Descartes' ideas (the plenist assumption that space is matter) were correct, then an evacuated vessel should collapse. Von Guericke's first air pump was rather like a large bicycle pump and in 1647, after much trouble with seals, he succeeded in imploding a copper sphere from which he pumped the air via an outlet at the bottom.

Although it seemed that Descartes was vindicated, von Guericke still had his doubts. He built a stronger vessel and succeeded in evacuating it without causing it to collapse. He also demonstrated that the sound of a bell is muffled and that a candle is extinguished as the air is removed, and gradually the theory that a vacuum cannot exist was discarded.

Von Guericke then turned to demonstrating the immense force that the pressure of the atmosphere exerts on an evacuated vessel. One of his most famous experiments was in 1654. A cylinder containing a well-fitting piston was connected to a rope passing over a pulley. Fifty strong men were unable to move the piston more than halfway up the cylinder, and when the closed end was evacuated they could not prevent the piston from descending.

Von Guericke went on to make his classic airpressure experiment, which was probably first performed at Magdeburg in 1657, in which two copper hemispheres with tight-fitting edges were placed together and the air pumped out. Two teams of horses were then harnessed to the hemispheres and proved unable to pull them apart. On admitting air to the hemispheres, they fell apart instantly.

Von Guericke's experiments and other observations on the elasticity of air led him to investigate the decrease of pressure with altitude, which Blaise Pascal (1623–1662) had demonstrated in his famous Puy de Dôme excursion in 1648. A natural consequence was the establishment of the link between atmospheric pressure and the weather, which von Guericke pursued as far as making weather forecasts with a water barometer and proposing a string of meteorological stations contributing data to a forecasting system – all this in 1660.

Von Guericke also interested himself in cosmology and magnetism. While experimenting with a globe of sulphur constructed to simulate the magnetic properties of the Earth, he discovered that it produced static electricity when rubbed and went on to develop a primitive machine for the production of static electricity. Von Guericke also demonstrated the magnetization of iron by hammering in a north–south direction. Another "first" with which he is credited is the observation of coloured shadows; these he observed in the early morning when an object illuminated by a candle cast a blue shadow on a white surface.

Von Guericke's remarkable blend of political and scientific activities was to be echoed by such figures as Count Rumford (1753–1814) and Benjamin Franklin (1706–1790) in the next century – although in the latter's case on an altogether grander scale. Von Guericke's discovery that the pressure of the atmosphere can be made to exert considerable force by the creation of a vacuum led directly to the development of steam engines in the 1700s.

Von Neumann, Johann (or John) (*1903-1957*), was a Hungarian-born American physicist and mathematician who originated Games Theory and developed the fundamental concepts involved in programming computers. He also made a valuable contribution to quantum mechanics.

Von Neumann was born at Budapest, Hungary, on 28 December 1903. He received private instruction until 1914, when he entered the Gymnasium, and even then continued to be tutored outside school in mathematics because of the exceptional ability that he displayed in the subject. Von Neumann left Hungary in 1919 in the wake of the disruptions arising as a result of the defeat suffered by Austria-Hungary in World War I. He attended several universities, studying in Berlin from 1921 until 1923 and then in Zurich until 1925. He received a degree in chemical engineering from the Zurich Institute in 1925, and was awarded a PhD in mathematics from the University of Budapest a year later. He then studied in Göttingen, where he worked with Robert Oppenheimer (1904-1967), and from 1927 until 1929 held the post of privatdozent (lecturer) in mathematics at the University of Berlin.

After a year as lecturer at the University of Hamburg, Von Neumann travelled to the United States in 1930. Holding first the position of Visiting Professor, he became Full Professor of Mathematics at the University of Princeton in 1931. He held this position until 1933, when he was invited to become the youngest member of the newly established Institute of Advanced Studies at Princeton University. Von Neumann was a member of this Institute for the rest of his career, although he also held a number of important advisory posts with the US government from 1940 to 1954.

During World War II, Von Neumann served as a consultant for various committees within the Navy, Army, the Atomic Energy Commission and the Office for Scientific Research and Development. He was associated with research projects at Los Alamos from 1943 until 1955, working under Oppenheimer on the A-bomb project and also under Edward Teller (1908-   ) on the H-bomb project. The importance of Von Neumann's scientific contributions brought him widespread recognition, including the award of the Medal of Freedom, the Albert Einstein Award and the Enrico Fermi Award - all in 1956. His health had begun to fail in 1955, and he died of cancer in Washington DC on 8 February 1957.

Pure mathematics was Von Neumann's primary scientific interest during the first years of his career. He made important contributions to the subjects of mathematical logic, set theory and operator theory and his theory of rings of operators is highly regarded.

In 1928 Von Neumann read a paper on Games Theory to a scientific meeting in Göttingen. This was an entirely new subject originated by Von Neumann himself. It consisted of proving that a quantitative mathematical model could be constructed for determining the best strategy, i.e. the one which, in the long term, would produce the optimal result with minimal losses for any game, even one of chance or one with more than two players. The sort of games for which this theory found immediate use were business, warfare and the social sciences - games in which strategies must be worked out for defeating an adversary. Games Theory has also found application in the behavioural sciences. Von Neumann began work on this subject in the late 1920s, but did not devote himself exclusively to it by any means.

Applied mathematics in the field of theoretical physics held a strong fascination for Von Neumann. He began to work on the axiomitization of quantum mechanics in 1927, and in 1932 published a book entitled *The Mathematical Foundations of Quantum Mechanics*. This defended mathematically the uncertainty principle of Werner Heisenberg (1901-1976). In 1944, Von Neumann made another very important contribution to quantum mechanics when he showed that the systems of matrix mechanics developed by Heisenberg and Max Born (1882-1970) and of wave mechanics developed by Erwin Schrödinger (1887-1961) were equivalent. Von Neumann also published papers with Subrahmanyan Chandrasekhar (1910-   ) on gravitational fields. Work on pure mathematics also continued and in particular he collaborated with Francis Murray in an investigation of non-commutative algebras during the latter part of the 1940s.

Work on the atom bomb project brought a variety of new problems, many of them completely different from those Von Neumann had previously encountered. The necessity for quickly producing approximate models for complex physical problems encouraged Von Neumann to examine and develop improvements for the available computing machines. During the war he contributed to work on hydrodynamics and on shock waves, and afterwards he spent a great deal of effort designing and then supervising the construction of the first computer able to use a flexible stored program (named MANIAC-1) at the Institute of Advanced Study in 1952. This work laid the foundations for the design of all subsequent programmable computers.

Von Neumann also developed his Games

Theory, and in 1944 published *Theory of Games and Economic Behavior* with Oskar Morgenstern, his major work on the subject. Games Theory was also used during the H-bomb project in the early 1950s, in which Von Neumann played an active role. The possibility of developing automata to the point where they might be self-producing, and the similarities between the nervous system and computers were areas which absorbed much of Von Neumann's interest during his last years.

Von Neumann was a mathematician with an exceptional talent for absorbing the essential features of all the important branches of both mathematics and theoretical physics, and he was also adept at the applications of his theoretical work. He demonstrated great originality and imagination in his pioneering efforts in the areas of computer design and especially in Games Theory.

Walton, Ernest Thomas Sinton (*1903–*), is an Irish physicist best known for his work with John Cockcroft (1897-1967) on the development of the first particle accelerator, which produced the first artificial transmutation in 1932. In recognition of this achievement, Walton and Cockcroft were awarded the 1951 Nobel Prize in Physics.

Walton was born in Dungarvan, County Waterford, on 6 October 1903. He attended the Methodist College in Belfast and went on to Trinity College, Dublin, where he earned his bachelor's degree in 1926. He was later awarded an MSc in 1928 and an MA in 1934 from the same institution. In 1927, Walton continued his studies at the Cavendish Laboratories at Cambridge University, remaining there until 1934. He obtained his PhD in 1931, and in 1934 returned to Ireland to become Fellow of Trinity College, Dublin. In 1947 Walton also became Professor of Natural and Experimental Philosophy at Trinity College. Since his retirement in 1974, Walton has held the post of Emeritus Fellow of Trinity College. He has received many honours in recognition of his scientific achievements. In particular Walton was the joint recipient with Cockcroft of the Hughes Medal of the Royal Society in 1938 as well as the Nobel Prize in Physics in 1951. His present residence is in Dublin.

Before Walton and Cockcroft began their investigation of artificial transmutation, the only means of changing one element into another was by bombarding it with alpha particles from a natural source, i.e. a radioactive substance. This placed a variety of constraints on the possible procedures in such work. Walton investigated several approaches for the production of fast particles. Two of the methods he attempted in 1928 failed because of difficulties in focusing the particles, and these methods were developed later by others to build the first successful betatron and the early linear accelerators.

In 1929 Walton and Cockcroft were joined at the Cavendish Laboratory by George Gamow (1904-1968). Gamow made calculations on the feasibility of producing transmutations by bombardment with proton beams. His results encouraged them to investigate the production of a high voltage multiplying the circuit which would enable them to produce particles of uniform energy. Protons were preferable to alpha particles because the smaller charge of the former makes them less susceptible to repulsive interactions with the target nuclei. Furthermore, hydrogen gas is more readily ionized than helium, so protons are produced more easily than are alpha particles.

The device that Cockcroft and Walton constructed, the first successful particle accelerator, used an arrangement of condensers to build up very high potentials and was completed in 1932. It could produce a beam of protons accelerated at over 500,000 electron volts. In 1932 Walton and Cockcroft used the proton beam to bombard lithium. They observed the production of large quantities of alpha particles, showing that the lithium nuclei had captured the protons and formed unstable beryllium nuclei which instantaneously decayed into two alpha particles travelling in opposite directions. Walton and Cockcroft detected these alpha particles with a fluorescent screen. They later investigated the transmutation of other light elements using proton beams, and also deuterons (nuclei of deuterium) derived from heavy water.

These experiments were a pioneering venture, representing the first investigations of artificial transmutation. The type of generator built by Cockcroft and Walton suffers electric breakdown at very high voltages, and has a limit of 1.5 MeV. Other generators, particularly that designed by Robert Van der Graaff (1907-1967) and the cyclotron developed by Ernest Lawrence (1901-1958) soon superseded it. The particle accelerator thereby became a vital research tool at an extremely turbulent time in the development of nuclear physics, and has been developed to a far more advanced state in recent years.

Waterston, John James (*1811-1883*), was a British physicist who first formulated the essential features of the kinetic theory of gases. Unfortunately, his work was not recognized during his lifetime and Waterston was considered to be an eccentric scientist of no outstanding merit, best known for his work on solar heat. This assessment of his abilities was considerably revised after his death when his contribution to kinetic theory came to light, but by that time the theory had been independently developed by others.

Waterston was born in Edinburgh in 1811. He attended Edinburgh High School and then joined a civil engineering firm. His employers permitted him to attend courses at Edinburgh University, and he studied a broad range of scientific and medical subjects. He showed particular aptitude in mathematics and physics, and began publishing scientific papers as early as 1830.

The expanding British railway system attracted many young engineers to its service, and Waterston moved to London in 1833 to do surveying and draughtsmanship work for it. He wrote papers on matters arising from his work and also continued to do experiments and research into pure science in his own time. He became affiliated with the Institute of Civil Engineers, and took a less time-consuming job in the Hydrographers' Department of the Admiralty in order to spend more time on science.

A complete change in Waterston's life came in 1839 when he went to India to take up a post as teacher of the East India Company's cadets in Bombay. He spent his spare time in the library of the Grant College in Bombay, and continued to write scientific papers which he sent back to Britain - including the ill-fated submission on kinetic theory.

Waterston spent nearly twenty years in Bombay, but when he had saved enough money he retired and in 1857 he returned to Edinburgh to devote all his efforts to research. He wrote papers on a variety of topics covering a broad scientific spectrum, but had difficulty in getting them published. He became increasingly bitter over this and towards the end of his life withdrew completely from all contacts with the rest of the scientific community. On 18 June 1883 he disappeared from his home and was never heard of again.

Waterston's first scientific paper, published when he was only 19 years old, concerned a model which he proposed might explain gravitational force without the necessity for postulating an effect which operated at great distances. This was a topic of lively debate at the time, and although he did not carry his work along these lines any further, the paper did contain some formative ideas which were developed in his kinetic theory of gases fifteen years later.

In 1843, Waterston wrote a book on the nervous system in which he attempted to apply molecular theory to physiology. It included several fundamental features of the kinetic theory of gases, among them the idea that temperature and pressure are related to the motion of molecules. However, Waterston's ideas on neurophysiology and psychology were ahead of their time and, perhaps for this very reason, the book aroused little interest.

The work of James Joule (1818-1889) on heat stimulated Waterston to consider more fully its application to the properties of gases. He produced a paper which contained the first formulation of the equipartition theory and was thus an early application of statistical mechanics, and submitted it to the Royal Society in 1845.

The Society, following its standard practice, had the paper read by two scientists who both commented unfavourably on the efforts of this obscure scientist writing from the other side of the globe, and the paper was firmly rejected. An abstract of the paper did appear in the Transactions of the Royal Society in 1846, and a short note was published on it by the British Association in 1851.

Waterston was unable to retrieve the paper from the Society, and as he had not kept a copy for himself, he was unable to publish his theory elsewhere. A longer abstract of the paper was the best he could provide, and that purely for private circulation. Hermann Helmholtz (1821-1894) published an abstract of his theory in a German journal, which may conceivably have stimulated interest in kinetic theory in Germany. But it was Rudolf Clausius (1822-1888), James Clerk Maxwell (1831-1879) and Ludwig Boltzmann (1844-1906) who received the credit for the development of the kinetic theory from 1857 onwards. The rejection of Waterston's work had delayed progress to the kinetic theory by about fifteen years. Waterston's priority was finally established by Lord Rayleigh (1842-1919), who discovered his 1845 paper on the kinetic theory in the Royal Society's vaults in 1891 and published it in the following year with an introduction warning young scientists of the resistance to new ideas often displayed by scientific societies.

Waterston did gain some recognition for a paper he presented to the British Association in 1853 on the basis for the generation of solar heat. He proposed that meteoric material falling into the Sun would produce heat. In 1857 he published an estimate of the solar temperature at 13 million degrees, which is not far from the present value accepted for the Sun's interior. Waterston wrote other papers on sound, capillarity, latent heat, and various aspects of astronomy. The rejection of two of his papers by the Royal Astronomical Society in 1878 may well have been related to his resignation from that society shortly thereafter, after having been a member for over a quarter of a century, and his subsequent progressive withdrawal from science.

Waterston must therefore be regarded rather as a tragic figure, a scientist whose originality and talent were frustrated to the detriment not only of himself but also of science as a whole.

Weber, Wilhelm Eduard (*1804-1891*), was a German physicist who made important advances in the measurement of electricity and magnetism by devising sensitive instruments and defining electric and magnetic units. In recognition of his achievements, the SI unit of magnetic flux density is called the weber. Weber was also the first to reach the conclusion that electricity consists of charged particles.

Weber was born at Wittenberg on 24 October 1804. The family was highly gifted, for Weber's father was Professor of Theology at the University of Wittenberg and his older brother Ernst Weber (1795-1878) became a pioneer in the physiology of perception. In 1814, the family moved to Halle, where Weber entered the University in 1822. He obtained his doctorate in 1826, and then became a lecturer at Halle, rising to an assistant professorship in 1828.

In 1831, Weber moved to Göttingen to become Professor of Physics and there began a close collaboration with Carl Gauss (1777-1855). He lost this post in 1837 following a protest at the suspension of the constitution by the new ruler of Hanover. However Weber managed to continue working at Göttingen and then in 1843 he obtained the position of Professor of Physics at Leipzig. In 1849, Weber returned to his former post at Göttingen. He remained in this position until he retired in the 1870s, and died at Göttingen on 23 June 1891.

Weber's work in magnetism dates from the time when he joined Gauss at Göttingen. They conceived absolute units of magnetism that were defined by expressions involving only length, mass and time, and Weber went on to construct highly sensitive magnetometers. He also built a 3-km telegraph to connect the physics laboratory with the astronomical observatory where Gauss worked, and this was the first practical telegraph to operate anywhere in the world. It was not subsequently developed as a commercial invention, and from 1836 to 1841 Gauss and Weber organized a network of observation stations to correlate measurements of terrestrial magnetism made around the world.

In 1840, Weber extended his work on magnetism into the realm of electricity. He defined an electromagnetic unit for electric current that was applied to measurements of current made by the deflection of the magnetic needle of a galvanometer. In 1846, he developed the electrodynamometer, in which a current causes a coil suspended within another coil to turn when a current is passed through both. This instrument could be used to measure alternating currents. Current could also be measured by the Coulomb torsion balance in electrostatic units, and in an experiment carried out with Rudolph Kohlrausch in 1855, Weber found that the ratio of the electromagnetic unit to the electrostatic unit is a constant equal to the velocity of light. They did this by discharging a condenser through a torsion balance and a ballistic galvanometer. Weber and Kohlrausch attached no great importance to their strange result, but it later proved to be vital to James Clerk Maxwell (1831-1879) in his development of the electromagnetic theory of light.

In 1852, Weber defined the absolute unit of electrical resistance and also began to conceive of electricity in terms of moving charged particles of positive and negative electricity, resistance being produced by a combining of the two particles that prevents current flow. In 1846, he had produced a general law of electricity that attempted to express electrical effects mathematically and although it was not successful, it did help Weber to develop his ideas on the nature of electricity. In a remarkable piece of foresight, he put forward in 1871 the view that atoms contain positive charges that are surrounded by rotating negative particles and that the application of an electric potential to a conductor causes the negative particles to migrate from one atom to another. It was not until 1913, with the proposal of the Rutherford-Bohr model of the atom, that Weber's ideas were seen to be essentially correct. Weber also provided similar explanations of thermal conduction and thermoelectricity that were later fully developed by others.

Weber also did important work in acoustics with his brother Ernst Weber. In 1825, they made the first experimental study of interference in sound. Their findings were important in enabling Hermann Helmholtz (1821-1894) to achieve explanations of the perception of sound and mechanism of hearing.

Weber's insistence on precise experimental work to produce correct definitions of electrical and magnetic units was very important to the development of these sciences and to electromagnetism. His far-reaching views on the nature of electricity were influential in creating a climate for the acceptance of such ideas when evidence for them was later found.

Wheatstone, Charles (*1802-1875*), was a British

physicist who is known principally for the Wheatstone bridge, a method of making accurate determination of electrical resistance. However, Wheatstone did not invent this method but popularized it. He in fact made several important but lesser-known original contributions to science, including the invention of the stereoscope and the rheostat, and the first determination of the velocity of electricity along a wire. He was also a pioneer of the telegraph, and he invented the concertina.

Wheatstone was born in Gloucester on 6 February 1802. His family were involved in the manufacture of musical instruments and he received no formal education in science. Wheatstone entered the music business as an apprentice to an uncle in 1816. He became an instrument maker, inventing the concertina in 1829, and also investigated the acoustic properties of instruments. Wheatstone's work in acoustics led to his appointment as Professor of Experimental Physics at King's College, London, in 1834, a position he retained for the rest of his life. His interests then extended to electricity and optics and in 1837, Wheatstone formed a partnership with William Cooke (1806–1879) to develop a commercial telegraph. This too continued for life and led to Wheatstone being knighted in 1868, Cooke receiving the same honour in the following year. Wheatstone died on a visit to Paris on 19 October 1875.

Wheatstone's early interest in acoustics was stimulated by his family's business, which was principally concerned with the manufacture of flutes. In 1827, he invented an ingenious device called the kaleidophone which visually demonstrated the vibration of sounding surfaces by causing an illuminated spot to vibrate and produce curves by the persistence of vision. Wheatstone went on to investigate the transmission of sound in instruments and subsequently discovered modes of vibration in air columns (1832) and vibrating plates (1833).

Wheatstone's contributions to light and optics are also important. In 1860, he demonstrated how the visual combination of two similar pictures in a stereoscope gives an illusion of three dimensions. However, work of greater significance came much earlier with a paper presented at the British Association meeting in Dublin in 1835 entitled *Prismatic Analysis of Electric Light*. There Wheatstone showed that different spectra are produced by spark discharges from metal electrodes, analysis of the spectra proving that different lines and colours are formed by different electrodes. He showed the sensitivity of the method and predicted correctly that with development, it would become a technique for the

analysis of elements. Wheatstone said, "We have a mode of discriminating metallic bodies more readily than by chemical examination and which may hereafter be employed for useful purposes." Many years were to pass before the classic development of spectroscopy by Robert Bunsen (1811–1899) and Gustav Kirchhoff (1824–1887) in 1860.

In 1848 Wheatstone described a polar clock, which was an instrument for telling the time based on the change in plane of polarization of sunlight in the direction of the Pole. With this clock, it was possible to tell the hour of the day by the light from the sky though the Sun might be obscured.

In 1834 Wheatstone began a series of important experiments with Cooke on the transmission of electricity along wires. The early work involved the pursuit of pure scientific knowledge, such as the determination of the velocity of electricity related below, but later work was directed towards the public transmission of messages, i.e. commercial telegraphy. A series of successes was achieved, the first being a patent in 1837 for the five-needle telegraph. This was an instrument in which five magnetic needles on a panel were deflected by electric signals to various positions that indicated letters of the alphabet, thus transmitting written messages. This device was developed by Wheatstone and Cooke, culminating in a portable two-needle telegraph in 1845 and a single-needle telegraph the following year. These instruments were direct ancestors of the teleprinter.

In the field of electricity, Wheatstone made several important contributions. In 1834, he made the first determination of the velocity of electricity through a wire by using a rotating mirror to determine the delay that occurred between sparks as a current produced several spark gaps in a long loop of wire. The result was very high – 30 per cent greater than the speed of light – possibly because the wire was not straight, but the method was taken up and used by Armand Fizeau (1819–1896) in 1849 to make the first accurate determination of the velocity of light.

Wheatstone also improved on early versions of the dynamo invented by Michael Faraday (1791–1867) by combining several armatures on one shaft so that current was generated continuously; previously only intermittent generation was possible. He also recognized the theoretical and practical importance of Ohm's law, developing the rheostat (variable resistance) and Wheatstone bridge method for the accurate determination of resistance. This important method was published in the *Transactions of the Royal Society* in 1843, but it had been invented ten years earlier by Samuel Christie (1784–1865). It involves placing an unknown resistance in a simple circuit with

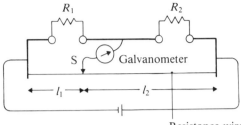

One practical form of the Wheatstone bridge compares two resistors R_1 and R_2 using a length of resistance wire (usually one metre long). The sliding contact S is moved along the wire until there is no deflection of the galvanometer. Then, if the lengths of wire are l_1 and l_2, $R_1/R_2 = l_1/l_2$.

three known resistances and varying one of them until no current flows through a galvanometer connected like a bridge to all four resistances. The unknown resistance can then be determined from the values of the other three resistances.

It is ironic that Wheatstone is mainly remembered for a device that he himself did not invent, and this must not blind us to the extraordinary range of his talents and great value of his original work in telegraphy, electricity, optics and acoustics.

Wien, Wilhelm (Carl Werner Otto Fritz Franz) *(1864–1928)*, was a German physicist whose work on thermal radiation led directly to the quantum theory. For his achievements, Wien was awarded the 1911 Nobel Prize in Physics.

Wien was born a farmer's son at Gaffken, East Prussia, on 13 January 1864. He began his education at gymnasia in Rastenburg and Königsberg, followed by university studies from 1882 to 1886 mainly at Berlin, where he was a student of Hermann Helmholtz (1821–1894), but with short spells at Göttingen and Heidelberg. Wien was awarded a doctorate in 1886 for a thesis on absorption phenomena associated with diffraction. He then returned home to manage his parents' farm, but in 1890 drought forced him to abandon this career and he went back to science and became an assistant to Helmholtz in Berlin. In 1896 Wien became Professor of Physics at Geissen in 1899, but soon moved to a similar position at Würzburg in 1900. He remained there until 1920, when he went to Munich to succeed Wilhelm Röntgen (1845–1923) as Professor of Physics. Wien died at Munich on 30 August 1928.

Wien's scientific activities included hydrodynamic studies, electric discharge in rarefied gases, cathode rays, positive rays and X-rays, but primarily he is remembered by his work on black-body radiation. This was an extension of the theories suggested by Ludwig Boltzmann (1844–1906), who in 1884 had deduced a law concerning the total energy emitted by a black body. A true black body is said to be achieved by a well-insulated heated cavity from which thermal radiation escapes through a small hole in one side. In 1893 Wien published a paper with a conclusion that the wavelength at which the maximum energy is radiated is inversely proportional to the absolute temperature of the body. In the paper, he showed that the energy density associated with the wavelength λ at the absolute temperature T is proportional to the product of the fifth power of the temperature and a function of the product λT. Wien's displacement law is derived from this statement. It states that $\lambda_m T$ is constant where λ_m is the wavelength when the energy density is a maximum. The work was extended by Otto Lummer (1860–1925) and Ernst Pringsheim (1859–1917), who produced evidence that the constant is 0.29 cm°C (0.0029 metre kelvin).

Wien's second important contribution to our knowledge of black-body radiation concerned his energy distribution formula, which was presented in 1896. This attempted to relate the distribution of energy in a continuous spectrum to the temperature in order to account for the different distributions of energy that occur at different temperatures, the peak wavelength becoming shorter at higher temperatures. The basis of this work was an assumption based on the summation of a very large number of oscillators having all possible wavelengths and in thermal equilibrium. Wien's law proved to be applicable at short wavelengths but had serious limitations at long wavelengths. Lord Rayleigh (1842–1919) found another formula that satisfied long wavelengths but not short wavelengths, and these errors provided Max Planck (1858–1947) with some clues to develop a treatment valid for the whole range of wavelengths. The result was his quantum theory, which was presented in 1900.

Wien also presented valuable ideas on positive rays initially discovered by Eugen Goldstein (1850–1930). He investigated their deflection in electrostatic and magnetic fields. He passed these rays through perforated cathodes and by their deflection was able to show in 1897 that they are positively charged particles.

Wien's radiation work marked the end of classical physics in trying to explain all phenomena. In providing Planck with the stimulus to develop new ideas beyond the classic theories, Wien helped to bring physics to the revolution that was needed to achieve further progress.

Wilson, Charles Thomson Rees *(1869–1959)*, was

a British physicist who invented the Wilson cloud chamber, the first instrument to detect the tracks of atomic particles. For this achievement, Wilson shared the 1927 Nobel Prize in Physics with Arthur Compton (1892–1962), who gained his award for the discovery of the Compton effect.

Wilson was born on 14 February 1869 at a farmhouse near Glencorse, just outside Edinburgh. His father, a successful farmer, died when Wilson was four and the family moved to Manchester. After studies at Owens College (now the University of Manchester), he gained a BSc in 1887 and then attended Sidney Sussex College, Cambridge, obtaining a BA in 1892 in natural sciences. After four years' teaching at Bradford Grammar School, Wilson returned to Cambridge where he was the Clerk Maxwell Student from 1896 to 1899. In 1900 he became a lecturer at Sidney Sussex College and in 1925 was appointed Jacksonian Professor of Natural Philosophy at Cambridge. Wilson held this post until 1934 and retired from Cambridge two years later. He continued to be active in research, producing his last paper (on thundercloud electricity) at the age of 87, by which time he was the oldest Fellow of the Royal Society. Wilson gained many honours, including the Society's Hughes Medal in 1911, the Royal Medal in 1922 and the Copley Medal in 1935. He died at Carlops, near Edinburgh, on 15 November 1959.

Wilson's great discovery of the cloud chamber was brought about by a thorough study of atmospheric cloud formation, an interest that began with observations of clouds on Ben Nevis (Britain's highest mountain) while on holiday in 1894. The wonderful optical effects fascinated Wilson and on his return to Cambridge, he tried to simulate them in his laboratory. In 1895, he began to construct a device to reproduce cloud formation and was successful in the production of an artificial cloud by causing the adiabatic expansion of moist air. From 1895 to 1899, Wilson carried out many experiments and established that the nucleation of droplets is able to take place in the absence of dust particles. Until this experiment, it was considered essential for each water droplet to form on a nucleus of dust. Wilson demonstrated that once supersaturated with water vapour, nucleation can occur and that furthermore it is greatly improved by exposure to X-rays. This showed that ions are the nucleation sites on which water droplets form in the absence of dust.

Another unforgettable experience on Ben Nevis in 1895 had inspired a life-long interest in atmospheric electricity. In Wilson's own words, "Mist hid the top of Ben Nevis; there was a faint muttering of distant thunder. Suddenly I felt my

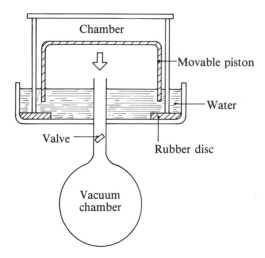

The cloud chamber devised by C.T.R. Wilson consisted originally of a cylindrical glass chamber fitted with a hollow piston which was connected, via a valve, to a large evacuated flask. The piston falls rapidly when the valve is opened, and water vapour condenses along the tracks of any particles in the chamber.

hair stand up; I did not await any further developments but started to run . . . the storm broke overhead with a bright flash and loud thunder just after I had left the summit. . . ." During the years from 1900 to 1910, Wilson's attentions were devoted to the study of electrical conduction in dust-free air. He devised a gold-leaf electroscope in which surface leakage from the leaf to the case was impossible. With this instrument, he was able to show that some electrical leakage always occurs in air, and that the conductivity of the air inside the electroscope is the same in daylight as in the dark, and is independent of the sign of the charge for leaf potential. Wilson hoped to establish some link with an outside source of ions, and he even undertook some experiments underground to collect data. Later work by others was to show cosmic radiation to be the probable explanation.

Wilson returned to the cloud chamber in 1910, having realized that it could possibly show the track of a charged particle moving through it because water droplets could condense along the particle's path. Applying a magnetic field to the chamber would cause the track to curve, giving a measure of the charge and mass of the particle. In 1911, after many attempts, Wilson succeeded in producing a working model of his cloud chamber. The chamber was constructed in the form of a short cylinder in which supersaturation was achieved and controlled by the movement of a piston through a determined distance. The condensation effects were monitored through the other end. The Wilson cloud chamber immediately became vital to the study of radioactivity. It was used to confirm the classic α particle scattering and transmutation experiments first performed by Ernest Rutherford (1871-1937), and Rutherford is reputed to have said it was "the most original apparatus in the whole history of physics".

The Wilson cloud chamber and its successors proved to be an indispensable tool in the investigation into the structure of the nucleus. Wilson himself was a lone researcher and did not contribute greatly to the development of his discovery. Modifications by Patrick Blackett (1897-1974) and Carl Anderson (1905-   ) brought about the discovery of the positron in 1932 and meson in 1936. The development of the cloud chamber into the bubble chamber by Donald Glaser (1926-   ) in 1952 produced a highly sensitive detector that has revealed whole families of new particles.

Y

Young, Thomas (*1773-1829*), was a British physicist and physician who discovered the principle of interference of light, showing it to be caused by light waves. He also made important discoveries in the physiology of vision and is also remembered for Young's modulus, the ratio of stress to strain in elasticity. In addition, Young was also an Egyptologist and was instrumental in the deciphering of hieroglyphics.

Young was born in Milverton, Somerset, on 13 June 1773. He was an infant prodigy, learning to read by the age of two, whereupon he read the whole Bible twice through. Young was largely self-taught, although he did attend school. He developed great ability at languages, taking particular interest in the ancient languages of the Middle East, and mastered mathematics, physics and chemistry while still a youth. He also showed great mechanical dexterity and for a short time made optical instruments.

In 1792, under the guidance of his great-uncle Richard Brocklesby (1722-1797), a distinguished London physician, Young commenced studying for the medical profession at St. Bartholomew's Hospital. At the young age of 21, he became a member of the Royal Society. He moved to Edinburgh to continue his medical studies in 1794 and then to Göttingen in 1795, where he was awarded his MD in 1796. He travelled throughout Germany for several months visiting museums before settling in Cambridge in 1797 for two years. He resided as a fellow-commoner at Emmanuel College, where he became known as "Phenomenon Young". At Cambridge Young used his time to pursue original scientific studies, and made his early investigations into interference.

Brocklesby left Young his London house and a fortune, and in 1800 Young returned to London and opened a medical practice there. In 1801, he was appointed Professor of Natural Philosophy at the Royal Institution and although he delivered many lectures, he was a disappointing lecturer to popular audiences. He resigned this post in July 1803 to concentrate on his practice as a physician. He was awarded an MB in 1803 from Cambridge University and an MD five years later. In 1811, Young became a physician at St. George's Hospital, London, and held this post until his death. He also held several other appointments, including Secretary of the Commission on Weights and Measures, Secretary of the Board of Longitude and Foreign Secretary of the Royal Society. Young died in London on 10 May 1829.

Young's early work was concerned with the physiology of vision. In 1793 he recognized that the mechanism of accommodation of the eye in focusing the eye on near or distant objects is due to a change of shape in the lens of the eye, the lens being composed of muscle fibres. Young confirmed this view in 1801 after having obtained experimental proof for it. He also showed that astigmatism, from which he himself suffered, is due to irregular curvature of the cornea. In 1801, Young was also the first to recognize that colour sensation is due to the presence in the retina of structures which respond to the three colours red, green and violet, showing that colour blindness is due to the inability of one or more of these structures to respond to light. Young's work in this field was elaborated into a proper theory of vision by Hermann Helmholtz (1821-1894) and James Clerk Maxwell (1831-1879).

Young also made a thorough study of optics at the same time. There was great controversy as to the nature of light – whether it consisted of streams of particles or of waves. In Britain, the particulate theory was strongly favoured because it had been advanced by Isaac Newton (1642-1727) a century before. In 1800, Young reopened the debate by suggesting that the wave theory of Christiaan Huygens (1629-1695) gave a more convincing explanation for the phenomena of reflection, refraction and diffraction. He assumed that light waves are propagated in a similar way to sound waves and are longitudinal vibrations but with a different medium and frequency. He also proposed that different colours consist of different frequencies.

In the following year, Young announced his discovery of the principle of interference. He explained that the bright bands of fringes in effects such as Newton's rings result from light waves interfering so that they reinforce each other. This was a hypothetical deduction and over the next two years, Young obtained experimental proof for the principle of interference by passing light through extremely narrow openings and observing the interference patterns produced.

Young's discovery of interference was convincing proof that light consists of waves, but it did not confirm that the waves are longitudinal. The discovery of the polarization of light by Étienne Malus (1775-1812) in 1808 led Young to suggest in 1817 that light waves may contain a transverse component. In 1821, Augustin Fresnel (1788-1827) proved that light waves are entirely transverse, and the wave nature of light was finally established.

In mechanics, Young established many important concepts in a course of lectures published in 1807. He was the first to use the terms "energy" for the product of the mass of a body with the square of its velocity and the expression "labour expended" (i.e. work done) for the product of the force exerted on a body "with the distance

through which it moved". He also stated that these two products are proportional to each other. He introduced absolute measurements in elasticity by defining the modulus as the weight which would double the length of a rod of unit cross-section. Today it is usually referred to as Young's modulus, and equals stress divided by strain in the elastic region of the loading of a material. Young also published in 1805 a theory of capillary action and accounted for the angle of contact in surface-tension effects for liquids.

From 1815 onwards, Young published papers on Egyptology mostly concerning the reading of tablets involving hieroglyphics. He was one of the first to interpret the writings on the Rosetta Stone, which was found at the mouth of the Nile in 1799. The hieroglyphic vocabulary that he established of approximately 200 signs has stood the test of time remarkably well.

Thomas Young was a scientist who possessed an extraordinary range of talents and a rare degree of insight, and he was able to initiate important paths of investigation that others were to take up and complete. His discoveries in vision are fundamental to an understanding of visual problems and to colour reproduction, and his discovery of interference was a vital step to a full explanation of the nature of light.

Yukawa, Hideki (*1907-*), is a Japanese physicist who is famous for his important theoretical work on elementary particles and nuclear forces, particularly for predicting the existence of the pi-meson (or pion) and the short-range strong nuclear force associated with this particle. He received numerous honours for his work, including the 1949 Nobel Prize in Physics, being the first Japanese to receive a Nobel Prize.

Yukawa was born in Kyoto on 23 January 1907 and was educated at Kyoto University (where his father was Professor of Geology), graduating in 1929. He then moved to Osaka University, where he both taught and studied for his doctorate, which he gained in 1938. In the following year he returned to Kyoto University and, except for various visiting professorships, remained there for the rest of his career - as Professor of Theoretical Physics from 1939 to 1950, Emeritus Professor from 1950 to 1953, and Director of the university's newly created Research Institute for Fundamental Physics from 1953. His visiting professorships included one to the Institute for Advanced Study, Princeton University (at the invitation of Julius Oppenheimer) from 1948 to 1949, and one to Columbia University from 1949 to 1953.

Yukawa proposed his new theory of nuclear forces in 1935 at a time when there was much

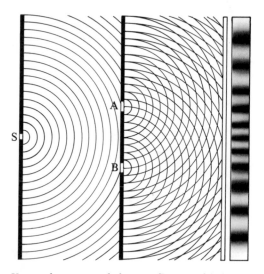

Young demonstrated the interference of light by passing monchromatic light through a narrow slit S (he originally used a small hole) and then letting it pass through a pair of closely spaced slits (A and B). Reinforcement and cancellation of the wave trains as they reached the screen produced characteristic interference fringes of alternate light and dark bands.

controversy over what holds the nucleus together. In 1932 James Chadwick had discovered the neutron but, Yukawa pointed out, this meant that because the nucleus contains only positively charged protons and neutral neutrons, the protons should repel each other and disrupt the integrity of the nucleus. He therefore postulated the existence of a nuclear "exchange force" that counteracted the mutual repulsion of the protons and therefore held the nucleus together. He predicted that this exchange force would involve the transfer of a particle (the existence of which was then unknown), that the force would be of very short range (effective over a distance of only about 10^{-8} m) and that it would be strong enough to overcome the repulsive forces between the protons yet decrease in intensity with sufficient rapidity so as to have a negligible effect on the innermost electrons. He also calculated – using quantum theory – that his predicted exchange particle would have a mass of about 200 times that of an electron (but would have the same charge as an electron) – about one-ninth the mass of a proton or neutron – and that the particle would be radioactive, with an extremely short half-life. At the time no particle having these characteristics had been found. In the following year (1936) Carl Anderson discovered the muon (or mu-meson) which possesses several of the properties of Yukawa's predicted particle but not all of them. In 1947, however, Cecil Powell discovered the pion (or pi-meson), a particle similar to Anderson's muon but which fulfilled all of the requirements of Yukawa's exchange particle.

Meanwhile, in 1936 Yukawa predicted that a nucleus could absorb one of the innermost orbiting electrons and that this would be equivalent to emitting a positron. These innermost electrons belong to the 1K electron shell, and this process of electron absorption by the nucleus is known as K capture. In 1947 Yukawa began working on a more detailed theory of elementary particles.

Z

Zeeman, Pieter (*1865–1943*), was a Dutch physicist who discovered the Zeeman effect, which is the splitting of spectral lines in an intense magnetic field. This achievement was important in determining the structure of the atom and Zeeman shared the 1902 Nobel Prize in Physics with Hendrik Lorentz (1853–1928), who had predicted the Zeeman effect.

Zeeman was born at Zonnemaire, Zeeland, on 25 May 1865. He was educated at local schools and at the Gymnasium in Delft before entering the University of Leiden in 1885. There Zeeman studied under Heike Kamerlingh Onnes (1853–1926) and Lorentz, gaining his PhD with a dissertation on the Kerr effect in 1893. He then remained at Leiden as a tutor and in 1897 moved to the University of Amsterdam to take up a lectureship. Zeeman became Professor of Physics at Amsterdam in 1900. He retained this position until he retired in 1935, and in 1923 became director of a new laboratory that was named the Zeeman Laboratory. In addition to the Nobel Prize, among his many honours was the award of the Royal Society's Rumford Medal in 1922. Zeeman died at Amsterdam on 9 October 1943.

While Zeeman was at Leiden, Lorentz proposed that light is caused by the vibration of electrons and suggested that imposing a magnetic field on light would result in a splitting of spectral lines by varying the wavelengths of the lines. Zeeman undertook the first experimental work in search of this in 1896. Using a sodium flare between the poles of a powerful electromagnet and producing spectra with a large concave diffraction grating, Zeeman was able to detect a broadening of the spectral lines when the current was activated. A similar effect was achieved with the sodium absorption spectra, so the changed shape of the flame was not responsible. In 1897, Zeeman refined the experiment and was successful in resolving the broadening of the narrow blue-green spectral line of cadmium produced in a vacuum discharge into a triplet of three component lines. Later work led Zeeman to evaluate the ratio e/m for the oscillating particles involved, which was in agreement with the value obtained for the electron by J.J. Thomson (1856–1940). This confirmed that the magnetic field was affecting the forces which control the electrons within the atom. However, Zeeman's subsequent experimental work suffered as a consequence of his promotion to the University of Amsterdam, where the facilities were much poorer than in Leiden. By the time he was able to acquire a purpose-built laboratory in 1923, many other workers had overtaken Zeeman's team in expertise and experience.

Study of the Zeeman effect led to important theoretical advances in physics. Zeeman's observations confirmed Lorentz's electromagnetic theory and later investigators were able to show that the spectral effects are caused by electron spin. As a result, the quantum theory was expanded to include these findings. Spectral observations of the Sun carried out by George Hale (1868–1938) in 1908 led him to believe that light emitted by sunspots is affected in a similar fashion to Zeeman's laboratory observations. The conclusion reached was that sunspots must be associated with intense magnetic fields within the Sun.

In later years, Zeeman's attention turned to the velocity of light in moving media and his experiments involved glass and quartz. Many difficulties were successfully overcome and Zeeman was able to show that the results were in agreement with the theory of relativity. He also studied isotopes, particularly argon, in which he identified a new isotope with a mass number of 38.

Glossary

Words which appear in italic type are explained in the glossary.

absolute zero The temperature at which a *molecule* has zero thermal energy; practically impossible to achieve. Absolute zero occurs at a temperature of about $-273°C$, and is used to define the temperature corresponding to zero on the *Kelvin scale of temperature*.

acoustics The study of sound, i.e. of the effects of *longitudinal* pressure *waves*.

adiabatic change A process which takes place without any heat entering or leaving the system.

alpha decay The disintegration of an unstable atomic *nucleus* which gives rise to the emission of *alpha particles*.

alpha particle A composite particle made up of two *protons* and two *neutrons*, and consequently carrying a net positive charge. Alpha particles are identical to helium *nuclei* and are sometimes emitted in the *radioactive decay* of *elements*.

alternating current A type of flow of electric *current* in which there is a complete reversal in direction once every cycle.

ampere The SI unit of electric current, symbol A.

Ampère's law The strength of the magnetic field B produced by a *current I* flowing through a conductor of length l is proportional to the product of the current and the length l.

amplitude For a wave motion, the *amplitude* is the maximum displacement from the position of equilibrium.

amplitude modulation A process in the transmission of *electromagnetic radiation*, especially *radio*, in which the *amplitude* of the *carrier wave* is *modulated* in relation to the frequency of the signal being transmitted.

angular momentum The rotational analogue of *momentum* in linear motion. It is the product of the moment of inertia of a body and its angular velocity. In *quantum mechanics* it is quantized in units of *Planck's constant* h; for example, the *spin* of the electron is h/2.

anode The positively charged electrode in a cell, discharge tube or *thermionic tube*.

antiferromagnetism A form of magnetism in which the neighbouring *dipoles* in a substance lie in opposite directions.

antimatter Matter made up of *antiparticles*, such as anti-*protons*, and positrons (anti-*electrons*).

antiparticle A particle of the same mass as one particular particle, but with equal and opposite charge (and other characteristics).

aperture The size of the opening admitting light into an optical instrument such as a telescope.

Appleton layer A region in the upper atmosphere where there is a large concentration of free *electrons*.

Archimedes' principle When a body is immersed in a *fluid*, it experiences an upward *force* equal to the weight of fluid displaced.

astigmatism An optical defect, in which rays in mutually perpendicular planes are out of focus relative to one another.

atom The smallest portion of an element that can take part in a chemical reaction.

atomic bomb A nuclear weapon whose explosive power is the result of *fission* occurring within it. Two masses of a fissile material, such as uranium-235, are brought together at detonation, the two masses combined being large enough to support a *chain reaction*. This proceeds explosively.

atomic number The number of *protons* in the *nucleus* of an *atom*. This is equal to the number of orbiting *electrons* on a neutral atom. Symbol Z.

atomic weight The average mass of an *atom* expressed in terms of the mass of 1/12 that of the atom carbon-12. Now termed relative atomic mass. See *mass number*.

Auger electron An *electron* emitted by an *atom* as a result of a change from an excited state to a lower energy state, without the emission of either *X-rays* or *gamma radiation*.

aurorae A sheet-like display of colour seen in high latitudes, as a result of the interaction with particles from the *solar wind* of *molecules* in the upper atmosphere.

Avogadro's hypothesis The number of *molecules* in two equal volumes of *gases* are the same, provided the two gases are at the same temperature and pressure.

Balmer series The visible *spectrum* of hydrogen, consisting of a series of distinct *spectral lines* with *wavelengths* in the visible region.

Bardeen–Cooper–Schrieffer theory A theory which accounts for the zero electrical resistance of some *superconducting* metals by invoking an attractive interaction between *electrons* binding them into "Cooper pairs".

barometer A device for measuring atmospheric *pressure*.

Bernoulli's theorem The sum of the *pressure*, *potential* and *kinetic energies* of a *fluid* flowing along a tube is constant, provided the flow is steady, incompressible and non-viscous.

beta decay The *radioactive decay* of an unstable *nucleus* involving the creation of *beta particles*.

beta particle An *electron* or *positron* emitted in the decay of an unstable atomic *nucleus*. The electron is the result of the conversion within the nucleus of a *neutron* into a *proton*, whereas the positron is the result of the change of a nuclear proton into a neutron.

Bhaba scattering A scattering process involving *electrons* and *positrons*.

Big-bang model A model in *cosmology* in which the Universe is taken as beginning in an enormous explosion which initiated the subsequent *Hubble expansion* of the galaxies. The theory is based upon Einstein's *general theory of relativity*.

birefringence See *double refraction*.

black-body radiation Radiation of a thermal nature emitted by a theoretically perfect emitter of radiation at a certain temperature.

Bohr model A semi-classical model of the *atom*, in which the *electrons* orbit the central *nucleus*, but are allowed to do so only in certain orbits, where their angular momentum is quantized. Emission and absorption of radiation is represented by jumps of electrons between certain orbits, the frequency of the radiation being given by another *quantum* relation.

Bose-Einstein statistics A treatment of particles which have integral *spin* in *statistical mechanics*, enabling properties of systems made up by such particles to be calculated.

bosons Particles obeying *Bose-Einstein statistics*, such as *photons*.

Boyle's law The volume of a *gas* held at constant temperature is inversely proportional to its pressure. This is strictly true only for a gas consisting of perfectly elastic *molecules*, each of which has zero volume or attractive or repulsive interaction with its neighbours, i.e. an *ideal* gas.

Bragg's law The maximum intensity of *X-rays* *diffracted* through a crystal occurs when the sine of the complement of the angle of incidence of the X-rays onto the crystal satisfies the relation $n\lambda = 2d\sin\theta$, where λ is the *wavelength* of the radiation, d is the lattice spacing and n is an integer.

bremsstrahlung *Electromagnetic radiation* produced by the rapid deceleration of charged

particles such as *electrons*, as occurs in the collison between electrons and *nuclei*.

Brewster's law The *refractive index* of a medium is given by the tangent of the angle at which maximum *polarization* occurs.

Brownian motion Motion affecting smoke and similarly sized microscopic particles as the result of impacts of *molecules* upon them. It appears as a random and erratic movement in the particles when viewed through a microscope.

bubble chamber A means of detecting and measuring the trajectories of high-energy ionizing particles. By keeping a substance such as liquid hydrogen heated to just above its boiling point, but holding it under *pressure* to prevent boiling, particles can be detected by the bubbles they form if the pressure is released just before they enter the chamber.

calculus A branch of higher mathematics that enables the rates of change of continuously varying quantities to be dealt with.

caloric theory A defunct theory of heat which views its flow as being the result of the flow of a substance known as "caloric".

calorimeter An instrument used in the determination of quantities of heat change.

canal rays Streams of positively charged *ions* produced from an *anode* in a discharge tube, in which gas is subjected to an electric discharge.

capacitance The ability of a system of electrical conductors and insulators to store charge.

Carnot's cycle A cycle of operations for a heat engine involving four distinct steps. Firstly, an *isothermal* expansion, then an *adiabatic* expansion, then an isothermal compression and finally an adiabatic compression.

Carnot's theorem A theorem in *thermodynamics* stating that the efficiency of any (reversible) heat engine depends only on the temperature range through which the machine operates.

carrier wave A wave of fixed *amplitude* and *frequency* generated by a radio transmitter.

cathode The negatively charged electrode in a cell, discharge tube or *thermionic tube*.

cathode rays Streams of *electrons* produced from the *cathode* in a discharge tube, in which a gas, at low pressure is subjected to an electric discharge.

centripetal force An inwardly directed *force* necessary to maintain a body in a circular trajectory.

chain reaction In nuclear *fission*, the disintegration of a fissile nucleus results in the release of two or three *neutrons*. Each one of these can go on to cause another disintegration in a chain reaction.

charge conservation A feature of *quantum mechanics*, in which reactions between *elementary particles* occur in such a way that there is no change in the total charge of the system after the event has occurred.

Charles' law The volume of a fixed mass of *gas* at constant *pressure* is directly proportional to the temperature of the gas.

Chladni figures Visual manifestations of sound waves resulting from the behaviour of small particles on plates vibrated in sympathy to a particular sound.

chromatic aberration An optical effect commonly found in simple lens instruments in which coloured fringes are seen around an image as a result of the *wavelength*-dependence of *refractive index* for glass.

Clausius–Clapeyron equation The relationship between the *pressure*, temperature and *latent heat* in a change of state, for example, liquid to gas.

cloud chamber A detection system that enables the tracks of ionizing particles to be detected. Its operation depends on the fact that water vapour contained within it condenses onto the charged *ions* more easily than onto the uncharged particles within the chamber.

Compton effect The collison and subsequent behaviour of a *photon* of *electromagnetic radiation* and a charged particle, such as an *electron*. In such a collision, the photon's energy is partly passed on to the massive charged particle, so there is a drop in *frequency* of the radiation, and a simultaneous rise in energy of the particle.

conduction The transport of thermal energy in a substance as a result of the transfer of higher *kinetic energy* of *molecules* at higher temperatures to those molecules with lower energies and temperatures.

continental drift A theory in geophysics which maintains that the continents, being part of vast tectonic plates, are capable of moving across the face of the Earth as the plates on which they shift move relative to one another.

convection The transport of thermal energy by the mass motion of the liquid or gas involved. Hotter regions of the fluid become less dense, rise to higher regions in the fluid column whilst cooler, denser fluid moves in to take its place. The result is a form of convective current.

Cooper pairs See *Bardeen–Cooper–Schrieffer theory*.

Coriolis force A special force that has to be invoked in dealing with the motion of bodies in certain types of rotating *frames of reference*.

cosmic rays Streams of very high energy particles, predominantely *protons*, originating from outer space, perhaps in supernova explosions, pulsars and the Sun.

cosmology The scientific study of the structure and evolution of the Universe.

coulomb The SI unit of electric charge, defined as the quantity of electricity transferred by an electric *current* of 1 *ampere* in one second. Symbol C.

Coulomb field The field of force surrounding an electric charge. Its intensity can be deduced from *Coulomb's law*.

Coulomb's law The *force* between two charged bodies varies directly as the product of the two charges, and inversely as the square of the distance between them.

CP violation The breaking of a fundamental *quantum theory* conservation rule by some unstable particles undergoing decay into other particles. C represent charge conjugation that relates particles to *antiparticles* and P stands for *parity*.

critical temperature The temperature above which a *gas* cannot be liquefied by *pressure* only.

Crooke's radiometer An instrument consisting of an evacuated glass dome in which sits a freely rotating system of vanes, whose opposite sides are white and black respectively. The rotation of the vanes when put near a source of heat is a demonstration of the *kinetic theory of gases*.

current An electric current is the result of the motion within a particular substance of the *electrons* or *ions* within it, as the result of some potential difference. Measured in amperes.

cryogenics The study of phenomena that occur at temperatures close to *absolute zero*.

cyclotron A particle accelerator which operates by imposing a magnetic force on changed particles held within a circular container.

Daniell cell A primary cell which uses a *cathode* of zinc, immersed in sulphuric acid contained in a porous pot which itself stands in a container of copper sulphate, in which the copper *anode* stands. An *electromotive force* of about 1.1 volts is produced by this cell.

De Broglie hypothesis A cornerstone of quantum physics which relates the wave nature of systems to their particle-like characteristics. For a particle with velocity v and mass m, one can associate a De Broglie wave of wavelength λ given by the De Broglie equation $\lambda = h/mv$, where h is *Planck's constant*.

density The ratio of the mass to the volume of a substance.

diamagnetism A form of magnetism induced in one substance by the magnetic field of another. Its basic cause lies in the shift of the orbital motion of the *electrons* of a substance resulting from the external magnetic field of the other substance. It occurs in all materials.

diffraction An example of an *interference*

phenomenon, which can be observed when light passes through an aperture and falls onto a screen; a series of light and dark bands occur which are the result of the wave nature of light.

dipole An electric or magnetic system consisting of two opposing charges or poles separated by a small distance.

direct current An electric *current* in which the direction of flow is always the same.

Doppler effect The apparent shift in the *frequency* of *electromagnetic radiation* (or sound) as a result of the motion of the source of the radiation relative to the observer. The shift is towards lower frequencies for a source receding from the observer, and to higher frequencies when approaching.

double refraction Birefringence. A crystal is said to permit double refraction if an unpolarized ray of light entering the crystal is split into two *polarized* rays, one of which does obey *Snell's law of refraction*, and the other does not. Calcite is such a crystal.

dry cell A source of *electromotive force* which does not contain a liquid. Usually taken to imply the *Leclanché* type of metal and paste cell.

dynamics The study of the action of *forces* upon bodies, which produce a change in the motion of the body. Classical dynamics is the study of such phenomena when velocities are much less than that of light. Relativistic dynamics, based on both *special* and *general theories of relativity*, is the corresponding study when velocities are close to that of light.

dynamo theory A theory of the origin of the magnetic fields of the Earth and other planets having magnetic fields in which the rotation of the planet as a whole sets up currents within the planet capable of producing a weak magnetic field.

eightfold-way A *quantum mechanical* scheme for the classification of *elementary particles* into families, grouped according to common properties as expressed by various *quantum numbers*.

elasticity The ability of a body to resume its former shape after having been deformed by an external *force*. Such an ability is retained by a body only as far as its elastic limit, beyond which any deformation becomes permanent. See *Hooke's law*.

electrodynamics The study of the effects of magnetic and electric *forces*.

electrolysis The decomposition of chemical substances by the passing of an electric *current* through them. This is the result of the migration of *ions* in the liquid state of these substances towards an electrode with the opposite charge, where the ions give up their charges.

electrolysis, laws of The first of (Faraday's) laws states that the chemical effect of an electric *current* is directly proportional to the amount of electricity that passes. The second states that the weights of substances deposited, or liberated, by a given quantity of electricity are directly proportional to the chemical equivalent of the substances.

electrolyte A substance whose liquid form and ionic composition permits the passage of an electric *current*, while being simultaneously decomposed by *electrolysis*.

electromagnetic force See *electromagnetic interaction*.

electromagnetic induction The process by which an *electromotive force* can be generated in a circuit when the *magnetic flux* through a circuit changes.

electromagnetic induction, Faraday's law of The induced *electromotive force* is equal to the rate of decrease of *magnetic flux*.

electromagnetic interaction The interaction between two charged particles (e.g. an *electron* and a *proton*) which appears as a *force* (attractive if the two charges are different in sign). In *quantum theory*, the electromagnetic interaction is carried between particles by *photons*.

electromagnetic radiation Emissions of *electromagnetic waves* as a result of the acceleration of electric charges.

electromagnetic spectrum The range of *frequencies* (or, equivalently, *wavelengths*) over which *electromagnetic radiation* is propagated. The lowest frequencies are usually taken as those of *radio* waves (less than 10^9 kilohertz) and the highest as *gamma* radiation, with frequencies upwards of 10^{16} kilohertz (kHz).

electromagnetic waves Waves of energy of a *transverse* nature, comprised of two mutually perpendicular magnetic and electric waves. They are produced by the acceleration of charges, such as occur in *alternating current* circuits.

electromotive force The basic driving force behind an electric *current*. Measured in volts.

electron An *elementary particle* having a mass of about 9×10^{-31} kg, and carrying a negative electric charge of 1.6×10^{-19} C. All *atoms* contain electrons, the particles being in orbit about a central, positively charged *nucleus*. The mass movement of electrons in a metal constitutes an electric *current*.

electrophorus A means of inducing a charge in one body into another. Usually consists of a metal plate with an insulating handle, the plate being capable of carrying *electrostatic* charges.

electrostatics The study of the effects of the *Coulomb fields* of electric charges.

element The basic atomic building blocks from which all chemicals can be made. An element is itself a substance comprised of *atoms* all of the same *atomic number*.

elementary particle One of a group of particles that make up all matter. Some, such as the *electron* and *proton*, are broadly stable, but many more decay very rapidly after being produced in high-energy nuclear reactions. Elementary particles are also involved in the description of *forces* in *quantum physics*, e.g. the *photon* is the carrier of the *electromagnetic force*.

energy, law of conservation of A fundamental principle of physics stating that energy can neither be created nor destroyed, but only changed from one form to another in a closed system.

entropy A mathematical device used in *thermodynamics* that may be interpreted as a measure of the amount of disorder in given system. In any process occurring in a closed system, the amount of entropy (i.e. of disorder) can never decrease; the total entropy of the Universe is always increasing.

etalon An instrument that uses *interference* phenomena to make possible very high resolution observations of *spectral lines*.

ether The now discarded concept of all-pervasive medium filling the entire Universe, allowing *electromagnetic radiation* to propagate. Such a medium is not required by the present understanding of *electromagnetism*, based on *Maxwell's equations*.

Faraday effect The rotation of the plane of *polarization* of polarized light by passing it through a transparent medium subjected to a transverse magnetic field.

feedback The coupling of the output from a particular process to the input.

Fermi-Dirac statistics A mathematical treatment of particles with half-integer *spin* in *statistical mechanics*, enabling properties of systems made up by such particles to be calculated.

fermions Particles obeying *Fermi-Dirac statistics*, such as *electrons*.

ferromagnetism A form of magnetism resulting from unbalanced *electron spins*, giving the *atoms* in which they lie the ability to form magnetic domains. Although ordinarily randomly orientated, the application of an external magnetic field lines up the domains, and the substance becomes magnetized.

fine structure A splitting of individual *spectral lines* seen when viewed under high resolution. This can be produced by external magnetic fields acting on *atoms*, for example.

fission The process by which a *nucleus* of an *element* with high *atomic number* (such as

uranium) splits into two approximately equal parts, releasing a vast amount of energy and some *neutrons* as a result. Such splitting can be achieved by the impact of neutrons with the nucleus. See *chain reaction*.

fluid Generic term for *gases* and *liquids*.

fluorescence An ability of some materials to absorb light of one *frequency* and emit it at a different one. The result is often a change in colour (wavelength) of the two types of light.

force When an object is acted upon is such a way that its state of rest or uniform motion in a straight line is changed, a force is said to act. By *Newton's laws of motion*, for a mass m to attain an acceleration a, a force F given by $F = ma$ must have acted on the body. Unit: the newton, symbol N.

Foucault pendulum A pendulum consisting of a long wire to which is attached a heavy weight, which is then free to swing in any plane. Once it starts swinging in one particular plane, the plane slowly rotates, this being the result of the rotation of the Earth beneath the pendulum.

frame of reference A set of axes fixed in such a way as to define uniquely the position of an object in space.

Fraunhofer lines Dark lines crossing the solar *spectrum*. They are caused by the absorption of light from hot regions of the Sun's surface by *gases* in the cooler, outer regions.

frequency The number of oscillations of a wave per unit time. One complete wave cycle per second is defined as one hertz, Hz.

frequency modulation The *modulation* of the *frequency* of the *carrier wave* of a radio transmission in such a way that it becomes free of static interference.

friction A force acting on a body preventing it moving relatively to another with which it is in contact.

fulcrum The point of balance of a system, e.g. the pivot of a lever.

fusion The fusing together of two light, low *atomic number*, *elements* to form a heavier one, with the release a large quantity of energy. Such a process can take place only at high temperatures, as only then do the fusing nuclei have sufficient *kinetic energy* to overcome their opposing *Coulomb fields*.

galvanometer An instrument that detects small changes in electric *current*, by making use of the magnetic effect of the current.

gamma rays A form of *electromagnetic radiation* of very high *frequency* and great penetrating power, often released in the *radioactive decay* of unstable *nuclei*.

gas A state of matter in which the constituent *molecules* (or *atoms*) move randomly relative to one another, but where each molecule (or atom) retains its identity.

geiger counter An instrument capable of detecting *alpha*, *beta* and *gamma* particle *emission* from materials. The incoming radiation creates *ions* within the counter, which are accelerated by electrical means and their effects counted.

geodesy The study of the Earth's shape and its effects on surveying and similar fields.

gluon A *quantum mechanical* concept which is used to explain the transmission of *forces* between *quarks*.

gravitation One of the four fundamental *forces* governing the Universe, and the most important on the cosmological scale, despite its being the weakest of the four forces. All bodies with mass experience the gravitational force, and according to the *general theory of relativity*, which views gravitation as curvature of space and time, massless objects such as *photons* can also be affected. For regions of relatively weak gravitational fields, Newton's law may be used. This states that the force of gravitation between two masses varies directly as the product of the masses, and inversely as the square of the distance between them. The constant of proportionality is G, Newton's *gravitational constant*. However, in regions such as exist near black holes for example, Newton's law breaks down, and general relativity must be used.

gravitational constant, G A fundamental constant of physics, which relates the force of *gravity* produced by a body to the masses involved and the separation. According to some physicists, its present value of 6.67×10^{-11} $m^3/kg\ s^2$ is decreasing at a rate proportional to the age of the Universe.

gyroscope A wheel mounted in such a way that it may rotate about any axis. Once set in rotation, the support of the wheel may be moved in any direction without changing the direction of the wheel relative to space. In addition, the application of a *force* will make the wheel rotate about an axis at right-angles to the axis about which the force is applied.

Hall effect An electric *current*-carrying conductor develops a *potential difference* across it when placed in a strong transverse magnetic field. This potential difference is at right-angles to both the magnetic field and the direction of current flow.

heat A property of a body resulting from the *kinetic energy* possessed by the constituents of the body, such as the *molecules* in a gas. Thus, heat is a form of energy, and as such can be transported by one of three means; *convection*, *conduction* and *radiation*.

heat capacity The amount of heat energy required to raise the temperature of a substance through one degree of temperature. See *specific heat capacity*.

heat death of the Universe According to the second *law of thermodynamics*, the *entropy* of the Universe, considered a closed system, is always increasing. It follows from this that there will eventually come a time in the history of the Universe when there is no further energy available, all processes having come into thermal equilibrium. The Universe will then no longer consist of hot bodies such as stars surrounded by cold space, all such disequilibrium having been eliminated. The resulting lack of any physical processes is called the heat death of the Universe.

Heaviside layer See *Kennelly-Heaviside layer*.

Hertzsprung–Russell diagram A plot of the temperature of stars and their luminosity, from which the evolution of stars can be deduced.

holography The process by which *lasers*, or any source of coherent light, are used to produce a three-dimensional image. Holograms are produced by splitting a beam of coherent light into two separate beams, the signal and reference beam. The former is *diffracted* by the object whose holographic image is required, the result falling onto a photographic plate. The reference beam is shone directly onto the plate, and the *interference* pattern of the combined beams form the hologram, which is recorded on the photographic plate. By illuminating the image with another coherent source of the same wavelength of light, the hologram acts as a diffraction grating, and the three-dimensional image can be seen in (or sometimes out of) the plate.

Hooke's law Within the elastic limit of a body possessing *elasticity*, the *stress* acting on the body produces a *strain* directly proportional to the size of the applied stress. See *elasticity*.

Hubble expansion The apparent recession of galaxies as seen from any point within the Universe, the velocity of recession being proportional to the distance of the galaxy from the observer.

hydrodynamics The study of the effects that *forces* have on *liquids* in motion.

hydrogen bomb A nuclear weapon in which the heat produced by an initial detonation of a fission, or *atom bomb*, is sufficiently high to allow an even greater release of energy from nuclear *fusion* to take place.

hydrometer An instrument capable of determining the density (relative or absolute) of a liquid. It makes use of *Archimedes' principle of hydrostatics*.

hydrostatics The study of the behaviour of *liquids* under the action of *forces* and *pressures* when the liquid is at rest.

hygrometer An instrument capable of determing the humidity of the air as determined by the ratio of the pressure of water vapour in the air at a given time to the pressure expected if the atmosphere was saturated at the same temperature.

hyperfine structure Very fine splitting of individual lines in a *spectrum*, which can be the result of the presence of different *isotopes* of an *element* in the source.

hyperon One of a group of unstable *elementary particles* with masses greater than that of the *neutron*.

ideal gas Perfect *gas*. A gas obeying the gas laws of *Boyle*, *Charles* and *Joule* exactly. This would imply that the gas consists of perfectly elastic *molecules*, each of which has zero volume and attractive or repulsive interaction with its neighbours.

inertia The property of a body measuring its reluctance to be affected dynamically by a *force*. Defined by *Newton's second law of motion*.

infrared radiation Part of the *electromagnetic spectrum*, corresponding to *wavelengths* between those of microwaves and visible light. Thus the wavelength band for infrared is about 10^{-6} m to 10^{-3} m.

interference The effect produced from the combining of waves. Constructive interference is said to be produced when the crest of one wave coincides with the crest of another. Such phenomena can be observed for all *electromagnetic radiation*, in particular light.

inverse square law The dependence of several of the most important interactions in physics including *gravitation* and *electrostatic Coulomb force*, obey the inverse square law, which implies that the strength of the *force* varies inversely as the square of the distance between the two interacting bodies.

ion An *atom* (or group of atoms) with a net electric charge. This charge is the result of an atom having either more or fewer *electrons* than the number needed for the atom to be electrically neutral. If more electrons (i.e. negatively charged), the result is an anion; if fewer (positively charged), then the result is a cation.

ionosphere A region in the Earth's upper atmosphere at a height of between about 60 and 500 km in which there are a large concentration of free *electrons* and *ions*. These are produced by the disruption of molecules at those heights by the *ultraviolet* and *X-ray radiation* produced by the Sun. The region is able to reflect *radio* waves as a result. Two regions of interest within the ionosphere are named the *Appleton layer* and the *Kennelly-Heaviside layer*, after the researchers who predicted and investigated their existence.

isothermal change A process which takes place without any change in temperature. See *adiabatic change*.

isotope An *atom* of an *element* with a particular *atomic number* but where the number of *neutrons* within the *nucleus* can differ from the original element. For example, uranium isotopes all have the same atomic number Z (92), but two examples of isotopes are uranium-235, which has a nucleus containing 92 protons and 143 neutrons, and uranium-238, which has a nucleus also containing 92 protons, but with 146 neutrons.

Josephson effect A *superconducting* ring interrupted by a thin layer of insulating material gives rise to an *alternating current* in the barrier when a steady external voltage is applied to it. This AC effect has a DC analogue, occurring when a steady magnetic field is applied to the insulating material.

Joule's electrical law The *heat H* in joules produced by the passing of a *current I* amps through a resistance of *R* ohms for a time *t* is given by $H = I^2 Rt$.

Joule's thermal law The internal energy of a *gas* at constant temperature is independent of its volume, provided the gas is *ideal*.

Joule-Thomson effect Or Joule-Kelvin effect. A means of cooling or heating a *gas* by passing it through a porous plug, under pressure. The temperature difference arises on the expansion of the gas on passing through the plug, and is due to the deviations of the gas involved from being an *ideal* gas, i.e. obeying *Joule's thermal law* and *Boyle's law* exactly.

Kelvin scale of temperature A scale of temperature whose zero point can be taken as *absolute zero*, so that 0 Kelvin corresponds to a temperature of about $-273°$ C.

Kennelly-Heaviside layer A region in the *ionosphere* capable of reflecting radio transmissions.

Kerr cell A device making use of the *Kerr effect*. The cell consists of a transparent container of a special liquid in which there are two electrodes, placed between two *polarizing* materials in the container. Only if the planes of polarization of all the various layers in the cell are aligned will light pass, and so the Kerr cell can be used as a shutter device.

Kerr effect The elliptical *polarization* of light as a result of the beam of light being reflected from a pole of an electromagnet. A similar effect also exists for liquids, if a *potential difference* is applied to the liquid itself, the angle of polarization depending on the size of the potential difference.

kinetic energy The energy possessed by a body by virtue of its motion. For speeds much less than the speed of light, the kinetic energy possessed by a body of mass m moving at a speed v is given by $mv^2/2$. *See potential energy*.

kinetic theory A theory which attempts to understand the properties of *gases* by considering them to consist of a vast number of *molecules* moving relative to one another. For example, the temperature of a gas is seen on this viewpoint to be the measure of the *kinetic energy* of the particles within the gas.

large number hypothesis A theory in *cosmology* that tries to understand the basic reason for an apparent coincidence of size in ratios of fundamental quantities in atomic and cosmological theory. If the apparent radius of the Universe is divided by the radius of the *electron*, the resulting large number (about 10^{43}) is remarkably similar to the ratio of the strengths of the *electrostatic (Coulomb)* and *gravitational force* between the *electron* and the *proton*. The reason for this is not clear at present, but if the relationship is to hold true for all time, it can be shown that on a *big-bang model* Universe the *gravitational constant* G must decrease with time, i.e. the strength of gravity must decrease.

Landé splitting factor A calculational device used in *quantum theory* that enables the *fine* and *hyperfine structure* of a *spectral line* to be determined by a knowledge of the various *spin* and orbital angular momenta of the *electrons* in the *atom*.

laser An acronym for light amplification by stimulated emission of radiation. By pumping *electromagnetic energy* into a special substance (such as a ruby crystal) it is possible to create a cascade of *photons*, with each new one created going on to produce another. By making this happen, in a resonant cavity, a wave is built up, which eventually has enough energy to burst out of one of the two mirror-like ends of the cavity in a pulse of single-*wavelength* (monochromatic) radiation that is also coherent (i.e. all the waves are in phase). See also *maser*.

latent heat The amount of heat released or absorbed in an *isothermal* change of state, such as from liquid to vapour (this is the *latent heat of vaporization*).

lattice The arrangement of positions in, for example, a crystal in which the *atoms*, *ions* or *molecules* remain virtually stationary.

Leclanché cell A primary cell in which the positive electrode (anode) is in the form of a rod of carbon in a mixture of manganese dioxide and carbon particles in a porous pot. The pot itself stands in a solution of ammonium chloride, in which stands the negative zinc electrode (cathode). The resultant e.m.f. is about 1.5 volts. Special types of Leclanché cell are possible in which the constituents are all non-liquid.

Lenz's law A law explaining an *induction*-related phenomenon. The induced electric current in a circuit relative to which a magnetic field is moving itself produces a magnetic field that tries to oppose the relative motion.

light, pressure of See *radiation pressure*.

light, theories of the nature of Prior to the advent of modern physics, theories of the basic nature of light fell into two camps: those whose viewed light as made up of a stream of particles (corpuscular theory), and those who viewed it as a wave motion (wave theory). Each attempted to explain all phenomena in optics, such as *reflection*, *refraction*, etc., on the basis of these two viewpoints. It is now known that light exists in *quanta* known as photons that exhibit both corpuscular and wave-like behaviour in certain circumstances.

light, velocity of Measured at about 299,793 km/s, this velocity cannot be reached by any body of a mass greater than zero. According to *Maxwell's laws of electromagnetism*, it is determined by two properties of space, one magnetic, the other electric.

line spectrum A *spectrum* made up of discrete lines of intensity at certain *wavelengths*, characterizing an *atom* in a particular state.

liquid A state of matter in which the *constituent molecules* can move freely relative to each other, with cohesive *forces* holding the whole together, unlike a *gas*.

Lissajous figures The path followed by a point subjected to two or more simultaneous simple wave motions, for example, at right-angles to one another.

longitude The longitude of a particular location is determined by angle between the great circle passing through it and the two poles of the Earth, and the circle passing through the poles and Greenwich, England (the Greenwich meridian), the angle being measured along the equator.

longitudinal wave A wave in which the vibrations take place in the direction of travel of the waves. See *transverse wave*.

Lorentz transformation A means of relating measurements of times and lengths made in one *frame of reference* to those made in another frame of reference moving at some velocity relative to the first. These formulae, which can be derived directly from Einstein's *theory of special relativity*, predict that at velocities approaching that of light, lengths appear to contract (the Lorentz contraction) and time intervals appear to increase (time dilation), as measured in a stationary frame of reference.

luminescence The emission of light from an object as a result of any process apart from direct heating.

Lyman series The series of lines in the *spectrum* of hydrogen that lie in the *ultraviolet* region of the spectrum.

Mach number The speed of an object divided by the speed of sound, about 332 m/s.

magic numbers Atomic *nuclei* which contain a magic number of *protons* or *neutrons* are very stable against *radioactive decay*. The numbers are 2, 8, 20, 28, 50, 82 and 126.

magnetic flux The product of the area of a circuit, for example, and the magnetic field strength at right-angles to that area.

magnetic flux density The *magnetic flux* passing through 1 m² of area of a magnetic field in a direction at right-angles to the magnetic force.

magnetic moment The product of the strength and length of a magnet.

magnetic monopole A prediction of one *quantum theory* (proposed by Dirac) that involves the existence of individual magnetic charges, analogous to the individual charges found in *electrostatics* (i.e. *electrons*). Such an entity has not yet been definitely observed to exist, but is expected to be rare in any case.

magnetic permeability The *magnetic flux density* in a body, divided by the external magnetic field strength producing it. It can be used as a way of classifying materials into different types of magnetism, such as *ferromagnetic*.

magnetohydrodynamics The study of the behaviour of *plasmas* under the influence of magnetic fields.

magnetosphere The region surrounding a planet in which ionized particles are trapped by the magnetic field of the planet itself. Because of the action of the *solar wind*, the magnetosphere is "blown" out into a tail in a direction away from the Sun.

Malus' law A law giving the intensity of light after having been *polarized* through a certain angle.

maser An acronym for microwave amplification by stimulated emission of radiation. A system for boosting microwave signals which operates in a similar way to the *laser*, except that the final burst of energy has a single *wavelength* which lies in the microwave region of the *electromagnetic spectrum*.

mass number The number of *neutrons* and *protons* in the nucleus of an *atom*.

mass spectrometer A means of analysing a substance in order to determine its basic chemical composition which makes use of the way in which the deflection of an *ion* in a magnetic and electric field depends on its mass to charge ratio.

matrix mechanics A mathematical description of subatomic phenomena which views certain characteristics of the particles involved as being matrices, and hence obeying the rules of matrix mathematics which differ in significant ways from the rules obeyed by ordinary arithmetic.

matter, continuous creation of A phenomenon invoked in certain cosmological theories, especially the *steady state model* of the Universe. In that particular theory, matter is considered to be constantly created, either evenly throughout space, or in localized regions of creation, so as to make up for the diluting effect the *Hubble expansion* of the Universe has on the average density of matter. By continually creating matter, it is then possible for the Universe to maintain a steady-state appearance.

Maxwell–Boltzmann distribution A mathematical function used in the *kinetic theory* of *gases* and derivable on the basis of *statistical mechanics*, giving the distribution of particle velocities in a gas at a particular temperature.

Maxwell's equations A set of four *vector* equations showing the interdependence of electricty and magnetism. The concepts of charge conservation are built into them, as are the experimental results of Faraday, Gauss and Ampère.

meson An unstable type of *elementary particle*, with a mass intermediate between that of the *proton* and *electron*. A number of such particles have been discovered (with the mu-meson now being considered not to belong to the meson family). The pi-mesons, or pions, make up a family of three mesons, with zero, positive and negative charges, and roughly the same masses.

meteorite Material, often stony or iron-like, which enters the Earth's atmosphere from interplanetary space and lands on the Earth's surface.

Michelson–Morley experiment An *interference* based experiment which attempted to find the absolute velocity of the Earth, i.e. its velocity relative to the *ether*, which would show up as a change in the *velocity of light* when measured at different angles to the direction of the Earth's motion. Despite this experiment's great accuracy, no such change was found, indicating that the speed of light was the same for all observers. This finding is the cornerstone of Einstein's *special theory of relativity*.

Milky Way The band of luminescence cutting the night sky in two, the faint light being the result of the presence within it of a vast number of stars. These stars occupy one arm of our Galaxy.

modulation The altering of some property of a wave, such as the *frequency*, by reference to some other wave motion.

molecule The smallest amount of a substance capable of retaining the basic properties of the substance and existing independently.

momentum The product of the velocity of a body and its mass.

monochromatic Literally, one colour, this is the property of some sources of radiation to emit waves of one *frequency* (or *wavelength*). *Lasers* and *masers* are examples.

Moseley's law The *frequency* of the characteristic *X-ray line spectra* for elements *is directly* proportional to the square of the *atomic number*, Z.

Mössbauer effect The ability for crystals at low temperatures to absorb *gamma rays* of a certain *wavelength* in such a way that the crystal as a whole may recoil, so that the gamma rays are emitted in an exceedingly narrow range of wavelengths, essentially unchanged from the original.

mu-meson See *meson*.

neutrino An *elementary particle* with no electric charge, a very low (if not zero) rest mass, carrying an intrinsic *spin* of matter, a great amount of material being needed to absorb one.

neutron An elementary particle of approximately the same mass as the *proton*, but zero electric charge. It is a constituent of the *nuclei* of all *atoms* apart from the hydrogen atom.

neutron star A star that has exhausted all its nuclear fuel required for *fusion*, collapsed, and reached a sufficiently high density that *quantum* effects have turned most of its material into *neutrons*.

Newton's law of cooling The rate of loss of *heat* from a body is directly proportional to the instantaneous temperature difference between the body and the surroundings. This leads to an exponential law of temperature decline.

Newton's laws of motion The first of these states that all bodies continue their motion in a straight line or state of rest unless acted upon by an external *force*. The resulting changes are described by the second law, which states that the rate of change of *momentum* of a body is proportional to the force applied, and take place

in the direction of the force. This gives rise to the formula that the force F giving rise to an acceleration a in a mass m is given by $F = ma$. The third law states that to every action there is an equal and opposite reaction.

Newton's rings An *interference* effect occurring in observations made of thin films separated by an air gap, *reflections* between various surfaces being allowed.

Nicol prism A device which uses the optical properties of calcite to produce plane *polarized* light by passing rays of light through it.

nuclear isomer *Atoms* of an *element* of a given mass that differ in their rates of *radioactive decay* are known as nuclear isomers.

nucleus The central part of an *atom*, generally made up of both *neutrons* and *electrons*. Although a hundred thousand times smaller than the size of the whole atom, virtually all the atom's mass is contained within the nucleus.

objective The system of lenses in a telescope or microscope nearest to the object being observed.

Ohm's law The *potential difference* in volts, across a *current*-carrying conductor is directly proportional to the current flowing in amps, the constant of proportionality being the resistance of the conductor, in ohms. Thus volts = amps × ohms in dimensional terms.

ortho-hydrogen *Molecules* of hydrogen in which the *spins* of the two *atoms* are parallel. See *para-hydrogen*.

oscilloscope Short for cathode ray oscilloscope (CRO). An intrument that allows one to see how electrical quantities vary with respect to each other, and also to time. The device operates by having the electrical change pass through onto deflection plates which alter the way *electrons* in the cathode tube strike the screen to give a visible image.

pair production The creation of an *electron* and anti-electron (*positron*) pair by the interaction between a high-energy particle or *photon* and the *electrostatic field* around a *nucleus*. It can also be used to describe the creation out of the vacuum state of particle–antiparticle pairs as allowed by Heisenberg's *uncertainty principle*.

para-hydrogen *Molecules* of hydrogen in which the *spins* of the two *atoms* are opposed.

parallelogram of forces A means of adding the effects of two non-parallel *forces* of given magnitude and direction to give their resultant effect in magnitude and direction.

paramagnetism Property of a material whose *magnetic permeability* is greater than unity. The origin of this form of magnetism lies in unbalanced electron *spins*, giving the *atom* as a whole the ability to be affected by an external magnetic field.

parity A concept in *quantum theory* related to the mirror-symmetry of the functions describing mathematically the behaviour of the particles.

Pascal's principle A law of *hydrostatics* stating that the application of *pressure* to a *fluid* results in that pressure being equally transmitted throughout the fluid, in all directions.

Pauli's exclusion principle A law of *quantum theory* that states that no two *electrons* in an uncharged *atom* can have the same set of *quantum numbers*.

periodic table The grouping of the chemical *elements* in such a way that the *atomic numbers* and basic chemical properties of elements in one region of it can be related to each other. The periodic law, which states that the properties of the elements vary periodically with the atomic number, can then be seen to operate.

photoelectric effect The transfer of energy from light rays falling onto a substance to the *electrons* within the substance. If the *frequency*, and hence the energy, of the radiation is high enough, it is possible to "boil" electrons, then known as photoelectrons, out of the substance. Being charge-carriers, these electrons can constitute a photoelectric current.

photometer An instrument used to measure the relative intensities of light sources. This is often achieved using the *photoelectric effect*.

photon The *quantum* of *electromagnetic radiation*. A photon can be considered as an *elementary particle* with zero mass and charge, which "carries" the *electromagnetic force* between charged particles.

photosynthesis The manufacture of carbohydrates from carbon dioxide, water and the energy from sunlight, by green plants.

pion See *meson*.

Planck's quantum constant A constant with a value of about 6.63×10^{-34} joule-seconds, which is the fundamental unit of *spin* angular momentum. Symbol $h/2\pi$.

Planck's radiation law The energy of *electromagnetic radiation* of a certain *frequency* is given by the product of the frequency and *Planck's constant*, h.

plasma A state of matter in which the *electrons* and *ions* making up the original *atoms* and *molecules* have been split up (often as the result of a very high temperature). The electrons and ions are present in roughly equal numbers.

Poisson's ratio The ratio of the lateral *strain* to the longitudinal strain in a wire held under tension.

polariscope An instrument that enables the rotation of the plane of polarization of *polarized* light to be determined.

polarization of light Being an *electromagnetic*

wave, light waves can be considered as made up of two mutually perpendicular vibrations of an electric and magnetic wave. In polarization, some restriction is put onto the plane of oscillation of one of these components (which is normally random).

potential difference A potential difference is said to exist between two points in a conductor, such as a wire, if some work has to be expended in pushing charges constituting an electric *current* between the two points.

potential energy The energy possessed by a body by virtue of its position (e.g. a compressed spring or a raised weight). See *kinetic energy*.

Poynting–Robertson effect The interaction of dust particles in interplanetary space with solar radiation causing a loss in orbital velocity of the dust around the Sun. This causes the dust particles to spiral into the Sun, if the effect is unopposed. However, under certain circumstances, *radiation pressure* is large enough to oppose the effect.

pressure The amount of *force* exerted per unit area. Measured in newtons, symbol N.

proton An *elementary particle* of mass about 1,836 times that of the *electron*, and an electric charge of the same magnitude but opposite sign (i.e. positive).

Prout's hypothesis The now-defunct proposal that all the chemical *elements* were made from the combination of different numbers of hydrogen *atoms*.

pyrometer A high-temperature thermometer.

quantum The name given to the smallest, indivisible unit of energy; every amount of energy is made up of an integral number of these packets.

quantum chromodynamics QCD The branch of high-energy physics that seeks to understand the nature of the *forces* between *quarks*.

quantum electrodynamics The theory of the electromagnetic field that includes *quantum* concepts, enabling the behaviour of *electrons* in *atoms* to be predicted to very high accuracy.

quantum mechanics The system of mechanics based on the concept of the *quantum*, which must be used when dealing with atomic and sub-atomic systems.

quantum number Integral or half-integral numbers defining the various properties of a system such as an *atom* in *quantum mechanical* terms. *Angular momentum*, *spin* and *strangeness* are examples.

quantum physics The branch of physics which takes into account the quantum nature of matter, energy and radiation.

quantum theory The approach to physical

problems based on the concept of the *quantum* of energy.

quark One of a set of particles that may be the fundamental constituents of all matter. By taking different permutations of quarks, and corresponding anti-quarks, it appears possible to explain the various common characteristics of certain *elementary particles* (as expressed in the *eightfold way*) in terms of the quarks they contain. Despite strenuous efforts, it has not so far been possible to observe a quark in isolation, outside its host particle.

radar *Radio* detecting and ranging. The use of high-*frequency* radio waves in guiding detecting and locating moving reflectors of *electromagnetic waves*, such as aircraft, missiles and ships.

radiation of heat The transfer of thermal energy by *electromagnetic waves* of *wavelengths* lying within the *infrared* region of the *electromagnetic spectrum*, i.e. between about 10^{-6} and 10^{-3} m.

radiation pressure The *pressure* exerted on an object by the *momentum* of *photons* of radiation striking its surface, giving rise to a *force* in accordance with *Newton's second law of motion*.

radio The transmission of *electromagnetic radiation* of *frequencies* from about 10 kHz to 100,000 MHz. Transmission of communication signals frequently involves the use of either *amplitude* or *frequency-modulated carrier waves*.

radioactive decay The spontaneous disintegration of the *nuclei* of certain compounds, which is accompanied by the emission of either *alpha* or *beta particles* and/or *gamma rays*. In certain circumstances it is possible to induce artificial radioactivity, by bombarding the nuclei with particles such as *neutrons*.

radiomicrometer An extremely sensitive detector of *infrared radiation*.

Raman effect The addition of certain *wavelengths* to the wavelength of light shone through a medium, produced by the change in energy of the incident *photons* on interacting with *molecules* vibrating within the medium. The other, subsidiary wavelengths are of very weak intensity, needing *laser* light of high power to make them readily observable.

Rayleigh–Jeans law A formula giving the intensity of *black-body radiation* at long *wavelengths* for a radiator at a certain temperature. It is thus an approximation to Planck's full formula for the black-body intensity based on *quantum* concepts.

rectifier A device capable of converting *alternating current* to *direct current* by having a much greater resistance to electric *current*

flowing in one direction than that flowing in the other.

reflection The reversing of the direction of *electromagnetic radiation* by a surface, according to specific laws.

reflection, laws of The original ray of light, the reflected ray of light and the right-angle to the reflecting surface all lie in the same plane. Secondly, the angle between the original, incident, ray and the right-angle is the same as that between the reflected ray and the right-angle to the surface.

refraction The change in the direction of a ray of light on passing through the surface between two different materials (e.g. air and water).

refraction, laws of The incident ray, the refracted ray and the normal to the surface between the two media at the point of incidence lie in the same plane. In addition, *Snell's law* states that the ratio of the sines of the angles of incidence and refraction is equal to a constant. See *refractive index*.

refractive index The ratio of the speed of light in a vacuum to the speed of light in a given material.

refractometer A device for determining the *refractive index* of a substance.

relativity, general theory A theory of gravitation, in which the effects of gravitation are explained in terms of the curvature of both space and time by the mass responsible for the gravitational field. Although Newton's theory is acceptable for weak fields, for the strong fields around black holes and in the Universe as a whole, the general theory must be used.

relativity, special theory A modification to the everyday laws of motion, based on the premises that the laws describing physical phenomena are the same for all observers, regardless of their particular (uniform) motion, and that the value for the speed of light is the same for all observers also. The theory enables the effects of very high velocity (approaching that of light) on the lengths and times to be calculated, and also the effects on masses.

resolving power The ability of an optical device to separate two closely spaced sources of light.

Rydberg's constant A constant which relates the *wavelength* of *spectral lines* in hydrogen like elements to the inverse-squares of integers.

scalar A mathematical representation of a quantity requiring just its magnitude for its complete definition. Examples: temperature, speed, mass.

Schrödinger's equation An equation that considers the *electron* in terms of a wave of probability, and which enables the behaviour of the electron in *atoms* and electric potentials to be calculated, and also the *spectra* of *atoms* to be predicted. It is the basis of *wave mechanics*.

Seebeck effect The ability of some metals, when joined, to give rise to an electric *current* when the opposite ends of the wires are kept at different temperatures.

semiconductor An electrical conducting material whose resistance decreases with temperature and th presence of impurities. Germanium and silicon have atomic structures permitting them to behave in this way, as do a variety of other metals.

Snell's law See *refraction, laws of*.

solar wind The stream of charged particles, such as *electrons* and *protons*, blown out from the Sun's outer atmosphere by the high thermal energy in that region.

solenoid A device consisting of a series of wires wound around a cylinder, which produces a magnetic field within the cylinder when a *current* flows through the wire windings. The intensity of the magnetic field depends directly on the number of turns of the wire.

solid state physics The study of materials in the solid state, investigating the magnetic thermal and electrical properties, for example.

specific heat capacity The amount of heat energy required to raise the temperature of unit mass (e.g. a kilogram) of a substance through one degree of temperature.

spectral line See *line spectrum*

spectroscope A device often consisting of two separate lens systems and a glass prism or *diffraction* grating separating the two, which enables observations of the various spectral lines in the *spectrum* of a substance to be made and their wavelengths determined. The chemical composition of the substance can then be deduced.

spectroscopy The use of a *spectroscope* to investigate the chemical composition of materials, and their state.

spectrum The display of the result of breaking *electromagnetic radiation*, e.g. light, into its constituent *wavelengths*. Such analysis can be carried out using a prism or a *diffraction* grating for example, and the wavelengths can be determined using a *spectroscope*. The spectra obtained from sources emitting electromagnetic radiation are called emission spectra, and those obtained when the radiation is analysed after passing through a transparent medium, in which absorption of certain wavelengths will take place, are called absorption spectra.

spherical aberration An optical error occurring when a lens or curved mirror does not bring all the incident rays of light to a sharp focus.

spin A *quantum number* that is related to the amount of *angular momentum*, which is quantized in *quantum mechanics* in units of *Planck's constant* divided by 2π, that a particle has intrinsically, as opposed for example, to orbital angular momentum. It is used to classify particles into various categories: all *fermions* have half-integer spin (e.g. the *electron*, with spin $\pm 1/2$), all *mesons* have integral spin (e.g. pions, with spin 0).

spin–orbit interaction An interaction between *electrons* orbiting a *nucleus* in an *atom* that arises from the magnetic field produced by the nucleus interacting with the spinning electron is to split the individual *spectral lines* in a *spectrum* into a number of components.

squid Superconducting Quantum Interference Device. A device which uses the *Josephson effect* to produce a highly sensitive magnetic field detection system, or an ultra-fast switching device for use in computers.

Stark effect The splitting of *spectral lines* into a number of components by a strong electric field.

statistical mechanics The mathematical description of the behaviour of large numbers of particles (such as make up a *gas* for example) using the theory of statistics to describe the overall effect of the behaviour of the particles.

steady-state Universe A model of the Universe in which the overall properties (rate of expansion, density, etc.) remain constant. This Universe has no birth or death.

Stefan–Boltzmann's law The relationship between the total energy E emitted over all *wavelengths* by a *black body* at temperature I per second per unit area, which is given by $E = \sigma T^4$, where σ is Stefan's constant.

Stokes' law The *terminal velocity* V reached by a small sphere of radius r, density d, falling under gravity in a medium of density D and viscosity η is given by $V = 2gr^2(d-D)/9\eta$, where g is the acceleration due to gravity.

strain The dimensional change produced by a *stress*, divided by the original dimension. Thus for a wire to which a weight is applied at one end, the strain is the difference between the stretched and unstretched lengths, divided by the original unstretched length.

strangeness A *quantum number* assigned to certain unstable *elementary particles* that decay much more slowly than was originally expected. Stable particles, such as *protons*, have a strangeness quantum number of zero. Others, such as the *hyperons*, have non-zero strangeness quantum numbers.

stress The *force* per unit area producing a *strain*.

strong nuclear force The strongest interaction in nature, and the one that binds the *protons* and *neutrons* together in the *nucleus* despite the mutual *electrostatic* repulsion the positively charged protons feel for each other. The interaction is very short range, being essentially zero outside the nucleus, and is related to the exchange of pi-*mesons* between protons and neutrons.

sunspot A region of intense magnetic fields, visible on the surface of the Sun as dark patches, resulting from the cooler temperatures in the regions relative to their surroundings. A cycle of activity of about 11 years has been identified for them.

superconductor A metal (e.g. tin) which when cooled to a temperature just above *absolute zero* loses its electrical resistance, becoming a perfect conductor.

superfluid A fluid with an anomalously high *thermal conductivity* capable of flowing virtually without *friction*. *Cryogenically* cooled helium can have such characteristics.

superheterodyne Supersonic heterodyne. A means of receiving *radio* transmissions involving the changing of the *frequency* of the *carrier wave* to an intermediate frequency above the limit of audible sound by a heterodyne process. In this, the received wave is combined with a slightly different frequency wave produced within the receiver. Once the intermediate frequency has been formed, the combined waves are amplified and the signal taken off by a demodulator.

surface tension An effect seen on the surface of liquids caused by the attraction between *molecules* of the liquid. The effect is to produce a "film" of tension over the surface.

synchrotron A particle accelerator which uses a system of constant electric field and modulated magnetic field to accelerate charged particles to high energy.

telegraphy A means of long distance communication by transmitting electric currents along wires.

terminal velocity When a *force* is velocity dependent, there is a specific velocity for which the corresponding force equals the force opposing the motion; this is the *terminal velocity*, which the body under the action of the two forces will then maintain, undergoing no further acceleration. An example is the air-resistance force, which depends on the square of the velocity. For a falling body, this force opposes that of *gravity*, and a terminal velocity is reached.

thermal conductivity The rate of *conduction* of *heat* through a material.

thermionic tube (valve). An evacuated metal or glass container enclosing a system of electrodes. The *cathode* emits *electrons* when heated, and these are attracted to a positively charged *anode*.

Perforated grid electrodes within the tube can be used to control the electron *current*.

thermionic valve See *thermionic tube*.

thermocouple A means of detecting and measuring temperature differences, generally involving two wires of different metals joined together. One junction is kept at a lower temperature, while the other is put on or in the substance whose temperature is to be determined. An electric *current* (related to the temperature difference) is then set up, which can be detected using a *galvanometer*.

thermodynamics The study of processes involving heat and energy.

thermodynamics, laws of The first states the *law of conservation of energy* for a closed system. The second states that heat cannot be transferred by any self-sustaining process from a colder to a hotter body; equivalently, the *entropy* of a closed system can never decrease. The third law states that *absolute zero* is unattainable; equivalently, the entropy change for a chemical reaction involving crystalline solids is zero at absolute zero.

transuranic element An *element* whose *atomic number Z* exceeds that of uranium, i.e. 92. Such elements the first of which is neptunium, with an atomic number of 93, do not occur naturally in the Universe.

transverse wave A wave in which the vibration takes place at right-angles to the direction of wave travel. See *longitudinal wave*.

tribology The study of *friction* and similar surface effects.

Tyndall effect Scattering of light to produce a visible beam.

ultrasonics The study of sound waves (i.e. *longitudinal pressure* waves) with *frequencies* above approximately 20 kHz, the audible frequency limit.

ultraviolet *electromagnetic radiation* lying between the wavelengths of visible light and *X-rays*.

uncertainty principle, Heisenberg's A principle of *quantum physics* stating the impossibility of simultaneously determining the position and *momentum* of a particle with limitless accuracy.

unified field theory An attempt to describe the laws of *electromagnetism* and *gravitation* in a single set of equations.

Van Allen belts Two belts of energetic charged particles about 4,000 and 16,000 km above the Earth. The inner belt is filled with particles produced by *cosmic ray*-atmospheric *molecule* collisons that have become trapped in the Earth's magnetic field, whereas the higher belt contains particles captured from the *solar wind*.

Van de Graaff generator An accelerator of *elementary particles* that uses an *electrostatic* field to raise the particles to high energies.

Van der Waals' force An interatomic and inter-molecular force of attraction resulting from the distortion of the *electron* distribution in one *atom* or *molecule* by another.

vector A mathematical representation of a quantity having both magnitude and direction in its definition, for example *force*, velocity and acceleration. See *scalar*.

wavelength The distance between each crest of a wave (or each trough). Measured in metres, the wavelength λ is related to frequency f by the velocity of the wave, v, according to the formula $\lambda = v/f$.

wave mechanics The branch of *quantum theory* that derives the various properties of *atoms* on the basis of every particle having an associated wave existing in a multidimensional space, representing probabilities of certain properties of the particles involved. *Schrödinger's equation* is the basis of wave mechanics, which has been shown to be equivalent to *matrix mechanics*.

weak interaction One of the four fundamental *forces* in nature. It is responsible for the decay of some *elementary particles* and of *atomic nuclei*.

Wheatstone bridge A special electrical circuit capable of determining resistances of conductors.

Wien's law The relationship between the intensity and *frequency* of *black-body radiation* at the high-frequency end of the *spectrum*. Wien's displacement law relates the *wavelength* of maximum intensity to the temperature of the black body.

X-ray diffraction The *diffraction* of X-rays, especially by the *lattice* of a crystal. Such an effect enables the structure of the lattice to be determined.

X-rays *Electromagnetic radiation* with *frequencies* between those of *ultraviolet* and *gamma* radiation, i.e. between about 10^{14} and 10^{17} kHz.

Zeeman effect The splitting of *spectral lines* of a substance placed in an intense magnetic field.

Index

The index entry in **bold** type will direct you to the main text entry in which the information you require is given.